3D Rotations

3D Rotations

Parameter Computation and Lie Algebra based Optimization

Kenichi Kanatani

CRC Press
Taylor & Francis Group
Boca Raton London New York

CRC Press is an imprint of the
Taylor & Francis Group, an **informa** business

First edition published 2020

by CRC Press
6000 Broken Sound Parkway NW, Suite 300, Boca Raton, FL 33487-2742

and by CRC Press
2 Park Square, Milton Park, Abingdon, Oxon, OX14 4RN

ISBN: 978-0-367-47133-0 (hbk)
ISBN: 978-0-367-49690-6 (pbk)
ISBN: 978-1-003-03767-5 (ebk)

Visit the Taylor & Francis Web site at
http://www.taylorandfrancis.com

and the CRC Press Web site at
http://www.crcpress.com

Contents

Preface

Many books have been published that deal with representation and analysis of rotation in the 3D space, but most of them are textbooks of physics. This is because 3D rotation is one of the most fundamental themes of classical mechanics and quantum physics. In fact, analysis of rigid body inertial motion is a key element of controlling rockets, satellites, and airplanes; analysis of spin, angular momentum, and energy of elementary particles such as atoms and electrons is the basis of quantum mechanics.

In recent years, however, 3D rotation analysis is widely encountered in everyday problems thanks to the development of computers. For example, sensing 3D using cameras and sensors, analyzing and modeling 3D for computer vision and computer graphics, and controlling and simulating robot motion all require 3D rotation computation. In this book, we focus on such "computational analysis" of 3D rotation, rather than classical "motion analysis."

The central issue of 3D rotation analysis for today's engineering application is the computation of parameters from input data, in particular when the observations contain measurement uncertainties, called "noise." To cope with this, we regard noise as random variables and model their probability distributions. Then, we pursue statistically optimal computation for maximizing the expected accuracy. This is a typical instance of nonlinear optimization. We illustrate how this proceeds and show some computer vision applications as examples.

Mathematically, the set of all 3D rotations forms a group denoted by $SO(3)$, and its properties have been studied by mathematicians for long. We first show that exploiting the group property of rotations, we can obtain an analytical solution for particular forms of nonlinear optimization that involves 3D rotation. In general, however, we need numerical search, for which we need to analyze the variations of the objective function induced by small variations of rotation arguments. It is known that small variations of rotation form a linear space called "Lie algebra." Based on this fact, we formulate in this book what we call the "Lie algebra method."

This book also proposes computing projects for readers who want to code the theories presented in this book, describing necessary 3D simulation setting as well as providing real GPS 3D measurement data.

To read this book, readers are not required to have knowledge of abstract mathematics such as group theory. However, familiarity with fundamentals of linear algebra is assumed. A brief overview of mathematical concepts related to 3D rotation, such as quaternions, singular value decomposition, Lie groups, and Lie algebras, is provided as Appendix at the end of the volume.

The author thanks Kokichi Sugihara, Professor Emeritus of the University of Tokyo, Osami Yasukura of Fukui University, Chikara Matsunaga of For-A, Co., Ltd., and Futoshi Magosaki of (formerly) Sumitomo Precision Products Co., Ltd. for helpful comments and suggestions. Parts of this work are based with permission on the auther's work *3D Rotations: Parameter Computation and Lie Algebra based Optimization* (in Japanese), ©Kyoritsu Shuppan Co., Ltd., 2019.

CHAPTER 1

Introduction

Here, we describe the background of the problems we discuss in this book. Then, we summarize the contents of the subsequent chapters.

1.1 3D ROTATIONS

As mentioned in Preface, 3D rotation has been historically an important theme of physics in relation to rigid body motion and quantum mechanics. In today's computer age, however, "computational" aspects of 3D rotation are important issues of 3D measurement using cameras and 3D sensors for computer vision and computer graphics applications as well as control and simulation of robots. As will be pointed out in the next chapter, 3D rotation is specified by a "rotation matrix" $\boldsymbol{R}$ (a 3×3 orthogonal matrix of determinant 1). A typical problem that needs to be solved is find rotations $\boldsymbol{R}_1$, $\boldsymbol{R}_2$, ..., $\boldsymbol{R}_M$ that optimize, i.e., minimize or maximize, a function

$$J = J(\cdots, \boldsymbol{R}_1, \boldsymbol{R}_2, ..., \boldsymbol{R}_M), \tag{1.1}$$

that includes these rotations in its arguments.

Consider, for example, computing from camera images the postures of the cameras that capture them and the objects seen in the images, which is a typical computer vision task called "3D reconstruction." By "posture." we mean the position and the orientation. The position is specified by the 3D coordinates of a prescribed reference point such as the centroid of the object or the lens center of the camera. The orientation is specified by the relative rotation between a coordinate system fixed to the object or the camera and a coordinate system fixed to the scene, called the "world coordinate system." The 3D reconstruction problem reduces to optimization of a function that includes rotations in its arguments in the form of Eq. (1.1).

Similar problems also occur in various other situations. For graphics applications, for example, we need to compute optimal postures of generated objects and the optimal illumination source arrangement. For robotics applications, we need to compute optimal postures of actuators such as robot hands, drones, and cameras. Such problems related to 3D orientations usually reduce to function optimization involving 3D rotations in the form of Eq. (1.1).

Considering such applications, we describe in Chapter 2 geometric meanings of 3D rotation and show how to represent 3D rotation using vectors and matrices. It is concluded that 3D rotation is specified by a rotation matrix, i.e., an orthogonal matrix of determinant 1. From this fact, we see that the nine elements of the rotation matrix are not independent of each other, having only three degrees of freedom. Then, we prove "Euler's theorem," which states that 3D rotation is a rotation around some axis by some angle. As a special case, we derive the matrix form for rotation around each coordinate axis.

In Chapter 3, we show how to describe a general rotation matrix $\boldsymbol{R}$ in terms of three parameters. The most straightforward way is the use of three rotation angles α, β, and γ around each coordinate axis, called the "roll," the "pitch," and the "yaw." We point out, however, that the resulting rotation depends on the order of composition. We also point out that this composition has different meanings, depending on whether each axial rotation takes place with respect to a coordinate system fixed to the object or with respect to a coordinate system fixed to the surrounding space. Taking this into consideration, we define the "Euler angles" θ, ϕ, and ψ of rotation, which are determined uniquely. We also discuss their potential singularities. Next, we derive the "Rodrigues formula," which specifies 3D rotation by an axis $\boldsymbol{l}$ and the angle Ω of rotation around it. Finally, we introduce the "quaternion representation" that specifies 3D rotation by four parameters q_0, q_1, q_2, and q_3 such that their sum of squares is 1 (hence the degree of freedom is 3). This is an extension of expressing 2D rotation on a plane by a complex number to 3D rotation in 3D.

1.2 ESTIMATION OF ROTATION

If we apply rotation $\boldsymbol{R}$ to N vectors $\boldsymbol{a}_1$, ..., $\boldsymbol{a}_N$, we obtain $\boldsymbol{a}'_1$, ..., $\boldsymbol{a}'_N$ such that $\boldsymbol{a}'_\alpha = \boldsymbol{R}\boldsymbol{a}_\alpha$, $\alpha = 1$, .., N. In Chapter 4, we consider its "inverse problem," namely, given two sets of vectors $\boldsymbol{a}_1$, ..., $\boldsymbol{a}_N$, and $\boldsymbol{a}'_1$, ..., $\boldsymbol{a}'_N$, we compute the rotation $\boldsymbol{R}$ between them. The solution is immediately obtained if there is no noise in the data so that $\boldsymbol{a}'_\alpha = \boldsymbol{R}\boldsymbol{a}_\alpha$, $\alpha = 1$, .., N, exactly holds for some $\boldsymbol{R}$. However, the important issue in practical applications is the case in which the data $\boldsymbol{a}_\alpha$ and $\boldsymbol{a}'_\alpha$ obtained via 3D sensing or camera images are not necessarily exact, namely the case in which

$$\boldsymbol{a}'_\alpha \approx \boldsymbol{R}\boldsymbol{a}_\alpha, \qquad \alpha = 1, .., N. \tag{1.2}$$

In practical situations, this problem arises in the process of estimating the motion between two 3D objects. A "motion" (or "Euclidean motion" to be strict) is a composition of translation and rotation. Given a 3D object in motion, we compute its translation and rotation from the locations before and after the motion. To do this, we first translate the object so that a specified reference point, such as its centroid, coincide before and after the motion. Then, the problem reduces to rotation estimation in the form of Eq. (1.2). In order to solve this problem, we need to give an interpretation of "≈" in Eq. (1.2) and mathematically model the data noise. The simplest and the most practical model is to assume that the noise is subject to an isotropic Gaussian distribution of constant variance. Then, the problem reduces to computing an $\boldsymbol{R}$ that minimizes the sum of the squares of the differences between the left and right sides of Eq. (1.2). The resulting $\boldsymbol{R}$ is called the "least-squares solution." Its computation is sometimes called the "Procrustes problem."

In Chapter 4, it is pointed out that this least-squares computation is "maximum likelihood estimation" from the viewpoint of statistics and that the solution is obtained by singular value decomposition of a matrix defined by the data. It is also pointed out that the same solution is obtained using the quaternion representation introduced in Chapter 3. We show an important application of this procedure: if we estimate the rotation $\boldsymbol{R}$ from data by some means, the computed $\boldsymbol{R}$ may not be an exact orthogonal matrix. In that case, we need to correct it to an exact orthogonal matrix. This problem arises in may engineering problems involving 3D configuration computation. The solution is obtained using the singular value decomposition.

The least-squares solution minimizes the sum of squares of the discrepancies of Eq. (1.2). In real applications, however, the measurement using 3D sensors often involves errors whose orientation is biased. For example, if we emit laser or ultrasonic waves for 3D measurement, the accuracy is generally different between the emission direction and directions orthogonal to it. The accuracy in the emission direction depends on the wavelength of the emission while the accuracy in directions orthogonal to it depends on the emission direction controller, e.g., servomotor. Such orientation dependence of the measurement accuracy is described by a matrix called the "covariance matrix." In Chapter 5, we study maximum likelihood estimation from biased data whose covariance matrix is provided. If the noise has no orientation dependence, the covariance matrix is a multiple of the identity matrix and the maximum likelihood solution coincides with the least-squares solution.

For computing the maximum-likelihood solution, we define a function $J(\boldsymbol{R})$ that evaluates the discrepancy from Eq. (1.2) in terms of the data covariance matrix and compute an $\boldsymbol{R}$ that minimizes it. In Chapter 5, we introduce two types of formulation:

- The rotation $\boldsymbol{R}$ is parameterized, and the function $J(\boldsymbol{R})$ is minimized with respect to the parameters.
- Without introducing parameters, the matrix $\boldsymbol{R}$ itself is regarded as an unknown, and $J(\boldsymbol{R})$ is minimized subject to the constraint that$\boldsymbol{R}$ represents a rotation.

In the first approach, we use the quaternion representation introduced in Chapter 3, expressing the rotation $\boldsymbol{R}$ in terms of a 4D vector $\boldsymbol{q}$. Then, Eq. (1.2) reduces to a linear expression in $\boldsymbol{q}$. This fact leads to various algorithms for systematically computing the maximum-likelihood solution. Here, we describe an algorithm called "FNS." In the second approach, we iteratively modify the matrix $\boldsymbol{R}$ in the 9-D space of its nine elements in such a way that after each step the function $J(\boldsymbol{R})$ decreases and at the same time $\boldsymbol{R}$ satisfies the constraint that it is a rotation. Here, we outline a procedure called "EFNS."

1.3 DERIVATIVE-BASED OPTIMIZATION

In Chapter 6, we consider minimization/maximization of a general function J in the form of Eq. (1.1). If the function J does not have a special property, the standard method is the use of the derivative. A straightforward method is first expressing the rotation matrix in terms of parameters, such as angle-axis, Euler angles, and quaternions, and then computing the derivative of the function J with respect to each parameter. The parameter value is chosen so that the value of J decreases/increases. Then, the derivative of J is reevaluated, and the process is iterated. This strategy is generally known as the "gradient method," and many variations have been proposed to improve the convergence properties, including "steepest descent" ("hill climbing"), "conjugate gradient," "Newton iterations," "Gauss–Newton iterations," and "Levenberg-Marquardt method."

However, if we are to adopt such a gradient-based approach, *we need not parameterize the rotation matrix* $\boldsymbol{R}$. After all, "derivative" is the rate of change of the function value when the variable is slightly incremented. Hence, all we need to know is the change of the function value when we add a small rotation to the given rotation. To be specific, we add a small rotation around each coordinate axis and evaluate the resulting change of the function value. After adding a small rotation that reduces/increases the function value, we update the rotation $\boldsymbol{R}$ and repeat the same process. Since the matrix $\boldsymbol{R}$ stored in the computer memory is updated at each step, no parameterization is necessary. Calling this scheme the "Lie algebra method," we describes the details of the computational procedure in Chapter 6. As real applications, we show how to compute the maximum likelihood estimati on of rotation discussed in Chapter 5. We also describe the computation of the "fundamental matrix" and the 3D reconstruction from images by "bundle adjustment"; both are fundamental procedures of computer vision [15, 29].

1.4 RELIABILITY EVALUATION OF ROTATION COMPUTATION

In Chapters 4–6, we introduce various algorithms for computing the rotation $\boldsymbol{R}$ from data, but the computed $\boldsymbol{R}$ has some errors if there is noise in the data. Chapter 7 discusses how to evaluate the accuracy of the computed $\boldsymbol{R}$. We point out that the accuracy is characterized by the "covariance matrix" $V[\boldsymbol{R}]$ of the computed rotation $\boldsymbol{R}$. The deviation of the computed rotation $\boldsymbol{R}$ from the true rotation $\bar{\boldsymbol{R}}$ is a small rotation around some axis by a small angle. The eigenvector of the covariance matrix $V[\boldsymbol{R}]$ for the largest eigenvalue indicates the axis direction around which the deviation is most likely to occur, and the corresponding eigenvalue is the variance of the deviated angle of rotation. As an example, we evaluate the covariance matrix of the rotation computed by maximum likelihood in the presence of anisotropic noise.

Next, we derive a theoretical accuracy bound such that the covariance matrix cannot be below that, whatever computational algorithm is used as long as there is noise in the data. This limit is called the "KCR lower bound." We show that it coincides with the covariance matrix of maximum likelihood estimation except for high order noise terms. This indicates that maximum likelihood estimation attains the theoretical accuracy bound except for high order noise terms.

1.5 COMPUTING PROJECTS

Readers may want to apply the theories described in this book to real engineering problems and numerically evaluate the solution. To this end, we propose two projects: one is a simulation experiment, and the other is real data analysis. For simulation, one can easily generate an arbitrary 3D object in 3D, using a graphics tool, but simulating realistic noise is not trivial, since noise is sensor-dependent. Here, we assume stereo vision for 3D sensing and describe how noise in stereo images affects the reconstructed 3D location in quantitative terms, which allows one to evaluate the covariance matrix of each measurement. Then, readers can compute the 3D rotation of the object using different methods of computation described in this book. Using different synthetic noise, one can also empirically evaluate the reliability of computation of each method and compare the result with the KCR lower bound described in Chapter 7. Next, we provide real GPS geodetic data of land deformation in northeast Japan. They describe the effect of a massive earthquake that took place on March 11, 2011. Readers can compute the land movement, using the GPS land data before and after the earthquake. For comparison, we show the data of a period in which no earthquake occurred, so that the effect of the earthquake can be grasped in quantitative terms.

1.6 RELATED TOPICS OF MATHEMATICS

Quaternion representation of 3D rotation is introduced in Chapter 3 and used for optimization computation in Chapters 4 and 5. The mathematical background of the Hamilton quaternion theory [22] is explained in Appendix A.

In the optimization procedure described in Chapter 4, the singular value decomposition of matrices plays a central role. It is also used as a basic component of computer vision application in Chapter 6. In Appendix B, related topics of linear algebra, including the singular value decomposition, are briefly summarized.

In relation to the "Lie algebra method" described in Chapter 6, we provide in Appendix C a brief introduction to basic concepts of abstract mathematics [17], including groups, topological spaces, manifolds, Lie groups, and Lie algebras.

CHAPTER 2

Geometry of Rotation

In this chapter, it is shown that the norms and the inner products of vectors and the determinants of matrices are preserved by a 3D rotation. It is concluded that a 3D rotation is represented by a "rotation matrix" (an "orthogonal matrix" of determinant 1) and has three degrees of freedom. We derive "Euler's theorem," which states that a 3D rotation is a rotation around some axis by some angle. We show expressions of 3D matrices that represent rotations around coordinate axes.

2.1 3D ROTATION

A *rotation* in the 3D space $\mathcal{R}^3$ is a linear transformation of $\mathcal{R}^3$ such that "lengths" and the "sense" are preserved. Preservation of lengths implies preservation of angles, because if three points A, B, and C are respectively mapped to A', B', and C', and if $\|\overrightarrow{AB}\|$, $\|\overrightarrow{BC}\|$, and $\|\overrightarrow{CA}\|$, where $\|\cdot\|$ denotes the norm of vectors, are equal to $\|\overrightarrow{A'B'}\|$, $\|\overrightarrow{B'C'}\|$, and $\|\overrightarrow{C'A'}\|$, respectively, the triangles $\triangle ABC$ and $\triangle A'B'C'$ are congruent to each other, so the corresponding angles are equal (Fig. 2.1(a)).

Preservation of norms also implies preservation of inner products, because if we write $\langle \boldsymbol{a}, \boldsymbol{b} \rangle$ for the inner product of $\boldsymbol{a}$ and $\boldsymbol{b}$, we see that $\|\boldsymbol{a}-\boldsymbol{b}\|^2 = \|\boldsymbol{a}\|^2 - 2\langle \boldsymbol{a}, \boldsymbol{b} \rangle + \|\boldsymbol{b}\|^2$ for arbitrary $\boldsymbol{a}$ and $\boldsymbol{b}$, so

$$\langle \boldsymbol{a}, \boldsymbol{b} \rangle = \frac{1}{2}(\|\boldsymbol{a}\|^2 + \|\boldsymbol{b}\|^2 - \|\boldsymbol{a}-\boldsymbol{b}\|^2). \tag{2.1}$$

Each term on the right side does not change after rotation.

By preservation of sense, we mean that if $\boldsymbol{a}$, $\boldsymbol{b}$, and $\boldsymbol{c}$ are a right-handed system, so are the transformed $\boldsymbol{a}'$, $\boldsymbol{b}'$, and $\boldsymbol{c}'$. This means that $|\boldsymbol{a}, \boldsymbol{b}, \boldsymbol{c}|$ and $|\boldsymbol{a}', \boldsymbol{b}', \boldsymbol{c}'|$ have the same sign, where $|\boldsymbol{a}, \boldsymbol{b}, \boldsymbol{c}|$ denotes the determinant of the matrix consisting of columns $\boldsymbol{a}$, $\boldsymbol{b}$, and $\boldsymbol{c}$ in that order. The determinant equals the signed volume of the parallelepiped made by the three columns. Since congruent shapes have the same volume, we conclude that $|\boldsymbol{a}', \boldsymbol{b}', \boldsymbol{c}'|$ $= |\boldsymbol{a}, \boldsymbol{b}, \boldsymbol{c}|$ after rotation.

There exist linear transformations that preserve lengths and angles but not the sense. Such a transformation is a composition of a rotation and a reflection (Fig. 2.1(b)). A *reflection* is a mapping into a position symmetric with respect to some plane passing through the origin. If a rotation is composed with a reflection, a right-handed system $\{\boldsymbol{a}, \boldsymbol{b}, \boldsymbol{c}\}$ is mapped to a left-handed system $\{\boldsymbol{a}', \boldsymbol{b}', \boldsymbol{c}'\}$. The volume of the parallelepipeds they define have reversed signs; $|\boldsymbol{a}', \boldsymbol{b}', \boldsymbol{c}'| = -|\boldsymbol{a}, \boldsymbol{b}, \boldsymbol{c}|$. Composition of a rotation and a reflection is sometimes called *improper rotation*, while the usual rotation is called *proper rotation*. In this book, rotations always mean proper rotations.

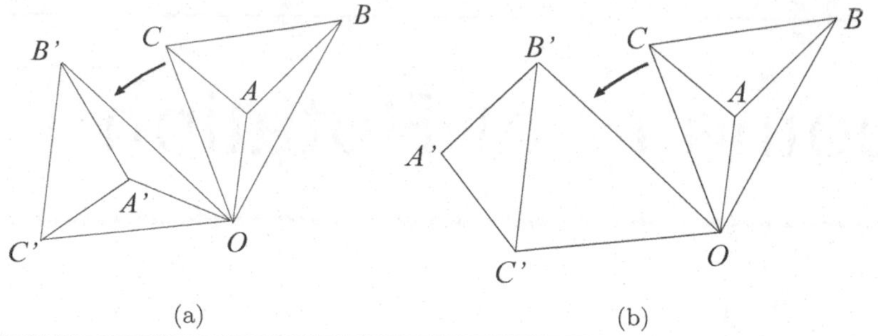

FIGURE 2.1 (a) Lengths and angles of vectors and the orientation of the space are preserved by a rotation in the 3D space $\mathcal{R}^3$. (b) The mapping is a composition of a rotation and a reflection if the orientation of the space is reversed, even though lengths and angles are preserved.

Thus, we can say that a rotation is a linear mapping $\boldsymbol{R}$ such that for arbitrary vectors $\boldsymbol{a}$, $\boldsymbol{b}$, and $\boldsymbol{c}$

$$\|\boldsymbol{Ra}\| = \|\boldsymbol{a}\|, \qquad |\boldsymbol{Ra}, \boldsymbol{Rb}, \boldsymbol{Rc}| = |\boldsymbol{a}, \boldsymbol{b}, \boldsymbol{c}| \tag{2.2}$$

hold. This implies that $\langle \boldsymbol{Ra}, \boldsymbol{Rb} \rangle = \langle \boldsymbol{a}, \boldsymbol{b} \rangle$ for arbitrary vectors $\boldsymbol{a}$, and $\boldsymbol{b}$.

2.2 ORTHOGONAL MATRICES AND ROTATION MATRICES

Let $\{\boldsymbol{e}_1, \boldsymbol{e}_2, \boldsymbol{e}_3\}$ be the standard basis of $\mathcal{R}^3$, where $\boldsymbol{e}_i$ denotes the unit vector whose ith component is 1, the other components being 0. Suppose they are rotated to vectors $\{\boldsymbol{r}_1, \boldsymbol{r}_2, \boldsymbol{r}_3\}$, respectively, by a rotation (Fig. 2.2). Then, this rotation is represented by a 3×3 matrix

$$\boldsymbol{R} = \begin{pmatrix} \boldsymbol{r}_1 & \boldsymbol{r}_2 & \boldsymbol{r}_3 \end{pmatrix}, \tag{2.3}$$

having these vectors as columns, since $\boldsymbol{r}_i = \boldsymbol{Re}_i$ holds from the definition of the vector $\boldsymbol{e}_i$.

The basis $\{\boldsymbol{e}_1, \boldsymbol{e}_2, \boldsymbol{e}_3\}$ is orthonormal, i.e., consisting of mutually orthogonal unit vectors. Since norms and angles are preserved by a rotation, $\{\boldsymbol{r}_1, \boldsymbol{r}_2, \boldsymbol{r}_3\}$ is also an orthonormal system. A matrix with orthonormal columns is called an *orthogonal matrix*. Since $\{\boldsymbol{r}_1, \boldsymbol{r}_2, \boldsymbol{r}_3\}$ has the same sense as $\{\boldsymbol{e}_1, \boldsymbol{e}_2, \boldsymbol{e}_3\}$, the matrix $\boldsymbol{R}$ has determinant 1. An orthogonal matrix of determinant 1 is called a *rotation matrix*. Thus, *a rotation is represented by a rotation matrix*. If $\{\boldsymbol{r}_1, \boldsymbol{r}_2, \boldsymbol{r}_3\}$ of Eq. (2.3) are a left-handed system, $\boldsymbol{R}$ has determinant -1. As pointed out earlier, a linear mapping specified by an orthogonal matrix of determinant -1 is a composition of a rotation and a reflection, i.e., an improper rotation. Thus, an orthogonal matrix represents either a proper rotation or an improper rotation.

The condition that $\{\boldsymbol{r}_1, \boldsymbol{r}_2, \boldsymbol{r}_3\}$ of Eq. (2.3) are an orthonormal system is written as

$$\langle \boldsymbol{r}_i, \boldsymbol{r}_j \rangle = \delta_{ij}, \tag{2.4}$$

where δ_{ij} is the *Kronecker delta*, taking on 1 for $i = j$ and 0 otherwise. It follows from Eq. (2.3) that

$$\begin{aligned} \boldsymbol{R}^\top \boldsymbol{R} &= \begin{pmatrix} \boldsymbol{r}_1^\top \\ \boldsymbol{r}_2^\top \\ \boldsymbol{r}_3^\top \end{pmatrix} \begin{pmatrix} \boldsymbol{r}_1 & \boldsymbol{r}_2 & \boldsymbol{r}_3 \end{pmatrix} = \begin{pmatrix} \langle \boldsymbol{r}_1, \boldsymbol{r}_1 \rangle & \langle \boldsymbol{r}_1, \boldsymbol{r}_2 \rangle & \langle \boldsymbol{r}_1, \boldsymbol{r}_3 \rangle \\ \langle \boldsymbol{r}_2, \boldsymbol{r}_1 \rangle & \langle \boldsymbol{r}_2, \boldsymbol{r}_2 \rangle & \langle \boldsymbol{r}_2, \boldsymbol{r}_3 \rangle \\ \langle \boldsymbol{r}_3, \boldsymbol{r}_1 \rangle & \langle \boldsymbol{r}_3, \boldsymbol{r}_2 \rangle & \langle \boldsymbol{r}_3, \boldsymbol{r}_3 \rangle \end{pmatrix} \\ &= \begin{pmatrix} 1 & 0 & 0 \\ 0 & 1 & 0 \\ 0 & 0 & 1 \end{pmatrix} = \boldsymbol{I}, \end{aligned} \tag{2.5}$$

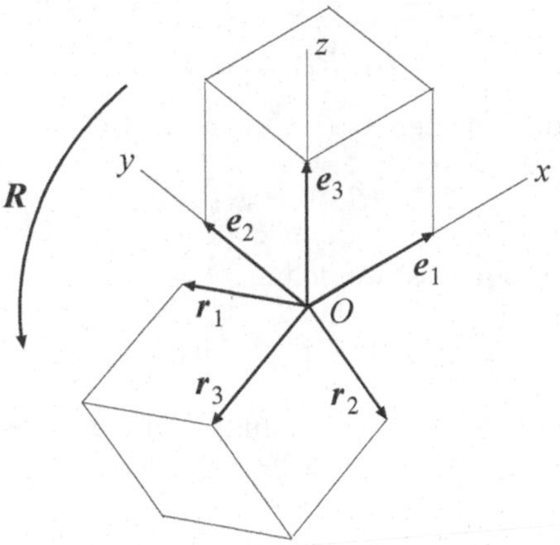

FIGURE 2.2 If the basis vectors $\{e_1, e_2, e_3\}$ of the 3D space $\mathcal{R}^3$ are rotated to $\{r_1, r_2, r_3\}$, respectively, the rotation is represented by a 3×3 matrix $\boldsymbol{R} = \begin{pmatrix} r_1 & r_2 & r_3 \end{pmatrix}$ having these vectors as columns.

where $\boldsymbol{I}$ is the identity matrix and $\top$ denotes transpose. Thus, we conclude that a matrix $\boldsymbol{R}$ is orthogonal if and only if $\boldsymbol{R}^\top \boldsymbol{R} = \boldsymbol{I}$ and that a matrix $\boldsymbol{R}$ represents a rotation if and only if $\boldsymbol{R}^\top \boldsymbol{R} = \boldsymbol{I}$ and $|\boldsymbol{R}| = 1$.

Recall that the determinant $|\boldsymbol{R}| = |\boldsymbol{r}_1, \boldsymbol{r}_2, \boldsymbol{r}_3|$ equals the signed volume of the parallelepiped defined by the columns $\boldsymbol{r}_1$, $\boldsymbol{r}_2$, and $\boldsymbol{r}_3$. An orthonormal system defines a cube of size 1. Hence, for an orthogonal matrix $\boldsymbol{R}$, the determinant is $|\boldsymbol{R}| = \pm 1$. It follows that we can say that $\boldsymbol{R}$ is a rotation matrix if and only if $\boldsymbol{R}^\top \boldsymbol{R} = \boldsymbol{I}$ and $|\boldsymbol{R}| > 0$.

The identity $\boldsymbol{R}^\top \boldsymbol{R} = \boldsymbol{I}$ of Eq. (2.5) implies that $\boldsymbol{R}^\top$ *equals the inverse* $\boldsymbol{R}^{-1}$:

$$\boldsymbol{R}\boldsymbol{R}^\top = \boldsymbol{R}\boldsymbol{R}^{-1} = \boldsymbol{I}. \tag{2.6}$$

Since $\boldsymbol{R}\boldsymbol{R}^\top = (\boldsymbol{R}^\top)^\top \boldsymbol{R}^\top$, we see that $\boldsymbol{R}^\top$ is also an orthogonal matrix. The columns of the transpose $\boldsymbol{R}^\top$ are the rows of $\boldsymbol{R}$, so *the columns and rows of an orthogonal matrix are both orthonormal systems*. Since the determinant is unchanged by transpose, we have $|\boldsymbol{R}^\top| = |\boldsymbol{R}|$. Hence, if $\boldsymbol{R}$ is a rotation matrix, so is $\boldsymbol{R}^\top$. Geometrically, $\boldsymbol{R}^\top$ $(= \boldsymbol{R}^{-1})$ represents the inverse of rotation $\boldsymbol{R}$.

Equation (2.4) consists of six identities in the elements for $(i, j) =$ (1,1), (2,2), (3,3), (1,2), (2,3), (3,1), which constrain the nine elements of $\boldsymbol{R}$. Hence, we can freely specify only $9 - 6 = 3$ elements. Namely, *a rotation matrix has three degrees of freedom* (the inequality $|\boldsymbol{R}| > 0$ does not affect the degree of freedom). Thus, a 3D rotation can be specified by at least three parameters, though not necessarily in a unique manner.

2.3 EULER'S THEOREM

We now derive "Euler's theorem," which states that an arbitrary rotation $\boldsymbol{R}$ in 3D is a rotation around some axis l by some angle Ω.

Let λ be an eigenvalue of $\boldsymbol{R}$, and $\boldsymbol{l}$ the corresponding unit eigenvector:

$$\boldsymbol{R}\boldsymbol{l} = \lambda \boldsymbol{l}. \tag{2.7}$$

The eigenvalue may have a complex value, and the eigenvector $\boldsymbol{l}$ may have complex components. Consider the inner product of Eq. (2.7) and its complex conjugate $\boldsymbol{R}\bar{\boldsymbol{l}} = \bar{\lambda}\bar{\boldsymbol{l}}$ on both sides:

$$\langle \boldsymbol{Rl}, \boldsymbol{R\bar{l}} \rangle = \lambda\bar{\lambda}\langle \boldsymbol{l}, \boldsymbol{\bar{l}} \rangle. \tag{2.8}$$

From Eq. (2.5), the left side is witten as (↪ Exercise 2.1).

$$\langle \boldsymbol{R}^\top \boldsymbol{Rl}, \boldsymbol{\bar{l}} \rangle = \langle \boldsymbol{l}, \boldsymbol{\bar{l}} \rangle = |\boldsymbol{l}|^2. \tag{2.9}$$

For a vector of complex components, we define

$$|\boldsymbol{l}|^2 = |l_1|^2 + |l_2|^2 + |l_3|^2 \quad (\geq 0), \tag{2.10}$$

where $|\cdot|$ denotes the absolute value (modulus) of a complex value. Since $\boldsymbol{l}$ is a nonzero eigenvector ($|\boldsymbol{l}|^2 > 0$) and the right side of Eq. (2.8) equals $|\lambda|^2|\boldsymbol{l}|^2$, we see from Eq. (2.9) that

$$|\lambda|^2 = 1. \tag{2.11}$$

Namely, the three eigenvalues λ_1, λ_2, and λ_3 of $\boldsymbol{R}$ all have absolute value 1. As is well known, the determinant of a matrix is the product of all its eigenvalues (↪ Exercise 2.2(2)), so

$$|\boldsymbol{R}| = \lambda_1\lambda_2\lambda_3 = 1. \tag{2.12}$$

On the other hand, the eigenvalues of a 3×3 matrix $\boldsymbol{R}$ are the roots of the characteristic polynomial $\phi(\lambda) = |\lambda\boldsymbol{I} - \boldsymbol{R}|$, i.e., the solutions of $\phi(\lambda) = 0$ (↪ Exercise 2.2(1)). This is a cubic polynomial in λ, so either its roots are all real or one is real and the remaining two are a complex conjugate pair. Since each has absolute value 1, we conclude that $\{\lambda_1, \lambda_2, \lambda_3\}$ $= \{1, 1, 1\}$, $\{1, -1, -1\}$ if all are real ($\{\cdots\}$ denotes the set of unordered elements). If one is a real numberλ and the other two are a complex conjugate pair α and $\bar{\alpha}$, we have $\lambda\alpha\bar{\alpha}$ $= \lambda|\alpha|^2 = \lambda = 1$ from Eq. (2.12). Whichever is the case, *at least one eigenvalue is 1*. The eigenvector $\boldsymbol{l}$ for a real eigenvalue λ is obtained from Eq. (2.7) by arithmetic operations and substitutions. Hence, it has real components. Thus, there exists a unit vector $\boldsymbol{l}$ such that

$$\boldsymbol{Rl} = \boldsymbol{l}. \tag{2.13}$$

This implies that the vector $\boldsymbol{l}$ is unchanged by the rotation $\boldsymbol{R}$, meaning that the line l in the direction $\boldsymbol{l}$ is invariant to the rotation $\boldsymbol{R}$. This line l is called the *axis of rotation*.

If a vector $\boldsymbol{a}$ is projected onto the line l, its projected length is $\langle \boldsymbol{l}, \boldsymbol{a} \rangle$ (↪ Exercise 2.3(1)). If $\boldsymbol{a}$ is rotated to $\boldsymbol{a}' = \boldsymbol{Ra}$ by rotation $\boldsymbol{R}$ (Fig. 2.3), we obtain from Eq. (2.13)

$$\langle \boldsymbol{l}, \boldsymbol{a}' \rangle = \langle \boldsymbol{l}, \boldsymbol{Ra} \rangle = \langle \boldsymbol{Rl}, \boldsymbol{Ra} \rangle = \langle \boldsymbol{l}, \boldsymbol{a} \rangle. \tag{2.14}$$

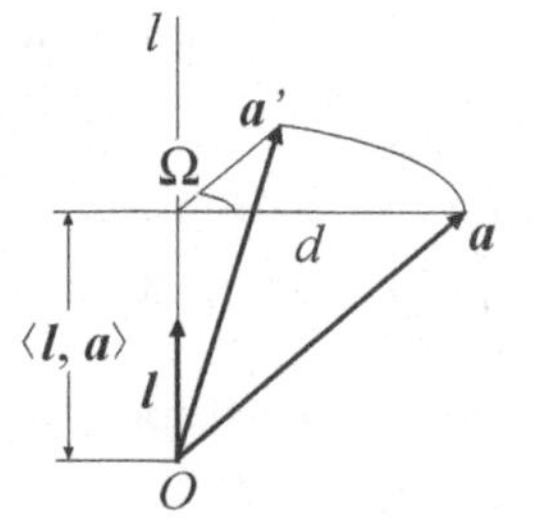

FIGURE 2.3 An arbitrary rotation $\boldsymbol{R}$ in 3D is a rotation around some axis l by some angle Ω.

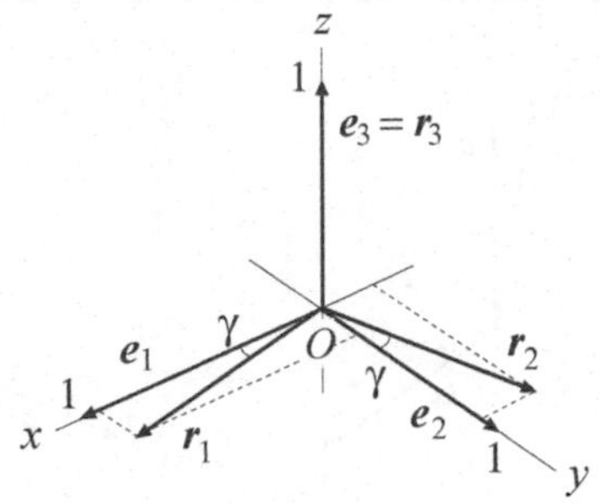

FIGURE 2.4 Rotation around the z-axis by angle γ.

The distance d between the endpoint of vector $\boldsymbol{a}$ and the line l is $d = \|\boldsymbol{a} - \langle \boldsymbol{l}, \boldsymbol{a}\rangle \boldsymbol{l}\|$ ($\hookrightarrow$ Exercise 2.3(2)). For the vector $\boldsymbol{a}' = \boldsymbol{R}\boldsymbol{a}$ after the rotation, we have

$$\begin{aligned} d' &= \|\boldsymbol{a}' - \langle \boldsymbol{l}, \boldsymbol{a}'\rangle \boldsymbol{l}\| = \|\boldsymbol{R}\boldsymbol{a} - \langle \boldsymbol{l}, \boldsymbol{R}\boldsymbol{a}\rangle \boldsymbol{l}\| = \|\boldsymbol{R}\boldsymbol{a} - \langle \boldsymbol{l}, \boldsymbol{R}\boldsymbol{a}\rangle \boldsymbol{R}\boldsymbol{l}\| \\ &= \|\boldsymbol{R}(\boldsymbol{a} - \langle \boldsymbol{l}, \boldsymbol{a}\rangle \boldsymbol{l})\| = \|\boldsymbol{a} - \langle \boldsymbol{l}, \boldsymbol{a}\rangle \boldsymbol{l}\| = d. \end{aligned} \tag{2.15}$$

Hence, for any vector $\boldsymbol{a}$, its projected length onto the line l and the distance d from the line l are both unaffected by the rotation $\boldsymbol{R}$. Thus, we obtain the following *Euler's theorem*: *any rotation $\boldsymbol{R}$ in 3D is a rotation around some axis l by some angle Ω.*

2.4 AXIAL ROTATIONS

Among rotations around axes, the most fundamental ones are those around the coordinate axes. In the following, the axis is regarded as oriented and the angle of rotation is regarded as positive or negative according to the right-hand rule.

First, consider the rotation around the z-axis by angle γ. If we rotate the basis vectors $\{\boldsymbol{e}_1, \boldsymbol{e}_2, \boldsymbol{e}_3\}$ around the z-axis by angle γ (Fig. 2.4), they are rotated, respectively, to

$$\boldsymbol{r}_1 = \begin{pmatrix} \cos\gamma \\ \sin\gamma \\ 0 \end{pmatrix}, \qquad \boldsymbol{r}_2 = \begin{pmatrix} -\sin\gamma \\ \cos\gamma \\ 0 \end{pmatrix}, \qquad \boldsymbol{r}_3 = \begin{pmatrix} 0 \\ 0 \\ 1 \end{pmatrix}. \tag{2.16}$$

As stated in Sec. 2.2, the corresponding rotation matrix $\boldsymbol{R}_z(\gamma)$ has these as columns in the form

$$\boldsymbol{R}_z(\gamma) = \begin{pmatrix} \cos\gamma & -\sin\gamma & 0 \\ \sin\gamma & \cos\gamma & 0 \\ 0 & 0 & 1 \end{pmatrix}. \tag{2.17}$$

Similarly, we obtain the rotation matrices around the x-axis by angle α and around the y-axis by angle β in the form (Fig. 2.5).

$$\boldsymbol{R}_x(\alpha) = \begin{pmatrix} 1 & 0 & 0 \\ 0 & \cos\alpha & -\sin\alpha \\ 0 & \sin\alpha & \cos\alpha \end{pmatrix}, \qquad \boldsymbol{R}_y(\beta) = \begin{pmatrix} \cos\beta & 0 & \sin\beta \\ 0 & 1 & 0 \\ -\sin\beta & 0 & \cos\beta \end{pmatrix}. \tag{2.18}$$

2.5 SUPPLEMENTAL NOTE

As stated in Introduction, 3D rotation plays a central role in analysis of dynamics of rigid bodies and angular momentum of elementary particles, and hence it has mostly been discussed by physicists. Classical textbooks still widely read today include [8, 10, 32]. 3D

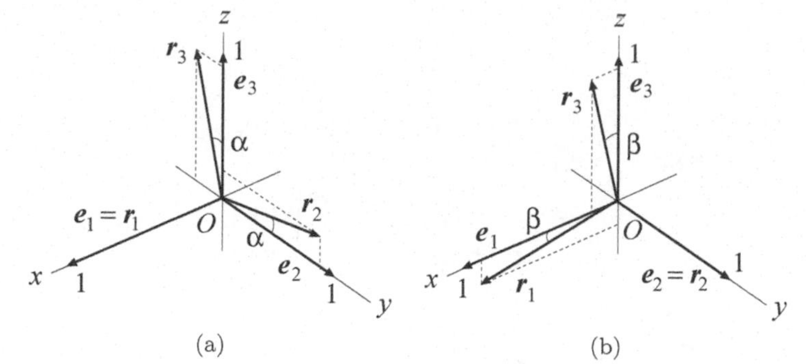

FIGURE 2.5 (a) Rotation around the x-axis by angle α. (b) Rotation around the y-axis by angle β.

rotation is also an important topic of computer vision research in relation to analysis of cameras and 3D scenes [17].

2.6 EXERCISES

2.1. Show that for an arbitrary matrix $\boldsymbol{A}$ and arbitrary vectors $\boldsymbol{x}$ and $\boldsymbol{y}$ the following identity holds:

$$\langle \boldsymbol{x}, \boldsymbol{A}\boldsymbol{y} \rangle = \langle \boldsymbol{A}^\top \boldsymbol{x}, \boldsymbol{y} \rangle. \tag{2.19}$$

2.2. (1) Show that an eigenvalue λ of matrix $\boldsymbol{A}$ is a root of the characteristic polynomial $\phi(\lambda) = |\lambda \boldsymbol{I} - \boldsymbol{A}|$.

(2) Show that the eigenvalues λ_1, λ_2, and λ_3 of matrix $\boldsymbol{A}$ satisfy the following identities:

$$\mathrm{tr}\boldsymbol{A} = \lambda_1 + \lambda_2 + \lambda_3, \qquad |\boldsymbol{A}| = \lambda_1 \lambda_2 \lambda_3. \tag{2.20}$$

2.3. (1) Show that the (signed) length of the projection of vector $\boldsymbol{a}$ onto line l having the unit direction vector $\boldsymbol{u}$ is given by $\langle \boldsymbol{u}, \boldsymbol{a} \rangle$ (Fig. 2.6).

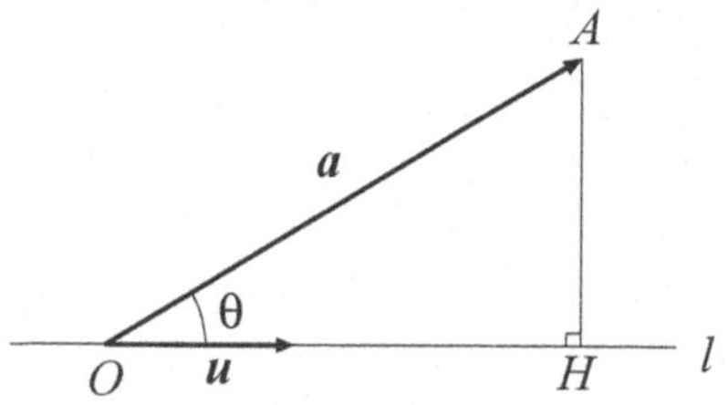

FIGURE 2.6 Projection of a vector $\boldsymbol{a}$ starting from a point on a line l onto the line l.

(2) Show that the distance between line l having the unit direction vector $\boldsymbol{u}$ and the endpoint of vector $\boldsymbol{a}$ starting from a point on l is given by $\|\boldsymbol{a} - \langle \boldsymbol{u}, \boldsymbol{a} \rangle \boldsymbol{u}\|$.

CHAPTER 3

Parameters of Rotation

We pointed out in the preceding chapter that 3D rotation has three degrees of freedom. In this chapter, we show various ways of representing a rotation matrix $\boldsymbol{R}$ by three parameters. The most naive way is the use of the rotation angles α, β, and γ, called "roll," "pitch," and "yaw," around the coordinate axes. We point out, however, that their designation depends on the order of the composition. We also show that rotation of the coordinate system relative of a fixed object and rotation of the object relative to a fixed coordinate system lead to different results. Considering these, we introduce the "Euler angles" that uniquely specify 3D rotation. We also point out its potential singularities. Then, we derive the "Rodrigues formula" that specifies 3D rotation by the axis $\boldsymbol{l}$ of rotation and the angle Ω around it. Finally, we introduce "quaternion representation," specifying 3D rotation by four parameters q_0, q_1, q_2, and q_3 whose square sum is unity (hence the degree of freedom is 3). This is an extension of complex numbers for describing 2D rotations in plane to 3D rotations in space.

3.1 ROLL, PITCH, YAW

As pointed out in Sec. 3.2, 3D rotation has three degrees of freedom. In principle, therefore, it can be specified by three parameters. Hence, It is natural to specify a 3D rotation by angles of rotation around the three coordinate axes. However, special care is necessary.

Rotations around the coordinate axes are traditionally called *roll*, *pitch*, and *yaw*. These terms are used for describing the posture of vehicles, ships, and airplanes. If we define the x-axis in the forward direction, the y-axis in the horizontal direction orthogonal to it, and the z-axis in the vertical direction[1], the rotations around them are the roll, the pitch, and the yaw, respectively (Fig. 3.1).

However, they are not sufficient for specifying a rotation, because if α, β, and γ are respectively the roll, the pitch, and the yaw, the final result *depends on the order of the rotation composition*. As we see from Fig. 3.2(a), (b), first rotating around the x-axis by 90° and then around the y-axis by 90° and first rotating around the y-axis by 90° and then around the x-axis by 90° produce different results. On the other hand, the same rotation can be obtained by composing different axial rotations. As shown in Fig. 3.2(a), (c), for example, rotation around the x-axis by 90° followed by rotation around the y-axis by 90°

[1]For airplanes and satellites, the y- and z-axes are often taken to be in the right-horizontal (facing forward) and down-vertical (earth-ward) directions, respectively (Fig. 3.1 does not follow this convention).

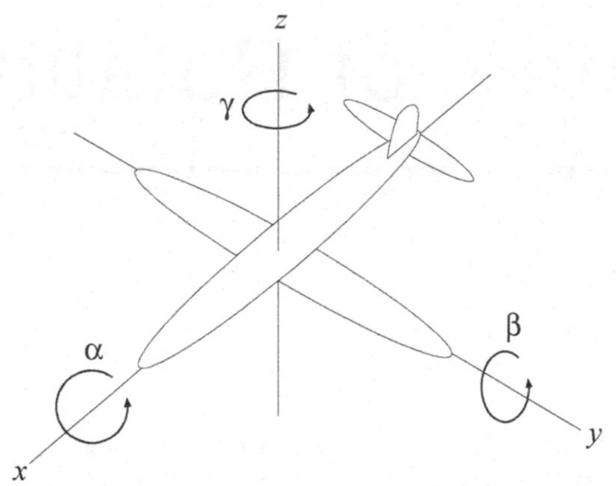

FIGURE 3.1 If we let the x-, y-, and z-axes be respectively the forward, the horizontal, and the vertical directions, the rotations around them are called roll, pitch, and yaw, respectively.

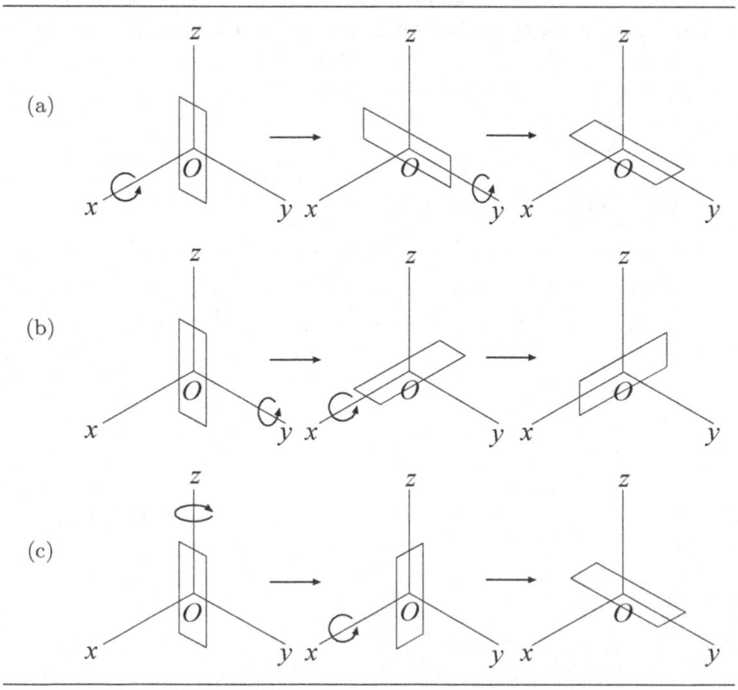

FIGURE 3.2 (a) Rotating around the x-axis by 90° and then around the y-axis by 90°. (b) Rotating around the y-axis by 90° and then around the x-axis by 90°. (c) Rotating around the z-axis by −90° and then around the x-axis by 90°. The results of (a) and (b) are different, while (a) and (c) result in the same rotation.

and rotation around the z-axis by $-90°$ followed by rotation around the x-axis by $90°$ both result in the same rotation[2].

Thus, we need to specify the order of composition. Still, a problem remains. If we consider rotations of roll α, pitch β, and yaw γ in that order, there remains *ambiguity of interpretation*. Consider Fig. 3.1, for example. Suppose we rotate the body around the x-axis by angle α. By this rotation, the y-axis is also rotated to a new direction if we regard it as fixed to the body. Is the next rotation around the *original* y-axis direction by β or around the *new* rotated y-axis, i.e., the wing direction? Mathematically, the former interpretation sounds reasonable. However, the roll, pitch, and yaw are the concepts defined in relation to the motion of the body, so the latter interpretation makes an engineering sense; the original y-axis is irrelevant to the current posture of the body. The same can be said of the yaw: is it a rotation around the "vertical" direction by γ or around the direction orthogonal to the "current" body axis?

If we compose rotations around the x-, y-, and z-axes of a "stationary" xyz coordinate system in space by angle α, β, and γ "in that order," the resulting rotation matrix is obtained from the matrices $\boldsymbol{R}_x(\alpha)$, $\boldsymbol{R}_y(\beta)$, and $\boldsymbol{R}_x(\alpha)$, of Eq. (2.17) in the form

$$\boldsymbol{R} = \boldsymbol{R}_z(\gamma)\boldsymbol{R}_y(\beta)\boldsymbol{R}_x(\alpha). \tag{3.1}$$

This is mathematically obvious. However, if we compose rotations around the x-, y-, and z-axes of the xyz coordinate system fixed to the body as defined in Fig. 3.1 by angle α, β, and γ "in that order," the resulting rotation is

$$\boldsymbol{R} = \boldsymbol{R}_x(\alpha)\boldsymbol{R}_y(\beta)\boldsymbol{R}_z(\gamma). \tag{3.2}$$

Namely, *the order of composition is reversed*. We explain the reason for this in the next section.

3.2 COORDINATE SYSTEM ROTATION

Consider an $\bar{x}\bar{y}\bar{z}$ coordinate system fixed in space. We call it the *world coordinate system*. Consider an object placed in space, and define an xyz coordinate system fixed to it such that its origin O coincides with the origin of the world $\bar{x}\bar{y}\bar{z}$ coordinate system. We call it the *object coordinate system*. Suppose this object coordinate system is rotated relative to the world coordinate system by $\boldsymbol{R}$. Let $\bar{\boldsymbol{e}}_1$, $\bar{\boldsymbol{e}}_2$, and $\bar{\boldsymbol{e}}_3$ be the basis vectors along the $\bar{x}$-, $\bar{y}$-, and $\bar{z}$-axes of the world coordinate system, respectively; $\bar{\boldsymbol{e}}_i$ is the unit vector with the ith component 1 and the others 0. Then, the basis vectors $\boldsymbol{e}_1$, $\boldsymbol{e}_2$, and $\boldsymbol{e}_3$ along the rotated x-, y-, and z-axes are, respectively,

$$\boldsymbol{e}_1 = \boldsymbol{R}\bar{\boldsymbol{e}}_1, \qquad \boldsymbol{e}_2 = \boldsymbol{R}\bar{\boldsymbol{e}}_2, \qquad \boldsymbol{e}_3 = \boldsymbol{R}\bar{\boldsymbol{e}}_3. \tag{3.3}$$

Let P be a point in space with world coordinates $(\bar{x}, \bar{y}, \bar{z})$. Then, what are the coordinates (x, y, z) of *that point* P with respect to the object coordinate system (Fig. 3.3)? How are $(\bar{x}, \bar{y}, \bar{z})$ and (x, y, z) related?

The precise meaning of P having world coordinates $(\bar{x}, \bar{y}, \bar{z})$ and object coordinates (x, y, z) is that we can write

$$\overrightarrow{OP} = \bar{x}\bar{\boldsymbol{e}}_1 + \bar{y}\bar{\boldsymbol{e}}_2 + \bar{z}\bar{\boldsymbol{e}}_3 = x\boldsymbol{e}_1 + y\boldsymbol{e}_2 + z\boldsymbol{e}_3. \tag{3.4}$$

[2]In Fig. 3.2(c), first rotating around the z-axis by $90°$ would result in the upside down configuration (rotation around the y-axis by $180°$).

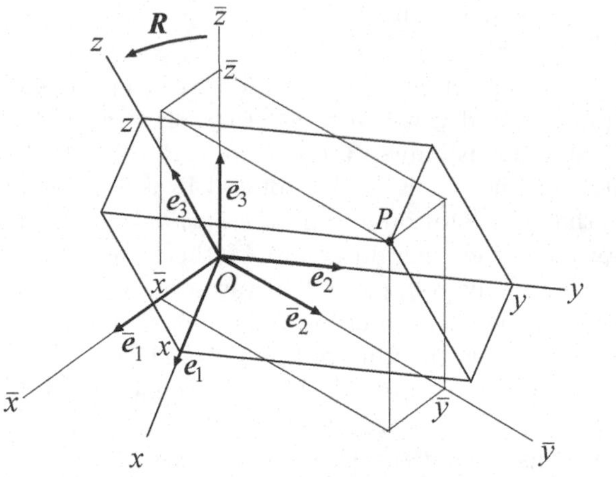

FIGURE 3.3 If the xyz coordinate system is rotated relative to the $\bar{x}\bar{y}\bar{z}$ coordinate system by $\boldsymbol{R}$, the basis vectors $\boldsymbol{e}_i$ of the xyz coordinate system are obtained by rotating the basis vectors $\bar{\boldsymbol{e}}_i$ of the $\bar{x}\bar{y}\bar{z}$ coordinate system by $\boldsymbol{R}$, $i = 1, 2, 3$. Then, a point P with coordinates $(\bar{x}, \bar{y}, \bar{z})$ with respect to the $\bar{x}\bar{y}\bar{z}$ coordinate system has coordinates (x, y, z) with respect to the xyz coordinate system.

From the definition of $\bar{\boldsymbol{e}}_1$, $\bar{\boldsymbol{e}}_2$, and $\bar{\boldsymbol{e}}_3$, the matrix consisting of them as columns is the identity matrix $\boldsymbol{I}$. As shown in Eq. (2.3), the matrix consisting of the vectors $\boldsymbol{e}_1$, $\boldsymbol{e}_2$, and $\boldsymbol{e}_3$ of Eq. (3.3) is $\boldsymbol{R}$. Hence, the vector $\overrightarrow{OP}$ of Eq. (3.4) is written in two ways as follows:

$$\overrightarrow{OP} = \begin{pmatrix} \bar{\boldsymbol{e}}_1 & \bar{\boldsymbol{e}}_2 & \bar{\boldsymbol{e}}_3 \end{pmatrix} \begin{pmatrix} \bar{x} \\ \bar{y} \\ \bar{z} \end{pmatrix} = \begin{pmatrix} \bar{x} \\ \bar{y} \\ \bar{z} \end{pmatrix},$$
$$\overrightarrow{OP} = \begin{pmatrix} \boldsymbol{e}_1 & \boldsymbol{e}_2 & \boldsymbol{e}_3 \end{pmatrix} \begin{pmatrix} x \\ y \\ z \end{pmatrix} = \boldsymbol{R} \begin{pmatrix} x \\ y \\ z \end{pmatrix}. \tag{3.5}$$

Equating them and multiplying both sides by $\boldsymbol{R}^\top$ $(= \boldsymbol{R}^{-1})$, we obtain

$$\begin{pmatrix} x \\ y \\ z \end{pmatrix} = \boldsymbol{R}^\top \begin{pmatrix} \bar{x} \\ \bar{y} \\ \bar{z} \end{pmatrix}. \tag{3.6}$$

This states that viewed from the object coordinate system, it seems as if a point P originally in the position $(\bar{x}, \bar{y}, \bar{z})$ rotates by $\boldsymbol{R}^\top$ $(= \boldsymbol{R}^{-1})$ and moves to the new position (x, y, z). In other words, viewed from a moving coordinate system, points outside seem to undergo a *reverse* motion, while they are in fact stationary, relative to which the coordinate system is moving[3] (Fig. 3.4). For example, the earth is in fact rotating around its axis from west to east relative to the sun, but viewed from the earth, the sun looks as if rotating around the earth from east to west.

In view of this, Eq. (3.2) is explained as follows. Consider an airplane, and define an xyz "airframe coordinate system" fixed to the airplane as shown in Fig. 3.1. Suppose it

[3]In tensor analysis, the vector $\boldsymbol{x}$ consisting of coordinate values is called a "contravariant vector" in the sense that it undergoes transformations "opposite to the coordinate system," and customarily denoted by x^i, $i = 1, 2, 3$, using upper indices [22].

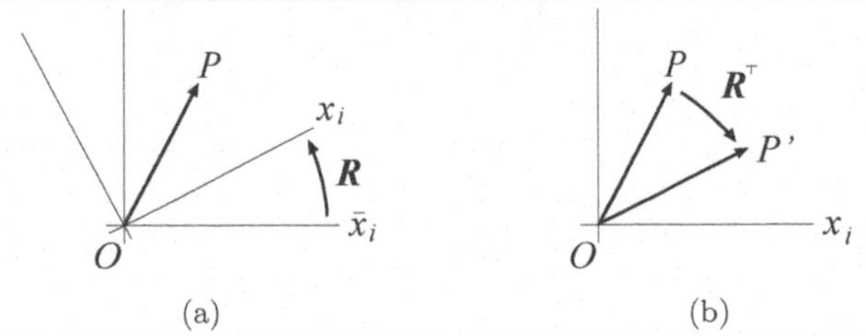

FIGURE 3.4 (a) The coordinate system is rotating relative to a point P fixed in the space. (b) If viewed from the rotating coordinate system, point P looks as if inversely rotating by $\boldsymbol{R}^\top$ $(= \boldsymbol{R}^{-1})$.

rotates around the x-axis by angle α. This rotation is represented by the matrix $\boldsymbol{R}_x(\alpha)$ of Fig. (2.18). However, if we look at a point P outside, e.g., on the control tower, we feel as if the outside world is rotating relative to the airplane by the inverse rotation $\boldsymbol{R}_x(\alpha)^{-1}$ $(= \boldsymbol{R}_x(\alpha)^\top)$. Suppose the airplane then rotates around its own y-axis by angle β. The outside world looks as if rotating relative to the xyz airframe coordinate system by $\boldsymbol{R}_y(\beta)^{-1}$ $(= \boldsymbol{R}_y(\beta)^\top)$. If the airplane further rotates around its own z-axis by angle γ, the outside world looks as if rotating relative to the xyz airframe coordinate system by $\boldsymbol{R}_z(\gamma)^{-1}$ $(= \boldsymbol{R}_z(\gamma)^\top)$. Composing these rotations, we feel as if the outside world is rotating relative to the airplane by $\boldsymbol{R}_z(\gamma)^\top \boldsymbol{R}_y(\beta)^\top \boldsymbol{R}_x(\alpha)^\top$. In reality, however, the outside world does not rotate but the airplane has undergone the inverse (= transpose) rotation given by (↪ Exercise 3.1(a))

$$(\boldsymbol{R}_z(\gamma)^\top \boldsymbol{R}_y(\beta)^\top \boldsymbol{R}_x(\alpha)^\top)^\top = \boldsymbol{R}_x(\alpha)\boldsymbol{R}_y(\beta)\boldsymbol{R}_z(\gamma). \tag{3.7}$$

Thus, we obtain Eq. (3.2).

3.3 EULER ANGLES

As pointed out in the preceding section, specification of a 3D rotation by roll α, pitch β, and γ depends on the order of composition, and ambiguity remains in interpretation. This is resolved by using the *Euler angles*. They are defined as a rotation of the $\bar{x}\bar{y}\bar{z}$ world coordinate system in the following three stages[4] (Fig. 3.5).

1. Define the xyz coordinate system by rotating the $\bar{x}\bar{y}\bar{z}$ coordinate system around the $\bar{z}$-axis by angle ϕ (Fig. 3.5(a)); the z-axis remains the same as the $\bar{z}$-axis.
2. Define the $x'y'z'$ coordinate system by rotating the xyz coordinate system around the x-axis by angle θ (Fig. 3.5(b)); the x'-axis remains the same as the x-axis.
3. Define the $x''y''z''$ coordinate system by rotating the $x'y'z'$ coordinate system around the z'-axis by angle ψ (Fig. 3.5(c)); the z''-axis remains the same as the z'-axis.

The x'-axis in Fig. 3.2(b), i.e., the intersection l of the $\bar{x}\bar{y}$ plane with the $x''y''$ plane, is called the *line of nodes*[5].

Viewed from the rotated xyz coordinate system, a point $P : (\bar{x}, \bar{y}, \bar{z})$ fixed to the $\bar{x}\bar{y}\bar{z}$ coordinate system looks like rotating around the z-axis (= the $\bar{z}$-axis) by angle $-\phi$. In

[4]Different conventions exist as to around which axis we rotate and in what order, depending on application domains. The description here follows the textbook of Goldstein et al. [10].

[5]This is a term for describing planet motions. For the earth, this is the intersection of the orbit plane of the sun viewed from the earth, called the "ecliptic plane," with the plane orthogonal to the axis of the earth, called the "equatorial plane."

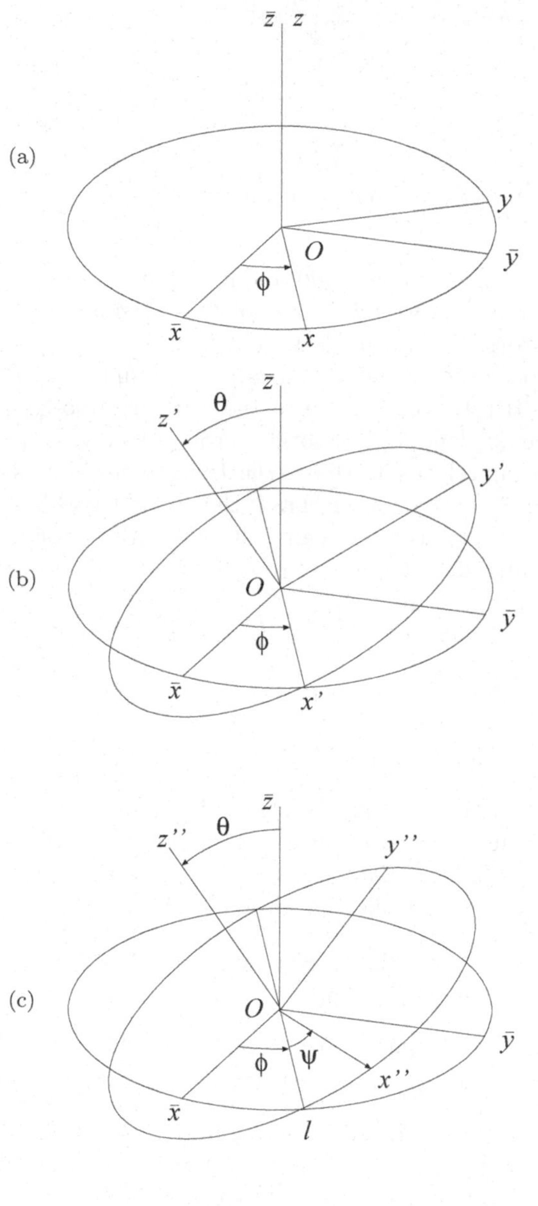

FIGURE 3.5 (a) The xyz coordinate system is obtained by rotating the $\bar{x}\bar{y}\bar{z}$ coordinate system around the $\bar{z}$-axis by angle ϕ (z-axis is the same as the $\bar{z}$-axis). (b) The $x'y'z'$ coordinate system is obtained by rotating the xyz coordinate system around the x-axis by angle θ (x'-axis is the same as the x-axis). (c) The $x''y''z''$ coordinate system is obtained by rotating the $x'y'z'$ coordinate system around the z-axis by angle ψ (z''-axis is the same as the z'-axis).

other words, using the expression in Eq. (2.18), the outside world rotates by $\boldsymbol{R}_z(-\phi)$ ($=\boldsymbol{R}_z(\phi)^\top$). Viewed from the further rotated $x'y'z'$ coordinate system, the point P looks like rotating around the x'-axis (= the x-axis) by angle $-\theta$. Namely, the outside world rotates by $\boldsymbol{R}_x(-\theta)$ ($=\boldsymbol{R}_x(\theta)^\top$). Viewed from the final $x''y''z''$ coordinate system, the point P looks like rotating around the z''-axis (=the z'-axis) by angle $-\psi$. Namely, the outside world looks like rotating by $\boldsymbol{R}_z(-\psi)$ ($=\boldsymbol{R}_z(\psi)^\top$). Composing these rotations, we find that the outside world rotates by $\boldsymbol{R}_z(\psi)^\top\boldsymbol{R}_x(\theta)^\top\boldsymbol{R}_z(\phi)^\top$. This is, however, due to the rotation of the coordinate system, and the coordinate rotation relative to the stationary $\bar{x}\bar{y}\bar{z}$ coordinate system is

$$\boldsymbol{R} = (\boldsymbol{R}_z(\psi)^\top\boldsymbol{R}_x(\theta)^\top\boldsymbol{R}_z(\phi)^\top)^\top = \boldsymbol{R}_z(\phi)\boldsymbol{R}_x(\theta)\boldsymbol{R}_z(\psi). \tag{3.8}$$

To this result, we can give another interpretation. Namely, the $x''y''z''$ coordinate system is alternatively obtained by the following operations.

1. Rotate the $\bar{x}\bar{y}\bar{z}$ coordinate system around the $\bar{z}$-axis by angle ψ.
2. Rotate the resulting coordinate system around the (original) $\bar{x}$-axis by angle θ.
3. Rotate the resulting coordinate system around the (original) $\bar{z}$-axis by angle ϕ.

As a result, the x''-axis and the $\bar{z}$-axis make angle θ, and the intersection l of the $x''y''$ plane with the $\bar{x}\bar{y}$ plane, i.e., the line of nodes, makes angle ϕ with the $\bar{x}$-axis. Also, the x''-axis make angle ψ with l. Mathematically, this description is more straightforward. Traditionally, however, the Euler angles are defined successively relative to the previous state of the rotating coordinate system. This is because of the convenience of applications such as navigation of vehicles, ships and airplanes and control of robot arms.

The Euler angles θ, ϕ, and ψ thus defined have no ambiguity of interpretation, but indeterminacy occurs when $\theta = 0$. This is because the direction of the line of nodes in Fig. 3.2(c) is indeterminate for $\theta = 0$. In fact, if we let $\theta = 0$ in Eq. (3.8), we see that due to $\boldsymbol{R}_x(0) = \boldsymbol{I}$

$$\boldsymbol{R} = \boldsymbol{R}_z(\phi)\boldsymbol{R}_z(\psi) = \boldsymbol{R}_z(\phi+\psi), \tag{3.9}$$

meaning that only the sum $\phi+\psi$ is determined. This phenomenon is known as *gimbal lock*[6]. If we control navigation based on Euler angles, the control becomes momentarily unstable in the instant of $\theta = 0$.

If Eqs. (2.17) and (2.18) are substituted, we see that the components of Eq. (3.8) are expressed as follows:

$$\boldsymbol{R} = \begin{pmatrix} \cos\phi\cos\psi - \sin\phi\cos\theta\sin\psi & -\cos\phi\sin\psi - \sin\phi\cos\theta\cos\psi & \sin\phi\sin\theta \\ \sin\phi\cos\psi + \cos\phi\cos\theta\sin\psi & -\sin\phi\sin\psi + \cos\phi\cos\theta\cos\psi & -\cos\phi\sin\theta \\ \sin\theta\sin\psi & \sin\theta\cos\psi & \cos\theta \end{pmatrix}. \tag{3.10}$$

This is the expression of the rotation matrix $\boldsymbol{R}$ in terms of the Euler angles θ, ϕ, and ψ. Conversely, we can express the Euler angles θ, ϕ, and ψ in terms of the elements of $\boldsymbol{R} = \begin{pmatrix} r_{ij} \end{pmatrix}$ (abbreviation of the matrix whose (i,j) element is r_{ij}). From the (3,3) element of Eq. (3.10), we see that

$$\theta = \cos^{-1} r_{33}, \qquad 0 \leq \theta \leq \pi. \tag{3.11}$$

[6]A "gimbal" is a kind of gyroscope used for navigation of ships and airplanes, having a rotating disk with a controllable axis. The axis direction is controlled by three rings, called the "gimbal rings," surrounding the rotating disk. The control becomes unstable when two of the three rings happen to be coplanar, the phenomenon called the "gimbal lock."

From the third column and the third row of Eq. (3.10), we see that if $\theta \neq 0$, we can determine ϕ and ψ from

$$\cos\phi = -\frac{r_{23}}{\sin\theta}, \qquad \sin\phi = \frac{r_{13}}{\sin\theta}, \qquad 0 \leq \phi < 2\pi, \tag{3.12}$$

$$\cos\psi = \frac{r_{32}}{\sin\theta}, \qquad \sin\psi = \frac{r_{31}}{\sin\theta}, \qquad 0 \leq \phi < 2\pi. \tag{3.13}$$

However, when $\theta \approx 0$, the numerators and the denominators of the expressions are both close to 0, causing instability of numerical computation. In the instance of $\theta = 0$, both ϕ and ψ are indeterminate (gimbal lock), in which case Eq. (3.10) reduces to $\boldsymbol{R}_z(\phi + \psi)$ as shown in Eq. (3.9). In that case, only $\phi + \psi$ is determined in the form

$$\cos(\phi + \psi) = r_{11}(= r_{22}), \qquad \sin(\phi + \psi) = r_{21}(= -r_{12}), \qquad 0 \leq \phi + \psi < 2\pi. \tag{3.14}$$

3.4 RODRIGUES FORMULA

The reason that 3D rotation is often represented as a composition of rotations around three coordinate axes is that in practical applications object postures are usually controlled by rotation around three orthogonal axes fixed to the object. As pointed out in Sec. 2.3, on the other hand, a 3D rotation is a rotation around some axis by some angle. Hence, it is also natural to represent 3D rotation by its axis and angle of rotation.

Suppose a vector $\boldsymbol{a}$ starting from the origin O is rotated by angle Ω around an axis l in the direction of $\boldsymbol{l}$ (unit vector) to $\boldsymbol{a}'$, where Ω is signed according to the right-hand rule with respect to $\boldsymbol{l}$ (Fig. 3.6). Let P and P' be the endpoints of $\boldsymbol{a}$ and $\boldsymbol{a}'$, respectively. Let H be the foot of the perpendicular from point P' to line OP. We see from Fig. 3.6 that

$$\boldsymbol{a}' = \overrightarrow{OQ} + \overrightarrow{QH} + \overrightarrow{HP'}. \tag{3.15}$$

Since $\overrightarrow{OQ}$ is the projection of $\boldsymbol{a}$ onto line l, we can write ($\hookrightarrow$ Exercise 2.3)

$$\overrightarrow{OQ} = \langle \boldsymbol{a}, \boldsymbol{l} \rangle \boldsymbol{l}. \tag{3.16}$$

Hence, $\overrightarrow{QP} = \boldsymbol{a} - \langle \boldsymbol{a}, \boldsymbol{l} \rangle \boldsymbol{l}$. Since $\overrightarrow{QH}$ is the projection of $\overrightarrow{QP'}$ onto the direction $\overrightarrow{QP}$, we can write

$$\begin{aligned}\overrightarrow{QH} &= \langle \overrightarrow{QP'}, \frac{\overrightarrow{QP}}{\|\overrightarrow{QP}\|} \rangle \frac{\overrightarrow{QP}}{\|\overrightarrow{QP}\|} = \frac{\langle \overrightarrow{QP'}, \overrightarrow{QP} \rangle}{\|\overrightarrow{QP}\|^2} \overrightarrow{QP} \\ &= \frac{\|\overrightarrow{QP}\|^2 \cos\Omega}{\|\overrightarrow{QP}\|^2} \overrightarrow{QP} = (\boldsymbol{a} - \langle \boldsymbol{a}, \boldsymbol{l} \rangle \boldsymbol{l}) \cos\Omega.\end{aligned} \tag{3.17}$$

Since $\|\overrightarrow{QP}'\| = \|\overrightarrow{QP}\|$, we see that $\|\overrightarrow{HP}'\| = \|\overrightarrow{QP}'\| \sin\Omega = \|\overrightarrow{QP}\| \sin\Omega$ and that for $0 < \Omega < \pi$ the direction of $\overrightarrow{HP}'$ is the direction of the vector product $\boldsymbol{l} \times \boldsymbol{a}$. Let θ be the angle made by vectors $\boldsymbol{l}$ and $\boldsymbol{a}$ as shown in Fig. 3.6. By the definition of vector product, $\|\boldsymbol{l} \times \boldsymbol{a}\|$ equals the area of the parallelogram made by vectors $\boldsymbol{l}$ and $\boldsymbol{a}$, so $\|\boldsymbol{l} \times \boldsymbol{a}\| = \|\boldsymbol{a}\| \sin\theta = \|\overrightarrow{QP}\|$. Hence, $\overrightarrow{HP}'$ is written as follows:

$$\overrightarrow{HP}' = \frac{\boldsymbol{l} \times \boldsymbol{a}}{\|\boldsymbol{l} \times \boldsymbol{a}\|} \|\overrightarrow{QP}\| \sin\Omega = \boldsymbol{l} \times \boldsymbol{a} \sin\Omega. \tag{3.18}$$

Substituting Eqs. (3.16), (3.17), and (3.18) into Eq. (3.15), we obtain

$$\boldsymbol{a}' = \boldsymbol{a} \cos\Omega + \boldsymbol{l} \times \boldsymbol{a} \sin\Omega + \langle \boldsymbol{a}, \boldsymbol{l} \rangle \boldsymbol{l} (1 - \cos\Omega). \tag{3.19}$$

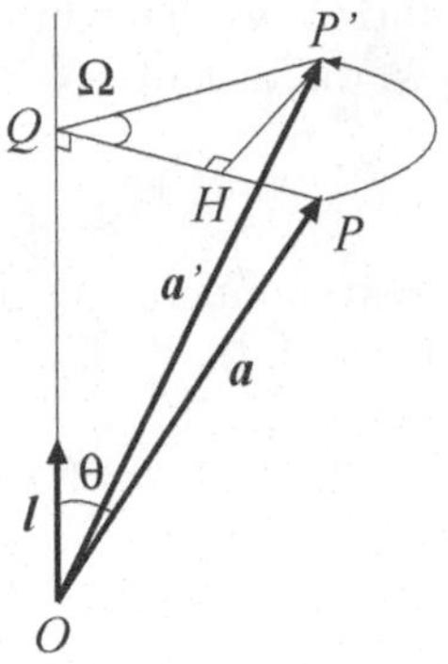

FIGURE 3.6 Rotation of vector $\boldsymbol{a}$ around axis $\boldsymbol{l}$ by angle Ω.

This is known as the *Rodrigues formula*.

Equation (3.19) can be expressed as the product of matrix $\boldsymbol{R}$ and vector $\boldsymbol{a}$ in the form $\boldsymbol{a}' = \boldsymbol{R}\boldsymbol{a}$ (↪ Exercise 3.2), where the matrix $\boldsymbol{R}$ is defined by

$$\boldsymbol{R} = \begin{pmatrix} \cos\Omega + l_1^2(1-\cos\Omega) & l_1l_2(1-\cos\Omega) - l_3\sin\Omega & l_1l_3(1-\cos\Omega) + l_2\sin\Omega \\ l_2l_1(1-\cos\Omega) + l_3\sin\Omega & \cos\Omega + l_2^2(1-\cos\Omega) & l_2l_3(1-\cos\Omega) - l_1\sin\Omega \\ l_3l_1(1-\cos\Omega) - l_2\sin\Omega & l_3l_2(1-\cos\Omega) + l_1\sin\Omega & \cos\Omega + l_3^2(1-\cos\Omega) \end{pmatrix}. \tag{3.20}$$

If we let $\boldsymbol{l} = (1,0,0)^\top$, $(0,1,0)^\top$, and $(0,0,1)^\top$ in this equation, we obtain $\boldsymbol{R}_x(\Omega)$, $\boldsymbol{R}_y(\Omega)$, and $\boldsymbol{R}_z(\Omega)$, respectively, as defined in Eqs. (2.17) and (2.18).

Equation (3.20) expresses the rotation matrix $\boldsymbol{R}$ in terms of the axis $\boldsymbol{l}$ and angle Ω. Conversely, we can express $\boldsymbol{l}$ and Ω in terms of $\boldsymbol{R}$. First, note that from $l_1^2 + l_2^2 + l_3^2 = 1$, the trace $\mathrm{tr}\boldsymbol{R}$ and non-diagonal elements of Eq. (3.20) satisfy the following relations:

$$\mathrm{tr}\boldsymbol{R} = 1 + 2\cos\Omega, \qquad \begin{pmatrix} r_{23} - r_{32} \\ r_{31} - r_{13} \\ r_{12} - r_{21} \end{pmatrix} = -2\sin\Omega \begin{pmatrix} l_1 \\ l_2 \\ l_3 \end{pmatrix}. \tag{3.21}$$

For $0 \leq \Omega < \pi$, we obtain Ω and $\boldsymbol{l}$ from these in the form

$$\Omega = \cos^{-1}\frac{\mathrm{tr}\boldsymbol{R} - 1}{2}, \qquad \boldsymbol{l} = -\mathcal{N}\left[\begin{pmatrix} r_{23} - r_{32} \\ r_{31} - r_{13} \\ r_{12} - r_{21} \end{pmatrix}\right], \tag{3.22}$$

where $\mathcal{N}[\,\cdot\,]$ denotes normalization to unit norm: $\mathcal{N}[\boldsymbol{a}] = \boldsymbol{a}/\|\boldsymbol{a}\|$. From Eqs. (3.21) and (3.22), we see that $\Omega = 0$ is a singularity and that the computation of $\boldsymbol{l}$ is numerically unstable when $\Omega \approx 0$. Geometrically, this reflects the fact that the axis is indeterminate for rotations by angle 0 (= the identity).

3.5 QUATERNION REPRESENTATION

"Quaternions" are extensions of complex numbers. Recall that a 2D rotation is described by a complex number. Let us identify a 2D vector $\boldsymbol{v} = (v_1, v_2)^\top$ with a complex number $z = v_1 + v_2 i$. Suppose $\boldsymbol{v}$ is rotated by angle θ to vector $\boldsymbol{v}'$. It is well known that the rotated $\boldsymbol{v}'$ corresponds to

$$z' = wz, \qquad w = \cos\theta + i\sin\theta \ \ (= e^{i\theta}). \tag{3.23}$$

For extending this to 3D rotation, we introduce, in addition to the imaginary unit i, two other imaginary units j and k, distinct from i, and consider the expression

$$q = q_0 + q_1 i + q_2 j + q_3 k, \tag{3.24}$$

where q_0, q_1, q_2, and q_3 are real numbers. We introduce a new operational rule: the three imaginary units i, j, and k are such that

$$i^2 = -1, \qquad j^2 = -1, \qquad k^2 = -1, \tag{3.25}$$

$$ij = k, \qquad jk = i, \qquad ki = j,$$

$$ji = -k, \qquad kj = -i, \qquad ik = -j. \tag{3.26}$$

The expression in the form of Eq. (3.24) is called a *quaternion* (see Appendix A for the mathematical background of quaternions). The real number q_0 and the remaining $q_1 i+q_2 j+q_3 k$ of Eq. (3.24) are called the *scalar part* and *vector part*, respectively, of q. If we identify the vector part $q_1 i + q_2 j + q_3 k$ with the vector $(q_1, q_2, q_3)^\top$, we can regard a quaternion as the sum of a scalar (real number) and a vector. Namely, we can write a quaternion q as the sum of a scalar α and a vector $\boldsymbol{a} = (a_1, a_2, a_3)^\top$ in the form

$$q = \alpha + \boldsymbol{a}, \tag{3.27}$$

where the second term on the right side is identified with $a_1 i + a_2 j + a_3 k$. Such a "sum" connected by "+" has only a formal meaning and is called the *formal sum*. However, we assume that the operation "+" obeys the same rules as in the case of real numbers, such as commutativity and distributivity.

Applying the rule of Eqs. (3.25) and (3.26), we can see that the product of quaternions $q = \alpha + \boldsymbol{a}$ and $q' = \beta + \boldsymbol{b}$ is written as (↪ Exercise 3.3)

$$qq' = \alpha\beta - \langle \boldsymbol{a}, \boldsymbol{b} \rangle + \alpha\boldsymbol{b} + \beta\boldsymbol{a} + \boldsymbol{a} \times \boldsymbol{b}, \tag{3.28}$$

where the last term on the right side is a quaternion identified with the vector product $\boldsymbol{a} \times \boldsymbol{b}$ of $\boldsymbol{a}$ and $\boldsymbol{b}$. In particular, the product of the vector parts $\boldsymbol{a}$ and $\boldsymbol{b}$ are written as the following formal sum:

$$\boldsymbol{ab} = -\langle \boldsymbol{a}, \boldsymbol{b} \rangle + \boldsymbol{a} \times \boldsymbol{b}. \tag{3.29}$$

For the quaternion q of Eq. (3.24), we define its *conjugate quaternion* $q^\dagger$ as the following expression (↪ Exercises 3.4, 3.5):

$$q^\dagger = q_0 - q_1 i - q_2 j - q_3 k. \tag{3.30}$$

We also define the *norm* $\|q\|$ of q as follows (↪ Exercises 3.6, 3.7).

$$\|q\| = \sqrt{q_0^2 + q_1^2 + q_2^2 + q_3^2}. \tag{3.31}$$

From this definition, the norm $\|\boldsymbol{a}\|$ of vector $\boldsymbol{a}$ is the same as the norm of $\boldsymbol{a}$ identified with a quaternion.

A quaternion of norm 1 is called a *unit quaternion*. Since $q_0^2 + q_1^2 + q_2^2 + q_3^2 = 1$ holds for a unit quaternion q, we see that there exists an angle Ω such that

$$q_0 = \cos\frac{\Omega}{2}, \qquad \sqrt{q_1^2 + q_2^2 + q_3^2} = \sin\frac{\Omega}{2}. \tag{3.32}$$

Hence, we can write q as the sum of its scalar and vector parts in the form

$$q = \cos\frac{\Omega}{2} + \boldsymbol{l}\sin\frac{\Omega}{2}, \tag{3.33}$$

where $\boldsymbol{l}$ is a unit vector ($\|\boldsymbol{l}\| = 1$). Then, for any vector $\boldsymbol{a}$, the quaternion

$$\boldsymbol{a}' = q\boldsymbol{a}q^\dagger \tag{3.34}$$

is a vector of the same norm as $\boldsymbol{a}$ ($\hookrightarrow$ Exercises 3.8, 3.9). In fact, this is the vector obtained by rotating $\boldsymbol{a}$ around $\boldsymbol{l}$ by angle Ω. This is shown as follows. First, note that

$$\begin{aligned}\boldsymbol{a}' &= q\boldsymbol{a}q^\dagger = (\cos\frac{\Omega}{2} + \boldsymbol{l}\sin\frac{\Omega}{2})\boldsymbol{a}(\cos\frac{\Omega}{2} - \boldsymbol{l}\sin\frac{\Omega}{2}) \\ &= \boldsymbol{a}\cos^2\frac{\Omega}{2} - \boldsymbol{al}\cos\frac{\Omega}{2}\sin\frac{\Omega}{2} + \boldsymbol{la}\sin\frac{\Omega}{2}\cos\frac{\Omega}{2} + \boldsymbol{lal}\sin^2\frac{\Omega}{2} \\ &= \boldsymbol{a}\cos^2\frac{\Omega}{2} + (\boldsymbol{la} - \boldsymbol{al})\cos\frac{\Omega}{2}\sin\frac{\Omega}{2} - \boldsymbol{lal}\sin^2\frac{\Omega}{2},\end{aligned} \tag{3.35}$$

where all vectors are identified with quaternions. From Eq. (3.29), we see that $\boldsymbol{la} - \boldsymbol{al} = 2\boldsymbol{l} \times \boldsymbol{a}$ and hence

$$\begin{aligned}\boldsymbol{lal} &= \boldsymbol{l}(-\langle\boldsymbol{a},\boldsymbol{l}\rangle + \boldsymbol{a}\times\boldsymbol{l}) = -\langle\boldsymbol{a},\boldsymbol{l}\rangle\boldsymbol{l} + \boldsymbol{l}(\boldsymbol{a}\times\boldsymbol{l}) = -\langle\boldsymbol{a},\boldsymbol{l}\rangle\boldsymbol{l} - \langle\boldsymbol{l},\boldsymbol{a}\times\boldsymbol{l}\rangle + \boldsymbol{l}\times(\boldsymbol{a}\times\boldsymbol{l}) \\ &= -\langle\boldsymbol{a},\boldsymbol{l}\rangle\boldsymbol{l} + \|\boldsymbol{l}\|^2\boldsymbol{a} - \langle\boldsymbol{l},\boldsymbol{a}\rangle\boldsymbol{l} = \boldsymbol{a} - 2\langle\boldsymbol{a},\boldsymbol{l}\rangle\boldsymbol{l},\end{aligned} \tag{3.36}$$

where we have noted that $\langle\boldsymbol{l},\boldsymbol{a}\times\boldsymbol{l}\rangle = |\boldsymbol{l},\boldsymbol{a},\boldsymbol{l}| = 0$ and used the formula of vector triple product ($\hookrightarrow$ Exercise 3.10)

$$\boldsymbol{a}\times(\boldsymbol{b}\times\boldsymbol{c}) = \langle\boldsymbol{a},\boldsymbol{c}\rangle\boldsymbol{b} - \langle\boldsymbol{a},\boldsymbol{b}\rangle\boldsymbol{c}. \tag{3.37}$$

It follows that Eq. (3.35) is written as

$$\begin{aligned}\boldsymbol{a}' &= \boldsymbol{a}\cos^2\frac{\Omega}{2} + 2\boldsymbol{l}\times\boldsymbol{a}\cos\frac{\Omega}{2}\sin\frac{\Omega}{2} - (\boldsymbol{a} - 2\langle\boldsymbol{a},\boldsymbol{l}\rangle\boldsymbol{l})\sin^2\frac{\Omega}{2} \\ &= \boldsymbol{a}(\cos^2\frac{\Omega}{2} - \sin^2\frac{\Omega}{2}) + 2\boldsymbol{l}\times\boldsymbol{a}\cos\frac{\Omega}{2}\sin\frac{\Omega}{2} + 2\sin^2\frac{\Omega}{2}\langle\boldsymbol{a},\boldsymbol{l}\rangle\boldsymbol{l} \\ &= \boldsymbol{a}\cos\Omega + \boldsymbol{l}\times\boldsymbol{a}\sin\Omega + \langle\boldsymbol{a},\boldsymbol{l}\rangle\boldsymbol{l}(1-\cos\Omega),\end{aligned} \tag{3.38}$$

which coincides with the Rodrigues formula of Eq. (3.19). Thus, Eqs. (3.33) and (3.34) are an extension of the Eq. (3.23) of 2D rotation to 3D rotation.

Letting $\boldsymbol{a} = a_1i + a_2j + a_3k$ and $\boldsymbol{a}' = a_1'i + a_2'j + a_3'k$ in Eq. (3.34) and substituting $q = q_0 + q_1i + q_2j + q_3k$, we can express Eq. (3.34) as the product of a matrix $\boldsymbol{R}$ and a vector $\boldsymbol{a}$ in the form

$$\boldsymbol{a}' = \boldsymbol{R}\boldsymbol{a}, \tag{3.39}$$

where the matrix $\boldsymbol{R}$ has the following form ($\hookrightarrow$ Exercise 3.11):

$$\boldsymbol{R} = \begin{pmatrix} q_0^2 + q_1^2 - q_2^2 - q_3^2 & 2(q_1q_2 - q_0q_3) & 2(q_1q_3 + q_0q_2) \\ 2(q_2q_1 + q_0q_3) & q_0^2 - q_1^2 + q_2^2 - q_3^2 & 2(q_2q_3 - q_0q_1) \\ 2(q_3q_1 - q_0q_2) & 2(q_3q_2 + q_0q_1) & q_0^2 - q_1^2 - q_2^2 + q_3^2 \end{pmatrix}. \tag{3.40}$$

Since Eq. (3.39) describes a 3D rotation, this matrix $\boldsymbol{R}$ should be the same matrix $\boldsymbol{R}$ of Eq. (3.20). In other words, Eq. (3.40) provides an expression of the rotation matrix $\boldsymbol{R}$ in terms of a quaternion q.

Conversely, if a rotation matrix $\boldsymbol{R} = \begin{pmatrix} r_{ij} \end{pmatrix}$ is given, we can determine a quaternion q that expresses $\boldsymbol{R}$ in the form of Eq. (3.40). Since $q_0^2 + q_1^2 + q_2^2 + q_3^2 = 1$, Eq. (3.40) implies

$$\mathrm{tr}\boldsymbol{R} = 3q_0^2 - q_1^2 - q_2^2 - q_3^2 = 3q_0^2 - (1 - q_0^2) = 4q_0^2 - 1. \tag{3.41}$$

Hence, we obtain

$$q_0 = \frac{\pm\sqrt{1 + \mathrm{tr}\boldsymbol{R}}}{2}. \tag{3.42}$$

Then, from

$$r_{23} - r_{32} = -4q_0q_1, \qquad r_{31} - r_{13} = -4q_0q_2, \qquad r_{12} - r_{21} = -4q_0q_3, \tag{3.43}$$

we obtain q_1, q_2, and q_3 in the form

$$\begin{pmatrix} q_1 \\ q_2 \\ q_3 \end{pmatrix} = -\frac{1}{q_0} \begin{pmatrix} r_{23} - r_{32} \\ r_{31} - r_{13} \\ r_{12} - r_{21} \end{pmatrix}. \tag{3.44}$$

This expression has a singularity for $q_0 = 0$, which, from Eq. (3.32), corresponds to $\Omega = \pi$ (half rotation). This reflects the fact that the sense of a half rotation is ambiguous. As we see from Eq. (3.34), the double sign $\pm$ of Eq. (3.42) corresponds to the fact that q and $-q$ represent the same rotation. In fact, we can write from Eq. (3.33)

$$-q = -\cos\frac{\Omega}{2} - \boldsymbol{l}\sin\frac{\Omega}{2} = \cos\frac{2\pi - \Omega}{2} - \boldsymbol{l}\sin\frac{2\pi - \Omega}{2}, \tag{3.45}$$

meaning that $-q$ represents a rotation by angle $2\pi - \Omega$ around axis $-\boldsymbol{l}$, which is the same as a rotation by angle Ω around axis $\boldsymbol{l}$.

3.6 SUPPLEMENTAL NOTES

As pointed out in Sec. 2.2, 3D rotation can be interpreted in two ways: an object rotating relative to a stationary coordinate system, and the coordinate system rotating relative to a stationary object. In 3D analysis of video images for computer vision, for example, we can regard the images either as capturing a static scene by a moving camera or as capturing a moving scene by a stationary camera. The two are equivalent and produce the same result. Hence, we can freely switch our interpretation from one to the other for the convenience of analysis. This is, however, prone to cause confusions and inconsistency of analysis.

Viewing a point as moving to a new position relative to a stationary coordinate system is known as *alibi*, a Latin word meaning "different place," while viewing the coordinate system as moving relative to a stationary point, thereby giving it a new set of coordinates, is know as *alias*, a Latin word meaning "different name." Mathematically, the two viewpoints produce relationships that are "inverse" of each other, as is pointed out in mechanics analysis (see, e.g., [10]) and computer vision analysis (see, e.g., [17]).

The Euler angles described in Sec. 3.3 was introduced by the Swiss mathematician-astronomer Leonhard Euler (1707–1783) for rigid body motion analysis. The Rodrigues formula described in Sec. 3.4 was due to the French mathematician Benjamin Olinde Rodrigues (1795–1851).

The quaternion described in Sec. 3.5 was invented by the Irish mathematician Sir William Rowan Hamilton (1805–1865) for extending complex numbers describing 2D rotations to 3D rotations. Its background is briefly summarized in Appendix A. Also, see [22] for more detalis and relationships to modern theories of geometry and algebra, Today's vector calculus was born from the operation rules of quaternions[7]. Because the resulting vector calculus can describe almost all phenomena of physics, quaternions are today no longer taught in beginners classes of most universities. However, Eq. (3.40) that expresses the rotation matrix $\boldsymbol{R}$ in terms of a quaternion q is still widely used for optimization of $\boldsymbol{R}$; we discuss this in the subsequent chapters. A system of symbols, such as quaternions, equipped with operation rules is called an *algebra*. A new system called *geometric algebra*, originated among others in the quaternion theory, has been attracting attention since the late 20th and the early 21st centuries (for the details, see [22]).

3.7 EXERCISES

3.1. (1) Show that the following identity holds for arbitrary matrices $\boldsymbol{A}_1$, $\boldsymbol{A}_2$, ..., $\boldsymbol{A}_N$:

$$(\boldsymbol{A}_1\boldsymbol{A}_2\cdots\boldsymbol{A}_N)^\top = \boldsymbol{A}_N^\top\cdots\boldsymbol{A}_2^\top\boldsymbol{A}_1^\top. \tag{3.46}$$

(2) Show that the following identity holds for arbitrary nonsingular matrices $\boldsymbol{A}_1$, $\boldsymbol{A}_2$, ..., $\boldsymbol{A}_N$:

$$(\boldsymbol{A}_1\boldsymbol{A}_2\cdots\boldsymbol{A}_N)^{-1} = \boldsymbol{A}_N^{-1}\cdots\boldsymbol{A}_2^{-1}\boldsymbol{A}_1^{-1}. \tag{3.47}$$

3.2. Show that from Eq. (3.19) we obtain the expression of Eq. (3.20) for the matrix $\boldsymbol{R}$.

3.3. Show that the rule of Eqs. (3.25) and (3.26) implies Eq. (3.28).

3.4. Show that the following relationships hold for quaternions q and q':

$$q^{\dagger\dagger} = q, \qquad (qq')^\dagger = q'^\dagger q^\dagger. \tag{3.48}$$

3.5. Show that for quaternion q the condition that its vector part is 0 and the condition that its scalar part is 0 are, respectively, given by

$$q^\dagger = q, \qquad q^\dagger = -q. \tag{3.49}$$

3.6. Show the following relation for quaternion q:

$$qq^\dagger = q^\dagger q = q_0^2 + q_1^2 + q_2^2 + q_3^2 \quad (= \|q\|^2). \tag{3.50}$$

3.7. Show that every quaternion $q \neq 0$ has its "inverse" q^{-1} such that

$$qq^{-1} = q^{-1}q = 1. \tag{3.51}$$

3.8. If $\boldsymbol{a}$ is a quaternion defined by a vector, show that the quaternion $\boldsymbol{a}'$ given by Eq. (3.34) is also defined by some vector, i.e., its scalar part is 0.

3.9. If q is a unit quaternion, show that $\boldsymbol{a}'$ of Eq. (3.34) has the same norm as $\boldsymbol{a}$, i.e., $\|\boldsymbol{a}'\| = \|\boldsymbol{a}\|$.

3.10. Show the vector triple product formula of Eq. (3.37).

3.11. By substituting $q = q_0 + q_1 i + q_2 j + q_3 k$ to Eq. (3.34), show that we can write it as $\boldsymbol{a}' = \boldsymbol{R}\boldsymbol{a}$ using the matrix $\boldsymbol{R}$ of Eq. (3.40).

[7] Today's vector calculus that does not use quaternions was formulated by the American physicist Josiah Willard Gibbs (1839–1903). It is said that some mathematicians, including the Scottish mathematician-physicist Peter Guthrie Tait (1831–1901), who contributed to the dissemination of the quaternion theory along with Hamilton, were fiercely opposed to it.

CHAPTER 4

Estimation of Rotation I: Isotropic Noise

In this chapter, we consider the "inverse problem" of rotating vectors, i.e., estimating the rotation from observing multiple vectors and their rotated positions. First, we show that if there is no noise in the observation, the rotation is determined by two sets of vector correspondences. Next, we consider the simplest case in which the observation has noise subject to an independent, isotropic, and homogeneous Gaussian distribution. We point out that in this case the least-squares solution is what is known in statistics as the "maximum likelihood solution," and show that the solution is computed using the singular value decomposition. We show that the solution is also obtained using the quaternion representation introduced in the preceding chapter. Finally, we apply these techniques to optimally correcting those matrices which are supposedly rotation matrices but not exactly so, due to noise.

4.1 ESTIMATING ROTATION

If N vectors $\boldsymbol{a}_1$, ..., $\boldsymbol{a}_N$ are rotated by $\boldsymbol{R}$, we observe $\boldsymbol{a}'_1$, ..., $\boldsymbol{a}'_N$ such that

$$\boldsymbol{a}'_\alpha = \boldsymbol{R}\boldsymbol{a}_\alpha, \qquad \alpha = 1, .., N. \tag{4.1}$$

Here, we consider the "inverse problem" of this. Namely, observing $2N$ vectors $\boldsymbol{a}_1$, ..., $\boldsymbol{a}_N$, $\boldsymbol{a}'_1$, ..., $\boldsymbol{a}'_N$, we want to determine a rotation $\boldsymbol{R}$ such that Eq. (4.1) holds. The solution is immediately obtained if there is no noise in the observation so that Eq. (4.1) exactly holds. However, it is when the vectors $\boldsymbol{a}_\alpha$ and $\boldsymbol{a}'_\alpha$ obtained by sensor measurement are not exact that this problem has a practical significance. So, we consider the case of

$$\boldsymbol{a}'_\alpha \approx \boldsymbol{R}\boldsymbol{a}_\alpha, \qquad \alpha = 1, .., N. \tag{4.2}$$

In real applications, this problem arises when we want to estimate a motion between two objects. A *motion*, or, to be strict, *rigid motion* or *Euclidean motion*, is a composition of translation and rotation. Consider how to compute the motion from a given 3D object position and its position after the motion. Suppose we measure N positions $\boldsymbol{x}_1$, ..., $\boldsymbol{x}_N$ by some sensing, e.g., image analysis or laser emission (Fig. 4.1). Let $\boldsymbol{x}'_1$, ..., $\boldsymbol{x}'_N$ be their corresponding positions after the motion. Assuming that it is a rigid motion, we want to know the translation $\boldsymbol{t}$ and rotation $\boldsymbol{R}$. For this, we first compute the centroids of the N

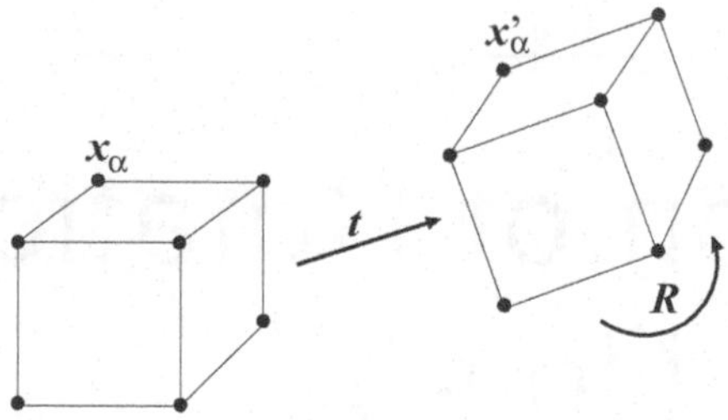

FIGURE 4.1 When N points $\{\boldsymbol{x}_\alpha\}$ move to $\{\boldsymbol{x}'_\alpha\}$, we want to know the translation $\boldsymbol{t}$ and the rotation $\boldsymbol{R}$.

positions before and after the motion:

$$\boldsymbol{x}_C = \frac{1}{N}\sum_{\alpha=1}^{N} \boldsymbol{x}_\alpha, \qquad \boldsymbol{x}'_C = \frac{1}{N}\sum_{\alpha=1}^{N} \boldsymbol{x}'_\alpha. \tag{4.3}$$

Next, we compute the deviations $\boldsymbol{a}_\alpha$ and $\boldsymbol{a}'_\alpha$ of $\boldsymbol{x}_\alpha$ and $\boldsymbol{x}'_\alpha$ from their centroids:

$$\boldsymbol{a}_\alpha = \boldsymbol{x}_\alpha - \boldsymbol{x}_C, \qquad \boldsymbol{a}'_\alpha = \boldsymbol{x}'_\alpha - \boldsymbol{x}'_C. \tag{4.4}$$

Then, the translation is given by $\boldsymbol{t} = \boldsymbol{x}'_C - \boldsymbol{x}_C$, and the rotation $\boldsymbol{R}$ is estimated so that Eq. (4.2) is satisfied.

To solve this problem, we need to give an interpretation of "$\approx$" in Eq. (4.2) based on some noise modeling. Before going into this, let us first consider the case in which there is no noise in the observation. If Eq. (4.1) is exact, the necessary number of data is $N = 2$. To be specific, we can construct from $\boldsymbol{a}_1$ and $\boldsymbol{a}_2$ an orthonormal system as follows. Since the vector product $\tilde{\boldsymbol{a}} = \boldsymbol{a}_1 \times \boldsymbol{a}_2$ is orthogonal to $\boldsymbol{a}_1$ and since the vector product $\tilde{\boldsymbol{b}} = \boldsymbol{a}_1 \times \tilde{\boldsymbol{a}}$ is orthogonal to both $\boldsymbol{a}_1$ and $\tilde{\boldsymbol{a}}$, the three vectors $\boldsymbol{a}_1$, $\tilde{\boldsymbol{a}}$, and $\tilde{\boldsymbol{b}}$ are a mutually orthogonal system (Fig. 4.2). W normalize them to obtain an orthonormal system $\{\boldsymbol{r}_1, \boldsymbol{r}_2, \boldsymbol{r}_3\}$,

$$\boldsymbol{r}_1 = \mathcal{N}[\boldsymbol{a}_1], \qquad \boldsymbol{r}_2 = \mathcal{N}[\boldsymbol{a}_1 \times \boldsymbol{a}_2], \qquad \boldsymbol{r}_3 = \mathcal{N}[\boldsymbol{a}_1 \times (\boldsymbol{a}_1 \times \boldsymbol{a}_2)], \tag{4.5}$$

where $\mathcal{N}[\,\cdot\,]$ denotes normalization to unit norm ($\hookrightarrow$ Eq. (3.22)). Similarly, we can construct an orthonormal system $\{\boldsymbol{r}'_1, \boldsymbol{r}'_2, \boldsymbol{r}'_3\}$ from $\boldsymbol{a}'_1$ and $\boldsymbol{a}'_2$. As stated in Sec. 2.2, the matrices having them as columns

$$\boldsymbol{R}_1 = \begin{pmatrix} \boldsymbol{r}_1 & \boldsymbol{r}_2 & \boldsymbol{r}_3 \end{pmatrix}, \qquad \boldsymbol{R}_2 = \begin{pmatrix} \boldsymbol{r}'_1 & \boldsymbol{r}'_2 & \boldsymbol{r}'_3 \end{pmatrix} \tag{4.6}$$

are orthogonal matrices, mapping the basis vectors $\{\boldsymbol{e}_1, \boldsymbol{e}_2, \boldsymbol{e}_3\}$ to $\{\boldsymbol{r}_1, \boldsymbol{r}_2, \boldsymbol{r}_3\}$ and $\{\boldsymbol{r}'_1, \boldsymbol{r}'_2, \boldsymbol{r}'_3\}$, respectively. Hence,

$$\boldsymbol{R} = \boldsymbol{R}_2 \boldsymbol{R}_1^\top \tag{4.7}$$

is the rotation matrix that maps $\{\boldsymbol{r}_1, \boldsymbol{r}_2, \boldsymbol{r}_3\}$ to $\{\boldsymbol{r}'_1, \boldsymbol{r}'_2, \boldsymbol{r}'_3\}$ (Fig. 4.3).

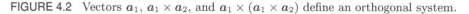

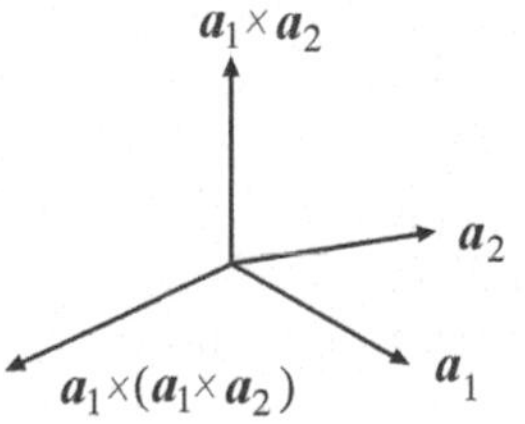

FIGURE 4.2 Vectors $\boldsymbol{a}_1$, $\boldsymbol{a}_1 \times \boldsymbol{a}_2$, and $\boldsymbol{a}_1 \times (\boldsymbol{a}_1 \times \boldsymbol{a}_2)$ define an orthogonal system.

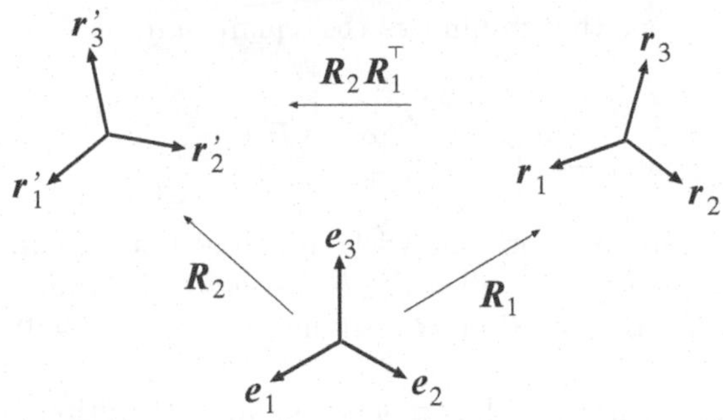

FIGURE 4.3 If the basis vectors $\{e_i\}$ are mapped to $\{r_i\}$ and $\{r'_i\}$ by rotations $\boldsymbol{R}_1$ and $\boldsymbol{R}_2$, respectively, the mapping of $\{r_i\}$ to $\{r'_i\}$ is given by $\boldsymbol{R}_2\boldsymbol{R}_1^\top$.

4.2 LEAST SQUARES AND MAXIMUM LIKELIHOOD

The above argument is for the noiseless case. The standard procedure to deal with noise is to regard noisy data as *random variables*. A random variable is a variable whose value is not definitive but is specified by a probability distribution. All observations in real situations are definitive values, and regarding them, or "modeling them" as random variables by introducing an artificial probability distribution is only a mathematical convenience. However, this can very well approximate the reality in many engineering problems where sensors are involved, providing a useful analytical tool.

The simplest and most practical assumption about noise probability distribution is to regard the noise as subject to an independent, homogeneous, and isotropic Gaussian distribution. By "independent," we mean the distribution of noise in different data is mutually independent; by "homogeneous," the distribution is the same for all data; by "isotropic," the distribution does not depend on directions in space.

We say that vector $\boldsymbol{x} = (x, y, z)^\top$ is subject to an isotropic Gaussian distribution of mean $\boldsymbol{0}$ and variance σ^2 if its probability density has the form

$$p(\boldsymbol{x}) = \frac{1}{\sqrt{(2\pi)^3}\sigma^3} e^{-\|\boldsymbol{x}\|^2/2\sigma^2}. \tag{4.8}$$

As we see, $p(\boldsymbol{x})$ is a function of the square norm $\|\boldsymbol{x}\|^2$, so the surface on which the probability density is constant, called the "equal probability surface," is a sphere (Fig. 4.4 depicts a two-dimensional case). If the discrepancy between the left and right sides of Eq. (4.2) is such an independent, homogeneous, and isotropic random variable, we can expect that the

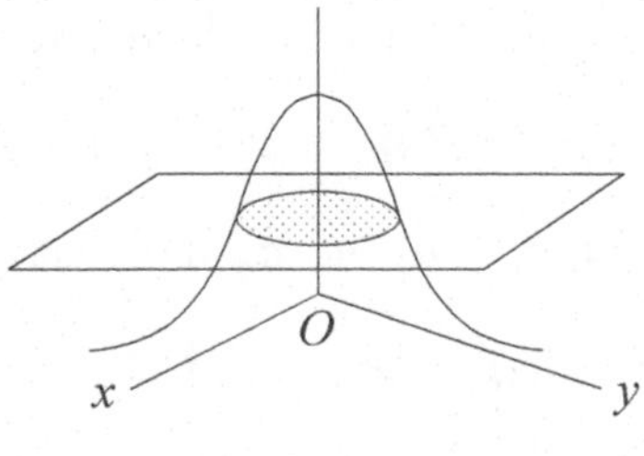

FIGURE 4.4 Probability density of an isotropic Gaussian distribution in two dimensions. The cross section with a plane parallel to the xy plane is a circle.

desired solution $\boldsymbol{R}$ is the one that minimizes the square sum of that discrepancy

$$J = \frac{1}{2}\sum_{\alpha=1}^{N} \|\boldsymbol{a}'_\alpha - \boldsymbol{R}\boldsymbol{a}_\alpha\|^2, \tag{4.9}$$

where "1/2" is only a formal coefficient without particular meaning. Since the solution minimizes the sum of squares, it is called the *least-squares solution*. For given $\boldsymbol{a}_\alpha$ and $\boldsymbol{a}'_\alpha$, $\alpha = 1, ..., N$, computing the rotation $\boldsymbol{R}$ that minimizes Eq. (4.9) is also known as the *Procrustes problem*.

When the data noise occurs according to a Gaussian distribution in the form of Eq. (4.8), it is intuitively reasonable to seek a least-squares solution that minimizes Eq. (4.9), but from the viewpoint of probability and statistics this is given the following justification. Let $\bar{\boldsymbol{a}}_\alpha$ and $\bar{\boldsymbol{a}}'_\alpha$ be the true values of $\boldsymbol{a}_\alpha$ and $\boldsymbol{a}'_\alpha$, respectively, and $\Delta\boldsymbol{a}_\alpha$ and $\Delta\boldsymbol{a}'_\alpha$ their respective noise terms. If $\Delta\boldsymbol{a}_\alpha$ and $\Delta\boldsymbol{a}'_\alpha$ are each subject to the Gaussian distribution of Eq. (4.8), their joint probability density for $\alpha = 1, ..., N$ is

$$\begin{aligned} p &= \prod_{\alpha=1}^{N} \frac{1}{\sqrt{(2\pi)^3}\sigma^3} e^{-\|\Delta\boldsymbol{a}_\alpha\|^2/2\sigma^2} \frac{1}{\sqrt{(2\pi)^3}\sigma^3} e^{-\|\Delta\boldsymbol{a}'_\alpha\|^2/2\sigma^2} \\ &= \left(\frac{1}{\sqrt{(2\pi)^3}\sigma^3}\right)^{2N} e^{-\sum_{\alpha=1}^{N}(\|\boldsymbol{a}_\alpha - \bar{\boldsymbol{a}}_\alpha\|^2 + \|\boldsymbol{a}'_\alpha - \bar{\boldsymbol{a}}'_\alpha\|^2)/2\sigma^2}. \end{aligned} \tag{4.10}$$

If regarded as a function of observations $\boldsymbol{a}_\alpha$ and $\boldsymbol{a}'_\alpha$, $\alpha = 1, ..., N$, this expression is called the *likelihood*. Estimating the parameters of the problem in question by maximizing their likelihood is called *maximum likelihood estimation*, or simply *maximum likelihood*. This is equivalent to minimizing the exponent of Eq. (4.10) multiplied by σ^2, i.e.,

$$J = \frac{1}{2}\sum_{\alpha=1}^{N}(\|\boldsymbol{a}_\alpha - \bar{\boldsymbol{a}}_\alpha\|^2 + \|\boldsymbol{a}'_\alpha - \bar{\boldsymbol{a}}'_\alpha\|^2). \tag{4.11}$$

This expression is called the *Mahalanobis distance*[1] of $\boldsymbol{a}_\alpha$ and $\boldsymbol{a}'_\alpha$ from $\bar{\boldsymbol{a}}_\alpha$ and $\bar{\boldsymbol{a}}'_\alpha$. In statistics, maximum likelihood is regarded as the standard criterion for optimal estimation.

In our problem, maximum likelihood is to compute $\bar{\boldsymbol{a}}_\alpha$, $\bar{\boldsymbol{a}}'_\alpha$, and $\boldsymbol{R}$ that minimize the Mahalanobis distance of Eq. (4.11) subject to the constraint that $\bar{\boldsymbol{a}}'_\alpha = \boldsymbol{R}_\alpha\bar{\boldsymbol{a}}_\alpha$. Introducing Lagrange multipliers to the constraint $\bar{\boldsymbol{a}}'_\alpha = \boldsymbol{R}_\alpha\bar{\boldsymbol{a}}_\alpha$, we can eliminate $\bar{\boldsymbol{a}}_\alpha$ and $\bar{\boldsymbol{a}}'_\alpha$ from Eq. (4.11) to see that the computation reduces to minimizing Eq. (4.9) (↪ Exercise 4.1). The function J of Eq. (4.9) is called the *residual sum of squares*, or simply the *residual*. The value $\boldsymbol{R}$ that minimizes this is the least-squares solution.

Alternatively, we can do the following reasoning. We write the discrepancies of the observations $\boldsymbol{a}_\alpha$ and $\boldsymbol{a}'_\alpha$ from the condition $\bar{\boldsymbol{a}}'_\alpha = \boldsymbol{R}_\alpha\bar{\boldsymbol{a}}_\alpha$, which should ideally hold, as

$$\boldsymbol{\varepsilon}_\alpha = \boldsymbol{a}'_\alpha - \boldsymbol{R}\boldsymbol{a}_\alpha, \qquad \alpha = 1, ..., N. \tag{4.12}$$

Substituting $\boldsymbol{a}_\alpha = \bar{\boldsymbol{a}}_\alpha + \Delta\boldsymbol{a}_\alpha$ and $\boldsymbol{a}'_\alpha = \bar{\boldsymbol{a}}'_\alpha + \Delta\boldsymbol{a}'_\alpha$ into this and noting that $\bar{\boldsymbol{a}}'_\alpha = \boldsymbol{R}\bar{\boldsymbol{a}}_\alpha$, we see that

$$\boldsymbol{\varepsilon}_\alpha = \Delta\boldsymbol{a}'_\alpha - \boldsymbol{R}\Delta\boldsymbol{a}_\alpha. \tag{4.13}$$

[1]Mathematically, the "Mahalanobis distance" is defined by removing the additive constant from the negative logarithm $-\log p$ of Eq. (4.10), or its square root. Here, we multiply it by σ^2 for analytical convenience.

If $\Delta\boldsymbol{a}_\alpha$ and $\Delta\boldsymbol{a}'_\alpha$ are isotropic Gaussian variables, the probability density of $\boldsymbol{R}\Delta\boldsymbol{a}_\alpha$ depends, by isotropy, only on $\|\boldsymbol{R}\Delta\boldsymbol{a}_\alpha\|^2 = \|\Delta\boldsymbol{a}_\alpha\|^2$. From the symmetry of the distribution, $\Delta\boldsymbol{a}'_\alpha$ and $-\Delta\boldsymbol{a}'_\alpha$ have the same probability density. If $\Delta\boldsymbol{a}_\alpha$ and $\Delta\boldsymbol{a}'_\alpha$ are independent Gaussian variables of variance σ^2, then due to the "reproductivity" of Gaussian variables, meaning that the sum of Gaussian variables is also Gaussian, the discrepancy $\boldsymbol{\varepsilon}_\alpha$ is a Gaussian variable of expectation $\mathbf{0}$ and variance $2\sigma^2$ ($\hookrightarrow$ Exercise 4.2). Hence, the Mahalanobis distance of $\boldsymbol{\varepsilon}_\alpha$, i.e., the sum of squares weighted by the inverse variance divided by 2 and multiplied by σ^2, is given by

$$\frac{\sigma^2}{2}\sum_{\alpha=1}^{N}\frac{\|\boldsymbol{\varepsilon}_\alpha\|^2}{2\sigma^2} = \frac{1}{4}\sum_{\alpha=1}^{N}\|\boldsymbol{a}'_\alpha - \boldsymbol{R}\boldsymbol{a}_\alpha\|^2. \tag{4.14}$$

Evidently, minimizing this is equivalent to minimizing the residual J of Eq. (4.9).

4.3 SOLUTION BY SINGULAR VALUE DECOMPOSITION

Expansion of the right side of Eq. (4.9) gives

$$\begin{aligned} J &= \frac{1}{2}\sum_{\alpha=1}^{N}\langle \boldsymbol{a}'_\alpha - \boldsymbol{R}\boldsymbol{a}_\alpha, \boldsymbol{a}'_\alpha - \boldsymbol{R}\boldsymbol{a}_\alpha\rangle = \frac{1}{2}\sum_{\alpha=1}^{N}\Big(\langle \boldsymbol{a}'_\alpha, \boldsymbol{a}'_\alpha\rangle - 2\langle \boldsymbol{R}\boldsymbol{a}_\alpha, \boldsymbol{a}'_\alpha\rangle + \langle \boldsymbol{R}\boldsymbol{a}_\alpha, \boldsymbol{R}\boldsymbol{a}_\alpha\rangle\Big) \\ &= \frac{1}{2}\sum_{\alpha=1}^{N}\|\boldsymbol{a}'_\alpha\|^2 - \sum_{\alpha=1}^{N}\langle \boldsymbol{R}\boldsymbol{a}_\alpha, \boldsymbol{a}'_\alpha\rangle + \frac{1}{2}\sum_{\alpha=1}^{N}\|\boldsymbol{a}_\alpha\|^2. \end{aligned} \tag{4.15}$$

In order to minimize this, we only need to compute the $\boldsymbol{R}$ that maximizes

$$K = \sum_{\alpha=1}^{N}\langle \boldsymbol{R}\boldsymbol{a}_\alpha, \boldsymbol{a}'_\alpha\rangle. \tag{4.16}$$

Noting the identity $\langle \boldsymbol{a}, \boldsymbol{b}\rangle = \mathrm{tr}(\boldsymbol{a}\boldsymbol{b}^\top)$ in vectors $\boldsymbol{a}$ and $\boldsymbol{b}$ ($\hookrightarrow$ Exercise 4.3), we can write K as

$$K = \mathrm{tr}\Big(\boldsymbol{R}\sum_{\alpha=1}^{N}\boldsymbol{a}_\alpha\boldsymbol{a}'^\top_\alpha\Big) = \mathrm{tr}(\boldsymbol{R}\boldsymbol{N}), \tag{4.17}$$

where we define the *correlation matrix* $\boldsymbol{N}$ by

$$\boldsymbol{N} = \sum_{\alpha=1}^{N}\boldsymbol{a}_\alpha\boldsymbol{a}'^\top_\alpha. \tag{4.18}$$

We now show that the rotation $\boldsymbol{R}$ that maximizes Eq. (4.17) is obtained from the "singular value decomposition" of the correlation matrix $\boldsymbol{N}$ (see Appendix B for the singular value decomposition and related concepts). Let

$$\boldsymbol{N} = \boldsymbol{U}\boldsymbol{\Sigma}\boldsymbol{V}^\top \tag{4.19}$$

be the singular value decomposition of $\boldsymbol{N}$, where $\boldsymbol{U}$ and $\boldsymbol{V}$ are orthogonal matrices and $\boldsymbol{\Sigma} = \mathrm{diag}(\sigma_1, \sigma_2, \sigma_3)$ is the diagonal matrix having the singular values σ_1, σ_2, and σ_3 (≥ 0) as diagonal elements in that order. Substituting Eq. (4.19), we can write Eq. (4.17) in the form

$$K = \mathrm{tr}(\boldsymbol{R}\boldsymbol{U}\boldsymbol{\Sigma}\boldsymbol{V}^\top) = \mathrm{tr}(\boldsymbol{V}^\top\boldsymbol{R}\boldsymbol{U}\boldsymbol{\Sigma}) = \mathrm{tr}(\boldsymbol{T}\boldsymbol{\Sigma}), \tag{4.20}$$

where we have noted the identity $\mathrm{tr}(\boldsymbol{AB}) = \mathrm{tr}(\boldsymbol{BA})$ for matrix trace (↪ Exercise 4.4) and put

$$\boldsymbol{T} = \boldsymbol{V}^\top \boldsymbol{R}\boldsymbol{U}. \tag{4.21}$$

Since $\boldsymbol{U}$ and $\boldsymbol{V}$ are orthogonal matrices and $\boldsymbol{R}$ is a rotation matrix, hence an orthogonal matrix, we see that $\boldsymbol{T}$ is also an orthogonal matrix. If we write $\boldsymbol{T} = \left(T_{ij}\right)$, we obtain

$$\mathrm{tr}(\boldsymbol{T\Sigma}) = \mathrm{tr}\left(\begin{pmatrix} T_{11} & T_{12} & T_{13} \\ T_{21} & T_{22} & T_{23} \\ T_{31} & T_{32} & T_{33} \end{pmatrix}\begin{pmatrix} \sigma_1 & & \\ & \sigma_2 & \\ & & \sigma_3 \end{pmatrix}\right) = \mathrm{tr}\begin{pmatrix} \sigma_1 T_{11} & \sigma_2 T_{12} & \sigma_3 T_{13} \\ \sigma_1 T_{21} & \sigma_2 T_{22} & \sigma_3 T_{23} \\ \sigma_1 T_{31} & \sigma_2 T_{32} & \sigma_3 T_{33} \end{pmatrix}$$
$$= \sigma_1 T_{11} + \sigma_2 T_{22} + \sigma_3 T_{33}. \tag{4.22}$$

An orthogonal matrix consists of columns (or rows) of unit vectors. Hence, the magnitude of any element is 1 or less ($|T_{ij}| \leq 1$). Since σ_1, σ_2, $\sigma_3 \geq 0$, we see that

$$\mathrm{tr}(\boldsymbol{T\Sigma}) \leq \sigma_1 + \sigma_2 + \sigma_3, \tag{4.23}$$

where the equality holds for $T_{11} = T_{22} = T_{33} = 1$, which means $\boldsymbol{T} = \boldsymbol{I}$. Hence, if the matrix $\boldsymbol{T}$ of Eq. (4.21) reduces to the identity $\boldsymbol{I}$ for some $\boldsymbol{R}$, then that $\boldsymbol{R}$ gives the rotation that maximizes K.

Equating Eq. (4.21) with $\boldsymbol{I}$ and multiplying it by $\boldsymbol{V}$ from left and $\boldsymbol{U}^\top$ from right, we see that such a matrix $\boldsymbol{R}$ is given by

$$\boldsymbol{R} = \boldsymbol{V}\boldsymbol{U}^\top. \tag{4.24}$$

If $|\boldsymbol{VU}|$ $(= |\boldsymbol{V}|\cdot|\boldsymbol{U}|) = 1$, then $|\boldsymbol{R}| = 1$, and hence $\boldsymbol{R}$ is a rotation matrix. However, $\boldsymbol{V}$ and $\boldsymbol{U}$ being orthogonal matrices only implies that their determinants are $|\boldsymbol{V}| = \pm 1$ and $|\boldsymbol{U}| = \pm 1$, not necessarily $|\boldsymbol{VU}| = 1$.

On the other hand, it can be shown (see Sec. 4.6) by using the variational principle that if $\boldsymbol{R}$ continuously changes over the set of all rotation matrices, the equality $|T_{11}| = |T_{22}| = |T_{33}| = 1$ holds for the value of $\boldsymbol{R}$ for which Eq. (4.21) takes an extremum value. Hence, if $T_{11} = T_{22} = T_{33} = 1$ does not hold for whatever choice of $\boldsymbol{R}$, we instead consider a rotation $\boldsymbol{R}$ such that

$$\mathrm{tr}(\boldsymbol{T\Sigma}) \leq \sigma_1 + \sigma_2 - \sigma_3 \tag{4.25}$$

by "sacrificing" the smallest singular value σ_3 of $\sigma_1 \geq \sigma_2 \geq \sigma_3$ (≥ 0) in Eq. (4.23). Then, the equality holds for $T_{11} = T_{22} = 1$, $T_{33} = -1$. Since the columns and rows of $\boldsymbol{T}$ are orthonormal systems, this means $\boldsymbol{T} = \mathrm{diag}(1, 1, -1)$. Equating Eq. (4.21) with $\mathrm{diag}(1, 1, -1)$ and multiplying it by $\boldsymbol{V}$ from left and $\boldsymbol{U}^\top$ from right, we see that such a matrix $\boldsymbol{R}$ has the form

$$\boldsymbol{R} = \boldsymbol{V}\begin{pmatrix} 1 & & \\ & 1 & \\ & & -1 \end{pmatrix}\boldsymbol{U}^\top. \tag{4.26}$$

If $|\boldsymbol{VU}| = 1$, then $|\boldsymbol{R}| = -1$, but if $|\boldsymbol{VU}| = -1$, then $|\boldsymbol{R}| = 1$, i.e., $\boldsymbol{R}$ is a rotation matrix.

It follows that the rotation matrix $\boldsymbol{R}$ that maximize K, i.e., the least-squares solution $\boldsymbol{R}$ that minimizes Eq. (4.9), is given by combining Eqs. (4.24) and (4.26) in the form

$$\boldsymbol{R} = \boldsymbol{V}\begin{pmatrix} 1 & & \\ & 1 & \\ & & |\boldsymbol{VU}| \end{pmatrix}\boldsymbol{U}^\top. \tag{4.27}$$

This result applies even when the number N of data is $N = 1, 2$. If $N = 2$, the correlation matrix $\boldsymbol{N}$ of Eq. (4.18) has rank 2 with $\boldsymbol{\Sigma} = \mathrm{diag}(\sigma_1, \sigma_2, 0)$ in Eq. (4.19). However, Eq. (4.27) uniquely determines $\boldsymbol{R}$. If no noise exists, the result coincides with the $\boldsymbol{R}$ determined by Eq. (4.7) in Sec. 4.1. If $N = 1$, the correlation matrix $\boldsymbol{N}$ has rank 1 with $\boldsymbol{\Sigma} = \mathrm{diag}(\sigma_1, 0, 0)$ in Eq. (4.19). Still, we can determine $\boldsymbol{R}$ by Eq. (4.27). However, the orthogonal matrices $\boldsymbol{U}$ and $\boldsymbol{V}$ of the singular value decomposition of Eq. (4.27) has indeterminacy for the second and third columns. This corresponds to the fact that for rotating $\boldsymbol{a}_1$ to $\boldsymbol{a}'_1$ we can add an arbitrary rotation around $\boldsymbol{a}_1$ before the rotation and an arbitrary rotation around $\boldsymbol{a}'_1$ after the rotation.

4.4 SOLUTION BY QUATERNION REPRESENTATION

We now show an alternative solution in terms of quaternions introduced in Sec. 3.5. Using the quaternion representation (3.40) of the rotation $\boldsymbol{R}$, the vector $\boldsymbol{R}\boldsymbol{a}_\alpha$ has components

$$\boldsymbol{R}\boldsymbol{a}_\alpha = \begin{pmatrix} (q_0^2+q_1^2-q_2^2-q_3^2)a_{\alpha(1)} + 2(q_1q_2-q_0q_3)a_{\alpha(2)} + 2(q_1q_3+q_0q_2)a_{\alpha(3)} \\ 2(q_2q_1+q_0q_3)a_{\alpha(1)} + (q_0^2-q_1^2+q_2^2-q_3^2)a_{\alpha(2)} + 2(q_2q_3-q_0q_1)a_{\alpha(3)} \\ 2(q_3q_1-q_0q_2)a_{\alpha(1)} + 2(q_3q_2+q_0q_1)a_{\alpha(2)} + (q_0^2-q_1^2-q_2^2+q_3^2)a_{\alpha(3)} \end{pmatrix}, \tag{4.28}$$

where $a_{\alpha(i)}$ denotes ith component of $\boldsymbol{a}_\alpha$. Hence, the function K of Eq. (4.16) has the form

$$\begin{aligned} K = \sum_{\alpha=1}^{N} \Big(& (q_0^2+q_1^2-q_2^2-q_3^2)a_{\alpha(1)}a'_{\alpha(1)} + 2(q_1q_2-q_0q_3)a_{\alpha(2)}a'_{\alpha(1)} \\ & +2(q_1q_3+q_0q_2)a_{\alpha(3)}a'_{\alpha(1)} + 2(q_2q_1+q_0q_3)a_{\alpha(1)}a'_{\alpha(2)} + (q_0^2-q_1^2+q_2^2-q_3^2)a_{\alpha(2)}a'_{\alpha(2)} \\ & +2(q_2q_3-q_0q_1)a_{\alpha(3)}a'_{\alpha(2)} + 2(q_3q_1-q_0q_2)a_{\alpha(1)}a'_{\alpha(3)} + 2(q_3q_2+q_0q_1)a_{\alpha(2)}a'_{\alpha(3)} \\ & +(q_0^2-q_1^2-q_2^2+q_3^2)a_{\alpha(3)}a'_{\alpha(3)} \Big) \\ = \sum_{\alpha=1}^{N} \Big(& q_0^2(a_{\alpha(1)}a'_{\alpha(1)} + a_{\alpha(2)}a'_{\alpha(2)} + a_{\alpha(3)}a'_{\alpha(3)}) + q_1^2(a_{\alpha(1)}a'_{\alpha(1)} - a_{\alpha(2)}a'_{\alpha(2)} \\ & -a_{\alpha(3)}a'_{\alpha(3)}) + q_2^2(-a_{\alpha(1)}a'_{\alpha(1)} + a_{\alpha(2)}a'_{\alpha(2)} - a_{\alpha(3)}a'_{\alpha(3)}) + q_3^2(-a_{\alpha(1)}a'_{\alpha(1)} \\ & -a_{\alpha(2)}a'_{\alpha(2)} + a_{\alpha(3)}a'_{\alpha(3)}) + 2q_0q_1(-a_{\alpha(3)}a'_{\alpha(2)} + a_{\alpha(2)}a'_{\alpha(3)}) + 2q_0q_2(a_{\alpha(3)}a'_{\alpha(1)} \\ & -a_{\alpha(1)}a'_{\alpha(3)}) + 2q_0q_3(-a_{\alpha(2)}a'_{\alpha(1)} + a_{\alpha(1)}a'_{\alpha(2)}) + 2q_2q_3(a_{\alpha(3)}a'_{\alpha(2)} + a_{\alpha(2)}a'_{\alpha(3)}) \\ & +2q_3q_1(a_{\alpha(3)}a'_{\alpha(1)} + a_{\alpha(1)}a'_{\alpha(3)}) + 2q_1q_2(a_{\alpha(2)}a'_{\alpha(1)} + a_{\alpha(1)}a'_{\alpha(2)})\Big). \end{aligned} \tag{4.29}$$

Noting that the (i, j) element of the correlation matrix $\boldsymbol{N}$ of Eq. (4.18) is written as $N_{ij} = \sum_{\alpha=1}^{N} a_{\alpha(i)}a'_{\alpha(j)}$ ($\hookrightarrow$ Exercise 4.3), we can rewrite the above equation as

$$\begin{aligned} K = & (q_0^2+q_1^2-q_2^2-q_3^2)N_{11} + 2(q_1q_2-q_0q_3)N_{21} + 2(q_1q_3+q_0q_2)N_{31} \\ & +2(q_2q_1+q_0q_3)N_{12} + (q_0^2-q_1^2+q_2^2-q_3^2)N_{22} + 2(q_2q_3-q_0q_1)N_{32} \\ & +2(q_3q_1-q_0q_2)N_{13} + 2(q_3q_2+q_0q_1)N_{23} + (q_0^2-q_1^2-q_2^2+q_3^2)N_{33} \\ = & q_0^2(N_{11}+N_{22}+N_{33}) + q_1^2(N_{11}-N_{22}-N_{33}) + q_2^2(-N_{11}+N_{22}-N_{33}) \\ & +q_3^2(-N_{11}-N_{22}+N_{33}) + 2q_0q_1(-N_{32}+N_{23}) + 2q_0q_2(N_{31}-N_{13}) \\ & +2q_0q_3(-N_{21}+N_{12}) + 2q_2q_3(N_{32}+N_{23}) + 2q_3q_1(N_{31}+N_{13}) \\ & +2q_1q_2(N_{21}+N_{12}). \end{aligned} \tag{4.30}$$

Define the following 4×4 symmetric matrix $\tilde{\boldsymbol{N}}$:

$$\tilde{\boldsymbol{N}} = \begin{pmatrix} N_{11}+N_{22}+N_{33} & -N_{32}+N_{23} & N_{31}-N_{13} & -N_{21}+N_{12} \\ -N_{32}+N_{23} & N_{11}-N_{22}-N_{33} & N_{21}+N_{12} & N_{31}+N_{13} \\ N_{31}-N_{13} & N_{21}+N_{12} & -N_{11}+N_{22}-N_{33} & N_{32}+N_{23} \\ -N_{21}+N_{12} & N_{31}+N_{13} & N_{32}+N_{23} & -N_{11}-N_{22}+N_{33} \end{pmatrix}. \tag{4.31}$$

In terms of the 4D vector $\boldsymbol{q} = (q_0, q_1, q_2, q_3)^\top$, Eq. (4.30) is written as

$$K = \langle \boldsymbol{q}, \tilde{\boldsymbol{N}}\boldsymbol{q} \rangle. \tag{4.32}$$

As pointed out in Sec. 3.5, a quaternion $q = q_0 + q_1 i + q_2 j + q_3 k$ that represents a rotation has unit norm: $\|\boldsymbol{q}\| = 1$. Hence, the vector $\boldsymbol{q}$ that maximizes the quadratic form of Eq. (4.32) is given by the unit eigenvector of the matrix $\tilde{\boldsymbol{N}}$ for the largest eigenvalue. Substituting that $\boldsymbol{q}$ into Eq. (3.40), we obtain the rotation $\boldsymbol{R}$ that maximizes K.

As in the case of Eq. (4.26), this procedure works for $N = 1, 2$, too. For $N = 1$, the largest eigenvalue of $\tilde{\boldsymbol{N}}$ is a multiple root, so the corresponding unit eigenvector has indeterminacy. The geometric meaning is the same as the case of Eq. (4.26).

4.5 OPTIMAL CORRECTION OF ROTATION

It often happens that an estimate $\hat{\boldsymbol{R}}$ of rotation computed from image or sensor data, which should be a rotation matrix if there is no noise in the data, is not necessarily an exact rotation matrix. Typically, this occurs when each element of $\hat{\boldsymbol{R}}$ is computed separately or when the nine elements of $\hat{\boldsymbol{R}}$ are computed by solving a set of linear equations that hold in the absence of noise. So, we consider the problem of optimally correcting $\hat{\boldsymbol{R}}$ to an exact rotation matrix $\boldsymbol{R}$. Let $\hat{\boldsymbol{r}}_1$, $\hat{\boldsymbol{r}}_2$, and $\hat{\boldsymbol{r}}_3$ be the three columns of $\hat{\boldsymbol{R}}$. The problem is regarded as optimally correcting these so that they form an exact orthonormal system.

Here, we define the "optimaility" in terms of matrix norm. To be specific, we want to compute a rotation matrix $\boldsymbol{R}$ such that $\|\boldsymbol{R} - \hat{\boldsymbol{R}}\|$ is minimized, where the *matrix norm* of an $m \times n$ matrix $\boldsymbol{A} = \left(A_{ij}\right)$ is defined by

$$\|\boldsymbol{A}\| = \sqrt{\sum_{i=1}^{m}\sum_{j=1}^{n} A_{ij}^2}. \tag{4.33}$$

This is also known as the *Frobenius norm* or *Euclid norm* (↪ Exercise 4.5).

For the matrix norm of Eq. (4.33), the following identity holds (↪ Exercise 4.6):

$$\|\boldsymbol{A}\|^2 = \mathrm{tr}(\boldsymbol{A}\boldsymbol{A}^\top) = \mathrm{tr}(\boldsymbol{A}^\top\boldsymbol{A}). \tag{4.34}$$

Using this, we can write $\|\boldsymbol{R} - \hat{\boldsymbol{R}}\|^2$ in the form

$$\begin{aligned} \|\boldsymbol{R} - \hat{\boldsymbol{R}}\|^2 &= \mathrm{tr}((\boldsymbol{R} - \hat{\boldsymbol{R}})(\boldsymbol{R} - \hat{\boldsymbol{R}})^\top) = \mathrm{tr}(\boldsymbol{R}\boldsymbol{R}^\top - \boldsymbol{R}\hat{\boldsymbol{R}}^\top - \hat{\boldsymbol{R}}\boldsymbol{R}^\top + \hat{\boldsymbol{R}}\hat{\boldsymbol{R}}^\top) \\ &= \mathrm{tr}\boldsymbol{I} - \mathrm{tr}(\boldsymbol{R}\hat{\boldsymbol{R}}^\top) - \mathrm{tr}((\boldsymbol{R}\hat{\boldsymbol{R}}^\top)^\top) + \mathrm{tr}(\hat{\boldsymbol{R}}\hat{\boldsymbol{R}}^\top) \\ &= 3 - 2\mathrm{tr}(\boldsymbol{R}\hat{\boldsymbol{R}}^\top) + \|\hat{\boldsymbol{R}}\|^2, \end{aligned} \tag{4.35}$$

where we have noted that the trace is invariant to transpose. Hence, the value $\boldsymbol{R}$ that minimizes $\|\boldsymbol{R} - \hat{\boldsymbol{R}}\|$ is the value $\boldsymbol{R}$ that maximizes $\mathrm{tr}(\boldsymbol{R}\hat{\boldsymbol{R}}^\top)$. Since the problem is the same as maximizing Eq. (4.17), the solution is obtained by the singular value decomposition of $\hat{\boldsymbol{R}}$. Let

$$\hat{\boldsymbol{R}} = \boldsymbol{U}\boldsymbol{\Sigma}\boldsymbol{V}^\top \tag{4.36}$$

be the singular value decomposition of $\hat{\boldsymbol{R}}$. Since $\hat{\boldsymbol{R}}^\top = \boldsymbol{V}\boldsymbol{\Sigma}\boldsymbol{U}^\top$, we obtain from Eq. (4.27)

$$\boldsymbol{R} = \boldsymbol{U}\begin{pmatrix} 1 & & \\ & 1 & \\ & & |\boldsymbol{U}\boldsymbol{V}| \end{pmatrix}\boldsymbol{V}^\top. \tag{4.37}$$

Note that the roles of $\boldsymbol{U}$ and $\boldsymbol{V}$ are interchanged. Thus, the desired rotation matrix $\boldsymbol{R}$ is obtained by replacing the singular values of the estimated $\hat{\boldsymbol{R}}$, which should ideally be 1, 1, and 1, by 1, 1, and $|\boldsymbol{U}\boldsymbol{V}|$.

For an appropriately designed estimation scheme, the determinant of the estimated $\hat{\boldsymbol{R}}$ should be positive (≈ 1). Then, this correction simply means *replacing all the singular values by 1*. However, for an configuration in which the data vectors are almost coplanar, the determinant of the resulting $\hat{\boldsymbol{R}}$ can be 0 or negative. Even in such a pathological case, Eq. (4.37) returns an $\boldsymbol{R}$ that optimally approximates the true rotation.

4.6 SUPPLEMENTAL NOTE

The solution using the singular value decomposition shown in Sec. 4.3 was first given by Arun et al. [1] for the case of $|\boldsymbol{V}\boldsymbol{U}| = 1$. (See Appendix B for the details of the singular value decomposition.) Extension to the case of $|\boldsymbol{V}\boldsymbol{U}| = -1$ was given by Kanatani [18, 19]. The analysis using the variational principle omitted in Sec. 4.3 goes as follows. First, consider the case of $\sigma_3 = 0$. Then, Eqs. (4.22) and (4.23) imply $\mathrm{tr}(\boldsymbol{T}\boldsymbol{\Sigma}) = \sigma_1 T_{11} + \sigma_2 T_{22} \leq \sigma_1 + \sigma_2$; the equality holds for $\boldsymbol{T} = \mathrm{diag}(1, 1, \pm 1)$. Hence, from Eq. (4.21) we obtain $\boldsymbol{R} = \boldsymbol{V}\mathrm{diag}(1, 1, \pm 1)\boldsymbol{U}^\top$, and we obtain a rotation marix $\boldsymbol{R}$ of $|\boldsymbol{R}| = 1$, using Eq. (4.27). So, consider the case of $\sigma_3 > 0$. Here, we show a sketch of how we obtain $|T_{11}| = |T_{22}| = |T_{33}| = 1$.

The matrix $\boldsymbol{T}$ defined by Eq. (4.21) is an orthogonal matrix, but its determinant is not necessarily 1. The fact that $\mathrm{tr}(\boldsymbol{T}\boldsymbol{\Sigma})$ takes its extremum means that it remains stationary for infinitesimal variation of $\boldsymbol{T}$. Note that even if $\boldsymbol{T}$ has determinant -1, i.e., if $\boldsymbol{T}$ is a composition of a rotation and a reflection, its small change is a small rotation. Hence, an infinitesimal variation of $\boldsymbol{T}$ is written as $\boldsymbol{T}+\boldsymbol{A}\boldsymbol{T}\delta t+\cdots$, where $\boldsymbol{A}$ is an antisymmetric matrix that determines the orientation of the infinitesimal rotation and δt is a small parameter that specifies the magnitude of the rotation. By "$\cdots$," we mean high order terms in δt (we will discuss the details of infinitesimal rotations in Chapter 6). It follows that we can write the infinitesimal variation of $\mathrm{tr}(\boldsymbol{T}\boldsymbol{\Sigma})$ as

$$\mathrm{tr}((\boldsymbol{T} + \boldsymbol{A}\boldsymbol{T}\delta t + \cdots)\boldsymbol{\Sigma}) = \mathrm{tr}(\boldsymbol{T}\boldsymbol{\Sigma}) + \mathrm{tr}(\boldsymbol{A}\boldsymbol{T}\boldsymbol{\Sigma})\delta t + \cdots. \tag{4.38}$$

Since this should be 0 for an arbitrary variation δt, we see that

$$\mathrm{tr}(\boldsymbol{A}\boldsymbol{T}\boldsymbol{\Sigma}) = 0. \tag{4.39}$$

This should holds for an arbitrary antisymmetric matrix $\boldsymbol{A}$, so we conclude that $\boldsymbol{T}\boldsymbol{\Sigma}$ is a symmetric matrix ($\hookrightarrow$ Exercise 4.7(4)). Hence,

$$\boldsymbol{T}\boldsymbol{\Sigma} = (\boldsymbol{T}\boldsymbol{\Sigma})^\top = \boldsymbol{\Sigma}^\top\boldsymbol{T}^\top = \boldsymbol{\Sigma}\boldsymbol{T}^\top, \tag{4.40}$$

so we obtain

$$\mathrm{tr}(\boldsymbol{T}^2\boldsymbol{\Sigma}) = \mathrm{tr}(\boldsymbol{T}\boldsymbol{T}\boldsymbol{\Sigma}) = \mathrm{tr}(\boldsymbol{T}\boldsymbol{\Sigma}\boldsymbol{T}^\top) = \mathrm{tr}(\boldsymbol{T}^\top\boldsymbol{T}\boldsymbol{\Sigma}) = \mathrm{tr}(\boldsymbol{\Sigma}), \tag{4.41}$$

where we use the identity of Eq. (4.47) shown below and note that $\boldsymbol{T}$ is an orthogonal matrix and hence $\boldsymbol{T}^\top\boldsymbol{T} = \boldsymbol{I}$. Let $\tilde{\boldsymbol{R}} = \boldsymbol{T}^2$. Since $\boldsymbol{T}$ is an orthogonal matrix, we see that $|\tilde{\boldsymbol{R}}| = |\boldsymbol{T}|^2 = 1$ and hence $\tilde{\boldsymbol{R}}$ is a rotation matrix. Using the reasoning of Eq. (4.22), we have

$$\mathrm{tr}(\tilde{\boldsymbol{R}}\boldsymbol{\Sigma}) = \sigma_1\tilde{R}_{11} + \sigma_2\tilde{R}_{22} + \sigma_3\tilde{R}_{33}. \tag{4.42}$$

On the other hand, we see from Eq. (4.41) that $\mathrm{tr}(\tilde{\boldsymbol{R}}\boldsymbol{\Sigma}) = \sigma_1 + \sigma_2 + \sigma_3$. Subtraction on both sides gives

$$(1 - \tilde{R}_{11})\sigma_1 + (1 - \tilde{R}_{22})\sigma_2 + (1 - \tilde{R}_{33})\sigma_3 = 0. \tag{4.43}$$

Since $\tilde{\boldsymbol{R}} = \left(\tilde{R}_{ij}\right)$ is a rotation matrix, we have $|\tilde{R}_{ij}| \leq 1$. We are also assuming that σ_1, σ_2, and σ_3 are all positive. Hence, each term of Eq. (4.43) is 0, which implies $\tilde{R}_{11} = \tilde{R}_{22} = \tilde{R}_{33} = 1$, namely $\tilde{\boldsymbol{R}}$ $(= \boldsymbol{T}^2) = \boldsymbol{I}$. The equality $\boldsymbol{T}^2 = \boldsymbol{T}\boldsymbol{T} = \boldsymbol{I}$ means $\boldsymbol{T} = \boldsymbol{T}^{-1}$. Since $\boldsymbol{T}$ is an orthogonal matrix, we conclude that $\boldsymbol{T}^{-1} = \boldsymbol{T}^\top$ and hence $\boldsymbol{T} = \boldsymbol{T}^\top$, meaning that $\boldsymbol{T}$ is a symmetric matrix. Thus, Eq. (4.40) implies $\boldsymbol{T}\boldsymbol{\Sigma} = \boldsymbol{\Sigma}\boldsymbol{T}$, i.e., $\boldsymbol{T}$ and $\boldsymbol{\Sigma}$ commute. It follows that $\boldsymbol{T}$ and $\boldsymbol{\Sigma}$ share the same eigenvectors if σ_1, σ_2, and σ_3 are distinct (↪ Exercise 4.8). Since $\boldsymbol{\Sigma}$ is a diagonal matrix, its eigenvectors are the basis vectors $\boldsymbol{e}_1$, $\boldsymbol{e}_2$, and $\boldsymbol{e}_3$. Hence, they are also the eigenvectors of $\boldsymbol{T}$, meaning that $\boldsymbol{T}$ is also diagonal. Thus, $\boldsymbol{T}^2 = \boldsymbol{I}$ means $\boldsymbol{T} = \mathrm{diag}(\pm1, \pm1, \pm1)$, i..e, $|T_{11}| = |T_{22}| = |T_{33}| = 1$. Here, we are assuming that σ_1, σ_2, and σ_3 are distinct, but if multiple roots exist, we can regard them as a limit of distinct roots and obtain the same conclusion. □

The problem of optimally correcting a matrix whose determinant is negative or is 0 (meaning that the rows or columns are coplanar) into a rotation matrix frequently appears in estimating the camera orientation for 3D scene reconstruction by computer vision [29]. The quaternion representation solution shown in Sec. 4.4 was first presented by Horn [16].

4.7 EXERCISES

4.1. Show that we obtain Eq. (4.14) by eliminating $\bar{\boldsymbol{a}}_\alpha$ and $\bar{\boldsymbol{a}}'_\alpha$ from the Mahalanobis distance of Eq. (4.11), using Lagrange multipliers for the constraint $\bar{\boldsymbol{a}}'_\alpha = \boldsymbol{R}\bar{\boldsymbol{a}}_\alpha$.

4.2. (1) Let $\boldsymbol{x}$ and $\boldsymbol{y}$ be independent nD random variables having probability densities $p_x(\boldsymbol{x})$ and $p_y(\boldsymbol{y})$, respectively. Show that the probability density of the sum $\boldsymbol{z} = \boldsymbol{x} + \boldsymbol{y}$ is given by

$$p_z(\boldsymbol{z}) = \int_{-\infty}^{\infty} p_x(\boldsymbol{x})p_y(\boldsymbol{z} - \boldsymbol{x})d\boldsymbol{x}, \tag{4.44}$$

where $\int_{-\infty}^{\infty} \cdots \int_{-\infty}^{\infty} (\cdots) dx_1 \cdots dx_n$ is abbreviated to $\int_{-\infty}^{\infty} (\cdots) d\boldsymbol{x}$.

(2) Show that if nD random variables $\boldsymbol{x}$ and $\boldsymbol{y}$ are independent and subject to a Gaussian distribution of mean $\boldsymbol{0}$ and variance σ^2, their sum $\boldsymbol{z} = \boldsymbol{x} + \boldsymbol{y}$ is subject to a Gaussian distribution of mean $\boldsymbol{0}$ and variance $2\sigma^2$.

4.3. Show that for arbitrary nD vectors $\boldsymbol{a} = \left(a_i\right)$ and $\boldsymbol{b} = \left(b_i\right)$, the (i, j) element of the $n \times n$ matrix $\boldsymbol{a}\boldsymbol{b}^\top$ is a_ib_j, i.e.,

$$\boldsymbol{a}\boldsymbol{b}^\top = \left(a_ib_j\right). \tag{4.45}$$

Also show that

$$\mathrm{tr}(\boldsymbol{a}\boldsymbol{b}^\top) = \langle \boldsymbol{a}, \boldsymbol{b} \rangle \tag{4.46}$$

holds.

4.4. Show that the identity

$$\mathrm{tr}(\boldsymbol{A}\boldsymbol{B}) = \mathrm{tr}(\boldsymbol{B}\boldsymbol{A}) \tag{4.47}$$

holds for for arbitrary $n \times n$ matrices $\boldsymbol{A}$ and $\boldsymbol{B}$.

4.5. Show that in terms of the matrix norm of Eq. (4.33), Eq. (4.9) can be written as

$$J = \frac{1}{2}\|\boldsymbol{A}' - \boldsymbol{R}\boldsymbol{A}\|^2, \tag{4.48}$$

where $\boldsymbol{A}$ and $\boldsymbol{A}'$ are $3 \times N$ matrices having columns $\boldsymbol{a}_1$, ..., $\boldsymbol{a}_N$ and $\boldsymbol{a}'_1$, ..., $\boldsymbol{a}'_N$, respectively.

4.6. Show that Eq. (4.34) holds for an arbitrary $n \times m$ matrix $\boldsymbol{A}$.

4.7. (1) Show that a square matrix $\boldsymbol{T}$ is uniquely decomposed into the sum

$$\boldsymbol{T} = \boldsymbol{T}^{(s)} + \boldsymbol{T}^{(a)} \tag{4.49}$$

of a symmetric matrix $\boldsymbol{T}^{(s)}$ and an antisymmetric matrix $\boldsymbol{T}^{(a)}$.

(2) Show that $\mathrm{tr}(\boldsymbol{S}\boldsymbol{A}) = 0$ holds for an arbitrary symmetric matrix $\boldsymbol{S}$ and an arbitrary antisymmetric matrix $\boldsymbol{A}$.

(3) Show that if a square matrix $\boldsymbol{T}$ is such that $\mathrm{tr}(\boldsymbol{S}\boldsymbol{T}) = 0$ for an arbitrary symmetric matrix $\boldsymbol{S}$, then $\boldsymbol{T}$ is an antisymmetric matrix.

(4) Show that if a square matrix $\boldsymbol{T}$ is such that $\mathrm{tr}(\boldsymbol{A}\boldsymbol{T}) = 0$ for an arbitrary antisymmetric matrix $\boldsymbol{A}$, then $\boldsymbol{T}$ is a symmetric matrix.

4.8. Show that if a symmetric matrix $\boldsymbol{A}$ has distinct eigenvalues and $\boldsymbol{A}\boldsymbol{B} = \boldsymbol{B}\boldsymbol{A}$ holds for some symmetric matrix $\boldsymbol{B}$, then $\boldsymbol{B}$ has the same eigenvectors as $\boldsymbol{A}$.

CHAPTER 5

Estimation of Rotation II: Anisotropic Noise

As in the preceding chapter, we consider the problem of computing from multiple vector data their rotation. Here, the data are assumed to contain anisotropic noise that depends on orientation. This is a usual circumstance of 3D measurement using sensors. The orientation dependence of noise is specified by a "covariance matrix." In this chapter, we formulate maximum likelihood estimation in general terms for a situation where covariance matrices for anisotropic Gaussian noise distribution are involved. We show that 3D rotation can be rewritten as a linear constraint in terms of quaternions introduced in Sec. 3.5 and that the solution can be obtained by an iterative scheme called "FNS." We also describe the outline of "EFNS" for computing the maximum likelihood solution without parameterizing the rotation matrix $\boldsymbol{R}$, regarding its nine elements as unknowns and optimizing them subject to the constraint that the nine elements define a 3D rotation.

5.1 ANISOTROPIC GAUSSIAN DISTRIBUTIONS

In the preceding chapter, we considered methods for optimally estimating rotation, assuming that the data contain isotropic Gaussian noise. In practice, however, sensor measurement has orientational bias to some extent. Today, various methods exist for 3D sensing including image analysis, laser and ultrasonic wave emission, and triangulation using multiple cameras; they are widely used for manufacturing inspection, human body measurement, cultural asset measurement, camera autofocusing, and many other applications [38]. Recently, an easy-to-use device called "kinect" is very popular.

Whatever method is used, however, the measurement accuracy is different in the depth direction, e.g., the camera optical axis or the laser emission direction, from the accuracy in the direction orthogonal to it. If images are used, for example, accuracy is high in visible directions of right, left, up, and down, but the accuracy in the depth direction depends on the position of auxiliary cameras. The depth accuracy of laser or ultrasonic wave emission depends on the wavelength of the emission, but the accuracy in the direction orthogonal to it depends on the emission controlling mechanisms, e.g., the servomotors. Here, we consider Gaussian noise distributions that depend on orientation.

We say that $\boldsymbol{x} = (x, y, z)^\top$ is subject to a general (not necessarily isotropic) Gaussian distribution of mean $\mathbf{0}$ if it has a probability density of the form

$$p(\boldsymbol{x}) = \frac{e^{-\langle \boldsymbol{x}, \boldsymbol{\Sigma}^{-1}\boldsymbol{x}\rangle/2}}{\sqrt{(2\pi)^3|\boldsymbol{\Sigma}|}}, \tag{5.1}$$

where

$$\boldsymbol{\Sigma} = \begin{pmatrix} \sigma_1^2 & \gamma_{12} & \gamma_{31} \\ \gamma_{12} & \sigma_2^2 & \gamma_{23} \\ \gamma_{31} & \gamma_{23} & \sigma_3^2 \end{pmatrix} \tag{5.2}$$

is called the *covariance matrix*; it is defined by

$$\boldsymbol{\Sigma} = E[\boldsymbol{x}\boldsymbol{x}^\top] \ \left(= \int_{\boldsymbol{x}} \boldsymbol{x}\boldsymbol{x}^\top p(\boldsymbol{x}) d\boldsymbol{x}\right). \tag{5.3}$$

The operation $E[\,\cdot\,]$ denotes expectation over the probability density $p(\boldsymbol{x})$. If we write x, y, and z as x_1, x_2, and x_3, respectively, Eqs. (5.2) and (5.3) imply

$$\sigma_i^2 = E[x_i^2], \qquad \gamma_{ij} = E[x_i x_j], \tag{5.4}$$

i.e., the diagonal element σ_i^2 of the covariance matrix $\boldsymbol{\Sigma}$ is the variance of x_i, and γ_{ij} is the covariance of x_i and x_j. The eigenvectors $\boldsymbol{u}_i$ of $\boldsymbol{\Sigma}$ are called the *principal axes* of the distribution. The principal axis for the largest eigenvalue is the direction in which the noise is the most likely to occur; the corresponding eigenvalue is the variance of noise in that direction. Conversely, the principal axis for the smallest eigenvalue is the direction in which the noise is the least likely to occur; the corresponding eigenvalue is the variance of noise in that direction.

In the xyz space, the equiprobability surface, i.e., the surface on which the value of $p(\boldsymbol{x})$ of Eq. (5.1) is constant, is an ellipsoid of the form

$$\langle \boldsymbol{x}, \boldsymbol{\Sigma}^{-1}\boldsymbol{x}\rangle = \text{const.}, \tag{5.5}$$

known as the *error ellipsoid*[1]. The three axes of symmetry of this ellipsoid are the principal axes of the covariance matrix $\boldsymbol{\Sigma}$, i.e. the directions of its eigenvectors $\boldsymbol{u}_i$, $i = 1, 2, 3$; the corresponding radii are proportional to the standard deviation of the noise in those directions (Fig. 5.1).

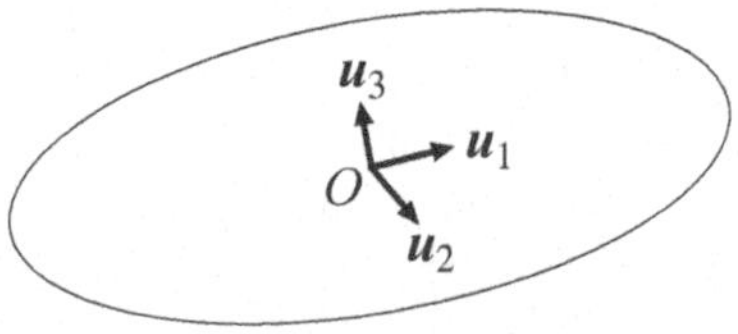

FIGURE 5.1 Equiprobability surface (error ellipsoid) of anisotropic Gaussian distribution. The eigenvectors $\boldsymbol{u}_i$ of the covariance matrix $\boldsymbol{\Sigma}$ are the axes of symmetry, and the radii in their directions are proportional to the standard deviation σ_i.

In particular, if $\sigma_1^2 = \sigma_2^2 = \sigma_3^2$ $(= \sigma^2)$ and $\gamma_{ij} = 0$, $i, j = 1, 2, 3$, the distribution is isotropic and we can write $\boldsymbol{\Sigma} = \sigma^2\boldsymbol{I}$. Then, Eq. (5.1) has the form of Eq. (4.8), and Eq. (5.5) reduces to the equation of a sphere.

[1]This is is called the "error ellipse" for two variables and the "confidence interval" for one variable.

5.2 ROTATION ESTIMATION BY MAXIMUM LIKELIHOOD

Given two sets of vectors $\boldsymbol{a}_1$, ..., $\boldsymbol{a}_N$ and $\boldsymbol{a}'_1$, ..., $\boldsymbol{a}'_N$, we regard them as perturbations of their true values $\bar{\boldsymbol{a}}_1$, ..., $\bar{\boldsymbol{a}}_N$ and $\bar{\boldsymbol{a}}'_1$, ..., $\bar{\boldsymbol{a}}'_N$ by noise and write

$$\boldsymbol{a}_\alpha = \bar{\boldsymbol{a}}_\alpha + \Delta\boldsymbol{a}_\alpha, \qquad \boldsymbol{a}'_\alpha = \bar{\boldsymbol{a}}'_\alpha + \Delta\boldsymbol{a}'_\alpha, \qquad \alpha = 1, ..., N, \tag{5.6}$$

where the noise terms $\Delta\boldsymbol{a}_\alpha$ and $\Delta\boldsymbol{a}'_\alpha$ are assumed to be independent (not necessarily isotropic) Gaussian variables of mean $\mathbf{0}$ and covariance matrices $V[\boldsymbol{a}_\alpha]$ and $V[\boldsymbol{a}'_\alpha]$, respectively. We assume that the true values $\bar{\boldsymbol{a}}_\alpha$ and $\bar{\boldsymbol{a}}'_\alpha$ satisfy

$$\bar{\boldsymbol{a}}'_\alpha = \boldsymbol{R}\bar{\boldsymbol{a}}_\alpha, \qquad \alpha = 1, ..., N, \tag{5.7}$$

for some rotation $\boldsymbol{R}$. Our task is to estimate that $\boldsymbol{R}$ from noisy observations $\boldsymbol{a}_\alpha$ and $\boldsymbol{a}'_\alpha$, $\alpha = 1, ..., N$.

For stereo vision using two cameras, we can theoretically derive the covariance matrix of 3D reconstruction based on triangulation from the camera configuration geometry and image processing accuracy (this will be discussed in detail in Chapter 8). For 3D measurement of the earth's surface using GPS, the position measurements and their covariance matrices are available on the websites of government agencies (this will also be discussed in Chapter 8). For many commercially available 3D sensors, the measurement covariance matrices are offered by the manufacturers.

In the following analysis, we write the covariance matrices $V[\boldsymbol{a}_\alpha]$ and $V[\boldsymbol{a}'_\alpha]$ as

$$V[\boldsymbol{a}_\alpha] = \sigma^2 V_0[\boldsymbol{a}_\alpha], \qquad V[\boldsymbol{a}'_\alpha] = \sigma^2 V_0[\boldsymbol{a}'_\alpha], \tag{5.8}$$

and call $V_0[\boldsymbol{a}_\alpha]$ and $V_0[\boldsymbol{a}'_\alpha]$ the *normalized covariance matrices*; these describe the sensor characteristics of the orientation dependence, which we assume are known. If the accuracy does not depend on orientation, we can write $V_0[\boldsymbol{a}_\alpha] = V_0[\boldsymbol{a}'_\alpha] = \boldsymbol{I}$. On the other hand, σ is a scalar that specifies the absolute magnitude of noise, which we call the *noise level*. We assume it to be unknown. Then, the probability density of $\Delta\boldsymbol{a}_\alpha$ and $\Delta\boldsymbol{a}'_\alpha$, $\alpha = 1, .., N$, has the form

$$\begin{aligned} p &= \prod_{\alpha=1}^{N} \frac{e^{-\langle \Delta\boldsymbol{a}_\alpha, V_0[\boldsymbol{a}_\alpha]^{-1}\Delta\boldsymbol{a}_\alpha\rangle/2\sigma^2}}{\sqrt{(2\pi)^3|V_0[\boldsymbol{a}_\alpha]|}\sigma^3} \frac{e^{-\langle \Delta\boldsymbol{a}'_\alpha, V_0[\boldsymbol{a}'_\alpha]^{-1}\Delta\boldsymbol{a}'_\alpha\rangle/2\sigma^2}}{\sqrt{(2\pi)^3|V_0[\boldsymbol{a}'_\alpha]|}\sigma^3} \\ &= \frac{e^{-\sum_{\alpha=1}^{N}(\langle \boldsymbol{a}_\alpha - \bar{\boldsymbol{a}}_\alpha, V_0[\boldsymbol{a}_\alpha]^{-1}(\boldsymbol{a}_\alpha - \bar{\boldsymbol{a}}_\alpha)\rangle + \langle \boldsymbol{a}'_\alpha - \bar{\boldsymbol{a}}'_\alpha, V_0[\boldsymbol{a}'_\alpha]^{-1}(\boldsymbol{a}'_\alpha - \bar{\boldsymbol{a}}'_\alpha)\rangle))/2\sigma^2}}{\prod_{\alpha=1}^{N}(2\pi)^3|V_0[\boldsymbol{a}_\alpha]||V_0[\boldsymbol{a}'_\alpha]|\sigma^6}. \end{aligned} \tag{5.9}$$

If viewed as a function of the observations $\boldsymbol{a}_\alpha$ and $\boldsymbol{a}'_\alpha$, $\alpha = 1, ..., N$, this gives their likelihood.

As stated in Sec. 4.2, maximum likelihood estimation is to estimate $\bar{\boldsymbol{a}}_\alpha$, $\bar{\boldsymbol{a}}'_\alpha$, $\alpha = 1, .., N$, and $\boldsymbol{R}$ that maximize this likelihood subject to the constraint $\bar{\boldsymbol{a}}'_\alpha = \boldsymbol{R}\bar{\boldsymbol{a}}_\alpha$. As mentioned in Sec. 4.2, this is also equivalent to minimizing the Mahalanobis distance

$$J = \frac{1}{2}\sum_{\alpha=1}^{N}(\langle \boldsymbol{a}_\alpha - \bar{\boldsymbol{a}}_\alpha, V_0[\boldsymbol{a}_\alpha]^{-1}(\boldsymbol{a}_\alpha - \bar{\boldsymbol{a}}_\alpha)\rangle + \langle \boldsymbol{a}'_\alpha - \bar{\boldsymbol{a}}'_\alpha, V_0[\boldsymbol{a}'_\alpha]^{-1}(\boldsymbol{a}'_\alpha - \bar{\boldsymbol{a}}'_\alpha)\rangle). \tag{5.10}$$

Eliminating $\bar{\boldsymbol{a}}_\alpha$ and $\bar{\boldsymbol{a}}'_\alpha$ using Lagrange multipliers for the constraint of Eq. (5.7), we can write Eq. (5.10) in the form (↪Exercise 5.1)

$$J = \frac{1}{2}\sum_{\alpha=1}^{N}\langle \boldsymbol{a}'_\alpha - \boldsymbol{R}\boldsymbol{a}_\alpha, \boldsymbol{W}_\alpha(\boldsymbol{a}'_\alpha - \boldsymbol{R}\boldsymbol{a}_\alpha)\rangle, \tag{5.11}$$

where we define the matrix $\boldsymbol{V}_\alpha$ by

$$\boldsymbol{V}_\alpha = \boldsymbol{R}V_0[\boldsymbol{a}_\alpha]\boldsymbol{R}^\top + V_0[\boldsymbol{a}'_\alpha], \tag{5.12}$$

and put

$$\boldsymbol{W}_\alpha = \boldsymbol{V}_\alpha^{-1}. \tag{5.13}$$

The value of $\boldsymbol{R}$ that minimizes the residual J of Eq. (5.11) is the maximum likelihood solution. It follows that we need not to know the unknown noise level σ. Namely, *it suffices to know covariance matrices up to scale*. If the noise distribution is isotropic, we have $V_0[\boldsymbol{a}_\alpha] = V_0[\boldsymbol{a}'_\alpha] = \boldsymbol{I}$ and hence $\boldsymbol{V}_\alpha = 2\boldsymbol{I}$ and $\boldsymbol{W}_\alpha = \boldsymbol{I}/2$, so Eq. (5.11) coincides with Eq. (4.9) up to a constant multiplier.

We can give an alternative interpretation to Eq. (5.11). The observed data do not necessarily satisfy Eq. (5.7), so let the discrepancy be, as in Sec. 4.2,

$$\boldsymbol{\varepsilon}_\alpha = \boldsymbol{a}'_\alpha - \boldsymbol{R}\boldsymbol{a}_\alpha, \qquad \alpha = 1, ..., N. \tag{5.14}$$

The true values satisfy Eq. (5.7), so substitution of Eq. (5.6) yields

$$\boldsymbol{\varepsilon}_\alpha = \Delta\boldsymbol{a}'_\alpha - \boldsymbol{R}\Delta\boldsymbol{a}_\alpha. \tag{5.15}$$

If $\Delta\boldsymbol{a}_\alpha$ and $\Delta\boldsymbol{a}'_\alpha$ are Gaussian variables, so is $\boldsymbol{\varepsilon}_\alpha$ due to the reproductivity of Gaussian variables ($\hookrightarrow$ Sec. 4.2). Since $\Delta\boldsymbol{a}_\alpha$ and $\Delta\boldsymbol{a}'_\alpha$ both have expectation $\boldsymbol{0}$, we have $E[\boldsymbol{\varepsilon}_\alpha] = \boldsymbol{0}$. From Eq. (5.3), the covariance matrix $V[\boldsymbol{\varepsilon}_\alpha]$ of $\boldsymbol{\varepsilon}_\alpha$ is

$$\begin{aligned} V[\boldsymbol{\varepsilon}_\alpha] &= E[\boldsymbol{\varepsilon}_\alpha\boldsymbol{\varepsilon}_\alpha^\top] = E[(\Delta\boldsymbol{a}'_\alpha - \boldsymbol{R}\Delta\boldsymbol{a}_\alpha)(\Delta\boldsymbol{a}'_\alpha - \boldsymbol{R}\Delta\boldsymbol{a}_\alpha)^\top] \\ &= E[\Delta\boldsymbol{a}'_\alpha\Delta\boldsymbol{a}'^\top_\alpha] - E[\Delta\boldsymbol{a}'_\alpha\Delta\boldsymbol{a}_\alpha^\top]\boldsymbol{R}^\top - \boldsymbol{R}E[\Delta\boldsymbol{a}_\alpha\Delta\boldsymbol{a}'^\top_\alpha] + \boldsymbol{R}E[\Delta\boldsymbol{a}_\alpha\Delta\boldsymbol{a}_\alpha^\top]\boldsymbol{R}^\top \\ &= \sigma^2 V_0[\boldsymbol{a}'_\alpha] + \sigma^2\boldsymbol{R}V_0[\boldsymbol{a}_\alpha]\boldsymbol{R}^\top = \sigma^2\boldsymbol{V}_\alpha. \end{aligned} \tag{5.16}$$

Note that $\Delta\boldsymbol{a}_\alpha$ and $\Delta\boldsymbol{a}'_\alpha$ are independent and hence $E[\Delta\boldsymbol{a}'_\alpha\Delta\boldsymbol{a}'^\top_\alpha] = \boldsymbol{O}$. The Mahalanobis distance of $\boldsymbol{\varepsilon}_\alpha$ is

$$J = \frac{\sigma^2}{2}\sum_{\alpha=1}^{N}\langle\boldsymbol{\varepsilon}_\alpha, V[\boldsymbol{\varepsilon}_\alpha]^{-1}\boldsymbol{\varepsilon}_\alpha\rangle = \frac{1}{2}\sum_{\alpha=1}^{N}\langle\boldsymbol{a}'_\alpha - \boldsymbol{R}\boldsymbol{a}_\alpha, \boldsymbol{W}_\alpha(\boldsymbol{a}'_\alpha - \boldsymbol{R}\boldsymbol{a}_\alpha)\rangle, \tag{5.17}$$

so we again obtain Eq. (5.11).

The standard strategy of minimizing Eq. (5.11) is to differentiate this with respect to the rotation $\boldsymbol{R}$. However, we defer this to the next chapter. Here, we introduce two alternative methods that do not employ differentiation with respect to $\boldsymbol{R}$.

(i) We parameterize the rotation $\boldsymbol{R}$. For this, the quaternion representation introduced in Sec. 3.5 is the most convenient, because it can reduce Eq. (5.7) to a "linear" equation in unknowns.

(ii) We regard Eq. (5.11) as a function of the nine elements of $\boldsymbol{R} = \left(R_{ij}\right)$ and minimize it subject to the constraint that $\{R_{ij}\}$, $i, j = 1, 2, 3$, define a rotation matrix.

5.3 ROTATION ESTIMATION BY QUATERNION REPRESENTATION

As shown in Sec. 3.5, if we represent a rotation $\boldsymbol{R}$ by a quaternion $q = q_0 + q_1 i + q_2 j + q_3 k$, rotation of vector $\boldsymbol{a}$ to vector $\boldsymbol{a}'$ is expressed by Eq. (3.34). Multiplying Eq. (3.34) by $\boldsymbol{q}$ on both sides and noting that $q^\dagger q = \|q\|^2 = 1$ ($\hookrightarrow$ Exercise 3.6), we obtain

$$\boldsymbol{a}'q = q\boldsymbol{a}. \tag{5.18}$$

This is a *linear* expression in q. Let $\boldsymbol{q}_l = q_1 i + q_2 j + q_3 k$ and identify this with vector $(q_1, q_2, q_3)^\top$. Substituting $q = q_0 + \boldsymbol{q}_l$ into Eq. (5.18) and noting Eq. (3.28), we obtain

$$-\langle \boldsymbol{a}', \boldsymbol{q}_l \rangle + q_0 \boldsymbol{a}' + \boldsymbol{a} \times \boldsymbol{q}_l = -\langle \boldsymbol{q}_l, \boldsymbol{a} \rangle + q_0 \boldsymbol{a} + \boldsymbol{q}_l \times \boldsymbol{a}. \tag{5.19}$$

From Eq. (3.33), $\boldsymbol{q}_l$ $(= \boldsymbol{l} \sin(\Omega/2))$ is a vector in the direction of the axis of rotation, so $\langle \boldsymbol{q}_l, \boldsymbol{a}' \rangle = \langle \boldsymbol{q}_l, \boldsymbol{a} \rangle$ holds ($\hookrightarrow$ Eq. (2.14)). Hence, Eq. (5.19) is rewritten as ($\hookrightarrow$ Exercise 5.2)

$$q_0(\boldsymbol{a}' - \boldsymbol{a}) + (\boldsymbol{a}' + \boldsymbol{a}) \times \boldsymbol{q}_l = \boldsymbol{0}, \tag{5.20}$$

or in component

$$\begin{aligned} q_0(a_1' - a_1) + (a_2' + a_2)q_3 - (a_3' + a_3)q_2 = 0, \\ q_0(a_2' - a_2) + (a_3' + a_3)q_1 - (a_1' + a_1)q_3 = 0, \\ q_0(a_3' - a_3) + (a_1' + a_1)q_2 - (a_2' + a_2)q_1 = 0. \end{aligned} \tag{5.21}$$

Define 4D vectors $\boldsymbol{\xi}^{(1)}$, $\boldsymbol{\xi}^{(2)}$, and $\boldsymbol{\xi}^{(3)}$ by

$$\boldsymbol{\xi}^{(1)} = \begin{pmatrix} a_1' - a_1 \\ 0 \\ -(a_3' + a_3) \\ a_2' + a_2 \end{pmatrix}, \quad \boldsymbol{\xi}^{(2)} = \begin{pmatrix} a_2' - a_2 \\ a_3' + a_3 \\ 0 \\ -(a_1' + a_1) \end{pmatrix}, \quad \boldsymbol{\xi}^{(3)} = \begin{pmatrix} a_3' - a_3 \\ -(a_2' + a_2) \\ a_1' + a_1 \\ 0 \end{pmatrix}. \tag{5.22}$$

If we express the quaternion q by a 4D vector $\boldsymbol{q} = (q_0, q_1, q_2, q_3)^\top$ $(= \begin{pmatrix} q_0 \\ \boldsymbol{q}_l \end{pmatrix})$, Eq. (5.21) is rewritten as

$$\langle \boldsymbol{\xi}^{(1)}, \boldsymbol{q} \rangle = 0, \qquad \langle \boldsymbol{\xi}^{(2)}, \boldsymbol{q} \rangle = 0, \qquad \langle \boldsymbol{\xi}^{(3)}, \boldsymbol{q} \rangle = 0. \tag{5.23}$$

Let $\bar{\boldsymbol{\xi}}_\alpha^{(k)}$ be the vector of Eq. (5.22) for the true values $\bar{\boldsymbol{a}}_\alpha$ and $\bar{\boldsymbol{a}}_\alpha'$. They satisfy

$$\langle \bar{\boldsymbol{\xi}}_\alpha^{(k)}, \boldsymbol{q} \rangle = 0, \qquad k = 1, 2, 3, \qquad \alpha = 1, ..., N. \tag{5.24}$$

On the other hand, if we write the vectors of Eq. (5.22) for the observed values $\boldsymbol{a}_\alpha$ and $\boldsymbol{a}_\alpha'$ as $\boldsymbol{\xi}_\alpha^{(k)}$, the inner product $\langle \boldsymbol{\xi}_\alpha^{(k)}, \boldsymbol{q} \rangle$ is not necessarily 0. However, Eq. (5.24) holds for the true values $\bar{\boldsymbol{a}}_\alpha$ and $\bar{\boldsymbol{a}}_\alpha'$, so if we write $\boldsymbol{\xi}_\alpha^{(k)} = \bar{\boldsymbol{\xi}}_\alpha^{(k)} + \Delta\boldsymbol{\xi}_\alpha^{(k)}$, we see that $\langle \boldsymbol{\xi}_\alpha^{(k)}, \boldsymbol{q} \rangle = \langle \Delta\boldsymbol{\xi}_\alpha^{(k)}, \boldsymbol{q} \rangle$. Let

$$\boldsymbol{\varepsilon}_\alpha = \begin{pmatrix} \langle \boldsymbol{\xi}_\alpha^{(1)}, \boldsymbol{q} \rangle \\ \langle \boldsymbol{\xi}_\alpha^{(2)}, \boldsymbol{q} \rangle \\ \langle \boldsymbol{\xi}_\alpha^{(3)}, \boldsymbol{q} \rangle \end{pmatrix} = \begin{pmatrix} \langle \Delta\boldsymbol{\xi}_\alpha^{(1)}, \boldsymbol{q} \rangle \\ \langle \Delta\boldsymbol{\xi}_\alpha^{(2)}, \boldsymbol{q} \rangle \\ \langle \Delta\boldsymbol{\xi}_\alpha^{(3)}, \boldsymbol{q} \rangle \end{pmatrix}. \tag{5.25}$$

Evidently, $E[\boldsymbol{\varepsilon}_\alpha] = \boldsymbol{0}$. The covariance matrix of $\boldsymbol{\varepsilon}_\alpha$ is

$$\begin{aligned} V[\boldsymbol{\varepsilon}_\alpha] &= E[\boldsymbol{\varepsilon}_\alpha \boldsymbol{\varepsilon}_\alpha^\top] \\ &= \begin{pmatrix} E[\langle \boldsymbol{q}, \Delta\boldsymbol{\xi}_\alpha^{(1)} \rangle \langle \Delta\boldsymbol{\xi}_\alpha^{(1)}, \boldsymbol{q} \rangle] & E[\langle \boldsymbol{q}, \Delta\boldsymbol{\xi}_\alpha^{(1)} \rangle \langle \Delta\boldsymbol{\xi}_\alpha^{(2)}, \boldsymbol{q} \rangle] & E[\langle \boldsymbol{q}, \Delta\boldsymbol{\xi}_\alpha^{(1)} \rangle \langle \Delta\boldsymbol{\xi}_\alpha^{(3)}, \boldsymbol{q} \rangle] \\ E[\langle \boldsymbol{q}, \Delta\boldsymbol{\xi}_\alpha^{(2)} \rangle \langle \Delta\boldsymbol{\xi}_\alpha^{(1)}, \boldsymbol{q} \rangle] & E[\langle \boldsymbol{q}, \Delta\boldsymbol{\xi}_\alpha^{(2)} \rangle \langle \Delta\boldsymbol{\xi}_\alpha^{(2)}, \boldsymbol{q} \rangle] & E[\langle \boldsymbol{q}, \Delta\boldsymbol{\xi}_\alpha^{(2)} \rangle \langle \Delta\boldsymbol{\xi}_\alpha^{(3)}, \boldsymbol{q} \rangle] \\ E[\langle \boldsymbol{q}, \Delta\boldsymbol{\xi}_\alpha^{(3)} \rangle \langle \Delta\boldsymbol{\xi}_\alpha^{(1)}, \boldsymbol{q} \rangle] & E[\langle \boldsymbol{q}, \Delta\boldsymbol{\xi}_\alpha^{(3)} \rangle \langle \Delta\boldsymbol{\xi}_\alpha^{(2)}, \boldsymbol{q} \rangle] & E[\langle \boldsymbol{q}, \Delta\boldsymbol{\xi}_\alpha^{(3)} \rangle \langle \Delta\boldsymbol{\xi}_\alpha^{(3)}, \boldsymbol{q} \rangle] \end{pmatrix} \\ &= \begin{pmatrix} \boldsymbol{q}^\top E[\Delta\boldsymbol{\xi}_\alpha^{(1)} \Delta\boldsymbol{\xi}_\alpha^{(1)\top}] \boldsymbol{q} & \boldsymbol{q}^\top E[\Delta\boldsymbol{\xi}_\alpha^{(1)} \Delta\boldsymbol{\xi}_\alpha^{(2)\top}] \boldsymbol{q} & \boldsymbol{q}^\top E[\Delta\boldsymbol{\xi}_\alpha^{(1)} \Delta\boldsymbol{\xi}_\alpha^{(3)\top}] \boldsymbol{q} \\ \boldsymbol{q}^\top E[\Delta\boldsymbol{\xi}_\alpha^{(2)} \Delta\boldsymbol{\xi}_\alpha^{(1)\top}] \boldsymbol{q} & \boldsymbol{q}^\top E[\Delta\boldsymbol{\xi}_\alpha^{(2)} \Delta\boldsymbol{\xi}_\alpha^{(2)\top}] \boldsymbol{q} & \boldsymbol{q}^\top E[\Delta\boldsymbol{\xi}_\alpha^{(2)} \Delta\boldsymbol{\xi}_\alpha^{(3)\top}] \boldsymbol{q} \\ \boldsymbol{q}^\top E[\Delta\boldsymbol{\xi}_\alpha^{(3)} \Delta\boldsymbol{\xi}_\alpha^{(1)\top}] \boldsymbol{q} & \boldsymbol{q}^\top E[\Delta\boldsymbol{\xi}_\alpha^{(3)} \Delta\boldsymbol{\xi}_\alpha^{(2)\top}] \boldsymbol{q} & \boldsymbol{q}^\top E[\Delta\boldsymbol{\xi}_\alpha^{(3)} \Delta\boldsymbol{\xi}_\alpha^{(3)\top}] \boldsymbol{q} \end{pmatrix}. \end{aligned} \tag{5.26}$$

From Eq. (5.22), the noise terms $\Delta\boldsymbol{\xi}_\alpha^{(k)}$ of $\boldsymbol{\xi}_\alpha^{(k)}$ are written in the form

$$\Delta\boldsymbol{\xi}_\alpha^{(1)} = \begin{pmatrix} \Delta a'_{\alpha(1)} - \Delta a_{\alpha(1)} \\ 0 \\ -(\Delta a'_{\alpha(3)} + \Delta a_{\alpha(3)}) \\ \Delta a'_{\alpha(2)} + \Delta a_{\alpha(2)} \end{pmatrix}, \qquad \Delta\boldsymbol{\xi}_\alpha^{(2)} = \begin{pmatrix} \Delta a'_{\alpha(2)} - \Delta a_{\alpha(2)} \\ \Delta a'_{\alpha(3)} + \Delta a_{\alpha(3)} \\ 0 \\ -(\Delta a'_{\alpha(1)} + \Delta a_{\alpha(1)}) \end{pmatrix},$$
$$\Delta\boldsymbol{\xi}_\alpha^{(3)} = \begin{pmatrix} \Delta a'_{\alpha(3)} - \Delta a_{\alpha(3)} \\ -(\Delta a'_{\alpha(2)} + \Delta a_{\alpha(2)}) \\ \Delta a'_{\alpha(1)} + \Delta a_{\alpha(1)} \\ 0 \end{pmatrix}, \tag{5.27}$$

where $\Delta a_{\alpha(i)}$ and $\Delta a'_{\alpha(i)}$ are the ith elements of $\Delta\boldsymbol{a}_\alpha$ and $\Delta\boldsymbol{a}'_\alpha$, respectively. Define 4×6 matrices $\boldsymbol{T}^{(1)}$, $\boldsymbol{T}^{(2)}$, and $\boldsymbol{T}^{(3)}$ by

$$\boldsymbol{T}^{(1)} = \begin{pmatrix} -1 & 0 & 0 & 1 & 0 & 0 \\ 0 & 0 & 0 & 0 & 0 & 0 \\ 0 & 0 & -1 & 0 & 0 & -1 \\ 0 & 1 & 0 & 0 & 1 & 0 \end{pmatrix}, \qquad \boldsymbol{T}^{(2)} = \begin{pmatrix} 0 & -1 & 0 & 0 & 1 & 0 \\ 0 & 0 & 1 & 0 & 0 & 1 \\ 0 & 0 & 0 & 0 & 0 & 0 \\ -1 & 0 & 0 & -1 & 0 & 0 \end{pmatrix},$$
$$\boldsymbol{T}^{(3)} = \begin{pmatrix} 0 & 0 & -1 & 0 & 0 & 1 \\ 0 & -1 & 0 & 0 & -1 & 1 \\ 1 & 0 & 0 & 1 & 0 & 0 \\ 0 & 0 & 0 & 0 & 0 & 0 \end{pmatrix}. \tag{5.28}$$

Then, Eq. (5.27) is written as

$$\Delta\boldsymbol{\xi}_\alpha^{(k)} = \boldsymbol{T}^{(k)} \begin{pmatrix} \Delta\boldsymbol{a}_\alpha \\ \Delta\boldsymbol{a}'_\alpha \end{pmatrix}. \tag{5.29}$$

The covariance matrix $V^{(kl)}[\boldsymbol{\xi}_\alpha]$ of $\Delta\boldsymbol{\xi}_\alpha^{(k)}$ and $\Delta\boldsymbol{\xi}_\alpha^{(l)}$ is given by

$$\begin{aligned} V^{(kl)}[\boldsymbol{\xi}_\alpha] &= E[\Delta\boldsymbol{\xi}_\alpha^{(k)}\Delta\boldsymbol{\xi}_\alpha^{(l)\top}] = \boldsymbol{T}^{(k)} \begin{pmatrix} E[\Delta\boldsymbol{a}_\alpha\Delta\boldsymbol{a}_\alpha^\top] & E[\Delta\boldsymbol{a}_\alpha\Delta\boldsymbol{a}'^\top_\alpha] \\ E[\Delta\boldsymbol{a}'_\alpha\Delta\boldsymbol{a}_\alpha^\top] & E[\Delta\boldsymbol{a}'_\alpha\Delta\boldsymbol{a}'^\top_\alpha] \end{pmatrix} \boldsymbol{T}^{(l)\top} \\ &= \sigma^2\boldsymbol{T}^{(k)} \begin{pmatrix} V_0[\boldsymbol{a}_\alpha] & \boldsymbol{O} \\ \boldsymbol{O} & V_0[\boldsymbol{a}'_\alpha] \end{pmatrix} \boldsymbol{T}^{(l)\top}. \end{aligned} \tag{5.30}$$

In the following, we denote this as follows:

$$V^{(kl)}[\boldsymbol{\xi}_\alpha] = \sigma^2 V_0^{(kl)}[\boldsymbol{\xi}_\alpha], \qquad V_0^{(kl)}[\boldsymbol{\xi}_\alpha] \equiv \boldsymbol{T}^{(k)} \begin{pmatrix} V_0[\boldsymbol{a}_\alpha] & \boldsymbol{O} \\ \boldsymbol{O} & V_0[\boldsymbol{a}'_\alpha] \end{pmatrix} \boldsymbol{T}^{(l)\top}. \tag{5.31}$$

Using this, we can write the covariance matrix $V[\boldsymbol{\varepsilon}_\alpha]$ of Eq. (5.26) in the form

$$V[\boldsymbol{\varepsilon}_\alpha] = \sigma^2\boldsymbol{V}_\alpha, \qquad \boldsymbol{V}_\alpha \equiv \begin{pmatrix} \langle\boldsymbol{q}, V_0^{(11)}[\boldsymbol{\xi}_\alpha]\boldsymbol{q}\rangle & \langle\boldsymbol{q}, V_0^{(12)}[\boldsymbol{\xi}_\alpha]\boldsymbol{q}\rangle & \langle\boldsymbol{q}, V_0^{(13)}[\boldsymbol{\xi}_\alpha]\boldsymbol{q}\rangle \\ \langle\boldsymbol{q}, V_0^{(21)}[\boldsymbol{\xi}_\alpha]\boldsymbol{q}\rangle & \langle\boldsymbol{q}, V_0^{(22)}[\boldsymbol{\xi}_\alpha]\boldsymbol{q}\rangle & \langle\boldsymbol{q}, V_0^{(23)}[\boldsymbol{\xi}_\alpha]\boldsymbol{q}\rangle \\ \langle\boldsymbol{q}, V_0^{(31)}[\boldsymbol{\xi}_\alpha]\boldsymbol{q}\rangle & \langle\boldsymbol{q}, V_0^{(32)}[\boldsymbol{\xi}_\alpha]\boldsymbol{q}\rangle & \langle\boldsymbol{q}, V_0^{(33)}[\boldsymbol{\xi}_\alpha]\boldsymbol{q}\rangle \end{pmatrix}. \tag{5.32}$$

Hence, the Mahalanobis distance of $\boldsymbol{\varepsilon}_\alpha$, $\alpha = 1, ..., N$, is

$$J = \frac{\sigma^2}{2}\sum_{\alpha=1}^{N}\langle\boldsymbol{\varepsilon}_\alpha, V[\boldsymbol{\varepsilon}_\alpha]^{-1}\boldsymbol{\varepsilon}_\alpha\rangle = \frac{1}{2}\sum_{\alpha=1}^{N}\langle\boldsymbol{\varepsilon}_\alpha, \boldsymbol{W}_\alpha\boldsymbol{\varepsilon}_\alpha\rangle, \tag{5.33}$$

where we define the matrix $\boldsymbol{W}_\alpha$ by

$$\boldsymbol{W}_\alpha = \boldsymbol{V}_\alpha^{-1}. \tag{5.34}$$

As pointed out in the preceding section, we need not know the noise level σ. Let $W_\alpha^{(kl)}$ be the (kl) element of the matrix $\boldsymbol{W}_\alpha$. Substituting Eq. (5.25), we can write the residual J of Eq. (5.33) in the form

$$J = \frac{1}{2}\sum_{\alpha=1}^{N}\sum_{k,l=1}^{3} W_\alpha^{(kl)}\langle \boldsymbol{\xi}_\alpha^{(k)}, \boldsymbol{q}\rangle\langle \boldsymbol{\xi}_\alpha^{(l)}, \boldsymbol{q}\rangle. \tag{5.35}$$

5.4 OPTIMIZATION BY FNS

In order to minimize Eq. (5.35), we differentiate it with respect to $\boldsymbol{q}$. First, we note that the following identity holds ($\hookrightarrow$ Exercise 5.3):

$$\nabla_{\boldsymbol{q}} W_\alpha^{(kl)} = -2\sum_{m,n=1}^{3} W_\alpha^{(km)} W_\alpha^{(ln)} V_0^{(mn)}[\boldsymbol{\xi}_\alpha]\boldsymbol{q}. \tag{5.36}$$

Using this, we can write the derivative of Eq. (5.35) in the form

$$\begin{aligned}
\nabla_{\boldsymbol{q}} J &= \sum_{\alpha=1}^{N}\sum_{k,l=1}^{3} W_\alpha^{(kl)}\langle \boldsymbol{\xi}_\alpha^{(l)}, \boldsymbol{q}\rangle \boldsymbol{\xi}_\alpha^{(k)} + \frac{1}{2}\sum_{\alpha=1}^{N}\sum_{k,l=1}^{3} \nabla_{\boldsymbol{q}} W_\alpha^{(kl)}\langle \boldsymbol{\xi}_\alpha^{(k)}, \boldsymbol{q}\rangle\langle \boldsymbol{\xi}_\alpha^{(l)}, \boldsymbol{q}\rangle \\
&= \sum_{\alpha=1}^{N}\sum_{k,l=1}^{3} W_\alpha^{(kl)} \boldsymbol{\xi}_\alpha^{(k)}\boldsymbol{\xi}_\alpha^{(l)\top}\boldsymbol{q} - \sum_{\alpha=1}^{N}\sum_{k,l,m,n=1}^{3} W_\alpha^{(km)} W_\alpha^{(ln)} V_0^{(mn)}[\boldsymbol{\xi}_\alpha]\langle \boldsymbol{\xi}_\alpha^{(k)}, \boldsymbol{q}\rangle\langle \boldsymbol{\xi}_\alpha^{(l)}, \boldsymbol{q}\rangle\boldsymbol{q} \\
&= \sum_{\alpha=1}^{N}\sum_{k,l=1}^{3} W_\alpha^{(kl)} \boldsymbol{\xi}_\alpha^{(k)}\boldsymbol{\xi}_\alpha^{(l)\top}\boldsymbol{q} - \sum_{\alpha=1}^{N}\sum_{,m,n=1}^{3} v_\alpha^{(m)} v_\alpha^{(n)} V_0^{(mn)}[\boldsymbol{\xi}_\alpha]\boldsymbol{q},
\end{aligned} \tag{5.37}$$

where $v_\alpha^{(k)}$ is defined by

$$v_\alpha^{(k)} = \sum_{l=1}^{3} W_\alpha^{(kl)}\langle \boldsymbol{\xi}_\alpha^{(l)}, \boldsymbol{q}\rangle. \tag{5.38}$$

If we define 4×4 matrices $\boldsymbol{M}$ and $\boldsymbol{L}$ by

$$\boldsymbol{M} = \sum_{\alpha=1}^{N}\sum_{k,l=1}^{3} W_\alpha^{(kl)}\boldsymbol{\xi}_\alpha^{(k)}\boldsymbol{\xi}_\alpha^{(l)\top}, \qquad \boldsymbol{L} = \sum_{\alpha=1}^{N}\sum_{k,l=1}^{3} v_\alpha^{(kl)} v_\alpha^{(l)} V_0^{(kl)}[\boldsymbol{\xi}_\alpha], \tag{5.39}$$

Eq. (5.37) is written as

$$\nabla_{\boldsymbol{q}} J = (\boldsymbol{M} - \boldsymbol{L})\boldsymbol{q}. \tag{5.40}$$

The solution $\boldsymbol{q}$ that makes this $\boldsymbol{0}$ is obtained by the following iterations called the *FNS* (*Fundamental Numerical Scheme*).

1. Let $\boldsymbol{q} = \boldsymbol{q}_0 = \boldsymbol{0}$ and $W_\alpha^{(kl)} = \delta_{kl}$ (Kronecker delta), $\alpha = 1, ..., N$, $k, l = 1, 2, 3$.

2. Compute the matrices $\boldsymbol{M}$ and $\boldsymbol{L}$ of Eq. (5.39), and let $\boldsymbol{X}$ be the 4×4 symmetric matrix

$$\boldsymbol{X} = \boldsymbol{M} - \boldsymbol{L}. \tag{5.41}$$

3. Solve the eigenvalue problem

$$Xq = \lambda q, \tag{5.42}$$

and obtain the unit eigenvector q for the smallest eigenvalue λ.

4. Stop if $q \approx q_0$ up to sign. Else, update

$$W_\alpha^{(kl)} \leftarrow \left(\langle q, V_0^{(kl)}[\xi_\alpha]q\rangle\right)^{-1}, \qquad q_0 \leftarrow q, \tag{5.43}$$

and go back to Step 2.

Here, the right side of the first equation of Eq. (5.43) designates the (kl) element of the inverse of the 3×3 matrix whose (kl) element is $\langle q, V_0^{(kl)}[\xi_\alpha]q\rangle$. The phrase "up to sign" in Step 4 is due to the fact that the sign of an eigenvector is indeterminate. Hence, we choose the sign of q so that $\langle q, q_0\rangle \geq 0$ holds and then compare q and q_0.

It can be shown that λ is necessarily 0 at the time of the convergence of the above iterations (↪ Exercise 5.4). Hence, we obtain the value of q that satisfies $\nabla_q J = \mathbf{0}$.

5.5 METHOD OF HOMOGENEOUS CONSTRAINTS

In this section, we formulate a method that treats the nine elements R_{ij}, $i, j = 1, 2, 3$, of the rotation matrix R as unknown variables. Namely, we regard the nine elements

$$\theta_1 = R_{11}, \qquad \theta_2 = R_{12}, \qquad ..., \qquad \theta_9 = R_{33} \tag{5.44}$$

of R as independent variables. The constraint $a' = Ra$ is written as

$$\begin{aligned} \theta_0 a_1' &= \theta_1 a_1 + \theta_2 a_2 + \theta_3 a_3, \\ \theta_0 a_2' &= \theta_4 a_1 + \theta_5 a_2 + \theta_6 a_3, \\ \theta_0 a_3' &= \theta_7 a_1 + \theta_8 a_2 + \theta_9 a_3, \end{aligned} \tag{5.45}$$

where we let $\theta_0 = 1$. Define 10D vectors $\xi^{(1)}$, $\xi^{(2)}$, and $\xi^{(3)}$ by

$$\begin{aligned} \xi^{(1)} &= (a_1, a_2, a_3, 0, 0, 0, 0, 0, 0, -a_1')^\top, \\ \xi^{(2)} &= (0, 0, 0, a_1, a_2, a_3, 0, 0, 0, -a_2')^\top, \\ \xi^{(3)} &= (0, 0, 0, 0, 0, 0, a_1, a_2, a_3, -a_3')^\top. \end{aligned} \tag{5.46}$$

Then, Eq. (5.45) is rewritten in the form

$$\langle \xi^{(1)}, \theta\rangle = 0, \qquad \langle \xi^{(2)}, \theta\rangle = 0, \qquad \langle \xi^{(3)}, \theta\rangle = 0, \tag{5.47}$$

where we define the 10D vector θ by

$$\theta = (\theta_1, \theta_2, \theta_3, \theta_4, \theta_5, \theta_6, \theta_7, \theta_8, \theta_9, \theta_0)^\top. \tag{5.48}$$

If we let $\xi_\alpha^{(1)}$, $\xi_\alpha^{(2)}$, and $\xi_\alpha^{(3)}$ be the values of the vector of Eq. (5.46) for noisy observations a_α and a_α', our task is to compute the θ that satisfies

$$\langle \xi_\alpha^{(k)}, \theta\rangle \approx 0, \qquad k = 1, 2, 3, \qquad \alpha = 1, ..., N, \tag{5.49}$$

subject to the condition that θ_1, ..., θ_9 constitute the elements of a rotation matrix $\boldsymbol{R}$. As pointed out in Sec. 2.3, the columns of $\boldsymbol{R}$ are unit vectors that are mutually orthogonal (as a result, the rows are also mutually orthogonal unit vectors). If we define

$$\begin{aligned} \phi_1(\boldsymbol{\theta}) &= \theta_1\theta_2 + \theta_4\theta_5 + \theta_7\theta_8, & \phi_4(\boldsymbol{\theta}) &= \theta_1^2 + \theta_4^2 + \theta_7^2 - \theta_0^2, \\ \phi_2(\boldsymbol{\theta}) &= \theta_2\theta_3 + \theta_5\theta_6 + \theta_8\theta_9, & \phi_5(\boldsymbol{\theta}) &= \theta_2^2 + \theta_5^2 + \theta_8^2 - \theta_0^2, \\ \phi_3(\boldsymbol{\theta}) &= \theta_3\theta_1 + \theta_6\theta_4 + \theta_9\theta_7, & \phi_6(\boldsymbol{\theta}) &= \theta_3^2 + \theta_6^2 + \theta_9^2 - \theta_0^2, \end{aligned} \tag{5.50}$$

the orthogonality condition is written as

$$\phi_i(\boldsymbol{\theta}) = 0, \qquad i = 1, ..., 6. \tag{5.51}$$

This is merely the condition that $\boldsymbol{R}$ is an orthogonal matrix; for it to be a rotation matrix, we further need the condition that its determinant be positive. However, an iterative scheme is a repetition of small changes, so as long as the initial determinant is positive, we need not consider its sign in the process of iterations.

The important thing here is that although we let $\theta_0 = 1$, *we need not consider this constraint*. This is because Eqs. (5.47) and (5.51) are *homogeneous polynomial equations*. Hence, if we multiply $\boldsymbol{\theta}$ by a constant, Eqs. (5.47) and (5.51) are not affected. It follows that if we solve the problem by regarding $\boldsymbol{\theta}$ as an unknown, only the ratio of θ_i, $i = 0, 1, ..., 9$, is determined. Hence, we only need to multiply the solution $\boldsymbol{\theta}$ by a constant so that $\theta_0 = 1$ in the end; in the course of the computation, we can arbitrarily normalize the $\boldsymbol{\theta}$. Here, we adopt the normalization

$$\|\boldsymbol{\theta}\| = 1 \tag{5.52}$$

for the sake of computational convenience.

Let $\bar{\boldsymbol{\xi}}_\alpha^{(k)}$ be the true value of the $\boldsymbol{\xi}_\alpha^{(k)}$ in Eq. (5.49) and write $\boldsymbol{\xi}_\alpha^{(k)} = \bar{\boldsymbol{\xi}}_\alpha^{(k)} + \Delta\boldsymbol{\xi}_\alpha^{(k)}$. Then, $\langle\bar{\boldsymbol{\xi}}_\alpha^{(k)}, \boldsymbol{\theta}\rangle = 0$. Let us vertically stack the left side expressions of Eq. (5.49) to define the vector

$$\boldsymbol{\varepsilon}_\alpha = \begin{pmatrix} \langle\boldsymbol{\xi}_\alpha^{(1)}, \boldsymbol{\theta}\rangle \\ \langle\boldsymbol{\xi}_\alpha^{(2)}, \boldsymbol{\theta}\rangle \\ \langle\boldsymbol{\xi}_\alpha^{(3)}, \boldsymbol{\theta}\rangle \end{pmatrix} = \begin{pmatrix} \langle\Delta\boldsymbol{\xi}_\alpha^{(1)}, \boldsymbol{\theta}\rangle \\ \langle\Delta\boldsymbol{\xi}_\alpha^{(2)}, \boldsymbol{\theta}\rangle \\ \langle\Delta\boldsymbol{\xi}_\alpha^{(3)}, \boldsymbol{\theta}\rangle \end{pmatrix}. \tag{5.53}$$

From Eq. (5.46), we see that the noise terms $\Delta\boldsymbol{\xi}_\alpha^{(k)}$ of $\boldsymbol{\xi}_\alpha^{(k)}$ are

$$\Delta\boldsymbol{\xi}_\alpha^{(1)} = \begin{pmatrix} \Delta a_{\alpha(1)} \\ \Delta a_{\alpha(2)} \\ \Delta a_{\alpha(3)} \\ 0 \\ 0 \\ 0 \\ 0 \\ 0 \\ 0 \\ -\Delta a_{\alpha(1)} \end{pmatrix}, \quad \Delta\boldsymbol{\xi}_\alpha^{(2)} = \begin{pmatrix} 0 \\ 0 \\ 0 \\ \Delta a_{\alpha(1)} \\ \Delta a_{\alpha(2)} \\ \Delta a_{\alpha(3)} \\ 0 \\ 0 \\ 0 \\ -\Delta a'_{\alpha(2)} \end{pmatrix}, \quad \Delta\boldsymbol{\xi}_\alpha^{(3)} = \begin{pmatrix} 0 \\ 0 \\ 0 \\ 0 \\ 0 \\ 0 \\ \Delta a_{\alpha(1)} \\ \Delta a_{\alpha(2)} \\ \Delta a_{\alpha(3)} \\ -\Delta a'_{\alpha(3)} \end{pmatrix}, \tag{5.54}$$

where $\Delta a_{\alpha(i)}$ and $\Delta a'_{\alpha(i)}$ are the i components of $\Delta\boldsymbol{a}_\alpha$ and $\Delta\boldsymbol{a}'_\alpha$, respectively. Define 10×6 matrices $\boldsymbol{T}^{(1)}$, $\boldsymbol{T}^{(2)}$, and $\boldsymbol{T}^{(3)}$ by

$$\boldsymbol{T}^{(1)} = \begin{pmatrix} 1 & 0 & 0 & 0 & 0 & 0 \\ 0 & 1 & 0 & 0 & 0 & 0 \\ 0 & 0 & 1 & 0 & 0 & 0 \\ 0 & 0 & 0 & 0 & 0 & 0 \\ 0 & 0 & 0 & 0 & 0 & 0 \\ 0 & 0 & 0 & 0 & 0 & 0 \\ 0 & 0 & 0 & 0 & 0 & 0 \\ 0 & 0 & 0 & 0 & 0 & 0 \\ 0 & 0 & 0 & 0 & 0 & 0 \\ 0 & 0 & 0 & -1 & 0 & 0 \end{pmatrix}, \qquad \boldsymbol{T}^{(2)} = \begin{pmatrix} 0 & 0 & 0 & 0 & 0 & 0 \\ 0 & 0 & 0 & 0 & 0 & 0 \\ 0 & 0 & 0 & 0 & 0 & 0 \\ 1 & 0 & 0 & 0 & 0 & 0 \\ 0 & 1 & 0 & 0 & 0 & 0 \\ 0 & 0 & 1 & 0 & 0 & 0 \\ 0 & 0 & 0 & 0 & 0 & 0 \\ 0 & 0 & 0 & 0 & 0 & 0 \\ 0 & 0 & 0 & 0 & 0 & 0 \\ 0 & 0 & 0 & 0 & -1 & 0 \end{pmatrix},$$

$$\boldsymbol{T}^{(3)} = \begin{pmatrix} 0 & 0 & 0 & 0 & 0 & 0 \\ 0 & 0 & 0 & 0 & 0 & 0 \\ 0 & 0 & 0 & 0 & 0 & 0 \\ 0 & 0 & 0 & 0 & 0 & 0 \\ 0 & 0 & 0 & 0 & 0 & 0 \\ 0 & 0 & 0 & 0 & 0 & 0 \\ 1 & 0 & 0 & 0 & 0 & 0 \\ 0 & 1 & 0 & 0 & 0 & 0 \\ 0 & 0 & 1 & 0 & 0 & 0 \\ 0 & 0 & 0 & 0 & 0 & -1 \end{pmatrix}. \tag{5.55}$$

Then, Eq. (5.54) is written in the form

$$\Delta\boldsymbol{\xi}_\alpha^{(k)} = \boldsymbol{T}^{(k)} \begin{pmatrix} \Delta\boldsymbol{a}_\alpha \\ \Delta\boldsymbol{a}'_\alpha \end{pmatrix}. \tag{5.56}$$

Let $V^{(kl)}[\boldsymbol{\xi}_\alpha]$ be the covariance matrix of $\Delta\boldsymbol{\xi}_\alpha^{(k)}$ and $\Delta\boldsymbol{\xi}_\alpha^{(l)}$. We see that

$$\begin{aligned} V^{(kl)}[\boldsymbol{\xi}_\alpha] &= E[\Delta\boldsymbol{\xi}_\alpha^{(k)}\Delta\boldsymbol{\xi}_\alpha^{(l)\top}] = \boldsymbol{T}^{(k)} \begin{pmatrix} E[\Delta\boldsymbol{a}_\alpha\Delta\boldsymbol{a}_\alpha^\top] & E[\Delta\boldsymbol{a}_\alpha\Delta\boldsymbol{a}'^\top_\alpha] \\ E[\Delta\boldsymbol{a}'_\alpha\Delta\boldsymbol{a}_\alpha^\top] & E[\Delta\boldsymbol{a}'_\alpha\Delta\boldsymbol{a}'^\top_\alpha] \end{pmatrix} \boldsymbol{T}^{(l)\top} \\ &= \sigma^2\boldsymbol{T}^{(k)} \begin{pmatrix} V_0[\boldsymbol{a}_\alpha] & \boldsymbol{O} \\ \boldsymbol{O} & V_0[\boldsymbol{a}'_\alpha] \end{pmatrix} \boldsymbol{T}^{(l)\top}. \end{aligned} \tag{5.57}$$

Hereafter, we write this as

$$V^{(kl)}[\boldsymbol{\xi}_\alpha] = \sigma^2 V_0^{(kl)}[\boldsymbol{\xi}_\alpha], \qquad V_0^{(kl)}[\boldsymbol{\xi}_\alpha] \equiv \boldsymbol{T}^{(k)} \begin{pmatrix} V_0[\boldsymbol{a}_\alpha] & \boldsymbol{O} \\ \boldsymbol{O} & V_0[\boldsymbol{a}'_\alpha] \end{pmatrix} \boldsymbol{T}^{(l)\top}. \tag{5.58}$$

Then, the covariance matrix $V[\boldsymbol{\varepsilon}_\alpha]$ of $\boldsymbol{\varepsilon}_\alpha$ of Eq. (5.53) is

$$\begin{aligned} V[\boldsymbol{\varepsilon}_\alpha] &= E[\boldsymbol{\varepsilon}_\alpha\boldsymbol{\varepsilon}_\alpha^\top] \\ &= \begin{pmatrix} E[\langle\boldsymbol{\theta},\Delta\boldsymbol{\xi}_\alpha^{(1)}\rangle\langle\Delta\boldsymbol{\xi}_\alpha^{(1)},\boldsymbol{\theta}\rangle] & E[\langle\boldsymbol{\theta},\Delta\boldsymbol{\xi}_\alpha^{(1)}\rangle\langle\Delta\boldsymbol{\xi}_\alpha^{(2)},\boldsymbol{\theta}\rangle] & E[\langle\boldsymbol{\theta},\Delta\boldsymbol{\xi}_\alpha^{(1)}\rangle\langle\Delta\boldsymbol{\xi}_\alpha^{(3)},\boldsymbol{\theta}\rangle] \\ E[\langle\boldsymbol{\theta},\Delta\boldsymbol{\xi}_\alpha^{(2)}\rangle\langle\Delta\boldsymbol{\xi}_\alpha^{(1)},\boldsymbol{\theta}\rangle] & E[\langle\boldsymbol{\theta},\Delta\boldsymbol{\xi}_\alpha^{(2)}\rangle\langle\Delta\boldsymbol{\xi}_\alpha^{(2)},\boldsymbol{\theta}\rangle] & E[\langle\boldsymbol{\theta},\Delta\boldsymbol{\xi}_\alpha^{(2)}\rangle\langle\Delta\boldsymbol{\xi}_\alpha^{(3)},\boldsymbol{\theta}\rangle] \\ E[\langle\boldsymbol{\theta},\Delta\boldsymbol{\xi}_\alpha^{(3)}\rangle\langle\Delta\boldsymbol{\xi}_\alpha^{(1)},\boldsymbol{\theta}\rangle] & E[\langle\boldsymbol{\theta},\Delta\boldsymbol{\xi}_\alpha^{(3)}\rangle\langle\Delta\boldsymbol{\xi}_\alpha^{(2)},\boldsymbol{\theta}\rangle] & E[\langle\boldsymbol{\theta},\Delta\boldsymbol{\xi}_\alpha^{(3)}\rangle\langle\Delta\boldsymbol{\xi}_\alpha^{(3)},\boldsymbol{\theta}\rangle] \end{pmatrix} \\ &= \begin{pmatrix} \boldsymbol{\theta}^\top E[\Delta\boldsymbol{\xi}_\alpha^{(1)}\Delta\boldsymbol{\xi}_\alpha^{(1)\top}]\boldsymbol{\theta} & \boldsymbol{\theta}^\top E[\Delta\boldsymbol{\xi}_\alpha^{(1)}\Delta\boldsymbol{\xi}_\alpha^{(2)\top}]\boldsymbol{\theta} & \boldsymbol{\theta}^\top E[\Delta\boldsymbol{\xi}_\alpha^{(1)}\Delta\boldsymbol{\xi}_\alpha^{(3)\top}]\boldsymbol{\theta} \\ \boldsymbol{\theta}^\top E[\Delta\boldsymbol{\xi}_\alpha^{(2)}\Delta\boldsymbol{\xi}_\alpha^{(1)\top}]\boldsymbol{\theta} & \boldsymbol{\theta}^\top E[\Delta\boldsymbol{\xi}_\alpha^{(2)}\Delta\boldsymbol{\xi}_\alpha^{(2)\top}]\boldsymbol{\theta} & \boldsymbol{\theta}^\top E[\Delta\boldsymbol{\xi}_\alpha^{(2)}\Delta\boldsymbol{\xi}_\alpha^{(3)\top}]\boldsymbol{\theta} \\ \boldsymbol{\theta}^\top E[\Delta\boldsymbol{\xi}_\alpha^{(3)}\Delta\boldsymbol{\xi}_\alpha^{(1)\top}]\boldsymbol{\theta} & \boldsymbol{\theta}^\top E[\Delta\boldsymbol{\xi}_\alpha^{(3)}\Delta\boldsymbol{\xi}_\alpha^{(2)\top}]\boldsymbol{\theta} & \boldsymbol{\theta}^\top E[\Delta\boldsymbol{\xi}_\alpha^{(3)}\Delta\boldsymbol{\xi}_\alpha^{(3)\top}]\boldsymbol{\theta} \end{pmatrix} \\ &= \sigma^2\boldsymbol{V}_\alpha, \end{aligned} \tag{5.59}$$

where we define

$$\boldsymbol{V}_\alpha \equiv \begin{pmatrix} \langle \boldsymbol{\theta}, V_0^{(11)}[\boldsymbol{\xi}_\alpha]\boldsymbol{\theta}\rangle & \langle \boldsymbol{\theta}, V_0^{(12)}[\boldsymbol{\xi}_\alpha]\boldsymbol{\theta}\rangle & \langle \boldsymbol{\theta}, V_0^{(13)}[\boldsymbol{\xi}_\alpha]\boldsymbol{\theta}\rangle \\ \langle \boldsymbol{\theta}, V_0^{(21)}[\boldsymbol{\xi}_\alpha]\boldsymbol{\theta}\rangle & \langle \boldsymbol{\theta}, V_0^{(22)}[\boldsymbol{\xi}_\alpha]\boldsymbol{\theta}\rangle & \langle \boldsymbol{\theta}, V_0^{(23)}[\boldsymbol{\xi}_\alpha]\boldsymbol{\theta}\rangle \\ \langle \boldsymbol{\theta}, V_0^{(31)}[\boldsymbol{\xi}_\alpha]\boldsymbol{\theta}\rangle & \langle \boldsymbol{\theta}, V_0^{(32)}[\boldsymbol{\xi}_\alpha]\boldsymbol{\theta}\rangle & \langle \boldsymbol{\theta}, V_0^{(33)}[\boldsymbol{\xi}_\alpha]\boldsymbol{\theta}\rangle \end{pmatrix}. \tag{5.60}$$

Hence, the Mahalanobis distance of $\boldsymbol{\varepsilon}_\alpha$, $\alpha = 1, ..., N$, is

$$J = \frac{\sigma^2}{2}\sum_{\alpha=1}^{N}\langle \boldsymbol{\varepsilon}_\alpha, V[\boldsymbol{\varepsilon}_\alpha]^{-1}\boldsymbol{\varepsilon}_\alpha\rangle = \frac{1}{2}\sum_{\alpha=1}^{N}\langle \boldsymbol{\varepsilon}_\alpha, \boldsymbol{W}_\alpha\boldsymbol{\varepsilon}_\alpha\rangle, \tag{5.61}$$

where we define the matrix $\boldsymbol{W}_\alpha$ by

$$\boldsymbol{W}_\alpha = \boldsymbol{V}_\alpha^{-1}. \tag{5.62}$$

Again, the noise level σ need not be known. Writing the (k, l) element of the matrix $\boldsymbol{W}_\alpha$ as $W_\alpha^{(kl)}$ and substituting Eq. (5.53) into Eq. (5.61), we can write the residual J in the form

$$J = \frac{1}{2}\sum_{\alpha=1}^{N}\sum_{k,l=1}^{3} W_\alpha^{(kl)}\langle \boldsymbol{\xi}_\alpha^{(k)}, \boldsymbol{\theta}\rangle\langle \boldsymbol{\xi}_\alpha^{(l)}, \boldsymbol{\theta}\rangle. \tag{5.63}$$

This has the same form as Eq. (5.35). Hence, it seems that we can compute the unit 10D vector $\boldsymbol{\theta}$ by the FNS scheme described in the preceding section. However, there is a big difference: the existence of the constraint of Eq. (5.51). Nevertheless, we can modify the FNS scheme so that Eq. (5.51) is satisfied at the time the iterations have converged. Here, we omit the details, but the key point is the fact that Eq. (5.51) is equivalently written as

$$\langle \nabla_{\boldsymbol{\theta}}\phi_i, \boldsymbol{\theta}\rangle = 0, \qquad i = 1, ..., 6. \tag{5.64}$$

This is shown as follows. Since $\phi_i(\boldsymbol{\theta})$, $i = 1, ..., 6$, are all homogeneous quadratic polynomials in $\boldsymbol{\theta}$, they satisfy $\phi_i(t\boldsymbol{\theta}) = t^2\phi_i(\boldsymbol{\theta})$ identically in $\boldsymbol{\theta}$ for an arbitrary real number t. Differentiation with respect to t yields $\langle \nabla_{\boldsymbol{\theta}}(t\boldsymbol{\theta}), \boldsymbol{\theta}\rangle = 2t\phi_i(\boldsymbol{\theta})$. Letting $t = 1$, we obtain

$$\langle \nabla_{\boldsymbol{\theta}}\phi_i, \boldsymbol{\theta}\rangle = 2\phi_i(\boldsymbol{\theta}). \tag{5.65}$$

Hence, Eqs. (5.51) and (5.64) are equivalent.

Note that $\nabla_{\boldsymbol{\theta}}\phi_i$ is the normal to the surface defined by $\phi_i(\boldsymbol{\theta}) = 0$ in the 10D space of $\boldsymbol{\theta}$. Equation (5.51) states that $\boldsymbol{\theta}$ is on 10 such surfaces defined by these equations. Due to Eq. (5.64), this is equivalent to saying that $\boldsymbol{\theta}$ is orthogonal to such 10 surfaces. Exploiting this fact, we project $\boldsymbol{\theta}$ at each step of the iterations onto the 4D subspace orthogonal to $\nabla_{\boldsymbol{\theta}}\phi_i$, $i = 1, ..., 6$. Modification of the FNS in this way is called the *EFNS* (*Extended Fundamental Numerical Scheme*). For this, too, we can prove that at the time of the convergence of the iterations we obtain the value of $\boldsymbol{\theta}$ that satisfies $\nabla_{\boldsymbol{\theta}}J = \boldsymbol{0}$ and at the same time Eq. (5.64) is met. We omit the details the procedure.

5.6 SUPPLEMENTAL NOTE

The problem we considered in this chapter can be generalized as follows. Suppose noise-free data $\bar{\boldsymbol{a}}_\alpha$, $\bar{\boldsymbol{a}}'_\alpha$, $\alpha = 1, ..., N$, satisfy equations of the form

$$F^{(k)}(\bar{\boldsymbol{a}}_\alpha, \bar{\boldsymbol{a}}'_\alpha, \boldsymbol{\theta}) = 0, \qquad k = 1, ..., L, \qquad \alpha = 1, ..., N, \tag{5.66}$$

where $\boldsymbol{\theta}$ is a parameter that specifies some relationship between $\bar{\boldsymbol{a}}_\alpha$ and $\bar{\boldsymbol{a}}'_\alpha$. For example, the relationship that they undergo a rigid rotation is described by equations such as Eqs. (5.7), (5.24), and (5.49), and the parameter $\boldsymbol{\theta}$ specifies that rotation (the rotation matrix $\boldsymbol{R}$, the quaternion q, or the vector $\boldsymbol{\theta}$ of Eq. (5.48)). However, we assume that we cannot directly observe $\bar{\boldsymbol{a}}_\alpha$ and $\bar{\boldsymbol{a}}'_\alpha$ but can only observe their noisy values $\boldsymbol{a}_\alpha$ and $\boldsymbol{a}'_\alpha$, $\alpha = 1, ..., N$. Our task is to estimate $\boldsymbol{\theta}$ from them.

To solve this problem, we introduce noise modeling and estimate the parameter $\boldsymbol{\theta}$ so that the true values $\bar{\boldsymbol{a}}_\alpha$ and $\bar{\boldsymbol{a}}'_\alpha$ are as close to the observations $\boldsymbol{a}_\alpha$ and $\boldsymbol{a}'_\alpha$ as possible subject to the constraint that $\bar{\boldsymbol{a}}_\alpha$ and $\bar{\boldsymbol{a}}'_\alpha$ satisfy Eq. (5.66). If the noise in $\boldsymbol{a}_\alpha$ and $\boldsymbol{a}'_\alpha$, $\alpha = 1, ..., N$, is Gaussian variables of mean $\boldsymbol{0}$ and covariance matrices of Eq. (5.8), the problem reduces to minimization of the Mahalanobis distance of Eq. (5.10) subject to Eq. (5.66). For computer vision problems involving image data, Eq. (5.10) is traditionally called the *reprojection error*.

The constraint of Eq. (5.66) is not restricted to rotation; it can describe various types of condition including rigid motion, affine transformation, and projective transformation. The computation of the *fundamental matrix* associated with camera imaging geometry (we will discuss this in Sec. 6.7) and the *homography matrix* also takes this form [29]. Maximum likelihood estimation of $\boldsymbol{\theta}$ reduces to minimization of the Mahalanobis distance, or the reprojection error, of Eq. (5.10) subject to the constraint of Eq. (5.66).

The main difference of this problem from the standard maximum likelihood estimation in statistics is that the unknown $\boldsymbol{\theta}$ is not included in the objective function of Eq. (5.10) to be minimized but instead included in the constraint of Eq. (5.66). Hence, we need to regard all $\boldsymbol{\theta}$, $\bar{\boldsymbol{a}}_\alpha$ and $\bar{\boldsymbol{a}}'_\alpha$, $\alpha = 1, ..., N$, as unknowns and search the high dimensional joint parameter space. For this type of problem, the unknown $\boldsymbol{\theta}$, which we really want to know, is called the *structural parameter*, while the accompanying, or ancillary, $\bar{\boldsymbol{a}}_\alpha$ and $\bar{\boldsymbol{a}}'_\alpha$, $\alpha = 1, ..., N$, are called the *nuisance parameters*.

If the constraint of Eq. (5.66) happens to be linear in $\bar{\boldsymbol{a}}_\alpha$, $\bar{\boldsymbol{a}}'_\alpha$, and $\boldsymbol{\theta}$, we can eliminate the nuisance parameters using Lagrange multipliers to obtain an objective function J of the structural parameter $\boldsymbol{\theta}$ alone such as Eqs. (5.11) and (5.35). Alternatively, we define a quantity $\boldsymbol{\varepsilon}_\alpha$, such as Eqs. (5.14), (5.25), and (5.53), that vanishes when noise does not exist and compute its covariance matrix $V[\boldsymbol{\varepsilon}_\alpha]$. From the Mahalanobis distance of $\boldsymbol{\varepsilon}_\alpha$, we can obtain the same form of the residual J.

However, even if Eq. (5.66) is not linear in $\bar{\boldsymbol{a}}_\alpha$ and $\bar{\boldsymbol{a}}'_\alpha$, we can still obtain a function J of $\boldsymbol{\theta}$ alone like Eqs. (5.11) and (5.35) by Taylor expansion, omitting high order terms. To be specific, we use Eq. (5.6) to replace $\bar{\boldsymbol{a}}_\alpha$ and $\bar{\boldsymbol{a}}'_\alpha$ by $\boldsymbol{a}_\alpha - \Delta\boldsymbol{a}_\alpha$ and $\boldsymbol{a}'_\alpha - \Delta\boldsymbol{a}'_\alpha$, respectively, ignore second and higher order terms in $\Delta\boldsymbol{a}_\alpha$ and $\Delta\boldsymbol{a}'_\alpha$, and introduce Lagrange multipliers. Alternatively, we evaluate the covariance matrix of $\boldsymbol{\varepsilon}_\alpha$, noting that the expectations of $\Delta\boldsymbol{a}_\alpha$ and $\Delta\boldsymbol{a}'_\alpha$ are $\boldsymbol{0}$, replacing the expectations of their second order terms by the corresponding covariance matrices, and omitting terms of fourth order and higher (the expectations of third order terms are $\boldsymbol{0}$ due to the symmetry of the probability distribution). The two approaches lead to the same result, and what we obtain is an approximation to the reprojection error, called the *Sampson error* after R. D. Sampson who first introduced this approximation to fitting an ellipse to a point sequence.

The FNS scheme we used in this chapter was first introduced by Chojnacki et al. [6] for minimizing the Sampson error of ellipse fitting and fundamental matrix computation. These are the cases in which $L = 1$, i.e., the constraint of Eq. (5.66) is a single equation. The extension of the FNS to $L > 1$ was given by Kanatani et al. [24] in relation to homography matrix computation. Although the Sampson error is an approximation to the reprojection error, we can first minimize the Sampson error by FNS and then modify the Sampson error using that solution. It can be shown that the Sampson error converges to the reprojection error if this process is repeated several times [27].

According to various experiments, however, the Sampson error is known to be a very good approximation to the reprojection error, and the value $\boldsymbol{\theta}$ that minimizes the Sampson error and the true maximum likelihood solution are almost the same; they usually coincide up to three or four significant digits. Thus, the Sampson error minimization and the reprojection error minimization are practically equivalent. For the rotation estimation of this chapter, on the other hand, the constraint is liner in $\bar{\boldsymbol{a}}_\alpha$ and $\bar{\boldsymbol{a}}'_\alpha$ from the beginning. Hence, the Sampson error and the reprojection error are the same, and an exact maximum likelihood solution is obtained by FNS.

The fact that the constraint of rotation can be rewritten as a linear equation in terms of quaternions, making possible a systematic computation of maximum likelihood, was first pointed out by Ohta and Kanatani [35]. Instead of FNS, they used a technique called *renormalization*, which, like FNS, iterates eigenvalue computations. This produces an optimal solution statistically equivalent to maximum likelihood. Analytically deriving the covariance matrix for triangulation by stereo vision (see Chapter 8 for the details), they computed the 3D rotation of an object on a turntable and evaluated the reliability of the computation (the reliability computation will be discussed in Chapter 7). The renormalization method belongs to a category of *algebraic method*, while FNS belongs to a category of *geometric method*. Their relationships are discussed in [28, 29].

The basic idea leading to the method for homogeneous constraints described in Sec. 5.5 was presented by Chojnacki et al. [7] as *CFNS* (*Constrained Fundamental Numerical Scheme*). Kanatani and Sugaya [26], however, pointed out that CFNS does not always produce a correct solution and modified it to *EFNS* (*Extended Fundamental Numerical Scheme*) so that a correct solution is always obtained. They applied it to the computation of the fundamental matrix over two images [26], and Kanatani and Matsunaga [23] applied it to computation of land movement, using GPS measurement data (see Chapter 8 for GPS land measurement). This method has the merit that it can not only compute rotations but also can be systematically applied to other different modes of motions, including rigid motions and affine deformations. However, if the iterations are started from a value very different from the solution, they may not necessarily converge. Hence, we need a good initial guess. For rotation estimation, we first use a method for isotropic noise, using singular value decomposition or quaternions discussed in Chapter 4, to obtain an approximate solution and use it to initialize the EFNS iterations.

5.7 EXERCISES

5.1. Show that Eq. (5.11) is obtained by eliminating $\bar{\boldsymbol{a}}_\alpha$ and $\bar{\boldsymbol{a}}'_\alpha$ from the Mahalanobis distance of Eq. (5.10) using Lagrange multipliers for the constraint of Eq. (5.7).

5.2. (1) Show that if vector $\boldsymbol{a}$ rotates around axis $\boldsymbol{l}$ (unit vector) by angle Ω to $\boldsymbol{a}'$ (Fig. 5.2), the following relation holds:

$$\boldsymbol{a}' - \boldsymbol{a} = 2\tan\frac{\Omega}{2}\boldsymbol{l} \times \frac{\boldsymbol{a}' + \boldsymbol{a}}{2}. \tag{5.67}$$

(2) Show that Eq. (5.20) is obtained from this.

5.3. Derive Eq. (5.36). Hint: $\boldsymbol{V}_\alpha \boldsymbol{W}_\alpha = \boldsymbol{I}$ holds from Eq. (5.34). Differentiate this with respect to $\boldsymbol{q}$.

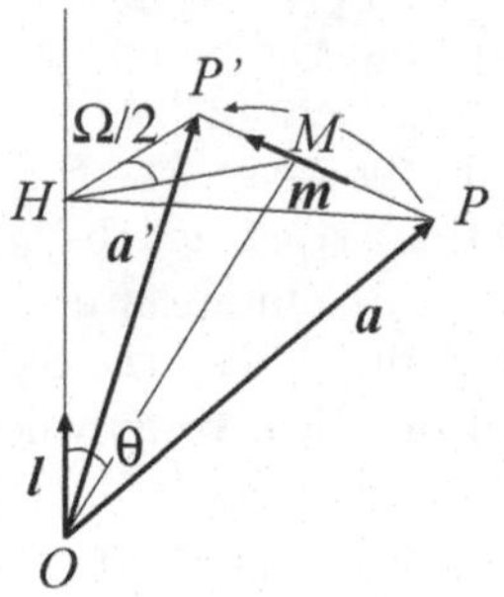

FIGURE 5.2 Vector $\boldsymbol{a}$ is rotated around axis $\boldsymbol{l}$ by angle Ω to $\boldsymbol{a}'$.

5.4. Show that the λ of Eq. (5.42) vanishes when the FNS iterations have converged.

CHAPTER 6

Derivative-based Optimization: Lie Algebra Method

In Chapters 4 and 5, we minimized a function $J(\boldsymbol{R})$ of a special form that represents maximum likelihood. Taking advantage of that form, we directly obtained the solution via the singular value decomposition and the quaternion representation. We also introduced eigenvalue computation iteration schemes such as the FNS. In this chapter, we consider the case of $J(\boldsymbol{R})$ having a general form. We first point out that we need not parametrize the rotation if we only consider small rotations, which define a linear space called the "Lie algebra." We study the relationship between small rotations and angular velocities to derive the exponential expression of rotation. Exploiting this fact, we derive a procedure, called the "Lie algebra method," for minimizing $J(\boldsymbol{R})$. We illustrate this procedure by applying it to maximum likelihood estimation of rotation and computation of the "fundamental matrix," which plays a central role in 3D reconstruction by computer vision. We also apply it to a 3D reconstruction scheme called "bundle adjustment."

6.1 DERIVATIVE-BASED OPTIMIZATION

In Chapters 4 and 5, we estimated the rotation $\boldsymbol{R}$ of observed data by minimizing some function $J(\boldsymbol{R})$ of $\boldsymbol{R}$. Exploiting the fact that $J(\boldsymbol{R})$ has a special form that represents maximum likelihood, we directly obtained the solution via the singular value decomposition and the quaternion representation or rewrite the rotation as a linear constraint to reduce the computation to eigenvalue computation iterations such as the FNS. In this chapter, we consider the case in which $J(\boldsymbol{R})$ has a general form.

What we can immediately think of is parameterizing the rotation matrix $\boldsymbol{R}$ via axis-angle, Euler numbers, quaternions, or some other parameteres, differentiating the function J with respect to them, incrementing them so that J decreases, and iterating this. Such a strategy is generally called a *gradient method*, for which various variations have been proposed for accelerating the convergence, including *steepest descent* (or *hill climbing*), *conjugate gradient*, *Newton iterations*, *Gauss–Newton iterations*, and the *Levenberg–Marquadt method*.

However, if we are to use such a gradient scheme, *we need not parameterize the rotation matrix* $\boldsymbol{R}$. After all, "differentiation" means evaluation of the change of the function value for a small variation of the variable. Hence, for differentiation with respect to rotation $\boldsymbol{R}$, we only need to evaluate the change of the function value when a small rotation is added to $\boldsymbol{R}$. To do this, it is sufficient to *parametrize a small rotation*. To be specific, we compute a small rotation that reduces the function value J, add it to the current rotation $\boldsymbol{R}$, regard the resulting rotation as a new current rotation $\boldsymbol{R}$, and iterate this process. As a result, the matrix $\boldsymbol{R}$ is updated at each iteration in the computer memory, so that there is no need to parametrize the matrix $\boldsymbol{R}$ itself. We call this the "Lie algebra method" and describe its procedure in this chapter.

This method has a big advantage over the parameterization, because any parameterization of rotation, such as axis-angle, Euler angles, and quaternions, has singularities at some special parameter values; they depend on parameterization but are likely to occur when $\boldsymbol{R}$ is the identity, a half-rotation, and a 360° rotation. At such singularities, the parameter values may have indeterminacy or their small changes may cause no rotations (except for high order terms). The gimbal lock of Euler angles described in Sec. 3.3 is a typical example. For numerical computation, numerical instability is likely to occur near such singularities. Theoretically, there exists no parameterization that does not have singularities, i.e., a smooth mapping onto the entire 3D space[1], though encountering such singularities is very rare in practical applications. Using the Lie algebra method, however, one need not worry about any singularities at all, because all we do is to update the current rotation by adding a small rotation. In a sense, this is obvious, but not many people understand this fact.

The "Lie algebra" is a linear space generated by infinitesimal rotations around coordinate axes. To explain this, we first show the relationship between small rotations and angular velocities. Next, we derive the exponential expression of rotation, and formalize the Lie algebra generated by infinitesimal rotations. We then show how it can be used for minimize $J(\boldsymbol{R})$ and apply the scheme to several typical problems.

6.2 SMALL ROTATIONS AND ANGULAR VELOCITY

If $\boldsymbol{R}$ represents a small rotation around some axis by a small angle $\Delta\Omega$, we can Taylor-expand it in the form

$$\boldsymbol{R} = \boldsymbol{I} + \boldsymbol{A}\Delta\Omega + O(\Delta\Omega)^2, \tag{6.1}$$

for some matrix $\boldsymbol{A}$, where $O(\Delta\Omega)^2$ denotes terms of second or higher orders in $\Delta\Omega$. Since $\boldsymbol{R}$ is a rotation matrix,

$$\begin{aligned}\boldsymbol{R}\boldsymbol{R}^\top &= (\boldsymbol{I} + \boldsymbol{A}\Delta\Omega + O(\Delta\Omega)^2)(\boldsymbol{I} + \boldsymbol{A}\Delta\Omega + O(\Delta\Omega)^2)^\top \\ &= \boldsymbol{I} + (\boldsymbol{A} + \boldsymbol{A}^\top)\Delta\Omega + O(\Delta\Omega)^2\end{aligned} \tag{6.2}$$

must be identically $\boldsymbol{I}$ for any $\Delta\Omega$. Hence, $\boldsymbol{A} + \boldsymbol{A}^\top = \boldsymbol{O}$, or

$$\boldsymbol{A}^\top = -\boldsymbol{A}. \tag{6.3}$$

This means that $\boldsymbol{A}$ is an antisymmetric matrix, so we can write it as

$$\boldsymbol{A} = \begin{pmatrix} 0 & -l_3 & l_2 \\ l_3 & 0 & -l_1 \\ -l_2 & l_1 & 0 \end{pmatrix} \tag{6.4}$$

[1]Mathematically, this is due to the fact that the parameter space of rotation has a different "topology" from the entire 3D space. See Sec. A.6 of Appendix A.

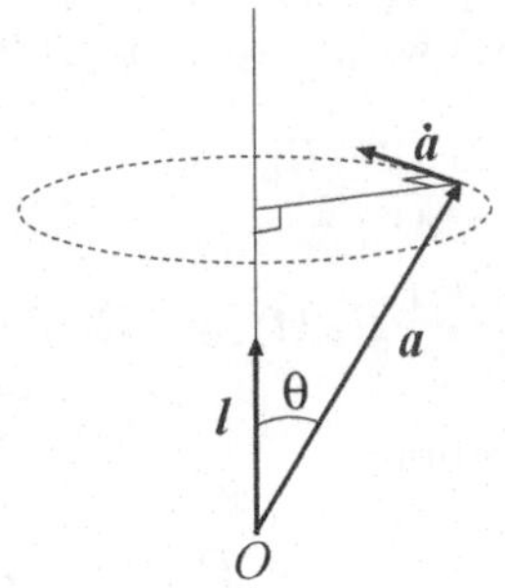

FIGURE 6.1 Vector $\boldsymbol{a}$ is rotating around an axis in the direction of the unit vector $\boldsymbol{l}$ with angular velocity ω. Its velocity vector is $\dot{\boldsymbol{a}}$.

for some l_1, l_2, and l_3. If a vector $\boldsymbol{a} = \begin{pmatrix} a_i \end{pmatrix}$ is rotated to $\boldsymbol{a}'$ by the rotation of Eq. (6.1), we obtain

$$\boldsymbol{a}' = (\boldsymbol{I} + \boldsymbol{A}\Delta\Omega + O(\Delta\Omega)^2)\boldsymbol{a} = \boldsymbol{a} + \begin{pmatrix} 0 & -l_3 & l_2 \\ l_3 & 0 & -l_1 \\ -l_2 & l_1 & 0 \end{pmatrix} \begin{pmatrix} a_1 \\ a_2 \\ a_3 \end{pmatrix} \Delta\Omega + O(\Delta\Omega)^2$$

$$= \boldsymbol{a} + \begin{pmatrix} l_2 a_3 - l_3 a_2 \\ l_3 a_1 - l_1 a_3 \\ l_1 a_2 - l_2 a_1 \end{pmatrix} \Delta\Omega + O(\Delta\Omega)^2 = \boldsymbol{a} + \boldsymbol{l} \times \boldsymbol{a}\Delta\Omega + O(\Delta\Omega)^2, \tag{6.5}$$

where we let $\boldsymbol{l} = \begin{pmatrix} l_i \end{pmatrix}$. Suppose this describes a continuous rotational motion over a small time interval Δt. Its velocity is given by

$$\dot{\boldsymbol{a}} = \lim_{\Delta t \to 0} \frac{\boldsymbol{a}' - \boldsymbol{a}}{\Delta t} = \omega \boldsymbol{l} \times \boldsymbol{a}, \tag{6.6}$$

where we define the *angular velocity* ω by

$$\omega = \lim_{\Delta t \to 0} \frac{\Delta\Omega}{\Delta t}. \tag{6.7}$$

Equation (6.6) states that the velocity $\dot{\boldsymbol{a}}$ is orthogonal to both $\boldsymbol{l}$ and $\boldsymbol{a}$ and that its magnitude equals ω times the area of the parallelogram made by $\boldsymbol{l}$ and $\boldsymbol{a}$. From the geometric consideration, the velocity $\dot{\boldsymbol{a}}$ is orthogonal to the axis of rotation and $\boldsymbol{a}$ itself (Fig. 6.1). If we let θ be the angle made by $\boldsymbol{a}$ and that axis, the distance of the endpoint of $\boldsymbol{a}$ from the axis is $\|\boldsymbol{a}\| \sin\theta$, and the definition of the angular velocity ω implies $\|\dot{\boldsymbol{a}}\| = \omega\|\boldsymbol{a}\| \sin\theta$. Since $\dot{\boldsymbol{a}}$ is orthogonal to $\boldsymbol{l}$ and $\boldsymbol{a}$ and since $\|\dot{\boldsymbol{a}}\| = \omega\|\boldsymbol{a}\| \sin\theta$ equals the area of the parallelogram made by $\boldsymbol{l}$ and $\boldsymbol{a}$, we conclude that $\boldsymbol{l}$ is *the unit vector along the axis of rotation*.

Equation (6.5) is also obtained from the Rodrigues formula of Eq. (3.20), which expresses the rotation matrix $\boldsymbol{R}$ in terms of the angle Ω and axis $\boldsymbol{l}$ (unit vector) (↪ Exercise 6.1). In physics, the vector $\boldsymbol{\omega} = \omega\boldsymbol{l}$ is known as the *angular velocity vector*. Using this notation, we can write Eq. (6.6) as

$$\dot{\boldsymbol{a}} = \boldsymbol{\omega} \times \boldsymbol{a}. \tag{6.8}$$

6.3 EXPONENTIAL EXPRESSION OF ROTATION

If we write $\boldsymbol{R}_{\boldsymbol{l}}(\Omega)$ to denote the rotation around axis $\boldsymbol{l}$ (unit vector) by angle Ω, Eq. (6.1) equals $\boldsymbol{R}_{\boldsymbol{l}}(\Delta\Omega)$. If we add it to rotation $\boldsymbol{R}_{\boldsymbol{l}}(\Omega)$, their composition is $\boldsymbol{R}_{\boldsymbol{l}}(\Delta\Omega)\boldsymbol{R}_{\boldsymbol{l}}(\Omega) = \boldsymbol{R}_{\boldsymbol{l}}(\Omega+$

$\Delta\Omega$). Hence, the derivative of $\boldsymbol{R}_l(\Omega)$ with respect to Ω is

$$\begin{aligned}\frac{d\boldsymbol{R}_l(\Omega)}{d\Omega} &= \lim_{\Delta\Omega\to 0}\frac{\boldsymbol{R}_l(\Omega+\Delta\Omega)-\boldsymbol{R}_l(\Omega)}{\Delta\Omega} = \lim_{\Delta\Omega\to 0}\frac{\boldsymbol{R}_l(\Delta\Omega)\boldsymbol{R}_l(\Omega)-\boldsymbol{R}_l(\Omega)}{\Delta\Omega}\\ &= \lim_{\Delta\Omega\to 0}\frac{\boldsymbol{R}_l(\Delta\Omega)-\boldsymbol{I}}{\Delta\Omega}\boldsymbol{R}_l(\Omega) = \boldsymbol{A}\boldsymbol{R}_l(\Omega).\end{aligned} \tag{6.9}$$

Differentiating this repeatedly, we obtain

$$\frac{d^2\boldsymbol{R}_l}{d\Omega^2} = \boldsymbol{A}\frac{d\boldsymbol{R}_l}{d\Omega} = \boldsymbol{A}^2\boldsymbol{R}_l, \qquad \frac{d^3\boldsymbol{R}_l}{d\Omega^2} = \boldsymbol{A}^2\frac{d\boldsymbol{R}_l}{d\Omega} = \boldsymbol{A}^3\boldsymbol{R}_l, \quad \cdots, \tag{6.10}$$

where the argument (Ω) is omitted. Since $\boldsymbol{R}_l(0) = \boldsymbol{I}$, the Taylor expansion of $\boldsymbol{R}_l(\Omega)$ around $\Omega = 0$ is given by

$$\begin{aligned}\boldsymbol{R}_l(\Omega) &= \boldsymbol{I} + \left.\frac{d\boldsymbol{R}}{d\Omega}\right|_{\Omega=0}\Omega + \frac{1}{2}\left.\frac{d^2\boldsymbol{R}}{d\Omega^2}\right|_{\Omega=0}\Omega^2 + \frac{1}{3!}\left.\frac{d^3\boldsymbol{R}}{d\Omega^3}\right|_{\Omega=0}\Omega^3 + \cdots\\ &= \boldsymbol{I} + \Omega\boldsymbol{A} + \frac{\Omega}{2}\boldsymbol{A}^2 + \frac{\Omega}{3!}\boldsymbol{A}^3 + \cdots = e^{\Omega\boldsymbol{A}},\end{aligned} \tag{6.11}$$

where we define the matrix exponential by the following series expansion[2]:

$$e^{\boldsymbol{X}} = \sum_{k=0}^{\infty}\frac{\boldsymbol{X}^k}{k!}. \tag{6.12}$$

In Eq. (6.11), the matrix $\boldsymbol{A}$ specifies the axis direction in the form of Eq. (6.4). Hence, this should coincide with the Rodrigues formula of Eq. (3.20).

In the following, we combine the axis $\boldsymbol{l}$ and angle Ω, as in the case of the angular velocity vector, as a single vector in the form of

$$\boldsymbol{\Omega} = \Omega\boldsymbol{l}, \tag{6.13}$$

which we call the *rotation vector*. We also write the matrix that represents the corresponding rotation as $\boldsymbol{R}(\boldsymbol{\Omega})$. Since $\Omega_1 = \Omega l_1$, $\Omega_2 = \Omega l_2$, and $\Omega_3 = \Omega l_3$, Eq. (6.4) is rewritten as

$$\Omega\boldsymbol{A} = \Omega_1\boldsymbol{A}_1 + \Omega_2\boldsymbol{A}_2 + \Omega_3\boldsymbol{A}_3, \tag{6.14}$$

where we define the matrices $\boldsymbol{A}_1$, $\boldsymbol{A}_2$, and $\boldsymbol{A}_3$ by

$$\boldsymbol{A}_1 = \begin{pmatrix}0&0&0\\0&0&-1\\0&1&0\end{pmatrix}, \quad \boldsymbol{A}_2 = \begin{pmatrix}0&0&1\\0&0&0\\-1&0&0\end{pmatrix}, \quad \boldsymbol{A}_3 = \begin{pmatrix}0&-1&0\\1&0&0\\0&0&0\end{pmatrix}. \tag{6.15}$$

Thus, Eq. (6.11) is also written as

$$\boldsymbol{R}(\boldsymbol{\Omega}) = e^{\Omega_1\boldsymbol{A}_1+\Omega_2\boldsymbol{A}_2+\Omega_3\boldsymbol{A}_3}, \tag{6.16}$$

which express the Rodrigues formula of Eq. (3.20).

[2]Matrix exponential is known to be always absolutely convergent.

6.4 LIE ALGEBRA OF INFINITESIMAL ROTATIONS

Consider a rotation $\boldsymbol{R}(t)$ continuously changing with parameter t, which can be interpreted as time or angle of rotation or some control parameter. We regard $t = 0$ as corresponding to the identity $\boldsymbol{I}$. We call a "linear" variation of $\boldsymbol{R}(t)$ around $t = 0$ an *infinitesimal rotation*. To be specific, we expand $\boldsymbol{R}(t)$ for a small change δt of t and ignore terms of order 2 and higher in δt. From Eq. (6.1), we see that an infinitesimal rotation is expressed in the form

$$\boldsymbol{I} + \boldsymbol{A}\delta t, \tag{6.17}$$

for some antisymmetric matrix $\boldsymbol{A}$, which we call the *generator* of the infinitesimal rotation. If we accumulate this infinitesimal rotation continuously, we obtain a finite rotation $e^{t\boldsymbol{A}}$ as shown in the preceding section.

Note that any multiple of an infinitesimal rotation is also an infinitesimal rotation. This may sound counterintuitive, but this is the consequence of our defining infinitesimal rotations as "linear" variations of rotations. If the parameter t is regarded as time, multiplication of a generator by a constant c means multiplication of the instantaneous velocity by c.

We also see that the composition of infinitesimal rotations is also an infinitesimal rotation. In fact, if infinitesimal rotations $\boldsymbol{I} + \boldsymbol{A}\delta t$ and $\boldsymbol{I} + \boldsymbol{A}'\delta t$ are composed, we obtain

$$(\boldsymbol{I} + \boldsymbol{A}'\delta t)(\boldsymbol{I} + \boldsymbol{A}\delta t) = \boldsymbol{I} + (\boldsymbol{A} + \boldsymbol{A}')\delta t \ \ (= (\boldsymbol{I} + \boldsymbol{A}\delta t)(\boldsymbol{I} + \boldsymbol{A}'\delta t)). \tag{6.18}$$

Recall that terms of order 2 and higher in δt are always ignored. From this, we see that, unlike finite rotations (↪ Sec. 3.1), the composition of infinitesimal rotations is *commutative*, i.e., it does not depend on the order of composition; the generator of the composed infinitesimal rotation is the *sum* of their generators. If we identify an infinitesimal rotation with its generator, we see that *the set of infinitesimal rotations constitute a linear space.*

A linear space is called an *algebra* if it is closed under some product operation. The set of all the generators of infinitesimal rotations can be regarded as an algebra if we define a product of generators $\boldsymbol{A}$ and $\boldsymbol{B}$ by

$$[\boldsymbol{A}, \boldsymbol{B}] = \boldsymbol{A}\boldsymbol{B} - \boldsymbol{B}\boldsymbol{A}, \tag{6.19}$$

called the *commutator* of $\boldsymbol{A}$ and $\boldsymbol{B}$. By definition, this is *anticommutative*:

$$[\boldsymbol{A}, \boldsymbol{B}] = -[\boldsymbol{B}, \boldsymbol{A}]. \tag{6.20}$$

The commutator is *bilinear*:

$$[\boldsymbol{A} + \boldsymbol{B}, \boldsymbol{C}] = [\boldsymbol{A}, \boldsymbol{C}] + [\boldsymbol{B}, \boldsymbol{C}], \qquad [c\boldsymbol{A}, \boldsymbol{B}] = c[\boldsymbol{A}, \boldsymbol{B}], \qquad c \in \mathcal{R}, \tag{6.21}$$

and the following *Jacobi identity* holds (↪ Exercise 6.2):

$$[\boldsymbol{A}, [\boldsymbol{B}, \boldsymbol{C}]] + [\boldsymbol{B}, [\boldsymbol{C}, \boldsymbol{A}]] + [\boldsymbol{C}, [\boldsymbol{A}, \boldsymbol{B}]] = \boldsymbol{O}. \tag{6.22}$$

An operation $[\,\cdot\,,\,\cdot\,]$ which maps two elements to another element is called a *Lie bracket* if the identities of Eqs. (6.20), (6.21), and (6.22) hold. Evidently, the commutator of Eq. (6.19) defines a Lie bracket. An algebra equipped with a Lie bracket is called a *Lie algebra.*

Thus, the set of infinitesimal rotations is a Lie algebra under the commutator. Since the generator $\boldsymbol{A}$ is an antisymmetric matrix, it has three degrees of freedom. Hence, the Lie algebra of infinitesimal rotations is three-dimensional with the matrices $\boldsymbol{A}_1$, $\boldsymbol{A}_2$, and $\boldsymbol{A}_3$ in Eq. (6.15) as its basis. It is easy to see that they satisfy the following (↪ Exercise 6.3):

$$[\boldsymbol{A}_2, \boldsymbol{A}_3] = \boldsymbol{A}_1, \qquad [\boldsymbol{A}_3, \boldsymbol{A}_1] = \boldsymbol{A}_2, \qquad [\boldsymbol{A}_1, \boldsymbol{A}_2] = \boldsymbol{A}_3. \tag{6.23}$$

In terms of this basis, an arbitrary generator $\boldsymbol{A}$ is expressed in the form

$$\boldsymbol{A} = \omega_1 \boldsymbol{A}_1 + \omega_2 \boldsymbol{A}_2 + \omega_3 \boldsymbol{A}_3, \tag{6.24}$$

for some ω_1, ω_2, and ω_3. From the definition of $\boldsymbol{A}_1$, $\boldsymbol{A}_2$, and $\boldsymbol{A}_3$ in Eq. (6.15), Eq. (6.24) is rewritten as

$$\boldsymbol{A} = \begin{pmatrix} 0 & -\omega_3 & \omega_2 \\ \omega_3 & 0 & -\omega_1 \\ -\omega_2 & \omega_1 & 0 \end{pmatrix}. \tag{6.25}$$

This defines a one-to-one correspondence between a generator $\boldsymbol{A}$ and a vector $\boldsymbol{\omega} = \begin{pmatrix}\omega_i\end{pmatrix}$. Let $\boldsymbol{\omega}' = \begin{pmatrix}\omega_i'\end{pmatrix}$ be the vector that corresponds to generator $\boldsymbol{A}'$. Then, the commutator of $\boldsymbol{A}$ and $\boldsymbol{A}'$ is

$$\begin{aligned}[\boldsymbol{A}, \boldsymbol{A}'] &= \begin{pmatrix} 0 & -\omega_3 & \omega_2 \\ \omega_3 & 0 & -\omega_1 \\ -\omega_2 & \omega_1 & 0 \end{pmatrix}\begin{pmatrix} 0 & -\omega_3' & \omega_2' \\ \omega_3' & 0 & -\omega_1' \\ -\omega_2' & \omega_1' & 0 \end{pmatrix} \\ &\quad - \begin{pmatrix} 0 & -\omega_3' & \omega_2' \\ \omega_3' & 0 & -\omega_1' \\ -\omega_2' & \omega_1' & 0 \end{pmatrix}\begin{pmatrix} 0 & -\omega_3 & \omega_2 \\ \omega_3 & 0 & -\omega_1 \\ -\omega_2 & \omega_1 & 0 \end{pmatrix} \\ &= \begin{pmatrix} 0 & -(\omega_1\omega_2' - \omega_2\omega_1') & \omega_3\omega_1' - \omega_1\omega_3' \\ \omega_1\omega_2' - \omega_2\omega_1' & 0 & -(\omega_2\omega_3' - \omega_3\omega_2') \\ -(\omega_3\omega_1' - \omega_1\omega_3') & \omega_2\omega_3' - \omega_3\omega_2' & 0 \end{pmatrix},\end{aligned} \tag{6.26}$$

which shows that the *vector product* $\boldsymbol{\omega} \times \boldsymbol{\omega}'$ corresponds to the commutator $[\boldsymbol{A}, \boldsymbol{A}']$.

Evidently, all the relations of Eqs. (6.20), (6.21), and (6.22) hold if the commutator $[\boldsymbol{A}, \boldsymbol{B}]$ is replaced by the vector product $\boldsymbol{a} \times \boldsymbol{b}$ (↪ Exercise 6.5). In other words, the vector product is a Lie bracket, and the set of vectors is also a Lie algebra under the Lie bracket $[\boldsymbol{a}, \boldsymbol{b}] = \boldsymbol{a} \times \boldsymbol{b}$. As shown above, the Lie algebra of vectors is the same as or, to be precise, *isomorphic* to, the Lie algebra of infinitesimal rotations. Indeed, the matrices $\boldsymbol{A}_1$, $\boldsymbol{A}_2$, and $\boldsymbol{A}_3$ in Eq. (6.15) represent infinitesimal rotations around the x-, y-, and z-axes, respectively, and Eq. (6.23) corresponds to the relationships $\boldsymbol{e}_2 \times \boldsymbol{e}_3 = \boldsymbol{e}_1$, $\boldsymbol{e}_3 \times \boldsymbol{e}_1 = \boldsymbol{e}_2$, and $\boldsymbol{e}_1 \times \boldsymbol{e}_2 = \boldsymbol{e}_3$ among the coordinate basis vectors $\boldsymbol{e}_1 = (1, 0, 0)^\top$, $\boldsymbol{e}_2 = (0, 1, 0)^\top$, and $\boldsymbol{e}_3 = (0, 0, 1)^\top$. The argument in Sec. 6.2 implies that identifying the generator $\boldsymbol{A}$ of Eq. (6.25) with the vector $\boldsymbol{\omega} = \begin{pmatrix}\omega_i\end{pmatrix}$ is nothing but *identifying an infinitesimal rotation with an instantaneous angular velocity vector*. In other words, we can think of the Lie algebra of infinitesimal rotations as *the set of all angular velocity vectors*.

6.5 OPTIMIZATION OF ROTATION

Given a function $J(\boldsymbol{R})$ of rotation $\boldsymbol{R}$, we now consider how to minimize it, assuming that the minimum exists. In general, the solution can be obtained by differentiating $J(\boldsymbol{R})$ with respect to $\boldsymbol{R}$ and finding the value of $\boldsymbol{R}$ for which the derivative vanishes. But, how should we interpret *differentiating with respect to* $\boldsymbol{R}$?

As is well known, the derivative of a function $f(x)$ is the rate of change of the function value $f(x)$ when the argument x is infinitesimally incremented to $x + \delta x$. By "infinitesimal increment," we mean considering the "linear" variation, ignoring high order terms in δx. In other words, if the function value changes to $f(x + \delta x) = f(x) + a\delta x + \cdots$, we call the coefficient a of δx the *differential coefficient*, or the *derivative*, of $f(x)$ with respect to x

and write $a = f'(x)$. This is equivalently written as $a = \lim_{\delta x \to 0}(f(x+\delta x) - f(x))/\delta x$. Evidently, if a function $f(x)$ takes its minimum at x, the function value does not change by infinitesimally incrementing x; the resulting change is of a high order in the increment. This is the principle of how we can minimize (or maximize) a function by finding the zero of its derivative. Thus, in order to minimize $J(\boldsymbol{R})$, we only need to find an $\boldsymbol{R}$ such that its infinitesimal variation does not change the value of $J(\boldsymbol{R})$ except for high order terms.

This consideration implies that "differentiation" of $J(\boldsymbol{R})$ with respect to $\boldsymbol{R}$ means evaluation of the rate of the change of $J(\boldsymbol{R})$ when an infinitesimal rotation is added to $\boldsymbol{R}$. If an infinitesimal rotation of Eq. (6.17) is added to $\boldsymbol{R}$, we obtain

$$(\boldsymbol{I} + \boldsymbol{A}\delta t)\boldsymbol{R} = \boldsymbol{R} + \boldsymbol{A}\boldsymbol{R}\delta t. \tag{6.27}$$

The generator $\boldsymbol{A}$ is represented by a vector $\boldsymbol{\omega}$ via Eq. (6.25). In the following, we combine the vector $\boldsymbol{\omega}$ and the parameter δt of infinitesimal variation as a single vector

$$\Delta\boldsymbol{\omega} = \boldsymbol{\omega}\delta t, \tag{6.28}$$

which we call the *small rotation vector*, an infinitesimal version of the finite rotation vector $\boldsymbol{\Omega}$ of Eq. (6.13). We also denote the antisymmetric matrix $\boldsymbol{A}$ corresponding to vector $\boldsymbol{\omega} = (\omega_1, \omega_2, \omega_3)^\top$ via Eq. (6.25) by[3] $\boldsymbol{A}(\boldsymbol{\omega})$. As shown in Eq. (6.5), the following identity holds for an arbitrary vector $\boldsymbol{a}$:

$$\boldsymbol{A}(\boldsymbol{\omega})\boldsymbol{a} = \boldsymbol{\omega} \times \boldsymbol{a}. \tag{6.29}$$

Using this notation, we can write Eq. (6.27) as $\boldsymbol{R} + \boldsymbol{A}(\Delta\boldsymbol{\omega})\boldsymbol{R}$ in terms of a small rotation vector $\Delta\boldsymbol{\omega}$. We substitute this into $J(\boldsymbol{R})$, and if $J(\boldsymbol{R} + \boldsymbol{A}(\Delta\boldsymbol{\omega})\boldsymbol{R})$ is written in the form

$$J(\boldsymbol{R} + \boldsymbol{A}(\Delta\boldsymbol{\omega})\boldsymbol{R}) = J(\boldsymbol{R}) + \langle \boldsymbol{g}, \Delta\boldsymbol{\omega}\rangle, \tag{6.30}$$

for some vector $\boldsymbol{g}$ by ignoring higher order terms in $\Delta\boldsymbol{\omega}$ (recall that $\langle \boldsymbol{a}, \boldsymbol{b}\rangle$ denotes the inner product of vectors $\boldsymbol{a}$ and $\boldsymbol{b}$), we call $\boldsymbol{g}$ the *gradient*, or the *first derivative*, of $J(\boldsymbol{R})$ with respect to $\boldsymbol{R}$.

Since $\boldsymbol{g}$ should vanish at $\boldsymbol{R}$ for which $J(\boldsymbol{R})$ takes its minimum, we need to solve $\boldsymbol{g} = \boldsymbol{0}$, but this is not easy in general. So, we do iterative search, starting from an initial value $\boldsymbol{R}$ and successively modifying it so that $J(\boldsymbol{R})$ reduces. Note that the value of the gradient $\boldsymbol{g}$ depends on $\boldsymbol{R}$, i.e., $\boldsymbol{g}$ is also a function of $\boldsymbol{R}$. If, after substituting $\boldsymbol{R} + \boldsymbol{A}(\Delta\boldsymbol{\omega})\boldsymbol{R}$ for $\boldsymbol{R}$ in $\boldsymbol{g}(\boldsymbol{R})$, we can write

$$\boldsymbol{g}(\boldsymbol{R} + \boldsymbol{A}(\Delta\boldsymbol{\omega})\boldsymbol{R}) = \boldsymbol{g}(\boldsymbol{R}) + \boldsymbol{H}\Delta\boldsymbol{\omega}, \tag{6.31}$$

for some symmetric matrix $\boldsymbol{H}$ by ignoring higher order terms in $\Delta\boldsymbol{\omega}$, we call the matrix $\boldsymbol{H}$ the *Hessian*, or the *second derivative*, of $J(\boldsymbol{R})$ with respect to $\boldsymbol{R}$. If the gradient $\boldsymbol{g}$ and the Hessian $\boldsymbol{H}$ are given, the value of $J(\boldsymbol{R} + \boldsymbol{A}(\Delta\boldsymbol{\omega})\boldsymbol{R})$ is approximated in the form

$$J(\boldsymbol{R} + \boldsymbol{A}(\Delta\boldsymbol{\omega})\boldsymbol{R}) = J(\boldsymbol{R}) + \langle \boldsymbol{g}, \Delta\boldsymbol{\omega}\rangle + \frac{1}{2}\langle \Delta\boldsymbol{\omega}, \boldsymbol{H}\Delta\boldsymbol{\omega}\rangle \tag{6.32}$$

by ignoring higher order terms in $\Delta\boldsymbol{\omega}$.

Now, we regard the "current" $\boldsymbol{R}$ as a fixed constant and regard the above expression as a function of $\Delta\boldsymbol{\omega}$. Since this is a quadratic polynomial in $\Delta\boldsymbol{\omega}$, its derivative with respect to $\Delta\boldsymbol{\omega}$ is $\boldsymbol{g} + \boldsymbol{H}\Delta\boldsymbol{\omega}$. Hence, this polynomial in $\Delta\boldsymbol{\omega}$ takes its minimum for

$$\Delta\boldsymbol{\omega} = -\boldsymbol{H}^{-1}\boldsymbol{g}. \tag{6.33}$$

[3]Some authors write this as $[\boldsymbol{\omega}]_\times$ or $(\boldsymbol{\omega}\times)$.

Namely, the rotation for which Eq. (6.32) takes its minimum is approximately $(\boldsymbol{I}+\boldsymbol{A}(\Delta\boldsymbol{\omega}))\boldsymbol{R}$ for that $\Delta\boldsymbol{\omega}$ (recall that the current value $\boldsymbol{R}$ is regarded as a fixed constant). However, $\boldsymbol{I}+\boldsymbol{A}(\Delta\boldsymbol{\omega})$ is not an exact rotation matrix, although the discrepancy is of higher order in δt. To make it an exact rotation matrix, we add higher order correction terms as an infinite series expansion in the form of Eq. (6.11). Thus, the rotation matrix for which Eq. (6.32) takes its minimum is approximated by $e^{\boldsymbol{A}(\Delta\boldsymbol{\omega})}\boldsymbol{R}$. Regarding this as the "new" value of the current rotation, we repeat this process. The procedure is described as follows.

1. Provide an initial value for $\boldsymbol{R}$.
2. Compute the gradient $\boldsymbol{g}$ and the Hessian $\boldsymbol{H}$ of $J(\boldsymbol{R})$.
3. Solve the following linear equation in $\Delta\boldsymbol{\omega}$:
$$\boldsymbol{H}\Delta\boldsymbol{\omega} = -\boldsymbol{g}. \tag{6.34}$$
4. Update $\boldsymbol{R}$ in the form
$$\boldsymbol{R} \leftarrow e^{\boldsymbol{A}(\Delta\boldsymbol{\omega})}\boldsymbol{R}. \tag{6.35}$$
5. If $\|\Delta\boldsymbol{\omega}\| \approx 0$, return $\boldsymbol{R}$ and stop. Else, go back to Step 2.

This is nothing but the well-known Newton iterations. For Newton iterations, we approximate the object function by a quadratic polynomial in the neighborhood of the current argument, proceed to the value that gives the minimum of that quadratic approximation, and repeat this. The difference of the above procedure from the usual Newton iterations is that we analyze the minimum of the quadratic approximation *not* in the space of the rotation $\boldsymbol{R}$ but *in the Lie algebra of infinitesimal rotations*. As we noted earlier, the space of $\boldsymbol{R}$ and its Lie algebra are not the same, having higher order discrepancies.

We can think of this situation as follows. The set of all rotations can be thought of as a "surface" defined by the "nonlinear" constraints $\boldsymbol{R}^\top\boldsymbol{R} = \boldsymbol{I}$ and $|\boldsymbol{R}| = 1$ in the 9D space of the nine elements of 3×3 matrices. This is called the *special orthogonal group*[4] of dimension 3, or the *group of rotations* for short, and denoted by $SO(3)$. It has the algebraic property that products and inverses of its elements are defined; such a set is called a *group*. It also has the geometric (or topological) property that the elements constitute a curved surface, or a *manifold* to be precise, in a high dimensional space. A set that has these two propperties is called a *Lie group*; $SO(3)$ is a typical Lie group. See Appendix C for groups, manifolds, and Lie groups.

On the other hand, the Lie algebra of infinitesimal rotations is defined by the "linear" constraint $\boldsymbol{A}+\boldsymbol{A}^\top = \boldsymbol{O}$. We can think of it as a "flat" space (imagine a "plane") that is "tangent" to $SO(3)$ at $\boldsymbol{R}$. This is a linear space with $\boldsymbol{R}$ as the origin $(0,0,0)$ equipped with coordinates $(\Delta\omega_1, \Delta\omega_2, \Delta\omega_3)$. We call it the *tangent space* of $SO(3)$ and denote it by $T_{\boldsymbol{R}}(SO(3))$. This space touches $SO(3)$ at $\boldsymbol{R}$ but deviates from it as we go away from $\boldsymbol{R}$. Hence, we "project" a point in the Lie algebra $T_{\boldsymbol{R}}(SO(3))$ to a nearby point of $SO(3)$. This is done by the exponential mapping $e^{\boldsymbol{A}(\Delta\boldsymbol{\omega})}$ of Eq. (6.11) (Fig. 6.2). See Appendix C for more about Lie algebras. Hereafter, we call this scheme of computing the update in the space of the Lie algebra and projecting it onto $SO(3)$ the *Lie algebra method*.

Note that in actual computation we need not compute the series expansion of Eq. (6.11) in Eq. (6.35). Simply compute the axis of the infinitesimal rotation by $\boldsymbol{l} = \mathcal{N}[\Delta\boldsymbol{\omega}]$ (normalization to unit norm) and its angle by $\Delta\Omega = \|\Delta\boldsymbol{\omega}\|$. Then, as noted in Sec.6.3, $e^{\boldsymbol{A}(\Delta\boldsymbol{\omega})}$ is the rotation with axis $\boldsymbol{l}$ and angle $\Delta\Omega$ given by the Rodrigues formula of Eq. (3.20).

[4]The term "special" means that the determinant is constrained to be 1.

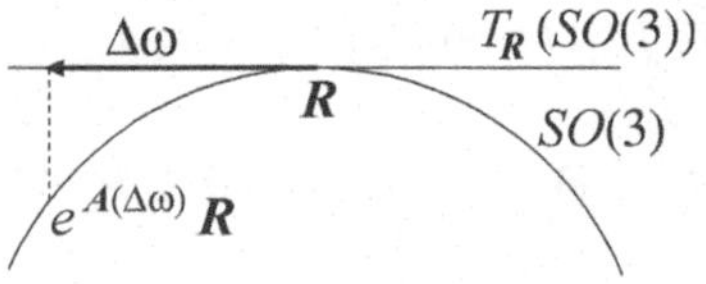

FIGURE 6.2 The Lie algebra of infinitesimal rotations can be thought of as the tangent space $T_{\boldsymbol{R}}(SO(3))$ to the group of rotations $SO(3)$ at $\boldsymbol{R}$. The increment $\Delta\boldsymbol{\omega}$ in the Lie algebra is projected to the point $e^{\boldsymbol{A}(\Delta\boldsymbol{\omega})}\boldsymbol{R}$ of $SO(3)$.

The criterion $\|\Delta\boldsymbol{\omega}\| \approx 0$ for convergence is set by a predetermined threshold. If $\Delta\boldsymbol{\omega}$ is $\boldsymbol{0}$, Eq. (6.33) implies $\boldsymbol{g} = \boldsymbol{0}$, producing a local minimum of $J(\boldsymbol{R})$. In general, iterative methods of this type are not necessarily guaranteed to converge when started from an arbitrary initial value (some methods are guaranteed, though). Hence, we need to start the iterations from a value close to the desired solution.

6.6 ROTATION ESTIMATION BY MAXIMUM LIKELIHOOD

We apply the above Lie algebra method to the maximum likelihood estimation for minimizing Eq. (5.11). Replacing $\boldsymbol{R}$ in Eq. (5.11) by $\boldsymbol{R}+\boldsymbol{A}(\Delta\boldsymbol{\omega})\boldsymbol{R}$, we see that the linear increment of J is given by

$$\Delta J = -\sum_{\alpha=1}^{N}\langle \boldsymbol{A}(\Delta\boldsymbol{\omega})\boldsymbol{R}\boldsymbol{a}_\alpha, \boldsymbol{W}_\alpha(\boldsymbol{a}'_\alpha - \boldsymbol{R}\boldsymbol{a}_\alpha)\rangle + \frac{1}{2}\sum_{\alpha=1}^{N}\langle \boldsymbol{a}'_\alpha - \boldsymbol{R}\boldsymbol{a}_\alpha, \Delta\boldsymbol{W}_\alpha(\boldsymbol{a}'_\alpha - \boldsymbol{R}\boldsymbol{a}_\alpha)\rangle, \tag{6.36}$$

where we have noted that the right side of Eq. (5.11) is symmetric with respect to the two $\boldsymbol{R}$'s in the expression so that we only need to consider the increment of one $\boldsymbol{R}$ and multiply the result by 2. Using the identity of Eq. (6.29), we can write the first term on the right side of Eq. (6.36) as

$$-\sum_{\alpha=1}^{N}\langle \Delta\boldsymbol{\omega} \times \boldsymbol{R}\boldsymbol{a}_\alpha, \boldsymbol{W}_\alpha(\boldsymbol{a}'_\alpha - \boldsymbol{R}\boldsymbol{a}_\alpha)\rangle = -\langle \Delta\boldsymbol{\omega}, \sum_{\alpha=1}^{N}(\boldsymbol{R}\boldsymbol{a}_\alpha) \times \boldsymbol{W}_\alpha(\boldsymbol{a}'_\alpha - \boldsymbol{R}\boldsymbol{a}_\alpha)\rangle, \tag{6.37}$$

where we have used the identity $\langle \boldsymbol{a}\times\boldsymbol{b}, \boldsymbol{c}\rangle = \langle \boldsymbol{a}, \boldsymbol{b}\times\boldsymbol{c}\rangle$ ($= |\boldsymbol{a}, \boldsymbol{b}, \boldsymbol{c}|$) for the scalar triple product (↪ Exercise 6.6). For evaluating $\Delta\boldsymbol{W}_\alpha$ in the second term on the right side of Eq. (6.36), we rewrite Eq. (5.13) as $\boldsymbol{W}_\alpha\boldsymbol{V}_\alpha = \boldsymbol{I}$, from which we obtain $\Delta\boldsymbol{W}_\alpha\boldsymbol{V}_\alpha + \boldsymbol{W}_\alpha\Delta\boldsymbol{V}_\alpha = \boldsymbol{O}$ for the linear increment. Using Eq. (5.13) again, we can write $\Delta\boldsymbol{W}_\alpha$ as

$$\Delta\boldsymbol{W}_\alpha = -\boldsymbol{W}_\alpha\Delta\boldsymbol{V}_\alpha\boldsymbol{W}_\alpha. \tag{6.38}$$

From Eq. (5.12), we obtain

$$\Delta\boldsymbol{W}_\alpha = -\boldsymbol{W}_\alpha(\boldsymbol{A}(\Delta\boldsymbol{\omega})\boldsymbol{R}V_0[\boldsymbol{a}_\alpha]\boldsymbol{R}^\top + \boldsymbol{R}V_0[\boldsymbol{a}_\alpha](\boldsymbol{A}(\Delta\boldsymbol{\omega})\boldsymbol{R})^\top)\boldsymbol{W}_\alpha, \tag{6.39}$$

which we substitute into the second term on the right side of Eq. (6.36). Note that the two terms on the right side of Eq. (6.39) are transpose of each other and that the second term on the right side of Eq. (6.36) is a quadratic form in $\boldsymbol{a}'_\alpha - \boldsymbol{R}\boldsymbol{a}_\alpha$. Hence, we only need to consider one term of Eq. (6.39) and multiply the result by 2 (↪ Exercise 6.7). Then, the second term on the right side of Eq. (6.36) is written as

$$
\begin{aligned}
&-\sum_{\alpha=1}^{N}\langle \boldsymbol{a}'_\alpha - \boldsymbol{R}\boldsymbol{a}_\alpha, \boldsymbol{W}_\alpha \boldsymbol{A}(\Delta\boldsymbol{\omega})\boldsymbol{R}V_0[\boldsymbol{a}_\alpha]\boldsymbol{R}^\top \boldsymbol{W}_\alpha(\boldsymbol{a}'_\alpha - \boldsymbol{R}\boldsymbol{a}_\alpha)\rangle \\
&= -\sum_{\alpha=1}^{N}\langle \boldsymbol{W}_\alpha(\boldsymbol{a}'_\alpha - \boldsymbol{R}\boldsymbol{a}_\alpha), \Delta\boldsymbol{\omega} \times \boldsymbol{R}V_0[\boldsymbol{a}_\alpha]\boldsymbol{R}^\top \boldsymbol{W}_\alpha(\boldsymbol{a}'_\alpha - \boldsymbol{R}\boldsymbol{a}_\alpha)\rangle \\
&= \sum_{\alpha=1}^{N}\langle \Delta\boldsymbol{\omega}, (\boldsymbol{W}_\alpha(\boldsymbol{a}'_\alpha - \boldsymbol{R}\boldsymbol{a}_\alpha)) \times \boldsymbol{R}V_0[\boldsymbol{a}_\alpha]\boldsymbol{R}^\top \boldsymbol{W}_\alpha(\boldsymbol{a}'_\alpha - \boldsymbol{R}\boldsymbol{a}_\alpha)\rangle.
\end{aligned} \tag{6.40}
$$

Combining this with Eq. (6.37), we can write Eq. (6.36) as

$$
\begin{aligned}
\Delta J = -\sum_{\alpha=1}^{N}\langle \Delta\boldsymbol{\omega}, &(\boldsymbol{R}\boldsymbol{a}_\alpha) \times \boldsymbol{W}_\alpha(\boldsymbol{a}'_\alpha - \boldsymbol{R}\boldsymbol{a}_\alpha) \\
&-(\boldsymbol{W}_\alpha(\boldsymbol{a}'_\alpha - \boldsymbol{R}\boldsymbol{a}_\alpha)) \times \boldsymbol{R}V_0[\boldsymbol{a}_\alpha]\boldsymbol{R}^\top \boldsymbol{W}_\alpha(\boldsymbol{a}'_\alpha - \boldsymbol{R}\boldsymbol{a}_\alpha)\rangle.
\end{aligned} \tag{6.41}
$$

Hence, from Eq. (6.30), the gradient of the function $J(\boldsymbol{R})$ of Eq. (5.11) is given by

$$
\boldsymbol{g} = -\sum_{\alpha=1}^{N}\Big((\boldsymbol{R}\boldsymbol{a}_\alpha) \times \boldsymbol{W}_\alpha(\boldsymbol{a}'_\alpha - \boldsymbol{R}\boldsymbol{a}_\alpha) - (\boldsymbol{W}_\alpha(\boldsymbol{a}'_\alpha - \boldsymbol{R}\boldsymbol{a}_\alpha)) \times \boldsymbol{R}V_0[\boldsymbol{a}_\alpha]\boldsymbol{R}^\top \boldsymbol{W}_\alpha(\boldsymbol{a}'_\alpha - \boldsymbol{R}\boldsymbol{a}_\alpha)\Big). \tag{6.42}
$$

Next, we consider the linear increment resulting from replacing $\boldsymbol{R}$ by $\boldsymbol{R} + \boldsymbol{A}(\Delta\boldsymbol{\omega})\boldsymbol{R}$ in this equation. Since we are computing an $\boldsymbol{R}$ such that $\boldsymbol{a}'_\alpha - \boldsymbol{R}\boldsymbol{a}_\alpha \approx \boldsymbol{0}$, we can ignore the increment of the first $\boldsymbol{R}$ in the first term on the right side of Eq. (6.42), assuming that $\boldsymbol{a}'_\alpha - \boldsymbol{R}\boldsymbol{a}_\alpha \approx \boldsymbol{0}$ as the iterations proceed. The second term is quadratic in $\boldsymbol{a}'_\alpha - \boldsymbol{R}\boldsymbol{a}_\alpha$, so we can ignore it. Only considering the increment of the second $\boldsymbol{R}$ in the first term, we obtain

$$
\begin{aligned}
\Delta\boldsymbol{g} &= \sum_{\alpha=1}^{N}(\boldsymbol{R}\boldsymbol{a}_\alpha) \times \boldsymbol{W}_\alpha \boldsymbol{A}(\Delta\boldsymbol{\omega})\boldsymbol{R}\boldsymbol{a}_\alpha) = \sum_{\alpha=1}^{N}(\boldsymbol{R}\boldsymbol{a}_\alpha) \times \boldsymbol{W}_\alpha(\Delta\boldsymbol{\omega} \times (\boldsymbol{R}\boldsymbol{a}_\alpha)) \\
&= -\sum_{\alpha=1}^{N}(\boldsymbol{R}\boldsymbol{a}_\alpha) \times \boldsymbol{W}_\alpha((\boldsymbol{R}\boldsymbol{a}_\alpha) \times \Delta\boldsymbol{\omega}).
\end{aligned} \tag{6.43}
$$

Now, we introduce new notations. For a vector $\boldsymbol{\omega}$ and a matrix $\boldsymbol{T}$, we define

$$
\boldsymbol{\omega} \times \boldsymbol{T} \equiv \boldsymbol{A}(\boldsymbol{\omega})\boldsymbol{T}, \qquad \boldsymbol{T} \times \boldsymbol{\omega} \equiv \boldsymbol{T}\boldsymbol{A}(\boldsymbol{\omega})^\top, \qquad \boldsymbol{\omega} \times \boldsymbol{T} \times \boldsymbol{\omega} \equiv \boldsymbol{A}(\boldsymbol{\omega})\boldsymbol{T}\boldsymbol{A}(\boldsymbol{\omega})^\top. \tag{6.44}
$$

The last one is the combination of the first two; whichever $\times$ we evaluate first, we obtain the same result. From Eq. (6.29), it is easily seen that $\boldsymbol{\omega} \times \boldsymbol{T}$ is "the matrix whose columns are the vector products of $\boldsymbol{\omega}$ and the three columns of $\boldsymbol{T}$" and that $\boldsymbol{T} \times \boldsymbol{\omega}$ is "the matrix whose rows are the vector products of the three rows of $\boldsymbol{T}$ and $\boldsymbol{\omega}$" (↪ Exercise 6.8). Using this notation and Eq. (6.29), we can write Eq. (6.43) as

$$
\Delta\boldsymbol{g} = -\sum_{\alpha=1}^{N}(\boldsymbol{R}\boldsymbol{a}_\alpha) \times \boldsymbol{W}_\alpha \boldsymbol{A}(\boldsymbol{R}\boldsymbol{a}_\alpha)\Delta\boldsymbol{\omega} = \sum_{\alpha=1}^{N}(\boldsymbol{R}\boldsymbol{a}_\alpha) \times \boldsymbol{W}_\alpha \times (\boldsymbol{R}\boldsymbol{a}_\alpha)\Delta\boldsymbol{\omega}, \tag{6.45}
$$

where we have noted that $\boldsymbol{A}(\boldsymbol{\omega})$ is antisymmetric: $\boldsymbol{A}(\boldsymbol{\omega})^\top = -\boldsymbol{A}(\boldsymbol{\omega})$. Comparing this and Eq. (6.31), we obtain the Hessian in the form

$$
\boldsymbol{H} = \sum_{\alpha=1}^{N}(\boldsymbol{R}\boldsymbol{a}_\alpha) \times \boldsymbol{W}_\alpha \times (\boldsymbol{R}\boldsymbol{a}_\alpha). \tag{6.46}
$$

Now that the gradient $\boldsymbol{g}$ and the Hessian $\boldsymbol{H}$ are given by Eqs. (6.42) and (6.46), we can minimize $J(\boldsymbol{R})$ by Newton iterations as described in the preceding section.

However, we have approximated the Hessian $\boldsymbol{H}$ by letting some quantities be zero in the course of the computation for minimizing those quantities. This convention is called *Gauss–Newton approximation*, and the Newton iterations using Gauss–Newton approximation are called *Gauss–Newton iterations*. From Eq. (6.33), we see that if $\Delta\boldsymbol{\omega}$ is $\mathbf{0}$ at the time of convergence, $\boldsymbol{g} = \mathbf{0}$ holds irrespective of the value of $\boldsymbol{H}$, returning an exact solution. In other words, *as long as the gradient* $\boldsymbol{g}$ *is correctly computed*, the Hessian $\boldsymbol{H}$ need not be exact. However, the value of $\boldsymbol{H}$ affects the speed of convergence.

If the Hessian $\boldsymbol{H}$ is not appropriate, we may overstep the minimum of $J(\boldsymbol{R})$ and the value of $J(\boldsymbol{R})$ may increase. Or we may proceed too slowly to reduce $J(\boldsymbol{R})$ meaningfully. A well-known measure to cope with this is add to $\boldsymbol{H}$ a multiple of the identity matrix $\boldsymbol{I}$ and adjust the constant c of $\boldsymbol{H} + c\boldsymbol{I}$. To be specific, we decrease c as long as $J(\boldsymbol{R})$ decreases and increase c if $J(\boldsymbol{R})$ increases. This modification is known as the *Levenberg–Marquardt method*. The procedure is written as follows.

1. Initialize $\boldsymbol{R}$, and let $c = 0.0001$.

2. Compute the gradient $\boldsymbol{g}$ and the (Gauss–Newton approximated) Hessian $\boldsymbol{H}$ of $J(\boldsymbol{R})$.

3. Solve the following linear equation in $\Delta\boldsymbol{\omega}$:

$$(\boldsymbol{H} + c\boldsymbol{I})\Delta\boldsymbol{\omega} = -\boldsymbol{g}. \tag{6.47}$$

4. Tentatively update $\boldsymbol{R}$ to

$$\tilde{\boldsymbol{R}} = e^{\boldsymbol{A}(\Delta\boldsymbol{\omega})}\boldsymbol{R}. \tag{6.48}$$

5. If $J(\tilde{\boldsymbol{R}}) < J(\boldsymbol{R})$ or $J(\tilde{\boldsymbol{R}}) \approx J(\boldsymbol{R})$ is not satisfied, let $c \leftarrow 10c$ and go back to Step 3.

6. If $\|\Delta\boldsymbol{\omega}\| \approx 0$, return $\tilde{\boldsymbol{R}}$ and stop. Else, update $\boldsymbol{R} \leftarrow \tilde{\boldsymbol{R}}$, $c \leftarrow c/10$ and go back to Step 2.

If we let $c = 0$, this reduces to Gauss–Newton iterations. In Steps 1, 5, and 6, the values 0.0001, $10c$, and $c/10$ are all empirical[5]. To start the iterations, we need appropriate initial values, for which we can compute the analytical homogeneous and isotropic noise solution using the singular value decomposition or the quaternion representation. The initial solution is sufficiently accurate in most practical applications, so the above Levenberg-Marquardt iterations usually converge after a few iterations.

6.7 FUNDAMENTAL MATRIX COMPUTATION

Consider two images of a 3D scene taken by two cameras. Suppose a point in the scene is imaged at (x, y) in the first camera image and at (x', y') in the second camera image. From the geometry of perspective imaging, the following *epipolar equation* holds [15, 29]:

$$\langle \begin{pmatrix} x/f_0 \\ y/f_0 \\ 1 \end{pmatrix}, \boldsymbol{F} \begin{pmatrix} x'/f_0 \\ y'/f_0 \\ 1 \end{pmatrix} \rangle = 0. \tag{6.49}$$

[5]In Eq. (6.47), we can alternatively use, instead of the identity $\boldsymbol{I}$, the diagonal matrix consisting of the diagonal elements of $\boldsymbol{H}$.

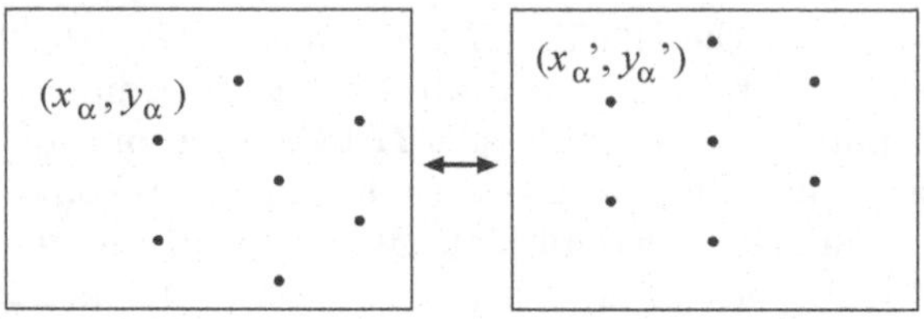

FIGURE 6.3 We compute the fundamental matrix $\boldsymbol{F}$ from point correspondences of two images.

Here, f_0 is an arbitrary scale constant; theoretically we could set it to 1, but it is better to let it have the magnitude of x/f and y/f for numerical stability of finite length computation [13]. The matrix $\boldsymbol{F}$ is called the *fundamental matrix* and is determined from the relative configuration of the two cameras and their internal parameters such as the focal length.

Computing the fundamental matrix $\boldsymbol{F}$ from point correspondences (x_α, y_α) and (x'_α, y'_α), $\alpha = 1, ..., N$, is a first step of many computer vision applications (Fig. 6.3). From the computed $\boldsymbol{F}$, one can reconstruct the 3D structure of the scene [15, 29]. The basic principle of its computation is minimizing the

$$J(\boldsymbol{F}) = \frac{f_0^2}{2} \sum_{\alpha=1}^{N} \frac{\langle \boldsymbol{x}_\alpha, \boldsymbol{F}\boldsymbol{x}'_\alpha \rangle^2}{\|\boldsymbol{P_k}\boldsymbol{F}\boldsymbol{x}'_\alpha\|^2 + \|\boldsymbol{P_k}\boldsymbol{F}^\top \boldsymbol{x}'_\alpha\|^2}, \tag{6.50}$$

where we define

$$\boldsymbol{x}_\alpha = \begin{pmatrix} x_\alpha/f_0 \\ y_\alpha/f_0 \\ 1 \end{pmatrix}, \qquad \boldsymbol{x}'_\alpha = \begin{pmatrix} x'_\alpha/f_0 \\ y'_\alpha/f_0 \\ 1 \end{pmatrix}, \qquad \boldsymbol{P_k} = \begin{pmatrix} 1 & 0 & 0 \\ 0 & 1 & 0 \\ 0 & 0 & 0 \end{pmatrix}. \tag{6.51}$$

By minimizing Eq. (6.50), we can obtain a maximum likelihood solution to a high accuracy, assuming that the noise terms Δx_α, Δy_α, $\Delta x'_\alpha$, and $\Delta y'_\alpha$ in the coordinates (x_α, y_α) and (x'_α, y'_α) are Gaussian variables of mean 0 with a constant variance. The function $J(\boldsymbol{F})$ of Eq. (6.50) is called the *Sampson error* (↪ Sec. 5.6). This form is obtained by minimizing the square sum of noises $\sum_{\alpha=1}^{N}(\Delta x_\alpha^2 + \Delta y_\alpha^2 + \Delta x'^2_\alpha + \Delta y'^2_\alpha)$, called the *reprojection error* (↪ Sec. 6.6, Exercise 5.1), subject to the constraint of Eq. (6.49), using Lagrange multipliers (↪ Exercise 6.9). Alternatively, it is obtained by evaluating the covariance matrix of the left side of Eq. (6.49) and computing the likelihood (↪ Exercise 6.10). The two results coincide.

Evidently, the fundamental matrix $\boldsymbol{F}$ has scale indeterminacy; Eqs. (6.49) and (6.50) are unchanged if $\boldsymbol{F}$ is multiplied by an arbitrary nonzero constant. So, we normalized $\boldsymbol{F}$ to $\|\boldsymbol{F}\|^2$ $(\equiv \sum_{i,j=1}^{3} F_{ij}^2) = 1$. Besides, there is an important requirement, called the *rank constraint* [15, 29]: $\boldsymbol{F}$ must have rank 2. Many strategies have been proposed to impose this constraint (we discuss this in Sec. 6.9), but the most straightforward one is to express $\boldsymbol{F}$ via the singular value decomposition in the form

$$\boldsymbol{F} = \boldsymbol{U} \begin{pmatrix} \sigma_1 & 0 & 0 \\ 0 & \sigma_2 & 0 \\ 0 & 0 & 0 \end{pmatrix} \boldsymbol{V}^\top, \tag{6.52}$$

where $\boldsymbol{U}$ and $\boldsymbol{V}$ are orthogonal matrices, and $\sigma_1 \geq \sigma_2$ (> 0) are the singular values (see Appendix B for the singular value decomposition); letting the third singular value σ_3 be 0 is the rank constraint. From the normalization $\|\boldsymbol{F}\|^2 = 1$, we have $\sigma_1^2 + \sigma_2^2 = 1$ (↪ Exercise 6.11), so we can let

$$\sigma_1 = \cos\phi, \qquad \sigma_2 = \sin\phi. \tag{6.53}$$

Substituting Eq. (6.52) into Eq. (6.50), we minimize $J(\boldsymbol{F})$ with respect to $\boldsymbol{U}$, $\boldsymbol{V}$, and ϕ.

Note that $\boldsymbol{U}$ and $\boldsymbol{V}$ are orthogonal matrices; they may not represent rotations depending on the sign of the determinant. However, *a small variation of an orthogonal matrix is a small rotation*. Hence, we can express the small variations of $\boldsymbol{U}$ and $\boldsymbol{V}$ in the form

$$\Delta\boldsymbol{U} = \boldsymbol{A}(\Delta\boldsymbol{\omega}_U)\boldsymbol{U}, \qquad \Delta\boldsymbol{V} = \boldsymbol{A}(\Delta\boldsymbol{\omega}_V)\boldsymbol{U}, \tag{6.54}$$

in terms of small rotation vectors $\Delta\boldsymbol{\omega}_U = \begin{pmatrix}\Delta\omega_{iU}\end{pmatrix}$ and $\Delta\boldsymbol{\omega}_V = \begin{pmatrix}\Delta\omega_{iV}\end{pmatrix}$. Incrementing $\boldsymbol{U}$, $\boldsymbol{V}$ and ϕ to $\boldsymbol{U}+\Delta\boldsymbol{U}$, $\boldsymbol{V}+\Delta\boldsymbol{V}$, and $\phi+\Delta\phi$ in Eq. (6.52), we can write the linear increment of $\boldsymbol{F}$, ignoring higher order terms, in the form

$$\begin{aligned}\Delta\boldsymbol{F} = {} & \boldsymbol{A}(\Delta\boldsymbol{\omega}_U)\boldsymbol{U}\mathrm{diag}(\cos\phi, \sin\phi, 0)\boldsymbol{V}^\top + \boldsymbol{U}\mathrm{diag}(\cos\phi, \sin\phi, 0)(\boldsymbol{A}(\Delta\boldsymbol{\omega}_V)\boldsymbol{V})^\top \\ & + \boldsymbol{U}\mathrm{diag}(-\sin\phi, \cos\phi, 0)\boldsymbol{V}^\top\Delta\phi.\end{aligned} \tag{6.55}$$

Taking out individual elements, we obtain

$$\begin{aligned}\Delta F_{11} &= \Delta\omega_{2U}F_{31} - \Delta\omega_{3U}F_{21} + \Delta\omega_{2V}F_{13} - \Delta\omega_{3V}F_{12} \\ &\quad +(U_{12}V_{12}\cos\phi - U_{11}V_{11}\sin\phi)\Delta\phi, \\ \Delta F_{12} &= \Delta\omega_{2U}F_{32} - \Delta\omega_{3U}F_{22} + \Delta\omega_{3V}F_{11} - \Delta\omega_{1V}F_{13} \\ &\quad +(U_{12}V_{22}\cos\phi - U_{11}V_{21}\sin\phi)\Delta\phi, \\ &\ \ \vdots \\ \Delta F_{33} &= \Delta\omega_{1U}F_{23} - \Delta\omega_{2U}F_{13} + \Delta\omega_{1V}F_{32} - \Delta\omega_{2V}F_{31} \\ &\quad +(U_{32}V_{32}\cos\phi - U_{31}V_{31}\sin\phi)\Delta\phi.\end{aligned} \tag{6.56}$$

Identify $\Delta\boldsymbol{F}$ with a 9D vector consisting of components ΔF_{11}, ΔF_{12}, ..., ΔF_{33}, and write

$$\Delta\boldsymbol{F} = \boldsymbol{F}_U\Delta\boldsymbol{\omega}_U + \boldsymbol{F}_V\Delta\boldsymbol{\omega}_V + \boldsymbol{\theta}_\phi\Delta\phi, \tag{6.57}$$

where we define the 9×3 matrices $\boldsymbol{F}_U$ and $\boldsymbol{F}_V$ and the 9D vector $\boldsymbol{\theta}_\phi$ by

$$\boldsymbol{F}_U = \begin{pmatrix} 0 & F_{31} & -F_{21} \\ 0 & F_{32} & -F_{22} \\ 0 & F_{33} & -F_{23} \\ -F_{31} & 0 & F_{11} \\ -F_{32} & 0 & F_{12} \\ -F_{33} & 0 & F_{13} \\ F_{21} & -F_{11} & 0 \\ F_{22} & -F_{12} & 0 \\ F_{23} & -F_{13} & 0 \end{pmatrix}, \qquad \boldsymbol{F}_V = \begin{pmatrix} 0 & F_{13} & -F_{12} \\ -F_{13} & 0 & F_{11} \\ F_{12} & -F_{11} & 0 \\ 0 & F_{23} & -F_{22} \\ -F_{23} & 0 & F_{21} \\ F_{22} & -F_{21} & 0 \\ 0 & F_{33} & -F_{32} \\ -F_{33} & 0 & F_{31} \\ F_{32} & -F_{31} & 0 \end{pmatrix}, \tag{6.58}$$

$$\boldsymbol{\theta}_\phi = \begin{pmatrix} \sigma_1U_{12}V_{12} - \sigma_2U_{11}V_{11} \\ \sigma_1U_{12}V_{22} - \sigma_2U_{11}V_{21} \\ \sigma_1U_{12}V_{32} - \sigma_2U_{11}V_{31} \\ \sigma_1U_{22}V_{12} - \sigma_2U_{21}V_{11} \\ \sigma_1U_{22}V_{22} - \sigma_2U_{21}V_{21} \\ \sigma_1U_{22}V_{32} - \sigma_2U_{21}V_{31} \\ \sigma_1U_{32}V_{12} - \sigma_2U_{31}V_{11} \\ \sigma_1U_{32}V_{22} - \sigma_2U_{31}V_{21} \\ \sigma_1U_{32}V_{32} - \sigma_2U_{31}V_{31} \end{pmatrix}. \tag{6.59}$$

Then, the linear increment ΔJ of the function $J(\boldsymbol{F})$ of Eq. (6.50) is given by

$$\begin{aligned}\Delta J &= \langle \nabla_{\boldsymbol{F}} J, \Delta \boldsymbol{F}\rangle = \langle \nabla_{\boldsymbol{F}} J, \boldsymbol{F}_U \Delta\boldsymbol{\omega}_U\rangle + \langle \nabla_{\boldsymbol{F}} J, \boldsymbol{F}_V \Delta\boldsymbol{\omega}_V\rangle + \langle \nabla_{\boldsymbol{F}} J, \boldsymbol{\theta}_\phi \Delta\phi\rangle \\ &= \langle \boldsymbol{F}_U^\top \nabla_{\boldsymbol{F}} J, \Delta\boldsymbol{\omega}_U\rangle + \langle \boldsymbol{F}_V^\top \nabla_{\boldsymbol{F}} J, \Delta\boldsymbol{\omega}_V\rangle + \langle \nabla_{\boldsymbol{F}} J, \boldsymbol{\theta}_\phi\rangle \Delta\phi, \end{aligned} \tag{6.60}$$

where $\nabla_{\boldsymbol{F}} J$ is the 9D vector consisting of components $\partial J/\partial F_{ij}$. From this, we obtain the gradients of J with respect to $\boldsymbol{U}_U$, $\boldsymbol{U}_V$, and ϕ in the form

$$\nabla_{\boldsymbol{\omega}_U} J = \boldsymbol{F}_U^\top \nabla_{\boldsymbol{F}} J, \qquad \nabla_{\boldsymbol{\omega}_V} J = \boldsymbol{F}_V^\top \nabla_{\boldsymbol{F}} J, \qquad \frac{\partial J}{\partial \phi} = \langle \nabla_{\boldsymbol{F}} J, \boldsymbol{\theta}_\phi\rangle. \tag{6.61}$$

Next, consider the second derivatives $\partial^2 J/\partial F_{ij}\partial F_{kl}$ of Eq. (6.50). We adopt the Gauss–Newton approximation of ignoring terms containing $\langle \boldsymbol{x}_\alpha, \boldsymbol{F}\boldsymbol{x}'_\alpha\rangle$, i.e., the left side of the epipolar equation of Eq. (6.49). It follows that we need not consider terms containing $\langle \boldsymbol{x}_\alpha, \boldsymbol{F}\boldsymbol{x}'_\alpha\rangle^2$ in the first derivative, i.e., we need not differentiate the denominator in Eq. (6.50). Hence, the first derivative is approximated to be

$$\frac{\partial J}{\partial F_{ij}} \approx \sum_{\alpha=1}^{N} \frac{f_0^2 x_{i\alpha} x'_{j\alpha} \langle \boldsymbol{x}_\alpha, \boldsymbol{F}\boldsymbol{x}'_\alpha\rangle}{\|\boldsymbol{P_k}\boldsymbol{F}\boldsymbol{x}'_\alpha\|^2 + \|\boldsymbol{P_k}\boldsymbol{F}^\top \boldsymbol{x}'_\alpha\|^2}, \tag{6.62}$$

where $x_{i\alpha}$ and $x'_{j\alpha}$ denote the ith components of $\boldsymbol{x}_\alpha$ and $\boldsymbol{x}'_\alpha$, respectively. For differentiating this with respect to F_{kl}, we need not differentiate the denominator because the numerator contains $\langle \boldsymbol{x}_\alpha, \boldsymbol{F}\boldsymbol{x}'_\alpha\rangle$. Differentiating only the numerator, we obtain

$$\frac{\partial^2 J}{\partial F_{ij}\partial F_{kl}} \approx \sum_{\alpha=1}^{N} \frac{f_0^2 x_{i\alpha} x'_{j\alpha} x_{k\alpha} x'_{l\alpha}}{\|\boldsymbol{P_k}\boldsymbol{F}\boldsymbol{x}'_\alpha\|^2 + \|\boldsymbol{P_k}\boldsymbol{F}^\top \boldsymbol{x}'_\alpha\|^2}. \tag{6.63}$$

Let us count the pairs of indices (i, j) = (1,1), (1,2), ..., (3,3), using a single running index I = 1, ..., 9. Similarly, we use a single running index J = 1, ..., 9 for pairs (k, l) and regard the right side of the above equation as the (I, J) element of a 9×9 matrix, which we write as $\nabla_{\boldsymbol{F}}^2 J$. Then, as in Eq. (6.60), we can write, using Eq. (6.57), the second derivation of J with respect to $\boldsymbol{U}$, $\boldsymbol{V}$, and ϕ in the form

$$\begin{aligned}\Delta^2 J &= \langle \Delta\boldsymbol{F}, \nabla_{\boldsymbol{F}}^2 J \Delta\boldsymbol{F}\rangle \\ &= \langle \boldsymbol{F}_U \Delta\boldsymbol{\omega}_U + \boldsymbol{F}_V \Delta\boldsymbol{\omega}_V + \boldsymbol{\theta}_\phi \Delta\phi, \nabla_{\boldsymbol{F}}^2 J(\boldsymbol{F}_U \Delta\boldsymbol{\omega}_U + \boldsymbol{F}_V \Delta\boldsymbol{\omega}_V + \boldsymbol{\theta}_\phi \Delta\phi\rangle \\ &= \langle \Delta\boldsymbol{\omega}_U, \boldsymbol{F}_U^\top \nabla_{\boldsymbol{F}}^2 J \boldsymbol{F}_U \Delta\boldsymbol{\omega}_U\rangle + \langle \Delta\boldsymbol{\omega}_U, \boldsymbol{F}_U^\top \nabla_{\boldsymbol{F}}^2 J \boldsymbol{F}_V \Delta\boldsymbol{\omega}_V\rangle \\ &\quad + \langle \Delta\boldsymbol{\omega}_V, \boldsymbol{F}_V^\top \nabla_{\boldsymbol{F}}^2 J \boldsymbol{F}_U \Delta\boldsymbol{\omega}_V\rangle + \langle \Delta\boldsymbol{\omega}_V, \boldsymbol{F}_V^\top \nabla_{\boldsymbol{F}}^2 J \boldsymbol{F}_V \Delta\boldsymbol{\omega}_V\rangle \\ &\quad + \langle \Delta\boldsymbol{\omega}_U, \boldsymbol{F}_U^\top \nabla_{\boldsymbol{F}}^2 J \boldsymbol{\theta}_\phi\rangle \Delta\phi + \langle \Delta\boldsymbol{\omega}_V, \boldsymbol{F}_V^\top \nabla_{\boldsymbol{F}}^2 J \boldsymbol{\theta}_\phi\rangle \Delta\phi \\ &\quad + \langle \Delta\boldsymbol{\omega}_U, \boldsymbol{F}_U^\top \nabla_{\boldsymbol{F}}^2 J \boldsymbol{\theta}_\phi\rangle \Delta\phi + \langle \Delta\boldsymbol{\omega}_V, \boldsymbol{F}_V^\top \nabla_{\boldsymbol{F}}^2 J \boldsymbol{\theta}_\phi\rangle \Delta\phi \\ &\quad + \langle \boldsymbol{\theta}_\phi, \nabla_{\boldsymbol{F}}^2 J \boldsymbol{\theta}_\phi\rangle \Delta\phi^2, \end{aligned} \tag{6.64}$$

from which we obtain the following second derivatives of J:

$$\nabla_{\boldsymbol{\omega}_U \boldsymbol{\omega}_U} J = \boldsymbol{F}_U^\top \nabla_{\boldsymbol{F}}^2 J \boldsymbol{F}_U, \qquad \nabla_{\boldsymbol{\omega}_V \boldsymbol{\omega}_V} J = \boldsymbol{F}_V^\top \nabla_{\boldsymbol{F}}^2 J \boldsymbol{F}_V, \qquad \nabla_{\boldsymbol{\omega}_U \boldsymbol{\omega}_V} J = \boldsymbol{F}_U^\top \nabla_{\boldsymbol{F}}^2 J \boldsymbol{F}_V,$$

$$\frac{\partial \nabla_{\boldsymbol{\omega}_U} J}{\partial \phi} = \boldsymbol{F}_U^\top \nabla_{\boldsymbol{F}}^2 J \boldsymbol{\theta}_\phi, \qquad \frac{\partial \nabla_{\boldsymbol{\omega}_V} J}{\partial \phi} = \boldsymbol{F}_V^\top \nabla_{\boldsymbol{F}}^2 J \boldsymbol{\theta}_\phi, \qquad \frac{\partial^2 J}{\partial \phi^2} = \langle \boldsymbol{\theta}_\phi, \nabla_{\boldsymbol{F}}^2 J \boldsymbol{\theta}_\phi\rangle. \tag{6.65}$$

Now that the first and second derivatives are given, the Levenberg–Marquardt procedure for minimizing J goes as follows:

1. Provide an initial value of $\boldsymbol{F}$ such that $|\boldsymbol{F}| = 0$ and $\|\boldsymbol{F}\| = 1$, and compute the singular value decomposition of Eq. (6.52). Evaluate the value J of Eq. (6.50), and let $c = 0.0001$.

2. Compute the first and second derivatives $\nabla_{\boldsymbol{F}} J$ and (Gauss–Newton approximated) $\nabla^2_{\boldsymbol{F}} J$ of J with respect to $\boldsymbol{F}$.

3. Compute the 9×3 matrices $\boldsymbol{F}_U$ and $\boldsymbol{F}_V$ of Eq. (6.58) and the 9D vector $\boldsymbol{\theta}_\phi$ of Eq. (6.59).

4. Compute the first derivatives $\nabla_{\boldsymbol{\omega}_U} J$, $\nabla_{\boldsymbol{\omega}_V} J$, and $\partial J/\partial \phi$ in Eq. (6.61) and the second derivatives $\nabla_{\boldsymbol{\omega}_U \boldsymbol{\omega}_U} J$, $\nabla_{\boldsymbol{\omega}_V \boldsymbol{\omega}_V} J$, $\nabla_{\boldsymbol{\omega}_U \boldsymbol{\omega}_V} J$, $\partial \nabla_{\boldsymbol{\omega}_U} J/\partial \phi$, $\partial \nabla_{\boldsymbol{\omega}_V} J/\partial \phi$, and $\partial^2 J/\partial \phi^2$ in Eq. (6.65) of J.

5. Solve the following linear equation in $\Delta \boldsymbol{\omega}_U$, $\Delta \boldsymbol{\omega}_V$, and $\Delta \phi$:

$$\left(\begin{pmatrix} \nabla_{\boldsymbol{\omega}_U \boldsymbol{\omega}_U} J & \nabla_{\boldsymbol{\omega}_U \boldsymbol{\omega}_V} J & \partial \nabla_{\boldsymbol{\omega}_U} J/\partial \phi \\ (\nabla_{\boldsymbol{\omega}_U \boldsymbol{\omega}_V} J)^\top & \nabla_{\boldsymbol{\omega}_V \boldsymbol{\omega}_V} J & \partial \nabla_{\boldsymbol{\omega}_V} J/\partial \phi \\ (\partial \nabla_{\boldsymbol{\omega}_U} J/\partial \phi)^\top & (\partial \nabla_{\boldsymbol{\omega}_V} J/\partial \phi)^\top & \partial^2 J/\partial \phi^2 \end{pmatrix} + c\boldsymbol{I} \right) \begin{pmatrix} \Delta \boldsymbol{\omega}_U \\ \Delta \boldsymbol{\omega}_V \\ \Delta \phi \end{pmatrix} = - \begin{pmatrix} \nabla_{\boldsymbol{\omega}_U} J \\ \nabla_{\boldsymbol{\omega}_V} J \\ \partial J/\partial \phi \end{pmatrix}. \tag{6.66}$$

6. Tentatively update $\boldsymbol{U}$, $\boldsymbol{V}$, and ϕ to

$$\tilde{\boldsymbol{U}} = e^{\boldsymbol{A}(\Delta \boldsymbol{\omega}_U)} \boldsymbol{U}, \qquad \tilde{\boldsymbol{V}} = e^{\boldsymbol{A}(\Delta \boldsymbol{\omega}_V)} \boldsymbol{V}, \qquad \tilde{\phi} = \phi + \Delta \phi. \tag{6.67}$$

7. Tentatively update $\boldsymbol{F}$ to

$$\tilde{\boldsymbol{F}} = \tilde{\boldsymbol{U}} \begin{pmatrix} \cos \tilde{\phi} & 0 & 0 \\ 0 & \sin \tilde{\phi} & 0 \\ 0 & 0 & 0 \end{pmatrix} \tilde{\boldsymbol{V}}^\top. \tag{6.68}$$

8. Let $\tilde{J}$ be the value of Eq. (6.50) for $\tilde{\boldsymbol{F}}$.

9. If $\tilde{J} < J$ or $\tilde{J} \approx J$ is not satisfied, let $c \leftarrow 10c$ and go back to Step 5.

10. If $\tilde{\boldsymbol{F}} \approx \boldsymbol{F}$, return $\tilde{\boldsymbol{F}}$ and stop. Else, update $\boldsymbol{F} \leftarrow \tilde{\boldsymbol{F}}$, $\boldsymbol{U} \leftarrow \tilde{\boldsymbol{U}}$, $\boldsymbol{V} \leftarrow \tilde{\boldsymbol{V}}$, $\tilde{\phi} \leftarrow \phi$, $c \leftarrow c/10$, and $J \leftarrow \tilde{J}$ and go back to Step 2.

We need an initial value of $\boldsymbol{F}$ for starting these iterations. Various simple schemes are known. The simplest one is the "least squares" that minimizes the square sum of the left side of the epipolar equation of Eq. (6.49), which is equivalent to ignoring the denominator on the left side of Eq. (6.50). Since the square sum is quadratic in $\boldsymbol{F}$, the solution is immediately obtained by eigenanalysis if the rank constraint is not considered. The rank constraint can be imposed by computing the singular value decomposition of the resulting $\boldsymbol{F}$ and replacing the smallest singular value by 0. Many other approximation schemes are known (see Sec. 6.9 for related topics).

6.8 BUNDLE ADJUSTMENT

We now consider *3D reconstruction*, i.e., the problem of reconstructing the 3D structure of the scene from multiple images taken by multiple cameras. One of the most fundamental methods is *bundle adjustment*: we optimally estimate all the 3D positions of the points we

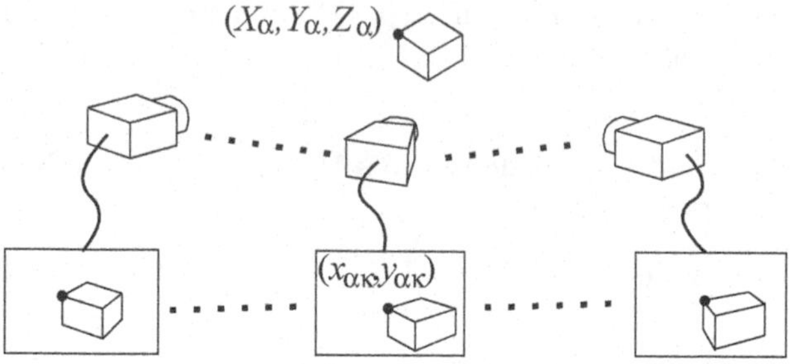

FIGURE 6.4 N points in the scene are viewed by M cameras. The αth point $(X_\alpha, Y_\alpha, Z_\alpha)$ is imaged at point $(x_{\alpha\kappa}, y_{\alpha\kappa})$ in the κth camera image.

are viewing and all the postures of the cameras as well as their internal parameters, in such a way that the bundle of rays, or lines of sight, will piece through the images appropriately.

We observe N particular points $(X_\alpha, Y_\alpha, Z_\alpha)$, $\alpha = 1, ..., N$, in 3D, which we call the *feature points* of the scene. Suppose the αth point is viewed at $(x_{\alpha\kappa}, y_{\alpha\kappa})$ in the image of the κth camera, $\kappa = 1, ..., M$ (Fig. 6.4). The imaging geometry of most of today's cameras is sufficiently modeled by perspective projection, for which the following relations hold [15, 29]:

$$x_{\alpha\kappa} = f_0 \frac{P_{\kappa(11)}X_\alpha + P_{\kappa(12)}Y_\alpha + P_{\kappa(13)}Z_\alpha + P_{\kappa(14)}}{P_{\kappa(31)}X_\alpha + P_{\kappa(32)}Y_\alpha + P_{\kappa(33)}Z_\alpha + P_{\kappa(34)}},$$
$$y_{\alpha\kappa} = f_0 \frac{P_{\kappa(21)}X_\alpha + P_{\kappa(22)}Y_\alpha + P_{\kappa(23)}Z_\alpha + P_{\kappa(24)}}{P_{\kappa(31)}X_\alpha + P_{\kappa(32)}Y_\alpha + P_{\kappa(33)}Z_\alpha + P_{\kappa(34)}}. \tag{6.69}$$

Here, f_0 is the scale constant we used in Eq. (6.49), and $P_{\kappa(ij)}$ are constants determined by the position, orientation, and internal parameters (e.g., the focal length, the principal point position, and the image distortion description) of the κth camera. We write the 3×4 matrix whose (i, j) element is $P_{\kappa(ij)}$ as $\boldsymbol{P}_\kappa$ and call it the *camera matrix* of the κth camera. From the geometry of perspective projection, we can write this in the form

$$\boldsymbol{P}_\kappa = \boldsymbol{K}_\kappa \boldsymbol{R}_\kappa^\top \begin{pmatrix} \boldsymbol{I} & -\boldsymbol{t}_\kappa \end{pmatrix}, \tag{6.70}$$

where $\boldsymbol{K}_\kappa$ is the 3×3 matrix, called the *intrinsic parameter matrix*, consisting of the internal parameters of the κth camera. The matrix $\boldsymbol{R}_\kappa$ specifies the rotation of the κth camera relative to the world coordinate system fixed to the scene, and $\boldsymbol{t}_\kappa$ is the position of the lens center of the κth camera. The principle of bundle adjustment is to minimize

$$E = \sum_{\alpha=1}^{N}\sum_{\kappa=1}^{M}\Big(\Big(\frac{x_{\alpha\kappa}}{f_0} - \frac{P_{\kappa(11)}X_\alpha + P_{\kappa(12)}Y_\alpha + P_{\kappa(13)}Z_\alpha + P_{\kappa(14)}}{P_{\kappa(31)}X_\alpha + P_{\kappa(32)}Y_\alpha + P_{\kappa(33)}Z_\alpha + P_{\kappa(34)}}\Big)^2$$
$$+\Big(\frac{y_{\alpha\kappa}}{f_0} - \frac{P_{\kappa(21)}X_\alpha + P_{\kappa(22)}Y_\alpha + P_{\kappa(23)}Z_\alpha + P_{\kappa(24)}}{P_{\kappa(31)}X_\alpha + P_{\kappa(32)}Y_\alpha + P_{\kappa(33)}Z_\alpha + P_{\kappa(34)}}\Big)^2\Big), \tag{6.71}$$

with respect to all the 3D positions $(X_\alpha, Y_\alpha, Z_\alpha)$ and all the camera matrices $\boldsymbol{P}_\kappa$ from observed $(x_{\alpha\kappa}, y_{\alpha\kappa})$, $\alpha = 1, ..., N$, $\kappa = 1, ..., M$, as the input so that Eq. (6.69) holds as accurately as possible. The expression E, called the *reprojection error*, measures the square sum of the discrepancies between the image positions predicted by the perspective projection geometry and their actually observed image positions.

Letting

$$
\begin{aligned}
p_{\alpha\kappa} &= P_{\kappa(11)}X_\alpha + P_{\kappa(12)}Y_\alpha + P_{\kappa(13)}Z_\alpha + P_{\kappa(14)},\\
q_{\alpha\kappa} &= P_{\kappa(21)}X_\alpha + P_{\kappa(22)}Y_\alpha + P_{\kappa(23)}Z_\alpha + P_{\kappa(24)},\\
r_{\alpha\kappa} &= P_{\kappa(31)}X_\alpha + P_{\kappa(32)}Y_\alpha + P_{\kappa(33)}Z_\alpha + P_{\kappa(34)},
\end{aligned}
\tag{6.72}
$$

we rewrite Eq. (6.71) in the form

$$
E = \sum_{\alpha=1}^{N}\sum_{\kappa=1}^{M}\Big(\Big(\frac{p_{\alpha\kappa}}{r_{\alpha\kappa}} - \frac{x_{\alpha\kappa}}{f_0}\Big)^2 + \Big(\frac{q_{\alpha\kappa}}{r_{\alpha\kappa}} - \frac{y_{\alpha\kappa}}{f_0}\Big)^2\Big). \tag{6.73}
$$

Using a single running index $k = 1, 2, \ldots$ for all the unknowns, i.e., all the 3D positions $(X_\alpha, Y_\alpha, Z_\alpha)$, $\alpha = 1, \ldots, N$, and all the camera matrices $\boldsymbol{P}_\kappa$, $\kappa = 1, \ldots, M$, we write all the unknowns as $\xi_1, \xi_2, \ldots$. The first derivative of the reprojection error E with respect to ξ_k is

$$
\begin{aligned}
\frac{\partial E}{\partial \xi_k} = \sum_{\alpha=1}^{N}\sum_{\kappa=1}^{M}\frac{2}{r_{\alpha\kappa}^2}\Big(&\Big(\frac{p_{\alpha\kappa}}{r_{\alpha\kappa}} - \frac{x_{\alpha\kappa}}{f_0}\Big)\Big(r_{\alpha\kappa}\frac{\partial p_{\alpha\kappa}}{\partial \xi_k} - p_{\alpha\kappa}\frac{\partial r_{\alpha\kappa}}{\partial \xi_k}\Big)\\
&+\Big(\frac{q_{\alpha\kappa}}{r_{\alpha\kappa}} - \frac{y_{\alpha\kappa}}{f_0}\Big)\Big(r_{\alpha\kappa}\frac{\partial q_{\alpha\kappa}}{\partial \xi_k} - q_{\alpha\kappa}\frac{\partial r_{\alpha\kappa}}{\partial \xi_k}\Big)\Big).
\end{aligned}
\tag{6.74}
$$

Next, we consider second derivatives. Noting that as Eq. (6.73) decreases in the course of iterations, we expect that $p_{\alpha\kappa}/r_{\alpha\kappa} - x_{\alpha\kappa}/f_0 \approx 0$, and $q_{\alpha\kappa}/r_{\alpha\kappa} - y_{\alpha\kappa}/f_0 \approx 0$. So, we adopt the Gauss–Newton approximation of ignoring them. Then, the second derivative of E is written as

$$
\begin{aligned}
\frac{\partial^2 E}{\partial \xi_k \partial \xi_l} = 2\sum_{\alpha=1}^{N}\sum_{\kappa=1}^{M}\frac{1}{r_{\alpha\kappa}^4}\Big(&\Big(r_{\alpha\kappa}\frac{\partial p_{\alpha\kappa}}{\partial \xi_k} - p_{\alpha\kappa}\frac{\partial r_{\alpha\kappa}}{\partial \xi_k}\Big)\Big(r_{\alpha\kappa}\frac{\partial p_{\alpha\kappa}}{\partial \xi_l} - p_{\alpha\kappa}\frac{\partial r_{\alpha\kappa}}{\partial \xi_l}\Big)\\
&+\Big(r_{\alpha\kappa}\frac{\partial q_{\alpha\kappa}}{\partial \xi_k} - q_{\alpha\kappa}\frac{\partial r_{\alpha\kappa}}{\partial \xi_k}\Big)\Big(r_{\alpha\kappa}\frac{\partial q_{\alpha\kappa}}{\partial \xi_l} - q_{\alpha\kappa}\frac{\partial r_{\alpha\kappa}}{\partial \xi_l}\Big)\Big).
\end{aligned}
\tag{6.75}
$$

As a result, for computing the first and second derivatives $\partial E/\partial \xi_k$ and $\partial^2 E/\partial \xi_k \partial \xi_l$ of E, *we only need to evaluate the first derivatives* $\partial p_{\alpha\kappa}/\partial \xi_k$, $\partial q_{\alpha\kappa}/\partial \xi_k$, *and* $\partial r_{\alpha\kappa}/\partial \xi_k$ *of* $p_{\alpha\kappa}$, $q_{\alpha\kappa}$, *and* $r_{\alpha\kappa}$.

Now, we apply the Lie algebra method to differentiation with respect to the rotation $\boldsymbol{R}_\kappa$ in Eq. (6.70); to other unknowns (the 3D positions $(X_\alpha, Y_\alpha, Z_\alpha)$, the camera positions $\boldsymbol{t}_\kappa$, and all the parameters contained in the intrinsic parameter matrix $\boldsymbol{K}_\kappa$), we can apply the usual chain rule straightforwardly.

The linear increment $\Delta \boldsymbol{P}_\kappa$ of Eq. (6.70) caused by a small change $\boldsymbol{A}(\boldsymbol{\omega}_\kappa)\boldsymbol{R}_\kappa$ of $\boldsymbol{R}_\kappa$ is written as

$$
\begin{aligned}
\Delta \boldsymbol{P}_\kappa &= \boldsymbol{K}_\kappa(\boldsymbol{A}(\Delta\boldsymbol{\omega}_\kappa)\boldsymbol{R}_\kappa)^\top\begin{pmatrix}\boldsymbol{I} & -\boldsymbol{t}_\kappa\end{pmatrix} = \boldsymbol{K}_\kappa\boldsymbol{R}_\kappa^\top\begin{pmatrix}\boldsymbol{A}(\boldsymbol{\omega}_\kappa)^\top & -\boldsymbol{A}(\boldsymbol{\omega}_\kappa)^\top\boldsymbol{t}_\kappa\end{pmatrix}\\
&= \boldsymbol{K}_\kappa\boldsymbol{R}_\kappa^\top\begin{pmatrix} 0 & \Delta\omega_{\kappa3} & -\Delta\omega_{\kappa2} & \Delta\omega_{\kappa2}t_{\kappa3} - \Delta\omega_{\kappa3}t_{\kappa2}\\ -\Delta\omega_{\kappa3} & 0 & \Delta\omega_{\kappa1} & \Delta\omega_{\kappa3}t_{\kappa1} - \Delta\omega_{\kappa1}t_{\kappa3}\\ \Delta\omega_{\kappa2} & -\Delta\omega_{\kappa1} & 0 & \Delta\omega_{\kappa1}t_{\kappa2} - \Delta\omega_{\kappa2}t_{\kappa1}\end{pmatrix},
\end{aligned}
\tag{6.76}
$$

where $\Delta\omega_{\kappa i}$ and $t_{\kappa i}$ are the ith components of $\Delta\boldsymbol{\omega}_\kappa$ and $\boldsymbol{t}_\kappa$, respectively. Rewriting the above equation in the form

$$
\Delta \boldsymbol{P}_\kappa = \frac{\partial \boldsymbol{P}_\kappa}{\partial \omega_{\kappa1}}\Delta\omega_{\kappa1} + \frac{\partial \boldsymbol{P}_\kappa}{\partial \omega_{\kappa2}}\Delta\omega_{\kappa2} + \frac{\partial \boldsymbol{P}_\kappa}{\partial \omega_{\kappa3}}\Delta\omega_{\kappa3}, \tag{6.77}
$$

we obtain the gradients $\partial \boldsymbol{P}_\kappa/\partial \omega_{\kappa 1}$, $\partial \boldsymbol{P}_\kappa/\partial \omega_{\kappa 2}$, and $\partial \boldsymbol{P}_\kappa/\partial \omega_{\kappa 3}$ of $\boldsymbol{P}_\kappa$ with respect to the small rotation vector $\Delta\boldsymbol{\omega}_\kappa$. Letting the components of the vector $\boldsymbol{\omega}_\kappa$ be included in the set of ξ_i, we obtain the first derivatives $\partial p_{\alpha\kappa}/\partial \xi_k$, $\partial q_{\alpha\kappa}/\partial \xi_k$, and $\partial r_{\alpha\kappa}/\partial \xi_k$ of Eq. (6.72) for the rotation. Note that the *value* of $\boldsymbol{\omega}_\kappa$ is not defined but its *differential* is defined. Using Eqs. (6.74) and (6.75), we can compute the first and second derivatives $\partial E/\partial \xi_k$ and $\partial^2 E/\partial \xi_k \partial \xi_l$ of the reprojection error E. The Levenberg–Marquardt bundle adjustment procedure has the following form.

1. Initialize the 3D positions $(X_\alpha, Y_\alpha, Z_\alpha)$ and the camera matrices $\boldsymbol{P}_\kappa$, and compute the associated reprojection error E. Let $c = 0.0001$.

2. Compute the first and second derivatives $\partial E/\partial \xi_k$ and $\partial^2 E/\partial \xi_k \partial \xi_l$ for all the unknowns.

3. Solve the following linear equation for $\Delta\xi_k$, $k = 1, 2, \ldots$:

$$\begin{pmatrix} \partial^2 E/\partial \xi_1^2 + c & \partial^2 E/\partial \xi_1 \partial \xi_2 & \partial^2 E/\partial \xi_1 \partial \xi_3 & \cdots \\ \partial^2 E/\partial \xi_2 \partial \xi_1 & \partial^2 E/\partial \xi_2^2 + c & \partial^2 E/\partial \xi_2 \partial \xi_3 & \cdots \\ \partial^2 E/\partial \xi_3 \partial \xi_1 & \partial^2 E/\partial \xi_3 \partial \xi_2 & \partial^2 E/\partial \xi_3^2 + c & \cdots \\ \vdots & \vdots & \vdots & \ddots \end{pmatrix} \begin{pmatrix} \Delta\xi_1 \\ \Delta\xi_2 \\ \Delta\xi_3 \\ \vdots \end{pmatrix} = - \begin{pmatrix} \partial E/\partial \xi_1 \\ \partial E/\partial \xi_2 \\ \partial E/\partial \xi_3 \\ \vdots \end{pmatrix}. \tag{6.78}$$

4. Tentatively update the unknowns ξ_k to $\tilde{\xi}_k = \xi_k + \Delta\xi_k$ *except the rotations* $\boldsymbol{R}_\kappa$, which are updated to $\tilde{\boldsymbol{R}}_\kappa = e^{\boldsymbol{A}(\Delta\boldsymbol{\omega}_\kappa)}\boldsymbol{R}_\kappa$.

5. Compute the corresponding reprojection error $\tilde{E}$. If $\tilde{E} > E$, let $c \leftarrow 10c$ and go back to Step 3.

6. Update the unknowns to $\xi_k \leftarrow \tilde{\xi}_k$. If $|\tilde{E} - E| \leq \delta$, then stop ($\delta$ is a small constant). Else, let $E \leftarrow \tilde{E}$ and $c \leftarrow c/10$ and go back to Step 2.

In usual numerical iterations, the variables are successively updated until they no longer change. However, the number of unknowns for bundle adjustment is thousands or even tens of thousands, so an impractically long computation time would be necessary if all variables were required to converge over significant digits. On the other hand, the purpose of bundle adjustment is to find a solution with a small reprojection error. So, it is a practical compromise to stop if the reprojection error almost ceases to decrease, as we describe in the above procedure.

6.9 SUPPLEMENTAL NOTES

As mentioned in Sec. 6.5, the set $SO(3)$ of 3D rotations, called the *special orthogonal group of dimension 3*, or simply the *group of rotations*, is a *group* in the sense that it is closed under composition and inverse, and at the same time a "surface," or a *manifold* to be precise, defined by equations of the nine elements of the 3×3 matrix in the 9D space. Namely, it is a *Lie group*. See Appendix C for the details of manifolds and Lie groups.

On the other hand, the *Lie algebra* of the group of rotations is a linear space spanned by generators of infinitesimal rotations equipped with the commutator product. Since a generator $\boldsymbol{A}$ is an antisymmetric matrix, it corresponds to a vector $\boldsymbol{\omega}$ one-to-one, and the commutator product corresponds to the vector product. Hence, the Lie algebra can be regarded as a set of vectors $\boldsymbol{\omega}$ that represent an infinitesimal rotation. From this viewpoint, it seems that we need not consider the commutator product at all. However, this is due to the specialty of three dimensions.

In general n dimensions, a "rotation" is defined by an orthogonal matrix of determinant 1. The corresponding Lie group is called the *special orthogonal group of dimension* n and denoted by $SO(n)$. Since Eqs. (6.1) and (6.2) hold in any dimensions, the generator $\boldsymbol{A}$ is an antisymmetric matrix. Except in 3 dimensions, however, it cannot be represented by an nD vector as in the form of Eq. (6.4), since an $n \times n$ antisymmetric matrix has $n(n-1)/2$ elements. Besides, the vector product is defined only in 3 dimensions. However, the commutator product can be defined in any dimensions, so we can define an n dimensional Lie algebra for which Eqs. (6.21) – (6.24) hold. This is not restricted to rotations; for groups of linear transformations in n dimensions, the associated Lie algebras are defined by introducing the commutator product to the linear space of their generators of infinitesimal transformations. See Appendix C for more about Lie groups and Lie algebras.

The importance of Lie algebras comes from the fact that almost all properties of Lie groups can be derived from the analysis of the associated Lie algebras. In 3 dimensions, however, the Lie groups and Lie algebras have very simple structures so that we need not much worry about them. An easy introduction to Lie groups and Lie algebras is found in [17]. The notation of Eq. (6.44) was introduced in [20] and frequently used in relation to optimization involving rotation [29, 35].

Lie algebras are used for formulating control of continuously changing poses, such as robot arms, using images [3, 9]. Recently, they are also used for *rotation averaging* [4, 12] to obtain a unique 3D reconstruction from images. If the pose is computed or measured for each object relative to other objects, the absolute pose depends, due to noise, on the path along which the computed relative poses are propagated. Hence, one needs to take an average of the differente poses resulting from different paths of composition. However, the average of rotation matrices is no longer a rotation matrix. Govindu [12] represented each rotation $\boldsymbol{R}$ by the rotation vector $\boldsymbol{\Omega}$ of Eq. (6.13) and averaged the resulting rotation vectors. Chatterjee and Govindu [4] optimized the computation so that the discrepancies of individual object poses are globally minimized, using Gauss-Newton iterations. This corresponds to the Lie algebra method described in this chapter. A similar averaging technique is used by Sakamoto and Kanatani [37] for seamlessly pasting images taken by rotating the camera over 360° to create an panoramic image. If we successively paste two consecutive images together, the initial image and the final image may not fit together due to error propagation, so the orientations of the camera must be optimized, which can be done by the Lie algebra method.

The fundamental matrix and the epipolar equation described in Sec. 6.7 are among the most fundamental concepts of computer vision for inferring 3D from images. The computation of the fundamental matrix from images and methods for 3D scene reconstruction from the computed fundamental matrix are discussed in many textbooks, including [15, 29].

The basic principle of fundamental matrix computation is to minimize a function that measures to what extent the epipolar equation is satisfied, such as the simple square sum, the Sampson error, and the reprojection error. To do this, we need to take into account the rank constraint, for which basically there are three approaches (Fig. 6.5). Detailed computational procedures for them are given in [29].

A posteriori correction We first do optimization without considering the rank constraint. Since an exact solution is obtained if there is no noise, the deviation from the rank constraint is small if the noise is small. Hence, we correct the computed solution $\boldsymbol{F}$ so that $|\boldsymbol{F}| = 0$ is satisfied a posteriori (Fig. 6.5(a)). The simplest method is to compute the singular value decomposition (SVD) of $\boldsymbol{F}$ and to replace the smallest singular value by 0, which is called the *SVD correction*. For higher accuracy, we

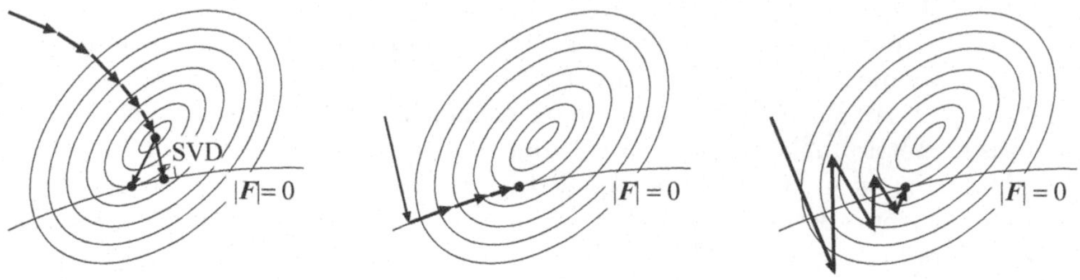

(a) A posteriori correction (b) Internal access (c) External access

FIGURE 6.5 (a) We go to the minimum of the objective function (its contours are shown in the figure) without considering the rank constraint. Then, we move to a nearby point on the hypersurface (shown as a curve in the figure) defined by $|\boldsymbol{F}| = 0$. For the SVD correction, we move perpendicularly to the hypersurface, while for the optimal correction we move in the direction in which the increase of the objective function is minimum. (b) We parameterize the hypersurface $|\boldsymbol{F}| = 0$ and search that hypersurface for the optimal parameter value. (c) We do iterations so that the objective function decreases in each step in such a way that the rank constraint is satisfied in the end.

analyze the statistical behavior of the solution in the presence of noise and impose the rank constraint in such away that the increase of the objective function is minimized, which is called the *optimal correction* [20]. The simple method of combining the least square solution mentioned at the end of Sec. 6.7 with the SVD correction is called *Hartley's 8-point method*[6] [13].

Internal access We parameterize the fundamental matrix $\boldsymbol{F}$ so that the rank constraint is identically satisfied and search that (internal) parameter space (Fig. 6.5(b)) . The method described in Sec. 6.7 belongs to this approach. The parameterization in terms of the singular value decomposition was proposed by Bartoli and Sturm [2], to which Sugaya and Kanatani [41] applied the Lie algebra method.

External access We do iterations in the (external) 9D space of the nine elements of the fundamental matrix $\boldsymbol{F}$ in such a way that the rank constraint is satisfied at the time of convergence and the objective function is guaranteed to be minimum. (Fig. 6.5(c)). As mentioned in Sec. 5.6, the basic idea was proposed by Chojnacki et al. [7] as *CFNS* (*Constrained Fundamental Numerical Scheme*) and improved by Kanatani and Sugaya [26] as *EFNS* (*Extended Fundamental Numerical Scheme*). This is based on the fact that $|\boldsymbol{F}| = 0$ is a homogeneous constraint of degree 3, and at each step of the FNS iterations the solution is projected to a direction in which the constraint is satisfied as mentioned in Sec. 5.5.

The fundamental matrix is determined by the intrinsic parameters of the two cameras and their relative pose. If the intrinsic parameters are known, it reduces to a matrix with a smaller degree of freedom, i.e., more constraints, called the *essential matrix*. The Lie algebra method can also be applied to its computation [43].

Bundle adjustment described in Sec. 6.8 is a process of adjusting the bundle of rays, or lines of sight, that start from the camera viewpoint, i.e., the lens center, and piece through

[6]The term "8-point" comes from the fact at least eight pairs of corresponding points are necessary.

the points we are viewing in such a way that the camera imaging geometry of perspective projection is satisfied. This term originates from photogrammetry for computing the 3D topography for map making from aerial photographs. Its origin dates back to the invention of photography and has been extensively studied mainly in Germany. Since the advent of computers in the second half of the 20th century, its algorithm has been produced by computer vision researchers. Today, various program codes are available on the Web. The best known is the *SBA* of Lourakis and Argyros [33]. Snavely et al. [39, 40] combined it with image correspondence extraction process and offered a tool called *bundler*. The procedure described in Sec. 6.8 is a modification of SBA for explicitly using the Lie algebra method for camera rotation optimization [29]; in most of currently available open software, the quaternion representation of rotations is used.

For actual implementation, many issues arise. One of them is the scale and orientation indeterminacy. This is a consequence of the fact that the world coordinate system can be arbitrarily defined and that imaging a small object by a nearby camera will produce the same image as imaging a large object by a faraway camera. To resolve this indeterminacy, we usually define the world coordinate system so that it coincides with the first camera frame and fix the scale so that the distance between the first and second cameras is unity. Normalization like this reduces the number of unknowns of Eq. (6.78). Also, all the points in the scene are not necessarily seen in all the images, so we must adjust the number of equations and unknowns of Eq. (6.78), accordingly.

Another issue is the computation time. Directly solving Eq. (6.78) would require hours or days of computation. One of the well known technique for reducing this is to separate the unknowns to the 3D point part and the camera matrix part; we solve for the unknowns of one part in terms of the unknowns of the other part and substitute the result into the remaining linear equations, which results in a smaller-size coefficient matrix known as the *Schur complement* [42]. The memory space is another issue; we need to retain all relevant information in the course of the iterations without writing all intermediate values in memory arrays, which might exhaust the memory resource. See [29] for implementation details and numerical examples using real image data.

6.10 EXERCISES

6.1. Consider a continuous rotation of angular velocity ω around axis $\boldsymbol{l}$ (unit vector). Show that if we let $\Omega = \omega t$ in the Rodrigues formula of Eq. (3.20) and differentiate it with respect to t, we see that at $t = 0$

$$\dot{\boldsymbol{R}} = \begin{pmatrix} 0 & -\omega l_3 & \omega l_2 \\ \omega l_3 & 0 & -\omega l_1 \\ -\omega l_2 & \omega l_1 & 0 \end{pmatrix}. \tag{6.79}$$

Show that Eq. (6.6) is obtained from this.

6.2. Show that the Jacobi identity of Eq. (6.22) holds.

6.3. Show that the Lie algebra basis $\{\boldsymbol{A}_1, \boldsymbol{A}_2, \boldsymbol{A}_3\}$ of Eq. (6.15) satisfies the relations of Eq. (6.23).

6.4. Prove the following vector triplet formulas:

$$\boldsymbol{a} \times (\boldsymbol{b} \times \boldsymbol{c}) = \langle \boldsymbol{a}, \boldsymbol{c} \rangle \boldsymbol{b} - \langle \boldsymbol{a}, \boldsymbol{b} \rangle \boldsymbol{c}, \qquad (\boldsymbol{a} \times \boldsymbol{b}) \times \boldsymbol{c} = \langle \boldsymbol{a}, \boldsymbol{c} \rangle \boldsymbol{b} - \langle \boldsymbol{b}, \boldsymbol{c} \rangle \boldsymbol{a}. \tag{6.80}$$

6.5. Show that Eq. (6.20) – (6.22) for the commutator $[\boldsymbol{A}, \boldsymbol{B}]$ holds if $[\boldsymbol{A}, \boldsymbol{B}]$ is replaced by the vector product $\boldsymbol{a} \times \boldsymbol{b}$.

6.6. Show the following identity for vector and inner products:

$$\langle \boldsymbol{a} \times \boldsymbol{b}, \boldsymbol{c} \rangle = \langle \boldsymbol{b} \times \boldsymbol{c}, \boldsymbol{a} \rangle = \langle \boldsymbol{c} \times \boldsymbol{a}, \boldsymbol{b} \rangle. \tag{6.81}$$

6.7. If we decompose an $n \times n$ matrix $\boldsymbol{A}$ into the sum $\boldsymbol{A} = \boldsymbol{A}^{(s)} + \boldsymbol{A}^{(a)}$ of a symmetric matrix $\boldsymbol{A}^{(s)}$ and an antisymmetric matrix $\boldsymbol{A}^{(a)}$ ($\hookrightarrow$ Exercise 4.7(1)), show that the following identity holds for an arbitrary nD vector $\boldsymbol{x}$:

$$\langle \boldsymbol{x}, \boldsymbol{A}\boldsymbol{x} \rangle = \langle \boldsymbol{x}, \boldsymbol{A}^\top \boldsymbol{x} \rangle = \langle \boldsymbol{x}, \boldsymbol{A}^{(s)} \boldsymbol{x} \rangle. \tag{6.82}$$

6.8. (1) Let $\boldsymbol{t}_1$, $\boldsymbol{t}_2$, and $\boldsymbol{t}_3$ be the three columns of matrix $\boldsymbol{T}$. Show that $\boldsymbol{\omega} \times \boldsymbol{T}$ is a matrix whose columns are the vector products of $\boldsymbol{\omega}$ and the vectors $\boldsymbol{t}_1$, $\boldsymbol{t}_2$, and $\boldsymbol{t}_3$, respectively, namely,

$$\boldsymbol{\omega} \times \begin{pmatrix} \boldsymbol{t}_1 & \boldsymbol{t}_2 & \boldsymbol{t}_3 \end{pmatrix} = \begin{pmatrix} \boldsymbol{\omega} \times \boldsymbol{t}_1 & \boldsymbol{\omega} \times \boldsymbol{t}_2 & \boldsymbol{\omega} \times \boldsymbol{t}_3 \end{pmatrix}. \tag{6.83}$$

(2) Let $\boldsymbol{t}_1^\top$, $\boldsymbol{t}_2^\top$, and $\boldsymbol{t}_3^\top$ be the three rows of $\boldsymbol{T}$. Show that $\boldsymbol{T} \times \boldsymbol{\omega}$ is a matrix whose rows are the vector product of $\boldsymbol{\omega}$ and the vectors $\boldsymbol{t}_1$, $\boldsymbol{t}_2$, and $\boldsymbol{t}_3$, respectively, namely,

$$\begin{pmatrix} \boldsymbol{t}_1^\top \\ \boldsymbol{t}_2^\top \\ \boldsymbol{t}_3^\top \end{pmatrix} \times \boldsymbol{\omega} = \begin{pmatrix} (\boldsymbol{\omega} \times \boldsymbol{t}_1)^\top \\ (\boldsymbol{\omega} \times \boldsymbol{t}_2)^\top \\ (\boldsymbol{\omega} \times \boldsymbol{t}_3)^\top \end{pmatrix}. \tag{6.84}$$

6.9. Show that the minimization of the reprojection error in the presence of noise

$$J = \frac{1}{2} \sum_{\alpha=1}^{N} (\Delta x_\alpha^2 + \Delta y_\alpha^2 + \Delta x_\alpha'^2 + \Delta y_\alpha'^2) \tag{6.85}$$

subject to the condition that the epipolar equation of Eq. (6.49) holds in the absence of noise reduces to the minimization of the Sampson error of Eq. (6.50) if higher order noise terms are ignored (the coefficient $1/2$ is merely formal with no particular meaning). Hint: Introduce Lagrange multipliers for Eq. (6.49).

6.10. By evaluating the covariance of the left side of Eq. (6.49) in the presence of noise in the coordinates of the corresponding points and by computing the likelihood, show that maximum likelihood estimation reduces to minimization of the Sampson error of Eq. (6.50) if higher order noise terms are ignored.

6.11. Show that the square norm $\|\boldsymbol{A}\|^2$ of an $n \times m$ matrix $\boldsymbol{A}$ is equal to the sum of the squares of its singular values.

CHAPTER 7

Reliability of Rotation Computation

This chapter deals with the problem of evaluating how much the rotation computed from sensor data is accurate. For this, we consider both experimental and theoretical evaluation. Experimental evaluation deals with the situation where a large number of values computed in similar circumstances or simulation results are obtained. In such a case, the standard approach is statistical analysis based on their sample means and sample variances. However, since a rotation is represented by a rotation matrix (an orthogonal matrix of determinant 1), evaluation of sample means and variances is not obvious, since the arithmetic average of rotation matrices is no longer a rotation matrix, as pointed out in Sec. 6.9. In order to resolve this issue, we define the sample means and sample covariance matrices in a consistent manner. For theoretical evaluation, on the other hand, we assume a probability distribution of noise in the input data and analyze the probability distribution of the deviations of the computed values from their true values. This is evaluated by the covariance matrix of the computation; the expectation of the deviation is usually 0. Here, we analyze the covariance matrix of maximum likelihood computation. Finally, we point out that there exists a theoretical accuracy bound on the covariance matrix, called the "KCR lower boud," whatever computational algorithms are used. We show that maximum likelihood computation achieves that bound up to high order noise terms.

7.1 ERROR EVALUATION FOR ROTATION

Consider again the problem of rotation estimation from sensor data. As in Sec. 5.2, let $\boldsymbol{a}_1$, ..., $\boldsymbol{a}_N$ and $\boldsymbol{a}'_1$, ..., $\boldsymbol{a}'_N$ be noisy observations of their respective true values $\bar{\boldsymbol{a}}_1$, ..., $\bar{\boldsymbol{a}}_N$ and $\bar{\boldsymbol{a}}'_1$, ..., $\bar{\boldsymbol{a}}'_N$, and write

$$\boldsymbol{a}_\alpha = \bar{\boldsymbol{a}}_\alpha + \Delta\boldsymbol{a}_\alpha, \qquad \boldsymbol{a}'_\alpha = \bar{\boldsymbol{a}}'_\alpha + \Delta\boldsymbol{a}'_\alpha, \qquad \alpha = 1, ..., N. \tag{7.1}$$

As before, we regard the noise terms $\Delta\boldsymbol{a}_\alpha$ and $\Delta\boldsymbol{a}'_\alpha$ as independent Gaussian variables of expectation $\mathbf{0}$ and covariance matrices $V[\boldsymbol{a}_\alpha] = \sigma^2 V_0[\boldsymbol{a}_\alpha]$ and $V[\boldsymbol{a}'_\alpha] = \sigma^2 V_0[\boldsymbol{a}'_\alpha]$, respectively, assuming that the true values $\bar{\boldsymbol{a}}_\alpha$ and $\bar{\boldsymbol{a}}'_\alpha$ satisfy

$$\bar{\boldsymbol{a}}'_\alpha = \boldsymbol{R}\bar{\boldsymbol{a}}_\alpha, \qquad \alpha = 1, ..., N, \tag{7.2}$$

for some rotation $\boldsymbol{R}$. Our task is to estimate $\boldsymbol{R}$ from noisy observations $\boldsymbol{a}_\alpha$ and $\boldsymbol{a}'_\alpha$, $\alpha = 1$, ..., N.

Suppose an estimate $\hat{\boldsymbol{R}}$ is obtained by some algorithm, e.g., the singular value decomposition method of Sec. 4.3 or the quaternion representation method of Sec. 4.4, both of which do not consider the data covariance matrices, or the quaternion-based FNS of Sec. 5.4, the EFNS of Sec. 5.5 using homogeneous constraints, or the Lie algebra method of Sec. 6.6, all of which take the data covariance matrices into consideration. Now, how can we tell how close the estimated $\hat{\boldsymbol{R}}$ is from the true rotation $\boldsymbol{R}$. A naive idea is to evaluate $\|\hat{\boldsymbol{R}} - \boldsymbol{R}\|$. However, if it is, say, $\|\hat{\boldsymbol{R}} - \boldsymbol{R}\| = 0.01$, not much useful information is obtained. This is because of the special nature of rotation operations.

If the problem is, on the other hand, to estimate translation $\boldsymbol{t}$, the analysis is straightforward. If another translation $\boldsymbol{t}'$ is added to $\boldsymbol{t}$, their composition is the "sum" $\boldsymbol{t}'' = \boldsymbol{t} + \boldsymbol{t}'$. Hence, it is reasonable to measure the deviation of $\boldsymbol{t}''$ from $\boldsymbol{t}$ by the "difference" $\boldsymbol{t}'' - \boldsymbol{t}$ $(= \boldsymbol{t}')$, which is the cause of the deviation of $\boldsymbol{t}$.

In contrast, if another rotation $\boldsymbol{R}'$ is added to $\boldsymbol{R}$, their composition is the "product" $\boldsymbol{R}''$ $= \boldsymbol{R}'\boldsymbol{R}$. Hence, it makes sense to measure the deviation of $\boldsymbol{R}''$ from $\boldsymbol{R}$ by the "quotient" $\boldsymbol{R}''\boldsymbol{R}^{-1}$ $(= \boldsymbol{R}')$, which is the cause of the deviation of $\boldsymbol{R}$.

From this consideration, it is appropriate to evaluate the deviation of $\hat{\boldsymbol{R}}$ from $\boldsymbol{R}$ by

$$\Delta\boldsymbol{R} = \hat{\boldsymbol{R}}\boldsymbol{R}^{-1} (= \hat{\boldsymbol{R}}\boldsymbol{R}^\top). \tag{7.3}$$

This is a rotation matrix that describes the rotation of $\hat{\boldsymbol{R}}$ relative to $\boldsymbol{R}$. Hence, it is a rotation around some axis $\boldsymbol{l}$ (unit vector) by some angle $\Delta\Omega$; $\boldsymbol{l}$ is the axis of deviation, and $\Delta\Omega$ is the deviation angle. The axis $\boldsymbol{l}$ and the angle $\Delta\Omega$ of $\Delta\boldsymbol{R}$ are computed by Eq. (3.22). Thus, if $\boldsymbol{l}$ and $\Delta\Omega$ are given, say $\Delta\Omega = 0.1°$, we can grasp the geometric meaning of the computation error. As pointed out in Sec. 6.3, the axis $\boldsymbol{l}$ and the angle $\Delta\Omega$ can be represented as a singl vector

$$\Delta\boldsymbol{\Omega} = \Delta\Omega\boldsymbol{l}. \tag{7.4}$$

We conclude that it is the most reasonable to evaluate the deviation of $\hat{\boldsymbol{R}}$ from $\boldsymbol{R}$ by this error vector $\Delta\boldsymbol{\Omega}$.

If the noise in the data is regarded as random variables as in Eq. (7.1), the rotation $\hat{\boldsymbol{R}}$ computed from the data is also a random variable and has a probability distribution. The statistical properties of the error vector $\Delta\boldsymbol{\Omega}$ are specified by its expectation and covariance matrix:

$$\boldsymbol{\mu}[\hat{\boldsymbol{R}}] = E[\Delta\boldsymbol{\Omega}], \qquad V[\hat{\boldsymbol{R}}] = E[\Delta\boldsymbol{\Omega}\Delta\boldsymbol{\Omega}^\top]. \tag{7.5}$$

The mean $\boldsymbol{\mu}[\hat{\boldsymbol{R}}]$ describes an average magnitude of the error and is called the *bias*. If $\boldsymbol{\mu}[\hat{\boldsymbol{R}}]$ $= \boldsymbol{0}$, the computation is expected to be correct on average. If $\boldsymbol{\mu}[\hat{\boldsymbol{R}}] \neq \boldsymbol{0}$, the solution is likely to deviate in a particular direction. The covariance matrix $V[\hat{\boldsymbol{R}}]$ describes the distribution of the axis of error rotation; the eigenvector for the largest eigenvalue is in the direction around which the deviation is the most likely to occur, and the corresponding eigenvalue equals the variance of the deviation angle.

Using these, we can evaluate the accuracy of the rotation estimation algorithm by simulated experiments: we artificially generate random values $\Delta\boldsymbol{a}_\alpha$ and $\Delta\boldsymbol{a}'_\alpha$ according to an assumed probability distribution and add them to the true values $\bar{\boldsymbol{a}}_\alpha$ and $\bar{\boldsymbol{a}}'_\alpha$. Let $\hat{\boldsymbol{R}}$ be the rotation obtained by some algorithm, e.g., the least squares, and let $\Delta\boldsymbol{\Omega}$ be its error vector. We repeat this N times, each time using different random noise. Let $\Delta\boldsymbol{\Omega}_1$, ..., $\Delta\boldsymbol{\Omega}_M$ be the resulting values. The bias and the covariance of the algorithm are experimentally evaluated by

$$\boldsymbol{\mu}[\hat{\boldsymbol{R}}] = \frac{1}{M}\sum_{k=1}^{M}\Delta\boldsymbol{\Omega}_k, \quad V[\hat{\boldsymbol{R}}] = \frac{1}{M}\sum_{k=1}^{M}(\Delta\boldsymbol{\Omega}_k - \boldsymbol{\mu}[\hat{\boldsymbol{R}}])(\Delta\boldsymbol{\Omega}_k - \boldsymbol{\mu}[\hat{\boldsymbol{R}}])^\top, \tag{7.6}$$

which describe the accuracy and the characteristics of that algorithm in quantitative terms.

7.2 ACCURACY OF MAXIMUM LIKELIHOOD

The discussion in the preceding section is an experimental evaluation. We now turn to theoretical evaluation. We take maximum likelihood estimation as an example and theoretically evaluate the accuracy of the solution. To be specific, we evaluate the deviation of the rotation $\hat{\boldsymbol{R}}$ that minimizes the function ($\hookrightarrow$ Eq. (5.11))

$$J(\boldsymbol{R}) = \frac{1}{2}\sum_{\alpha=1}^{N}\langle \boldsymbol{a}'_\alpha - \boldsymbol{R}\boldsymbol{a}_\alpha, \boldsymbol{W}_\alpha(\boldsymbol{a}'_\alpha - \boldsymbol{R}\boldsymbol{a}_\alpha)\rangle, \qquad \boldsymbol{W}_\alpha \equiv (\boldsymbol{R}V_0[\boldsymbol{a}_\alpha]\boldsymbol{R}^\top + V_0[\boldsymbol{a}'_\alpha])^{-1}, \quad (7.7)$$

from the true rotation $\bar{\boldsymbol{R}}$.

According to our assumption, the noise terms $\Delta\boldsymbol{a}_\alpha$ and $\Delta\boldsymbol{a}'_\alpha$ of Eq. (7.1) have expectation $\boldsymbol{0}$ and covariance matrices $\sigma^2V_0[\boldsymbol{a}_\alpha]$ and $\sigma^2V_0[\boldsymbol{a}'_\alpha]$. We assume that σ is sufficiently small so that the deviation of $\hat{\boldsymbol{R}}$ from $\bar{\boldsymbol{R}}$ is $O(\sigma)$. As discussed in the preceding chapter, we can write $\hat{\boldsymbol{R}}$ as

$$\hat{\boldsymbol{R}} = \bar{\boldsymbol{R}} + \Delta\boldsymbol{\omega}\times\bar{\boldsymbol{R}} + O(\sigma^2) \quad (7.8)$$

for some vector $\Delta\boldsymbol{\omega}$, where and hereafter we use the notation of Eq. (6.44). Note that $\Delta\boldsymbol{\omega}$ is $O(\sigma)$. Substituting Eqs. (7.1) and (7.8) into Eq. (7.7) and noting that $\bar{\boldsymbol{a}}'_\alpha = \bar{\boldsymbol{R}}\bar{\boldsymbol{a}}_\alpha$, we obtain

$$J(\boldsymbol{R}) = \frac{1}{2}\sum_{\alpha=1}^{N}\langle \Delta\boldsymbol{a}'_\alpha - \bar{\boldsymbol{R}}\Delta\boldsymbol{a}_\alpha - \Delta\boldsymbol{\omega}\times\bar{\boldsymbol{R}}\bar{\boldsymbol{a}}_\alpha, \bar{\boldsymbol{W}}_\alpha(\Delta\boldsymbol{a}'_\alpha - \bar{\boldsymbol{R}}\Delta\boldsymbol{a}_\alpha - \Delta\boldsymbol{\omega}\times\bar{\boldsymbol{R}}\bar{\boldsymbol{a}}_\alpha)\rangle + O(\sigma^3), \quad (7.9)$$

where $\bar{\boldsymbol{W}}_\alpha$ is the true value of $\boldsymbol{W}_\alpha$, i.e., the value for $\bar{\boldsymbol{R}}$. Here, we do not consider the error of $\boldsymbol{W}_\alpha$ because it is multiplied by a quantity of $O(\sigma^2)$ so that the error of $\boldsymbol{W}_\alpha$, which is of $O(\sigma)$, is absorbed in the last term of $O(\sigma^3)$. We can rewrite Eq. (7.9) in the following form:

$$\begin{aligned}
J(\boldsymbol{R}) &= \frac{1}{2}\sum_{\alpha=1}^{N}\Big(\langle \Delta\boldsymbol{a}'_\alpha - \bar{\boldsymbol{R}}\Delta\boldsymbol{a}_\alpha, \bar{\boldsymbol{W}}_\alpha(\Delta\boldsymbol{a}'_\alpha - \bar{\boldsymbol{R}}\Delta\boldsymbol{a}_\alpha)\rangle - \langle \Delta\boldsymbol{a}'_\alpha - \bar{\boldsymbol{R}}\Delta\boldsymbol{a}_\alpha, \bar{\boldsymbol{W}}_\alpha\Delta\boldsymbol{\omega}\times\bar{\boldsymbol{R}}\bar{\boldsymbol{a}}_\alpha\rangle \\
&\quad -\langle \Delta\boldsymbol{\omega}\times\bar{\boldsymbol{R}}\bar{\boldsymbol{a}}_\alpha, \bar{\boldsymbol{W}}_\alpha(\Delta\boldsymbol{a}'_\alpha - \bar{\boldsymbol{R}}\Delta\boldsymbol{a}_\alpha)\rangle + \langle \Delta\boldsymbol{\omega}\times\bar{\boldsymbol{R}}\bar{\boldsymbol{a}}_\alpha, \bar{\boldsymbol{W}}_\alpha\Delta\boldsymbol{\omega}\times\bar{\boldsymbol{R}}\bar{\boldsymbol{a}}_\alpha\rangle\Big) + O(\sigma^3) \\
&= \frac{1}{2}\sum_{\alpha=1}^{N}\langle \Delta\boldsymbol{a}'_\alpha - \bar{\boldsymbol{R}}\Delta\boldsymbol{a}_\alpha, \bar{\boldsymbol{W}}_\alpha(\Delta\boldsymbol{a}'_\alpha - \bar{\boldsymbol{R}}\Delta\boldsymbol{a}_\alpha)\rangle \\
&\quad -\sum_{\alpha=1}^{N}\langle \Delta\boldsymbol{\omega}\times\bar{\boldsymbol{R}}\bar{\boldsymbol{a}}_\alpha, \bar{\boldsymbol{W}}_\alpha(\Delta\boldsymbol{a}'_\alpha - \bar{\boldsymbol{R}}\Delta\boldsymbol{a}_\alpha)\rangle \\
&\quad +\frac{1}{2}\sum_{\alpha=1}^{N}\langle \Delta\boldsymbol{\omega}\times\bar{\boldsymbol{R}}\bar{\boldsymbol{a}}_\alpha, \bar{\boldsymbol{W}}_\alpha(\bar{\boldsymbol{R}}\bar{\boldsymbol{a}}_\alpha)\times\Delta\boldsymbol{\omega}\rangle\Big) + O(\sigma^3) \\
&= \frac{1}{2}\sum_{\alpha=1}^{N}\langle \Delta\boldsymbol{a}'_\alpha - \bar{\boldsymbol{R}}\Delta\boldsymbol{a}_\alpha, \bar{\boldsymbol{W}}_\alpha(\Delta\boldsymbol{a}'_\alpha - \bar{\boldsymbol{R}}\Delta\boldsymbol{a}_\alpha)\rangle \\
&\quad -\sum_{\alpha=1}^{N}\langle \Delta\boldsymbol{\omega}, (\bar{\boldsymbol{R}}\bar{\boldsymbol{a}}_\alpha)\times\bar{\boldsymbol{W}}_\alpha(\Delta\boldsymbol{a}'_\alpha - \bar{\boldsymbol{R}}\Delta\boldsymbol{a}_\alpha)\rangle \\
&\quad +\frac{1}{2}\sum_{\alpha=1}^{N}\langle \Delta\boldsymbol{\omega}, (\bar{\boldsymbol{R}}\bar{\boldsymbol{a}}_\alpha)\times\bar{\boldsymbol{W}}_\alpha\times(\bar{\boldsymbol{R}}\bar{\boldsymbol{a}}_\alpha)\Delta\boldsymbol{\omega}\rangle + O(\sigma^3).
\end{aligned} \quad (7.10)$$

Differentiating this with respect to $\Delta\omega$, we obtain

$$\nabla_{\Delta\omega}J = -\sum_{\alpha=1}^{N}(\bar{\boldsymbol{R}}\bar{\boldsymbol{a}}_\alpha)\times\bar{\boldsymbol{W}}_\alpha(\Delta\boldsymbol{a}'_\alpha-\bar{\boldsymbol{R}}\Delta\boldsymbol{a}_\alpha)+\sum_{\alpha=1}^{N}(\bar{\boldsymbol{R}}\bar{\boldsymbol{a}}_\alpha)\times\bar{\boldsymbol{W}}_\alpha\times(\bar{\boldsymbol{R}}\bar{\boldsymbol{a}}_\alpha)\Delta\boldsymbol{\omega}+O(\sigma^3). \quad (7.11)$$

For $\boldsymbol{R} = \hat{\boldsymbol{R}}$ that minimizes $J(\boldsymbol{R})$, this is $\boldsymbol{0}$:

$$\sum_{\alpha=1}^{N}(\bar{\boldsymbol{R}}\bar{\boldsymbol{a}}_\alpha)\times\bar{\boldsymbol{W}}_\alpha\times(\bar{\boldsymbol{R}}\bar{\boldsymbol{a}}_\alpha)\Delta\boldsymbol{\omega} = \sum_{\alpha=1}^{N}(\bar{\boldsymbol{R}}\bar{\boldsymbol{a}}_\alpha)\times\bar{\boldsymbol{W}}_\alpha(\Delta\boldsymbol{a}'_\alpha-\bar{\boldsymbol{R}}\Delta\boldsymbol{a}_\alpha)+O(\sigma^3). \quad (7.12)$$

Multiplying both sides by their respective transpose, we obtain

$$\begin{aligned}
&\Big(\sum_{\alpha=1}^{N}(\bar{\boldsymbol{R}}\bar{\boldsymbol{a}}_\alpha)\times\bar{\boldsymbol{W}}_\alpha\times(\bar{\boldsymbol{R}}\bar{\boldsymbol{a}}_\alpha)\Big)\Delta\boldsymbol{\omega}\Delta\boldsymbol{\omega}^\top\Big(\sum_{\beta=1}^{N}(\bar{\boldsymbol{R}}\bar{\boldsymbol{a}}_\beta)\times\bar{\boldsymbol{W}}_\beta\times(\bar{\boldsymbol{R}}\bar{\boldsymbol{a}}_\beta)\Big)\\
&=\sum_{\alpha,\beta=1}^{N}(\bar{\boldsymbol{R}}\bar{\boldsymbol{a}}_\alpha)\times\bar{\boldsymbol{W}}_\alpha(\Delta\boldsymbol{a}'_\alpha-\bar{\boldsymbol{R}}\Delta\boldsymbol{a}_\alpha)(\Delta\boldsymbol{a}'_\beta-\bar{\boldsymbol{R}}\Delta\boldsymbol{a}_\beta)^\top\bar{\boldsymbol{W}}_\beta^\top\boldsymbol{A}(\bar{\boldsymbol{R}}\bar{\boldsymbol{a}}_\beta)^\top+O(\sigma^3)\\
&=\sum_{\alpha,\beta=1}^{N}(\bar{\boldsymbol{R}}\bar{\boldsymbol{a}}_\alpha)\times\bar{\boldsymbol{W}}_\alpha(\Delta\boldsymbol{a}'_\alpha-\bar{\boldsymbol{R}}\Delta\boldsymbol{a}_\alpha)(\Delta\boldsymbol{a}'_\beta-\bar{\boldsymbol{R}}\Delta\boldsymbol{a}_\beta)^\top\bar{\boldsymbol{W}}_\beta\times(\bar{\boldsymbol{R}}\bar{\boldsymbol{a}}_\beta)+O(\sigma^3),
\end{aligned} \quad (7.13)$$

where we have noted that $\bar{\boldsymbol{W}}_\beta$ is a symmetric matrix and used the notation of Eq. (6.44). Evaluating expectation on both sides, we obtain

$$\begin{aligned}
&\Big(\sum_{\alpha=1}^{N}\bar{\boldsymbol{R}}\bar{\boldsymbol{a}}_\alpha\times\bar{\boldsymbol{W}}_\alpha\times(\bar{\boldsymbol{R}}\bar{\boldsymbol{a}}_\alpha)\Big)E[\Delta\boldsymbol{\omega}\Delta\boldsymbol{\omega}^\top]\Big(\sum_{\beta=1}^{N}\bar{\boldsymbol{R}}\bar{\boldsymbol{a}}_\beta\times\bar{\boldsymbol{W}}_\beta\times(\bar{\boldsymbol{R}}\bar{\boldsymbol{a}}_\beta)\Big)\\
&=\sum_{\alpha,\beta=1}^{N}(\bar{\boldsymbol{R}}\bar{\boldsymbol{a}}_\alpha)\times\bar{\boldsymbol{W}}_\alpha E[(\Delta\boldsymbol{a}'_\alpha-\bar{\boldsymbol{R}}\Delta\boldsymbol{a}_\alpha)(\Delta\boldsymbol{a}'_\beta-\bar{\boldsymbol{R}}\Delta\boldsymbol{a}_\beta)^\top]\bar{\boldsymbol{W}}_\beta\times(\bar{\boldsymbol{R}}\bar{\boldsymbol{a}}_\beta)+O(\sigma^4),
\end{aligned} \quad (7.14)$$

where we have noted that expectation of terms of $O(\sigma^3)$ is 0 due to the symmetry of the noise distribution. Since $\Delta\boldsymbol{\omega} = O(\sigma)$ and since expectation of $O(\sigma^3)$ is 0, the covariance matrix $V[\hat{\boldsymbol{R}}]$ defined by Eq. (7.5) is written from Eq. (7.8) as

$$V[\hat{\boldsymbol{R}}] = E[\Delta\boldsymbol{\omega}\Delta\boldsymbol{\omega}^\top]+O(\sigma^4). \quad (7.15)$$

On the other hand, $\Delta\boldsymbol{a}_\alpha$ and $\Delta\boldsymbol{a}'_\alpha$ are independent for different α, so we see from Eq. (5.16) that

$$E[(\Delta\boldsymbol{a}'_\alpha-\bar{\boldsymbol{R}}\Delta\boldsymbol{a}_\alpha)(\Delta\boldsymbol{a}'_\beta-\bar{\boldsymbol{R}}\Delta\boldsymbol{a}_\beta)^\top] = \sigma^2\delta_{\alpha\beta}\bar{\boldsymbol{V}}_\alpha, \quad (7.16)$$

where $\bar{\boldsymbol{V}}_\alpha$ is the value of Eq. (5.12) with $\boldsymbol{R}$ replaced by $\bar{\boldsymbol{R}}$. Substituting the above expression into Eq. (7.14) and writing

$$\bar{\boldsymbol{H}} = \sum_{\alpha=1}^{N}(\bar{\boldsymbol{R}}\bar{\boldsymbol{a}}_\alpha)\times\bar{\boldsymbol{W}}_\alpha\times(\bar{\boldsymbol{R}}\bar{\boldsymbol{a}}_\alpha), \quad (7.17)$$

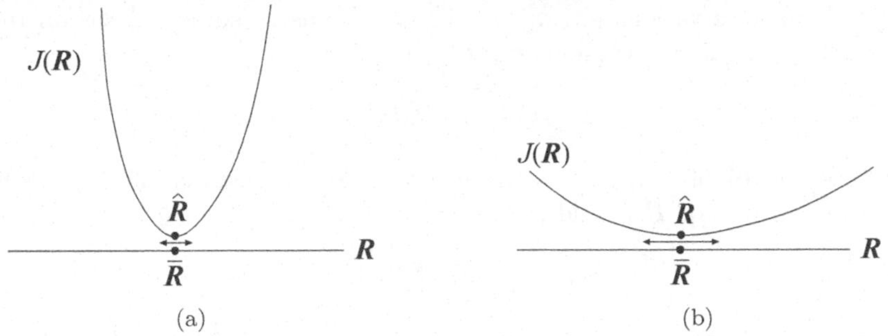

FIGURE 7.1 (a) If the Hessian $\bar{\boldsymbol{H}}$ of the function $J(\boldsymbol{R})$ is large, the position of its minimum has high certainty. (b) If it is small, the minimum position is susceptible to noise and becomes uncertain.

as in Eq. (6.46), we obtain

$$\begin{aligned}\bar{\boldsymbol{H}}V[\hat{\boldsymbol{R}}]\bar{\boldsymbol{H}} &= \sigma^2\sum_{\alpha=1}^{N}(\bar{\boldsymbol{R}}\bar{\boldsymbol{a}}_\alpha)\times\bar{\boldsymbol{W}}_\alpha\bar{\boldsymbol{V}}_\alpha\bar{\boldsymbol{W}}_\alpha\times(\bar{\boldsymbol{R}}\bar{\boldsymbol{a}}_\alpha)+O(\sigma^4)\\ &= \sigma^2\sum_{\alpha=1}^{N}(\bar{\boldsymbol{R}}\bar{\boldsymbol{a}}_\alpha)\times\bar{\boldsymbol{W}}_\alpha\times(\bar{\boldsymbol{R}}\bar{\boldsymbol{a}}_\alpha)+O(\sigma^4)\\ &= \sigma^2\bar{\boldsymbol{H}}+O(\sigma^4),\end{aligned}\tag{7.18}$$

where we have noted that Eq. (5.13) implies $\bar{\boldsymbol{W}}_\alpha\bar{\boldsymbol{V}}_\alpha\bar{\boldsymbol{W}}_\alpha=\bar{\boldsymbol{W}}_\alpha$. Multiplying Eq. (7.18) by $\bar{\boldsymbol{H}}^{-1}$ from left and right, we can express $V[\hat{\boldsymbol{R}}]$ in the form

$$V[\hat{\boldsymbol{R}}]=\sigma^2\bar{\boldsymbol{H}}^{-1}+O(\sigma^4).\tag{7.19}$$

This result can be given the following interpretation. As seen from Eq. (7.10), $\langle\Delta\boldsymbol{\omega},\bar{\boldsymbol{H}}\Delta\boldsymbol{\omega}\rangle$ is the second order term in $\Delta\boldsymbol{\omega}$ in the expansion of the function $J(\boldsymbol{R})$ of Eq. (7.7) in the neighborhood of $\bar{\boldsymbol{R}}$. Namely, $\bar{\boldsymbol{H}}$ is the Hessian of the expansion. Equation (7.19) states that the covariance matrix $V[\hat{\boldsymbol{R}}]$ that specifies the uncertainty of the solution $\hat{\boldsymbol{R}}$ is, except for high order noise terms, proportional to $\bar{\boldsymbol{H}}^{-1}$.

If we imagine a "graph" of the function $J(\boldsymbol{R})$, the Hessian $\bar{\boldsymbol{H}}$ describes the "curvature" of the graph. Equation (7.19) means that as the curvature becomes larger, i.e., the "valley" of the graph is deeper, the true value is closer to its bottom (Fig. 7.1(a)). Conversely, as the curvature specified by the Hessian $\bar{\boldsymbol{H}}$ is smaller, the graph spreads flatter and the true value is more susceptible to noise and more likely to deviate. (Fig. 7.1(b)). This observation is not limited to maximum likelihood estimation; this generally applies when parameter estimation is reduced to minimization of some function.

If we use the Lie algebra method of Sec. 6.6 for maximum likelihood estimation, the Hessian of Eq. (6.46) is evaluated in each iteration step. When the iterations have converged, we obtain not only the maximum likelihood estimate $\hat{\boldsymbol{R}}$ but as a byproduct also the covariance matrix $V[\hat{\boldsymbol{R}}]\approx\sigma^2\boldsymbol{H}^{-1}$ that describes its reliability. This is one of the merits of using the iteration scheme of Sec. 6.6.

7.3 THEORETICAL ACCURACY BOUND

We now show that there exists a theoretical lower bound on the covariance matrix, which we cannot fall below whatever algorithm is used for the computation. Let $\hat{\boldsymbol{R}}$ be a rotation estimated from observations $\boldsymbol{a}_\alpha$, $\boldsymbol{a}'_\alpha$, $\alpha = 1, ..., N$, using some algorithm. In other words, $\hat{\boldsymbol{R}}$ is a function of the observations $\boldsymbol{a}_\alpha$, $\boldsymbol{a}'_\alpha$, $\alpha = 1, ..., N$:

$$\hat{\boldsymbol{R}} = \hat{\boldsymbol{R}}(\boldsymbol{a}_1, ..., \boldsymbol{a}_N, \boldsymbol{a}'_1, ..., \boldsymbol{a}'_N). \tag{7.20}$$

Such a function of observations is generally called an *estimator*. We assume that it is *unbiased*. An estimator $\hat{\boldsymbol{R}}$ is said to be unbiased if

$$E[\hat{\boldsymbol{R}}] = \bar{\boldsymbol{R}}. \tag{7.21}$$

This means that even though individual results may vary, the estimation is correct "on average." Such an estimator is called an *unbiased estimator*.

In Eq. (7.21), $E[\,\cdot\,]$ denotes expectation with respect to an assumed probability distribution. Here, we must be careful about the probability distribution of the observations $\boldsymbol{a}_\alpha$, $\boldsymbol{a}'_\alpha$, $\alpha = 1, ..., N$. From the assumption of Eq. (7.1), the probability density of $\boldsymbol{a}_\alpha$ and $\boldsymbol{a}'_\alpha$ has the form

$$\begin{aligned} p_\alpha(\boldsymbol{a}_\alpha, \boldsymbol{a}'_\alpha) &= \frac{e^{-\langle \boldsymbol{a}_\alpha - \bar{\boldsymbol{a}}_\alpha, V_0[\boldsymbol{a}_\alpha]^{-1}(\boldsymbol{a}_\alpha - \bar{\boldsymbol{a}}_\alpha)\rangle/2\sigma^2}}{\sigma^3\sqrt{(2\pi)^3|V_0[\boldsymbol{a}_\alpha]|}} \frac{e^{-\langle \boldsymbol{a}'_\alpha - \bar{\boldsymbol{a}}'_\alpha, V_0[\boldsymbol{a}'_\alpha]^{-1}(\boldsymbol{a}'_\alpha - \bar{\boldsymbol{a}}'_\alpha)\rangle/2\sigma^2}}{\sigma^3\sqrt{(2\pi)^3|V_0[\boldsymbol{a}'_\alpha]|}} \\ &= \frac{e^{-(\langle \boldsymbol{a}_\alpha - \bar{\boldsymbol{a}}_\alpha, V_0[\boldsymbol{a}_\alpha]^{-1}(\boldsymbol{a}_\alpha - \bar{\boldsymbol{a}}_\alpha)\rangle + \langle \boldsymbol{a}'_\alpha - \bar{\boldsymbol{a}}'_\alpha, V_0[\boldsymbol{a}'_\alpha]^{-1}(\boldsymbol{a}'_\alpha - \bar{\boldsymbol{a}}'_\alpha)\rangle)/2\sigma^2}}{\sigma^6(2\pi)^3\sqrt{|V_0[\boldsymbol{a}_\alpha]||V_0[\boldsymbol{a}'_\alpha]|}}, \end{aligned} \tag{7.22}$$

which is parameterized by $\bar{\boldsymbol{a}}_\alpha$ and $\bar{\boldsymbol{a}}'_\alpha$. However, we are assuming that they are constrained to be $\bar{\boldsymbol{a}}'_\alpha = \bar{\boldsymbol{R}}\bar{\boldsymbol{a}}_\alpha$ as in Eq. (7.2). In other words, $\bar{\boldsymbol{R}}$ is also an indirect parameter of the distribution. Strictly speaking, therefore, Eq. (7.22) should be written as $p_\alpha = p_\alpha(\boldsymbol{a}_\alpha, \boldsymbol{a}'_\alpha | \bar{\boldsymbol{a}}_\alpha, \bar{\boldsymbol{a}}'_\alpha, \bar{\boldsymbol{R}})$. Since we are assuming that the noise is independent for each α, the probability density of $\boldsymbol{a}_\alpha$ and $\boldsymbol{a}'_\alpha$, $\alpha = 1, ..., N$, equals $p_1 \cdots p_N$, which is parameterized by $\bar{\boldsymbol{a}}_\alpha$, $\bar{\boldsymbol{a}}'_\alpha$, $\alpha = 1, ..., N$, and $\bar{\boldsymbol{R}}$.

The statement that $\hat{\boldsymbol{R}}$ is an unbiased estimator is a property of the "algorithm" for estimation computation, not of particular parameter values. In other words, the unbiasedness property

$$E[\hat{\boldsymbol{R}} - \bar{\boldsymbol{R}}] = \boldsymbol{O} \tag{7.23}$$

is an "identity" in all the parameters $\bar{\boldsymbol{a}}_1, ..., \bar{\boldsymbol{a}}_N, \bar{\boldsymbol{a}}'_1, ..., \bar{\boldsymbol{a}}'_N$, and $\bar{\boldsymbol{R}}$ that satisfy $\bar{\boldsymbol{a}}'_\alpha = \bar{\boldsymbol{R}}\bar{\boldsymbol{a}}_\alpha$. We can write Eq. (7.23) as

$$\int (\hat{\boldsymbol{R}} - \bar{\boldsymbol{R}}) p_1 \cdots p_N d\boldsymbol{a} = \boldsymbol{O}, \tag{7.24}$$

where $\int (...) d\boldsymbol{a}$ is an abbreviation of $\int \cdots \int (...) d\boldsymbol{a}_1 d\boldsymbol{a}'_1 \cdots d\boldsymbol{a}_N d\boldsymbol{a}'_N$. Since Eq. (7.24) is an identity in $\bar{\boldsymbol{a}}_\alpha$, $\bar{\boldsymbol{a}}'_\alpha$, and $\bar{\boldsymbol{R}}$ that satisfy $\bar{\boldsymbol{a}}'_\alpha = \bar{\boldsymbol{R}}\bar{\boldsymbol{a}}_\alpha$, its variation is 0 for arbitrary infinitesimal variations $\bar{\boldsymbol{a}}_\alpha \to \bar{\boldsymbol{a}}_\alpha + \delta\bar{\boldsymbol{a}}_\alpha$ and $\bar{\boldsymbol{a}}'_\alpha \to \bar{\boldsymbol{a}}'_\alpha + \delta\bar{\boldsymbol{a}}'_\alpha$ that preserve $\bar{\boldsymbol{a}}'_\alpha = \bar{\boldsymbol{R}}\bar{\boldsymbol{a}}_\alpha$, where by "infinitesimal variations" we mean considering "linear" variations by ignoring higher order terms in the expansion as stated in Sec. 6.4. The property that something does not change for infinitesimal variations is called a *variational principle*. Hereafter, we call an infinitesimal variation simply a *variation*.

As pointed out in Sec. 6.5, the variation $\delta\bar{\boldsymbol{R}}$ of a rotation matrix $\bar{\boldsymbol{R}}$ is written as $\delta\boldsymbol{\omega} \times \bar{\boldsymbol{R}}$ for some infinitesimal vector $\delta\boldsymbol{\omega}$, where we are using the notation of Eq. (6.44). Hence, the variation of $\bar{\boldsymbol{a}}'_\alpha = \bar{\boldsymbol{R}}\bar{\boldsymbol{a}}_\alpha$ on both sides is

$$\delta\bar{\boldsymbol{a}}'_\alpha = \bar{\boldsymbol{R}}\delta\bar{\boldsymbol{a}}_\alpha + \delta\boldsymbol{\omega} \times \bar{\boldsymbol{R}}\bar{\boldsymbol{a}}_\alpha. \tag{7.25}$$

For variations that satisfy this, the variation of the left side of Eq. (7.24) is

$$\delta\int(\hat{\boldsymbol{R}}-\bar{\boldsymbol{R}})p_1\cdots p_N d\boldsymbol{a}=\int(-\delta\bar{\boldsymbol{R}})p_1\cdots p_N d\bar{\boldsymbol{a}}+\sum_{\alpha=1}^{N}\int(\hat{\boldsymbol{R}}-\bar{\boldsymbol{R}})p_1\cdots\delta p_\alpha\cdots p_N d\bar{\boldsymbol{a}}$$
$$=-\delta\bar{\boldsymbol{R}}+\int(\hat{\boldsymbol{R}}-\bar{\boldsymbol{R}})\sum_{\alpha=1}^{N}p_1\cdots\delta p_\alpha\cdots p_N d\bar{\boldsymbol{a}}. \tag{7.26}$$

Note that the estimator $\hat{\boldsymbol{R}}$ is a function of "observations" $\boldsymbol{a}_1,\ldots,\boldsymbol{a}_N$ and $\boldsymbol{a}'_1,\ldots,\boldsymbol{a}'_N$, so its variation is $\delta\hat{\boldsymbol{R}}=\boldsymbol{O}$ for the variations of the "true values" $\bar{\boldsymbol{a}}_1,\ldots\bar{\boldsymbol{a}}_N$, $\bar{\boldsymbol{a}}'_1,\ldots\bar{\boldsymbol{a}}'_N$, and $\bar{\boldsymbol{R}}$. Also note that $\int p_1\cdots p_N d\bar{\boldsymbol{a}}=1$.

The variation of p_α of Eq. (7.22) is written as

$$\delta p_\alpha=p_\alpha\delta\log p_\alpha=p_\alpha(\langle\nabla_{\bar{\boldsymbol{a}}_\alpha}\log p_\alpha,\delta\bar{\boldsymbol{a}}_\alpha\rangle+\langle\nabla_{\bar{\boldsymbol{a}}'_\alpha}\log p_\alpha,\delta\bar{\boldsymbol{a}}'_\alpha\rangle)$$
$$=(\langle\boldsymbol{l}_\alpha,\delta\bar{\boldsymbol{a}}_\alpha\rangle+\langle\boldsymbol{l}'_\alpha,\delta\bar{\boldsymbol{a}}'_\alpha\rangle)p_\alpha, \tag{7.27}$$

where we define $\boldsymbol{l}_\alpha$ and $\boldsymbol{l}'_\alpha$ by[1]

$$\boldsymbol{l}_\alpha\equiv\nabla_{\bar{\boldsymbol{a}}_\alpha}\log p_\alpha,\qquad \boldsymbol{l}'_\alpha\equiv\nabla_{\bar{\boldsymbol{a}}'_\alpha}\log p_\alpha. \tag{7.28}$$

Hence, Eq. (7.26) is rewritten as

$$\delta\bar{\boldsymbol{R}}=\int(\hat{\boldsymbol{R}}-\bar{\boldsymbol{R}})\sum_{\alpha=1}^{N}(\langle\boldsymbol{l}_\alpha,\delta\bar{\boldsymbol{a}}_\alpha\rangle+\langle\boldsymbol{l}'_\alpha,\delta\bar{\boldsymbol{a}}'_\alpha\rangle)p_1\cdots p_N d\bar{\boldsymbol{a}}$$
$$=E[(\hat{\boldsymbol{R}}-\bar{\boldsymbol{R}})\sum_{\alpha=1}^{N}(\langle\boldsymbol{l}_\alpha,\delta\bar{\boldsymbol{a}}_\alpha\rangle+\langle\boldsymbol{l}'_\alpha,\delta\bar{\boldsymbol{a}}'_\alpha\rangle)]. \tag{7.29}$$

Since $\hat{\boldsymbol{R}}-\bar{\boldsymbol{R}}$ $(=O(\sigma))$ is a small rotation, Eq. (7.8) implies that we can write this as $\Delta\boldsymbol{\omega}\times\bar{\boldsymbol{R}}+O(\sigma^2)$ for some error vector $\Delta\boldsymbol{\omega}$ $(=O(\sigma))$. Hence, Eq. (7.29) is written as

$$\delta\boldsymbol{\omega}\times\bar{\boldsymbol{R}}=E[(\Delta\boldsymbol{\omega}\times\bar{\boldsymbol{R}}+O(\sigma^2))\sum_{\alpha=1}^{N}(\langle\boldsymbol{l}_\alpha,\delta\bar{\boldsymbol{a}}_\alpha\rangle+\langle\boldsymbol{l}'_\alpha,\delta\bar{\boldsymbol{a}}'_\alpha\rangle)]. \tag{7.30}$$

Multiplying this by $\bar{\boldsymbol{R}}^\top$ from right on both sides, we obtain

$$\delta\boldsymbol{\omega}\times\boldsymbol{I}=E[(\Delta\boldsymbol{\omega}\times\boldsymbol{I}+O(\sigma^2))\sum_{\alpha=1}^{N}(\langle\boldsymbol{l}_\alpha,\delta\bar{\boldsymbol{a}}_\alpha\rangle+\langle\boldsymbol{l}'_\alpha,\delta\bar{\boldsymbol{a}}'_\alpha\rangle)]. \tag{7.31}$$

From the definition of Eq. (6.44), the left side $\delta\boldsymbol{\omega}\times\boldsymbol{I}$ $(=\boldsymbol{A}(\delta\boldsymbol{\omega}))$ is an antisymmetric matrix consisting of $\delta\boldsymbol{\omega}$ as nondiagonal elements in the form of Eq. (6.25). It follows that $\Delta\boldsymbol{\omega}\times\boldsymbol{I}+O(\sigma^2)$ on the right side is also an antisymmetric matrix and can be written as $\Delta\tilde{\boldsymbol{\omega}}\times\boldsymbol{I}$ for some vector $\Delta\tilde{\boldsymbol{\omega}}$. Noting that $\Delta\tilde{\boldsymbol{\omega}}=\Delta\boldsymbol{\omega}+O(\sigma^2)$, we obtain from Eq. (7.31)

$$\delta\boldsymbol{\omega}=E[\Delta\tilde{\boldsymbol{\omega}}\sum_{\alpha=1}^{N}(\langle\boldsymbol{l}_\alpha,\delta\bar{\boldsymbol{a}}_\alpha\rangle+\langle\boldsymbol{l}'_\alpha,\delta\bar{\boldsymbol{a}}'_\alpha\rangle)]. \tag{7.32}$$

[1] In statistics, they are called the *scores* of $\bar{\boldsymbol{a}}_\alpha$ and $\bar{\boldsymbol{a}}'_\alpha$ for p_α.

This holds for arbitrary variations $\delta\bar{\boldsymbol{a}}_\alpha$, $\delta\bar{\boldsymbol{a}}'_\alpha$, and $\delta\boldsymbol{\omega}$ that satisfy Eq. (7.25). In particular, this holds for the following variations:

$$\delta\bar{\boldsymbol{a}}_\alpha = -V_0[\boldsymbol{a}_\alpha]\bar{\boldsymbol{R}}^\top\bar{\boldsymbol{W}}_\alpha(\delta\boldsymbol{\omega}\times\bar{\boldsymbol{R}}\bar{\boldsymbol{a}}_\alpha), \qquad \delta\bar{\boldsymbol{a}}'_\alpha = V_0[\boldsymbol{a}'_\alpha]\bar{\boldsymbol{W}}_\alpha(\delta\boldsymbol{\omega}\times\bar{\boldsymbol{R}}\bar{\boldsymbol{a}}_\alpha). \tag{7.33}$$

It is easy to see that these satisfy Eq. (7.25) (↪ Exercise 7.1). Substituting these into Eq. (7.32), we obtain

$$\begin{aligned}
\delta\boldsymbol{\omega} &= E[\Delta\tilde{\boldsymbol{\omega}}\sum_{\alpha=1}^{N}(-\langle\boldsymbol{l}_\alpha, V_0[\boldsymbol{a}_\alpha]\bar{\boldsymbol{R}}^\top\bar{\boldsymbol{W}}_\alpha(\delta\boldsymbol{\omega}\times\bar{\boldsymbol{R}}\bar{\boldsymbol{a}}_\alpha)\rangle + \langle\boldsymbol{l}'_\alpha, V_0[\boldsymbol{a}'_\alpha]\bar{\boldsymbol{W}}_\alpha(\delta\boldsymbol{\omega}\times\bar{\boldsymbol{R}}\bar{\boldsymbol{a}}_\alpha)\rangle)] \\
&= E[\Delta\tilde{\boldsymbol{\omega}}\sum_{\alpha=1}^{N}(-\langle\bar{\boldsymbol{W}}_\alpha\bar{\boldsymbol{R}}V_0[\boldsymbol{a}_\alpha]\boldsymbol{l}_\alpha, \delta\boldsymbol{\omega}\times\bar{\boldsymbol{R}}\bar{\boldsymbol{a}}_\alpha\rangle + \langle\bar{\boldsymbol{W}}_\alpha V_0[\boldsymbol{a}'_\alpha]\boldsymbol{l}'_\alpha, \delta\boldsymbol{\omega}\times\bar{\boldsymbol{R}}\bar{\boldsymbol{a}}_\alpha\rangle)] \\
&= E[\Delta\tilde{\boldsymbol{\omega}}\sum_{\alpha=1}^{N}\langle\bar{\boldsymbol{W}}_\alpha(V_0[\boldsymbol{a}'_\alpha]\boldsymbol{l}'_\alpha - \bar{\boldsymbol{R}}V_0[\boldsymbol{a}_\alpha]\boldsymbol{l}_\alpha), \delta\boldsymbol{\omega}\times\bar{\boldsymbol{R}}\bar{\boldsymbol{a}}_\alpha\rangle \\
&= -E[\Delta\tilde{\boldsymbol{\omega}}\sum_{\alpha=1}^{N}\langle\bar{\boldsymbol{W}}_\alpha(V_0[\boldsymbol{a}'_\alpha]\boldsymbol{l}'_\alpha - \bar{\boldsymbol{R}}V_0[\boldsymbol{a}_\alpha]\boldsymbol{l}_\alpha)\times(\bar{\boldsymbol{R}}\bar{\boldsymbol{a}}_\alpha), \delta\boldsymbol{\omega}\rangle \\
&= -E[\Delta\tilde{\boldsymbol{\omega}}\sum_{\alpha=1}^{N}\langle\boldsymbol{m}_\alpha, \delta\boldsymbol{\omega}\rangle)] = -E[\Delta\tilde{\boldsymbol{\omega}}\sum_{\alpha=1}^{N}\boldsymbol{m}_\alpha^\top]\delta\boldsymbol{\omega},
\end{aligned} \tag{7.34}$$

where we define $\boldsymbol{m}_\alpha$ by

$$\boldsymbol{m}_\alpha \equiv \bar{\boldsymbol{W}}_\alpha(V_0[\boldsymbol{a}'_\alpha]\boldsymbol{l}'_\alpha - \bar{\boldsymbol{R}}V_0[\boldsymbol{a}_\alpha]\boldsymbol{l}_\alpha)\times(\bar{\boldsymbol{R}}\bar{\boldsymbol{a}}_\alpha). \tag{7.35}$$

Since Eq. (7.34) holds for an arbitrary variation $\delta\boldsymbol{\omega}$, we obtain

$$E[\Delta\tilde{\boldsymbol{\omega}}\sum_{\alpha=1}^{N}\boldsymbol{m}_\alpha^\top] = -\boldsymbol{I}, \tag{7.36}$$

and hence

$$\begin{aligned}
E\Big[\begin{pmatrix}\Delta\tilde{\boldsymbol{\omega}} \\ \sum_{\alpha=1}^{N}\boldsymbol{m}_\alpha\end{pmatrix}\begin{pmatrix}\Delta\tilde{\boldsymbol{\omega}} \\ \sum_{\beta=1}^{N}\boldsymbol{m}_\beta\end{pmatrix}^\top\Big] &= \begin{pmatrix} E[\Delta\tilde{\boldsymbol{\omega}}\Delta\tilde{\boldsymbol{\omega}}^\top] & E[\Delta\tilde{\boldsymbol{\omega}}\sum_{\alpha=1}^{N}\boldsymbol{m}_\alpha^\top] \\ E[(\Delta\tilde{\boldsymbol{\omega}}\sum_{\alpha=1}^{N}\boldsymbol{m}_\alpha^\top)^\top] & E[\sum_{\alpha=1}^{N}\boldsymbol{m}_\alpha\sum_{\beta=1}^{N}\boldsymbol{m}_\beta^\top]\end{pmatrix} \\
&= \begin{pmatrix} V[\tilde{\boldsymbol{R}}] & -\boldsymbol{I} \\ -\boldsymbol{I} & \boldsymbol{M}\end{pmatrix},
\end{aligned} \tag{7.37}$$

where we define

$$V[\tilde{\boldsymbol{R}}] \equiv E[\Delta\tilde{\boldsymbol{\omega}}\Delta\tilde{\boldsymbol{\omega}}^\top], \qquad \boldsymbol{M} \equiv E[\sum_{\alpha=1}^{N}\boldsymbol{m}_\alpha\sum_{\beta=1}^{N}\boldsymbol{m}_\beta^\top]. \tag{7.38}$$

The form of the left side Eq. (7.37) implies that this is a positive semidefinite symmetric matrix (↪ Exercise 7.2). Hence, if $\boldsymbol{M}$ is a nonsingular matrix, the following inequality holds (↪ Exercise 7.3).

$$V[\tilde{\boldsymbol{R}}] \succ \boldsymbol{M}^{-1}. \tag{7.39}$$

By the symbol $\succ$, we mean that the difference of the left side from the right side is a positive semidefinite symmetric matrix.

7.4 KCR LOWER BOUND

Since $\Delta\tilde{\omega} = \Delta\omega + O(\sigma^2)$, the matrix $V[\tilde{\boldsymbol{R}}]$ of Eq. (7.38) differs from $E[\Delta\omega\Delta\omega^\top]$ by $O(\sigma^4)$. Recall that the expectation of odd order terms in noise is 0. Hence, $V[\tilde{\boldsymbol{R}}]$ is practically the same as the covariance matrix $V[\hat{\boldsymbol{R}}]$ of Eq. (7.15). Equation (7.39) states that *this cannot be made smaller than* $\boldsymbol{M}^{-1}$ *whatever algorithm is used for estimation*, in the sense that the difference is a positive semidefinite symmetric matrix. Hence, $\boldsymbol{M}^{-1}$ can be regarded as a theoretical accuracy bound; we call it the *KCR lower bound*. We now evaluate this in more concrete terms.

From Eq. (7.22), $\log p_\alpha$ has the form

$$\log p_\alpha = -\frac{1}{2\sigma^2}(\langle \boldsymbol{a}_\alpha - \bar{\boldsymbol{a}}_\alpha, V_0[\boldsymbol{a}_\alpha]^{-1}(\boldsymbol{a}_\alpha - \bar{\boldsymbol{a}}_\alpha)\rangle + \langle \boldsymbol{a}'_\alpha - \bar{\boldsymbol{a}}'_\alpha, V_0[\boldsymbol{a}'_\alpha]^{-1}(\boldsymbol{a}'_\alpha - \bar{\boldsymbol{a}}'_\alpha)\rangle) + ..., \tag{7.40}$$

where "..." denotes the logarithm of the normalization constant, which does not contain $\bar{\boldsymbol{a}}_\alpha$ or $\bar{\boldsymbol{a}}'_\alpha$. Hence, the vectors $\boldsymbol{l}_\alpha$ and $\boldsymbol{l}'_\alpha$ of Eq. (7.28) have the form

$$\boldsymbol{l}_\alpha = \nabla_{\bar{\boldsymbol{a}}_\alpha} \log p_\alpha = \frac{1}{\sigma^2} V_0[\boldsymbol{a}_\alpha]^{-1}(\boldsymbol{a}_\alpha - \bar{\boldsymbol{a}}_\alpha),$$
$$\boldsymbol{l}'_\alpha = \nabla_{\bar{\boldsymbol{a}}'_\alpha} \log p_\alpha = \frac{1}{\sigma^2} V_0[\boldsymbol{a}'_\alpha]^{-1}(\boldsymbol{a}'_\alpha - \bar{\boldsymbol{a}}'_\alpha). \tag{7.41}$$

Substituting these into Eq. (7.35), we obtain

$$\begin{aligned}
\boldsymbol{m}_\alpha &= \bar{\boldsymbol{W}}_\alpha(V_0[\boldsymbol{a}'_\alpha]\boldsymbol{l}'_\alpha - \bar{\boldsymbol{R}}V_0[\boldsymbol{a}_\alpha]\boldsymbol{l}_\alpha) \times (\bar{\boldsymbol{R}}\bar{\boldsymbol{a}}_\alpha) \\
&= \frac{1}{\sigma^2}\bar{\boldsymbol{W}}_\alpha(V_0[\boldsymbol{a}'_\alpha]V_0[\boldsymbol{a}'_\alpha]^{-1}(\boldsymbol{a}'_\alpha - \bar{\boldsymbol{a}}'_\alpha) - \bar{\boldsymbol{R}}V_0[\boldsymbol{a}_\alpha]V_0[\boldsymbol{a}_\alpha]^{-1}(\boldsymbol{a}_\alpha - \bar{\boldsymbol{a}}_\alpha)) \times (\bar{\boldsymbol{R}}\bar{\boldsymbol{a}}_\alpha) \\
&= \frac{1}{\sigma^2}\bar{\boldsymbol{W}}_\alpha(\boldsymbol{a}'_\alpha - \bar{\boldsymbol{a}}'_\alpha - \bar{\boldsymbol{R}}(\boldsymbol{a}_\alpha - \bar{\boldsymbol{a}}_\alpha)) \times (\bar{\boldsymbol{R}}\bar{\boldsymbol{a}}_\alpha) \\
&= -\frac{1}{\sigma^2}(\bar{\boldsymbol{R}}\bar{\boldsymbol{a}}_\alpha) \times \bar{\boldsymbol{W}}_\alpha(\boldsymbol{a}'_\alpha - \bar{\boldsymbol{a}}'_\alpha - \bar{\boldsymbol{R}}(\boldsymbol{a}_\alpha - \bar{\boldsymbol{a}}_\alpha)).
\end{aligned} \tag{7.42}$$

Evidently, $E[\boldsymbol{m}_\alpha] = \boldsymbol{0}$. Since $\boldsymbol{m}_\alpha$ and $\boldsymbol{m}_\beta$ are independent for $\alpha \neq \beta$, we see that

$$E[\boldsymbol{m}_\alpha \boldsymbol{m}_\beta^\top] = E[\boldsymbol{m}_\alpha]E[\boldsymbol{m}_\beta]^\top = \boldsymbol{O}, \qquad \alpha \neq \beta. \tag{7.43}$$

Hence, the matrix $\boldsymbol{M}$ of Eq. (7.38) has the form

$$\begin{aligned}
\boldsymbol{M} &= E[\sum_{\alpha=1}^N \boldsymbol{m}_\alpha \sum_{\beta=1}^N \boldsymbol{m}_\beta^\top] = E[\sum_{\alpha,\beta=1}^N \boldsymbol{m}_\alpha \boldsymbol{m}_\beta^\top] = E[\sum_{\alpha=1}^N \boldsymbol{m}_\alpha \boldsymbol{m}_\alpha^\top] \\
&= \frac{1}{\sigma^4}E[\sum_{\alpha=1}^N (\bar{\boldsymbol{R}}\bar{\boldsymbol{a}}_\alpha) \times \bar{\boldsymbol{W}}_\alpha(\boldsymbol{a}'_\alpha - \bar{\boldsymbol{a}}'_\alpha - \bar{\boldsymbol{R}}(\boldsymbol{a}_\alpha - \bar{\boldsymbol{a}}_\alpha)) \\
&\quad (\boldsymbol{a}'_\alpha - \bar{\boldsymbol{a}}'_\alpha - \bar{\boldsymbol{R}}(\boldsymbol{a}_\alpha - \bar{\boldsymbol{a}}_\alpha))^\top \bar{\boldsymbol{W}}_\alpha^\top((\bar{\boldsymbol{R}}\bar{\boldsymbol{a}}_\alpha)\times)^\top] \\
&= \frac{1}{\sigma^4}E[\sum_{\alpha=1}^N (\bar{\boldsymbol{R}}\bar{\boldsymbol{a}}_\alpha) \times \bar{\boldsymbol{W}}_\alpha((\boldsymbol{a}'_\alpha - \bar{\boldsymbol{a}}'_\alpha)(\boldsymbol{a}'_\alpha - \bar{\boldsymbol{a}}'_\alpha)^\top - (\boldsymbol{a}'_\alpha - \bar{\boldsymbol{a}}'_\alpha)(\boldsymbol{a}_\alpha - \bar{\boldsymbol{a}}_\alpha)\bar{\boldsymbol{R}}^\top \\
&\quad -\bar{\boldsymbol{R}}(\boldsymbol{a}_\alpha - \bar{\boldsymbol{a}}_\alpha)(\boldsymbol{a}'_\alpha - \bar{\boldsymbol{a}}'_\alpha)^\top + \bar{\boldsymbol{R}}(\boldsymbol{a}_\alpha - \bar{\boldsymbol{a}}_\alpha)(\boldsymbol{a}_\alpha - \bar{\boldsymbol{a}}_\alpha)^\top \bar{\boldsymbol{R}}^\top)\bar{\boldsymbol{W}}_\alpha \times (\bar{\boldsymbol{R}}\bar{\boldsymbol{a}}_\alpha)] \\
&= \frac{1}{\sigma^4}\sum_{\alpha=1}^N (\bar{\boldsymbol{R}}\bar{\boldsymbol{a}}_\alpha) \times \bar{\boldsymbol{W}}_\alpha(E[(\boldsymbol{a}'_\alpha - \bar{\boldsymbol{a}}'_\alpha)(\boldsymbol{a}'_\alpha - \bar{\boldsymbol{a}}'_\alpha)^\top] \\
&\quad +\bar{\boldsymbol{R}}E[(\boldsymbol{a}_\alpha - \bar{\boldsymbol{a}}_\alpha)(\boldsymbol{a}_\alpha - \bar{\boldsymbol{a}}_\alpha)^\top]\bar{\boldsymbol{R}}^\top)\bar{\boldsymbol{W}}_\alpha \times (\bar{\boldsymbol{R}}\bar{\boldsymbol{a}}_\alpha)
\end{aligned}$$

$$
\begin{aligned}
&= \frac{1}{\sigma^2}\sum_{\alpha=1}^{N}(\bar{\boldsymbol{R}}\bar{\boldsymbol{a}}_\alpha)\times\bar{\boldsymbol{W}}_\alpha(V_0[\boldsymbol{a}'_\alpha]+\bar{\boldsymbol{R}}V_0[\boldsymbol{a}_\alpha]\bar{\boldsymbol{R}}^\top)\bar{\boldsymbol{W}}_\alpha\times(\bar{\boldsymbol{R}}\bar{\boldsymbol{a}}_\alpha)\\
&= \frac{1}{\sigma^2}\sum_{\alpha=1}^{N}(\bar{\boldsymbol{R}}\bar{\boldsymbol{a}}_\alpha)\times\bar{\boldsymbol{W}}_\alpha\bar{\boldsymbol{V}}_\alpha\bar{\boldsymbol{W}}_\alpha\times(\bar{\boldsymbol{R}}\bar{\boldsymbol{a}}_\alpha) = \frac{1}{\sigma^2}\sum_{\alpha=1}^{N}(\bar{\boldsymbol{R}}\bar{\boldsymbol{a}}_\alpha)\times\bar{\boldsymbol{W}}_\alpha\times(\bar{\boldsymbol{R}}\bar{\boldsymbol{a}}_\alpha)\\
&= \frac{1}{\sigma^2}\bar{\boldsymbol{H}},
\end{aligned}
\tag{7.44}
$$

where we have used the relations of Eqs. (5.12) and (5.13) and the definition of $\bar{\boldsymbol{H}}$ in Eq. (7.17). Thus, the inequality of Eq. (7.39) is written in the form

$$
V[\tilde{\boldsymbol{R}}] \succ \sigma^2\bar{\boldsymbol{H}}^{-1}. \tag{7.45}
$$

Comparing this with Eq. (7.19) and noting that $V[\hat{\boldsymbol{R}}]$ and $V[\tilde{\boldsymbol{R}}]$ differ only by $O(\sigma^4)$, we conclude that *maximum likelihood estimation attains the KCR lower bound up to $O(\sigma^4)$*.

7.5 SUPPLEMENTAL NOTES

In 3D computation of the scene from images by computer vision, the accuracy of a computed rotation $\hat{\boldsymbol{R}}$ has often been evaluated simply by the difference $\|\hat{\boldsymbol{R}}-\boldsymbol{R}\|$ from its true value $\boldsymbol{R}$. Evaluation in terms of the error vector $\Delta\boldsymbol{\Omega}$ and the covariance matrix $V[\hat{\boldsymbol{R}}]$ as in this chapter was first used by Ohta and Kanatani [35], who showed that maximum likelihood estimation reduces to minimization of Eq. (7.7). To solve this, they used a numerical scheme called "renormalization" which iterates eigenvalue computation, as mentioned in Sec. 5.6. They also showed the KCR lower bound of Eq. (7.45), but the derivation details were omitted.

We showed in Sec. 7.2 that the covariance matrix of the maximum likelihood estimate of the rotation is given by Eq. (7.19), where the noise level σ is assumed to be known. If it is unknown, we need to estimate it by some means. It can be estimated from the minimum value $J(\hat{\boldsymbol{R}})$ of Eq. (7.7) attained by the maximum likelihood estimate $\hat{\boldsymbol{R}}$. Equation (7.7), i.e., Eq. (5.11) is written as Eq. (5.17). Suppose the true value $\boldsymbol{R}$ is known. Then, as seen from Eq. (5.16), the quantity $\boldsymbol{\varepsilon}_\alpha$ of Eq. (5.15) is a Gaussian variable of expectation $\boldsymbol{0}$ and covariance matrix $\sigma^2\boldsymbol{V}_\alpha$. It follows that, as is well known in statistics, $\langle\boldsymbol{\varepsilon}_\alpha, V[\boldsymbol{\varepsilon}_\alpha]^{-1}\boldsymbol{\varepsilon}_\alpha\rangle$ is a χ^2 variable of three degrees of freedom and that the sum of independent χ^2 variables is also a χ^2 variable whose degree of freedom equals the sum of the degrees of freedom of individual variables ($\hookrightarrow$ Exercise 7.4). From Eq. (5.17), we see that $2J/\sigma^2$ is the sum of N independent χ^2 variables of three degrees of freedom. Hence, it has $3N$ degrees of freedom. Since the expectation of a χ^2 variable equals its degree of freedom, the following holds for the maximum likelihood estimate $\hat{\boldsymbol{R}}$:

$$
\sigma^2 \approx \frac{2J(\hat{\boldsymbol{R}})}{3N}. \tag{7.46}
$$

This inference relies on the assumption that $\boldsymbol{R}$ in Eq. (5.16) is the true value and hence $\boldsymbol{R}$ and $\boldsymbol{W}_\alpha$ in Eq. (5.17) are both their true values. In practice, however, we evaluate the residual $J(\hat{\boldsymbol{R}})$ using, instead of the true $\boldsymbol{R}$, the maximum likelihood estimate $\hat{\boldsymbol{R}}$, i.e., the value of $\boldsymbol{R}$ that minimizes $J(\boldsymbol{R})$. This causes some bias and makes Eq. (7.46) an underestimation. If the constraint satisfied by the true data value is linear in parameters, it is known that this bias is corrected by replacing the denominator $3N$ on the right side of Eq. (7.46) by $3N - d$, where d is the number of parameters [20]. However, such an analysis is difficult for nonlinear constraints involving rotations[2].

For estimation of the geometric structure from noisy observations using a constraint of form of Eq. (5.66), i.e., for estimating the parameter $\boldsymbol{\theta}$ when the true observations $\bar{\boldsymbol{a}}_\alpha$ and $\bar{\boldsymbol{a}}'_\alpha$ satisfy Eq. (5.66) from noisy observations $\boldsymbol{a}_\alpha$ and $\boldsymbol{a}'_\alpha$, $\alpha = 1, ..., N$, under (generally inhomogeneous and anisotropic) Gaussian noise, there exists a lower bound on the covariance matrix $V[\hat{\boldsymbol{\theta}}]$ of the computed estimate $\hat{\boldsymbol{\theta}}$ independent of the estimation algorithm. This fact was first pointed out by Kanatani [20]. Since the principle of its derivation is the same as the *Cramer–Rao lower bound* known in statistical estimation, he called the resulting lower bound simply the "Cramer–Rao lower bound." However, Chernov and Lesort [5] pointed out that it has a different meaning from the Cramer-Rao lower bound and proposed to call it the *KCR* (*Kanatani–Cramer–Rao*) *lower bound*. It differs from the Cramer–Rao lower bound in the following respects.

1. The Cramer–Rao lower bound concerns the problem of *statistical estimation* formalized as estimation of the parameters of an unknown data generating mechanism, called the *statistical model*, described as a parameterized probability density, from repeated observations. In contrast, the KCR lower bound does not concern the data generating mechanism; the noise in the data is assumed to follow a known Gaussian distribution. Rather, it concerns estimation of the parameters in the equation, called the *constraint* (↪ Sec. 5.6), that observed data are supposed to satisfy were it not for noise.

2. The Cramer–Rao lower bound, or statistical estimation in general for this matter, concerns the behavior of the estimate in the asymptotic limit $N \to \infty$ of N repeated observations. In contrast, the KCR lower bound does not concern the number of observed data; it can be small. Rather, it concerns the behavior of the estimate in the asymptotic limit $\sigma \to 0$ of the small noise level [21].

3. If we regard the problem in the form of Eq. (5.66) as statistical estimation and compute the Cramer–Rao lower bound, we obtain a lower bound on all the parameters including the *structural parameter* $\boldsymbol{\theta}$ and the *nuisance parameters* $\bar{\boldsymbol{a}}$ and $\bar{\boldsymbol{a}}'$, $\alpha = 1, ..., N$, (↪ Sec. 5.6) in the form of a very large size matrix[3] [34]. For the KCR lower bound, in contrast, the uncertainty in the nuisance parameters are eliminated[4], resulting in a lower bound on only the structural parameters in the form of a very small size matrix.

The general theory of the KCR lower bound is found in [20], and detailed analysis is given in the particular case of Eq. (5.66) being linear in the parameter $\boldsymbol{\theta}$, having the form

$$\langle \bar{\boldsymbol{\xi}}^{(k)}(\bar{\boldsymbol{a}}_\alpha, \bar{\boldsymbol{a}}'_\alpha), \boldsymbol{\theta} \rangle = 0, \qquad k = 1, ..., L, \qquad \alpha = 1, ..., N, \tag{7.47}$$

where $\bar{\boldsymbol{\xi}}^{(k)}(\bar{\boldsymbol{a}}_\alpha, \bar{\boldsymbol{a}}'_\alpha)$ is some nonlinear function of $\bar{\boldsymbol{a}}_\alpha$ and $\bar{\boldsymbol{a}}'_\alpha$. Many problems of computer vision have this form. In particular, if the constraint is given as a polynomial in $\bar{\boldsymbol{a}}_\alpha$ and $\bar{\boldsymbol{a}}'_\alpha$, it is rewritten in this form by regarding all the coefficients of the monomials as unknowns.

Typical examples include the epipolar equation ($L = 1$) and the fundamental matrix ($L = 1$) discussed in Sec. 6.7 [29]. Another example is the *homography matrix* ($L = 2$), which

[2]Evaluating the expectation of the residual as an expression of the involved parameters is a central problem of *geometric model selection*, inferring what kind of constraints, or models, the data should satisfy in the absence of noise. For constraints that are linear in the parameters, a criterion called the *geometric AIC* is proposed [20, 23].

[3]This is given as the inverse of a large size matrix, called the *Fisher information matrix* [34]. However, the inversion computation is often difficult for large size matrices.

[4]For the problem of this chapter, the substitution of Eq. (7.33) corresponds to that elimination.

appears when a planar surface or an infinitely far away scene is imaged by two cameras [29]. The problem of fitting an ellipse to projections of circular objects in the scene ($L = 1$) also has this form [28]. For these problems, the theoretical analysis of the KCR lower bound for $L = 1$ is given in [28], and general analysis for $L \geq 1$ is found in [29]. Analysis of simple problems such as fitting a line to a sequence of points in plane is given in [21]. These analyses show that, irrespective of particulars of the problems, maximum likelihood estimation attains the KCR lower bound up to $O(\sigma^4)$.

7.6 EXERCISES

7.1. Show that the variations $\delta\bar{\boldsymbol{a}}_\alpha$ and $\delta\bar{\boldsymbol{a}}'_\alpha$ of Eq. (7.33) satisfy Eq. (7.25).

7.2. Show that $\boldsymbol{A} = \boldsymbol{a}\boldsymbol{a}^\top$ is a positive semidefinite symmetric matrix for any vector $\boldsymbol{a}$.

7.3. (1) Show that if $\boldsymbol{A}$ is a positive semidefinite symmetric matrix, so is the matrix $\boldsymbol{B} = \boldsymbol{U}^\top\boldsymbol{A}\boldsymbol{U}$ for an arbitrary nonsingular matrix $\boldsymbol{U}$.

(2) Show that the fact that Eq. (7.37) is a positive semidefinite matrix implies Eq. (7.39).

7.4. Show that if an nD vector $\boldsymbol{x}$ is a Gaussian variable of mean $\boldsymbol{0}$ and covariance matrix $\boldsymbol{\Sigma}$, then $\langle \boldsymbol{x}, \boldsymbol{\Sigma}^{-1}\boldsymbol{x} \rangle$ is a χ^2 variable of n degrees of freedom and its expectation is n.

CHAPTER 8

Computing Projects

For readers who want to apply the theories described in this book to real engineering problems and numerically evaluate the solution, we provide two computing projects: one is a simulation experiment, and the other is real data analysis. For simulation, one can easily generate an arbitrary 3D object in 3D, using a graphics tool, but simulating realistic noise is not trivial, since noise is sensor-dependent. Here, we assume stereo vision for 3D sensing and present a mathematical framework for describing how noise in stereo images affects the reconstructed 3D location, allowing one to evaluate the covariance matrix of each measurement. Readers can then compute the 3D rotation of the object using different methods described in this book. They can also apply the theory in Chapter 7 to evaluate the reliability of computation. Next, we show real GPS geodetic data of land deformation in northeast Japan. They describe the effect of a massive earthquake that took place on March 11, 2011. Readers can compute the land movement, using the GPS land data before and after the earthquake to grasp the effect of the earthquake in quantitative terms.

8.1 STEREO VISION EXPERIMENT

In this experiment, we first define a 3D object in 3D. The shape is arbitrary. This can be easily done by using a graphics tool. We translate and rotate it in 3D and add random noise to corresponding feature points before and after the motion. From them, we estimate the object motion: we subtract the displacement of the centroid of the object and compute the rotation, using the methods described in Chapters 4, 5, and 6.

The difficult part is generation of realistic noise, since noise characteristics depend on the sensor for location measurement. Here, we assume stereo vision. Figure 8.1 is a schematic illustration, where the object is a curved grid surface. Defining two perspective cameras in the scene that view the object before and after the motion, we obtain two pairs of images. The imaging geometry of stereo vision is modeled as follows.

Assume a fixed XYZ world coordinate system and regard the reference camera position as placed at the coordinate origin O with the optical axis aligned to the Z-axis. The xy image coordinate system is defined in such a way that its origin o is at the *principal point* (the intersection with the optical axis) and the x- and y-axis are parallel to the X- and Y-axis of the world coordinate system, respectively. Then, the camera is rotated around the world coordinate origin O by $\boldsymbol{R}$ (rotation matrix) and translated by $\boldsymbol{t}$ from the reference position. We call $\{\boldsymbol{R}, \boldsymbol{t}\}$ the *motion parameters* of the camera. If the camera focal length is f, a 3D point (X, Y, Z) in the scene is projected onto a 2D point (x, y) by the following

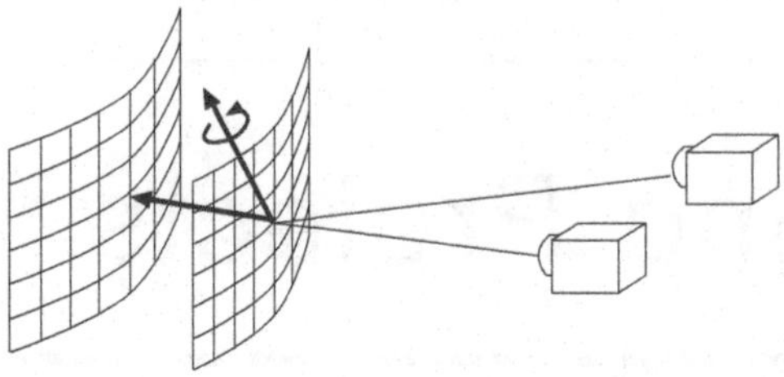

FIGURE 8.1 A grid surface is rotated and translated in 3D. The 3D position of the grid points are measured by stereo vision before and after the motion.

relationship [15, 29]:

$$\boldsymbol{x} \simeq \boldsymbol{P}\boldsymbol{X}, \qquad \boldsymbol{x} \equiv \begin{pmatrix} x/f_0 \\ y/f_0 \\ 1 \end{pmatrix}, \qquad \boldsymbol{X} \equiv \begin{pmatrix} X \\ Y \\ Z \\ 1 \end{pmatrix}. \tag{8.1}$$

The symbol $\simeq$ means equality up to a nonzero constant multiplier, and f_0 is a scale constant of approximately the image size for stabilizing finite length computation [13]. The 3×4 matrix $\boldsymbol{P}$, called the *camera matrix*, has the form

$$\boldsymbol{P} = \begin{pmatrix} f/f_0 & 0 & 0 \\ 0 & f/f_0 & 0 \\ 0 & 0 & 1 \end{pmatrix} \begin{pmatrix} \boldsymbol{R}^\top & -\boldsymbol{R}^\top \boldsymbol{t} \end{pmatrix}, \tag{8.2}$$

where the *aspect ratio* (the ratio of scale in the horizontal and vertical directions of the image frame) is set to 1 with no *skews* (i.e., the pixel array is orthogonal). For real cameras, the aspect ratio may not only eqaual 1 or have some skew, but also the principal point may not be at the frame center and the image may be distorted due to lens imperfection. Although Eq. (8.2) is the simplest idealization, it is a practically sufficient modeling of perspective cameras.

To simulate stereo vision, we define two cameras with motion parameters $\{\boldsymbol{R}, \boldsymbol{t}\}$ and $\{\boldsymbol{R}', \boldsymbol{t}'\}$ with focal lengths f and f', respectively. Let $\boldsymbol{P}$ and $\boldsymbol{P}'$ be their respective camera matrices. Then, the images of a point (X, Y, Z) in 3D observed by the respective cameras are computed by Eq. (8.2), resulting in two pairs of stereo images of the object before and after the motion as shown in Fig. 8.2.

8.2 OPTIMAL CORRECTION OF STEREO IMAGES

To simulate the fact that image processing for correspondence detection entails uncertainty to some extent, we add independent isotropic Gaussian noise of mean $\boldsymbol{0}$ and standard deviation σ (pixels) to each of the feature points of the object in the generated stereo images. As a result, the corresponding positions $\boldsymbol{x}$ and $\boldsymbol{x}'$ of the stereo pair no longer satisfy the epipolar constraint of Eq. (6.49), meaning that no 3D point is associated to them. So, we correct $\boldsymbol{x}$ and $\boldsymbol{x}'$ to $\hat{\boldsymbol{x}}$ and $\hat{\boldsymbol{x}}'$, respectively, so that they exactly satisfy Eq. (6.49) to define a unique 3D point. This is done as follows.

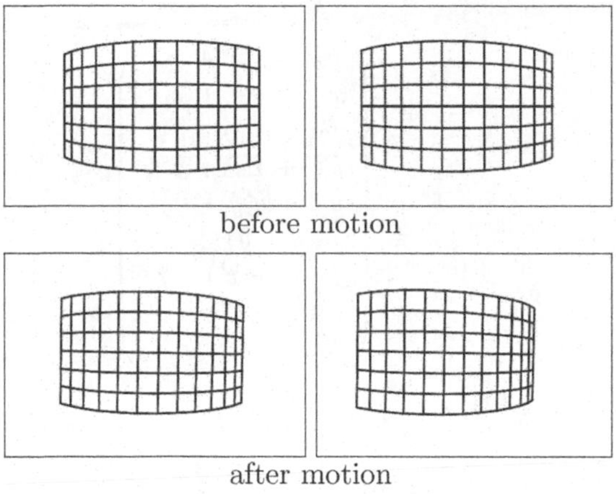

FIGURE 8.2 Simulated stereo image pairs.

For the camera modeling of Eq. (8.2), the fundamental matrix $\boldsymbol{F}$ in Eq. (6.49) is given by [15, 29]

$$\boldsymbol{F} \simeq \begin{pmatrix} 1 & 0 & 0 \\ 0 & 1 & 0 \\ 0 & 0 & f/f_0 \end{pmatrix} (\boldsymbol{t}' - \boldsymbol{t}) \times \boldsymbol{R}'\boldsymbol{R}^\top \begin{pmatrix} 1 & 0 & 0 \\ 0 & 1 & 0 \\ 0 & 0 & f'/f_0 \end{pmatrix}, \tag{8.3}$$

where the multiplication notation of Eq. (6.44) is used. In the following computation, we express the fundamental matrix $\boldsymbol{F} = (F_{ij})$ as the 9D vector $\boldsymbol{f} = (F_{11}, F_{12}, F_{13}, F_{21}, F_{22}, F_{23}, F_{31}, F_{32}, F_{33})^\top$. Let (x, y) and (x', y') be a pair of corresponding points in the stereo images that do not necessarily satisfy the epipolar constraint. We optimally correct them to $(\hat{x}, \hat{y})$ and $(\hat{x}', \hat{y}')$, where by "optimally" we mean that we minimize the *reprojection error*

$$E = \frac{1}{2}\Big((\bar{x} - x)^2 + (\bar{y} - y)^2 + (\bar{x}' - x')^2 + (\bar{y}' - y')^2\Big) \tag{8.4}$$

with respect to $(\bar{x}, \bar{y})$ and $(\bar{x}', \bar{y}')$, which we regard as the true values, subject to the constraint that they satisfy Eq. (6.49). Let $(\hat{x}, \hat{y})$ and $(\hat{x}', \hat{y}')$ be the corrected values, respectively. The correction procedure goes as follows ($\hookrightarrow$ Exercise 8.1):

1. Let $E_0 = \infty$ (a sufficiently large number), $\hat{x} = x$, $\hat{y} = y$, $\hat{x}' = x'$, $\hat{y}' = y'$, and $\tilde{x} = \tilde{y} = \tilde{x}' = \tilde{y}' = 0$.

2. Compute the following 9×9 matrix $V_0[\hat{\boldsymbol{\xi}}]$ and the 9D vector $\boldsymbol{\xi}^*$:

$$V_0[\hat{\boldsymbol{\xi}}] = \begin{pmatrix} \hat{x}^2 + \hat{x}'^2 & \hat{x}'\hat{y}' & f_0\hat{x}' & \hat{x}\hat{y} & 0 & 0 & f_0\hat{x} & 0 & 0 \\ \hat{x}'\hat{y}' & \hat{x}^2 + \hat{y}'^2 & f_0\hat{y}' & 0 & \hat{x}\hat{y} & 0 & 0 & f_0\hat{x} & 0 \\ f_0\hat{x}' & f_0\hat{y}' & f_0^2 & 0 & 0 & 0 & 0 & 0 & 0 \\ \hat{x}\hat{y} & 0 & 0 & \hat{y}^2 + \hat{x}'^2 & \hat{x}'\hat{y}' & f_0\hat{x}' & f_0\hat{y} & 0 & 0 \\ 0 & \hat{x}\hat{y} & 0 & \hat{x}'\hat{y}' & \hat{y}^2 + \hat{y}'^2 & f_0\hat{y}' & 0 & f_0\hat{y} & 0 \\ 0 & 0 & 0 & f_0\hat{x}' & f_0\hat{y}' & f_0^2 & 0 & 0 & 0 \\ f_0\hat{x} & 0 & 0 & f_0\hat{y} & 0 & 0 & f_0^2 & 0 & 0 \\ 0 & f_0\hat{x} & 0 & 0 & f_0\hat{y} & 0 & 0 & f_0^2 & 0 \\ 0 & 0 & 0 & 0 & 0 & 0 & 0 & 0 & 0 \end{pmatrix}, \tag{8.5}$$

$$\boldsymbol{\xi}^* = \begin{pmatrix} \hat{x}\hat{x}' + \hat{x}'\tilde{x} + \hat{x}\tilde{x}' \\ \hat{x}\hat{y}' + \hat{y}'\tilde{x} + \hat{x}\tilde{y}' \\ f_0(\hat{x} + \tilde{x}) \\ \hat{y}\hat{x}' + \hat{x}'\tilde{y} + \hat{y}\tilde{x}' \\ \hat{y}\hat{y}' + \hat{y}'\tilde{y} + \hat{y}\tilde{y}' \\ f_0(\hat{y} + \tilde{y}) \\ f_0(\hat{x}' + \tilde{x}') \\ f_0(\hat{y}' + \tilde{y}') \\ f_0^2 \end{pmatrix}. \tag{8.6}$$

3. Update $\tilde{x}$, $\tilde{y}$, $\tilde{x}'$, $\tilde{y}'$, $\hat{x}$, $\hat{y}$, $\hat{x}'$, and $\hat{y}'$ as follows:

$$\begin{pmatrix} \tilde{x} \\ \tilde{y} \end{pmatrix} \leftarrow \frac{\langle \boldsymbol{f}, \boldsymbol{\xi}^* \rangle}{\langle \boldsymbol{f}, V_0[\hat{\boldsymbol{\xi}}]\boldsymbol{f} \rangle} \begin{pmatrix} F_{11} & F_{12} & F_{13} \\ F_{21} & F_{22} & F_{23} \end{pmatrix} \begin{pmatrix} \hat{x}' \\ \hat{y}' \\ 1 \end{pmatrix},$$
$$\begin{pmatrix} \tilde{x}' \\ \tilde{y}' \end{pmatrix} \leftarrow \frac{\langle \boldsymbol{f}, \boldsymbol{\xi}^* \rangle}{\langle \boldsymbol{f}, V_0[\hat{\boldsymbol{\xi}}]\boldsymbol{f} \rangle} \begin{pmatrix} F_{11} & F_{21} & F_{31} \\ F_{12} & F_{22} & F_{32} \end{pmatrix} \begin{pmatrix} \hat{x} \\ \hat{y} \\ 1 \end{pmatrix}, \tag{8.7}$$

$$\hat{x} \leftarrow x - \tilde{x}, \qquad \hat{y} \leftarrow y - \tilde{y}, \qquad \hat{x}' \leftarrow x' - \tilde{x}', \qquad \hat{y}' \leftarrow y' - \tilde{y}'. \tag{8.8}$$

4. Compute the reprojection error E by

$$E = \tilde{x}^2 + \tilde{y}^2 + \tilde{x}'^2 + \tilde{y}'^2. \tag{8.9}$$

If $E \approx E_0$, return $(\hat{x}, \hat{y})$ and $(\hat{x}', \hat{y}')$ and stop. Else, let $E_0 \leftarrow E$ and go back to Step 2.

8.3 TRIANGULATION OF STEREO IMAGES

Let (x, y) and (x', y') be a pair of corresponding points in the stereo images that satisfy the epipolar constraint. Then, the corresponding 3D point is easily reconstructed; this process is called *triangulation*. Since both sides of Eq. (8.1) are equal up to a nonzero constant, we can elliminate it by writing Eq. (8.1) as componentwise ratios in the form ($\hookrightarrow$ Eq. (6.69))

$$x = f_0 \frac{P_{11}X + P_{12}Y + P_{13}Z + P_{14}Y}{P_{31}X + P_{32}Y + P_{33}Z + P_{34}Y},$$
$$y = f_0 \frac{P_{21}X + P_{22}Y + P_{23}Z + P_{24}Y}{P_{31}X + P_{32}Y + P_{33}Z + P_{34}Y}, \tag{8.10}$$

where P_{ij} is the (i, j) element of $\boldsymbol{P}$. We obtain similar equations for (x', y') viewed by the second camera. Canceling the denominators, we obtain four lincar equations, which can be written in matrix form as

$$\begin{pmatrix} f_0P_{11} - xP_{31} & f_0P_{12} - xP_{32} & f_0P_{13} - xP_{33} \\ f_0P_{21} - yP_{31} & f_0P_{22} - yP_{32} & f_0P_{23} - yP_{33} \\ f_0P'_{11} - x'P'_{31} & f_0P'_{12} - x'P'_{32} & f_0P'_{13} - x'P_{33} \\ f_0P'_{21} - y'P'_{31} & f_0P'_{22} - y'P'_{32} & f_0P'_{23} - y'P_{33} \end{pmatrix} \begin{pmatrix} X \\ Y \\ Z \end{pmatrix} = \begin{pmatrix} f_0P_{14} - xP_{34} \\ f_0P_{24} - yP_{34} \\ f_0P'_{14} - x'P'_{34} \\ f_0P'_{24} - y'P'_{34} \end{pmatrix}, \tag{8.11}$$

where P'_{ij} is the (i, j) element of the matrix $\boldsymbol{P}'$ of the second camera. This gives four linear equations for three unknowns, so we can pick out arbitrary three equations to solve for

X, Y, and Z. The solution is identical whichever three equations are selected. In fact, the epipolar equation of Eq. (6.49) is obtained as the necessary and sufficient condition that Eq. (8.11) has a unique solution (↪ Exercise 8,2). In actual computation, however, it is more convenient to solve Eq. (8.11) using all the four equations, rather than selecting three, by least squares. Namely, solve

$$\boldsymbol{T}^\top \boldsymbol{T} \begin{pmatrix} X \\ Y \\ Z \end{pmatrix} = -\boldsymbol{A}^\top \boldsymbol{p}, \tag{8.12}$$

where $\boldsymbol{T}$ is the 4×3 coefficient matrix and $\boldsymbol{p}$ is the 4D vector that appear on the left and right side of Eq. (8.11), respectively (↪ Exercise 8.3). We obtain the same solution since Eq. (8.11) is guaranteed to have a unique solution.

8.4 COVARIANCE EVALUATION OF STEREO RECONSTRUCTION

From the corrected positions $\hat{\boldsymbol{x}}$ and $\hat{\boldsymbol{x}}'$ obtained by the optimal correction procedure of Sec. 8.2, the corresponding 3D position $\hat{\boldsymbol{r}} = (X, Y, Z)^\top$ is uniquely computed by the above triangulation procedure. Note that although we add independent isotropic noise to $\boldsymbol{x}$ and $\boldsymbol{x}'$, the noise in the *corrected* positions $\hat{\boldsymbol{x}}$ and $\hat{\boldsymbol{x}}'$ is no longer independent or isotropic; the distribution is anisotropic having correlations. The normalized covariance matrices $V_0[\hat{\boldsymbol{x}}]$ and $V_0[\hat{\boldsymbol{x}}']$ and the normalized correlation matrices $V_0[\hat{\boldsymbol{x}}, \hat{\boldsymbol{x}}']$ and $V_0[\hat{\boldsymbol{x}}', \hat{\boldsymbol{x}}]$ of corrected positions are given by

$$\begin{aligned} V_0[\hat{\boldsymbol{x}}] &= \frac{1}{f_0^2}\Big(\boldsymbol{P_k} - \frac{(\boldsymbol{P_k}\boldsymbol{F}\hat{\boldsymbol{x}}')(\boldsymbol{P_k}\boldsymbol{F}\hat{\boldsymbol{x}}')^\top}{\|\boldsymbol{P_k}\boldsymbol{F}\hat{\boldsymbol{x}}'\|^2 + \|\boldsymbol{P_k}\boldsymbol{F}^\top\hat{\boldsymbol{x}}\|^2}\Big), \\ V_0[\hat{\boldsymbol{x}}'] &= \frac{1}{f_0^2}\Big(\boldsymbol{P_k} - \frac{(\boldsymbol{P_k}\boldsymbol{F}^\top\hat{\boldsymbol{x}})(\boldsymbol{P_k}\boldsymbol{F}^\top\hat{\boldsymbol{x}})^\top}{\|\boldsymbol{P_k}\boldsymbol{F}\hat{\boldsymbol{x}}'\|^2 + \|\boldsymbol{P_k}\boldsymbol{F}^\top\hat{\boldsymbol{x}}\|^2}\Big), \\ V_0[\hat{\boldsymbol{x}}, \hat{\boldsymbol{x}}'] &= \frac{1}{f_0^2}\Big(-\frac{(\boldsymbol{P_k}\boldsymbol{F}\hat{\boldsymbol{x}}')(\boldsymbol{P_k}\boldsymbol{F}^\top\hat{\boldsymbol{x}})^\top}{\|\boldsymbol{P_k}\boldsymbol{F}\hat{\boldsymbol{x}}'\|^2 + \|\boldsymbol{P_k}\boldsymbol{F}^\top\hat{\boldsymbol{x}}\|^2}\Big) = V_0[\hat{\boldsymbol{x}}', \hat{\boldsymbol{x}}]^\top, \end{aligned} \tag{8.13}$$

where $\boldsymbol{F}$ is the fundamental matrix, and we define $\boldsymbol{P_k} \equiv \mathrm{diag}(1,1,0)$ (↪ Exercise 8.4). Since the vector $\hat{\boldsymbol{X}}$ reconstructed from $\hat{\boldsymbol{x}}$ and $\hat{\boldsymbol{x}}'$ satisfies the projection relationship of Eq. (8.1), vectors $\hat{\boldsymbol{x}}$ and $\boldsymbol{P}\hat{\boldsymbol{X}}$ are parallel, and so are $\hat{\boldsymbol{x}}'$ and $\boldsymbol{P}'\hat{\boldsymbol{X}}$. Hence,

$$\hat{\boldsymbol{x}} \times \boldsymbol{P}\hat{\boldsymbol{X}} = \boldsymbol{0}, \qquad \hat{\boldsymbol{x}}' \times \boldsymbol{P}'\hat{\boldsymbol{X}} = \boldsymbol{0}. \tag{8.14}$$

It follows that if the noise in $\hat{\boldsymbol{x}}$ and $\hat{\boldsymbol{x}}'$ is $\Delta\hat{\boldsymbol{x}}$ and $\Delta\hat{\boldsymbol{x}}'$, respectively, the noise $\Delta\hat{\boldsymbol{X}}$ in $\hat{\boldsymbol{X}}$ satisfies to a first approximation

$$\Delta\hat{\boldsymbol{x}} \times \boldsymbol{P}\hat{\boldsymbol{X}} + \hat{\boldsymbol{x}} \times \boldsymbol{P}\Delta\hat{\boldsymbol{X}} = \boldsymbol{0}, \qquad \Delta\hat{\boldsymbol{x}}' \times \boldsymbol{P}'\hat{\boldsymbol{X}}' + \hat{\boldsymbol{x}}' \times \boldsymbol{P}'\Delta\hat{\boldsymbol{X}} = \boldsymbol{0}. \tag{8.15}$$

These are combined into one equation in the form

$$\begin{pmatrix} \hat{\boldsymbol{x}} \times \tilde{\boldsymbol{P}} \\ \hat{\boldsymbol{x}}' \times \tilde{\boldsymbol{P}}' \end{pmatrix} \Delta\hat{\boldsymbol{r}} = \begin{pmatrix} (\boldsymbol{P}\hat{\boldsymbol{X}}) \times \boldsymbol{I} & \boldsymbol{O} \\ \boldsymbol{O} & (\boldsymbol{P}'\hat{\boldsymbol{X}}) \times \boldsymbol{I} \end{pmatrix} \begin{pmatrix} \Delta\hat{\boldsymbol{x}} \\ \Delta\hat{\boldsymbol{x}}' \end{pmatrix}, \tag{8.16}$$

where $\Delta\hat{\boldsymbol{r}}$ is the 3D vector of the first three components of $\Delta\hat{\boldsymbol{X}}$ and $\tilde{\boldsymbol{P}}$ and $\tilde{\boldsymbol{P}}'$ are the left 3×3 submatrices of the 3×4 projection matrices $\boldsymbol{P}$ and $\boldsymbol{P}'$, respectively. Here, we are using the notation of Eq. (6.44). Multiplying both sides by the transpose of the left side from left, we obtain

$$\Big((\hat{\boldsymbol{x}}\times\tilde{\boldsymbol{P}})^\top(\hat{\boldsymbol{x}}\times\tilde{\boldsymbol{P}})+(\hat{\boldsymbol{x}}'\times\tilde{\boldsymbol{P}}')^\top(\hat{\boldsymbol{x}}'\times\tilde{\boldsymbol{P}}')\Big)\Delta\hat{\boldsymbol{r}}$$
$$=\Big((\hat{\boldsymbol{x}}\times\tilde{\boldsymbol{P}})^\top((\boldsymbol{P}\hat{\boldsymbol{X}})\times\boldsymbol{I})\ \ (\hat{\boldsymbol{x}}'\times\tilde{\boldsymbol{P}}')^\top((\boldsymbol{P}'\hat{\boldsymbol{X}})\times\boldsymbol{I})\Big)\begin{pmatrix}\Delta\hat{\boldsymbol{x}}\\ \Delta\hat{\boldsymbol{x}}'\end{pmatrix}, \tag{8.17}$$

which can be rewritten in the form (↪ Exercise 8.5)

$$\boldsymbol{A}\Delta\hat{\boldsymbol{r}}=\boldsymbol{B}\begin{pmatrix}\Delta\hat{\boldsymbol{x}}\\ \Delta\hat{\boldsymbol{x}}'\end{pmatrix}, \tag{8.18}$$

$$\boldsymbol{A}\equiv\tilde{\boldsymbol{P}}^\top(\|\hat{\boldsymbol{x}}\|^2\boldsymbol{I}-\hat{\boldsymbol{x}}\hat{\boldsymbol{x}}^\top)\tilde{\boldsymbol{P}}+\tilde{\boldsymbol{P}}'^\top(\|\hat{\boldsymbol{x}}'\|^2\boldsymbol{I}-\hat{\boldsymbol{x}}\hat{\boldsymbol{x}}'^\top)\tilde{\boldsymbol{P}}', \tag{8.19}$$

$$\boldsymbol{B}\equiv\Big(\tilde{\boldsymbol{P}}^\top\big((\hat{\boldsymbol{x}},\boldsymbol{P}\hat{\boldsymbol{X}})\boldsymbol{I}-(\boldsymbol{P}\hat{\boldsymbol{X}})\hat{\boldsymbol{x}}^\top\big)\ \ \tilde{\boldsymbol{P}}'^\top\big((\hat{\boldsymbol{x}}',\boldsymbol{P}'\hat{\boldsymbol{X}})\boldsymbol{I}-(\boldsymbol{P}'\hat{\boldsymbol{X}})\hat{\boldsymbol{x}}'^\top\big)\Big). \tag{8.20}$$

From Eq. (8.18), we obtain

$$\Delta\hat{\boldsymbol{r}}\Delta\hat{\boldsymbol{r}}^\top=\boldsymbol{A}^{-1}\boldsymbol{B}\begin{pmatrix}\Delta\hat{\boldsymbol{x}}\Delta\hat{\boldsymbol{x}}^\top & \Delta\hat{\boldsymbol{x}}\Delta\hat{\boldsymbol{x}}'^\top\\ \Delta\hat{\boldsymbol{x}}'\Delta\hat{\boldsymbol{x}}^\top & \Delta\hat{\boldsymbol{x}}'\Delta\hat{\boldsymbol{x}}'^\top\end{pmatrix}\boldsymbol{B}^\top(\boldsymbol{A}^{-1})^\top. \tag{8.21}$$

Taking expectation on both sides, we obtain the normalized covariance matrix $V_0[\hat{\boldsymbol{r}}]$ of the reconstructed position $\hat{\boldsymbol{r}}$ in the following form:

$$V_0[\hat{\boldsymbol{r}}]=\boldsymbol{A}^{-1}\boldsymbol{B}\begin{pmatrix}V_0[\hat{\boldsymbol{x}}] & V_0[\hat{\boldsymbol{x}},\hat{\boldsymbol{x}}']\\ V_0[\hat{\boldsymbol{x}}',\hat{\boldsymbol{x}}] & V_0[\hat{\boldsymbol{x}}']\end{pmatrix}\boldsymbol{B}^\top(\boldsymbol{A}^{-1})^\top. \tag{8.22}$$

Thus, we can reconstruct the 3D positions $\hat{\boldsymbol{r}}$ of all the feature points of the object by doing the triangulation of Sec. 8.3 and computing their (normalized) covariance matrices $V_0[\hat{\boldsymbol{r}}]$ by the above procedure. We do the same for the object after it is moved. Using the resulting 3D positions and their covariance matrices before and after the object motion, we can do the following experiment:

- Compute the object rotation (after subtracting the centroid displacement) by the methods described in Chapters 4, 5, and 6.
- Repeat the computation, each time changing the noise to add to the stereo images and experimentally evaluate $\boldsymbol{\mu}[\hat{\boldsymbol{R}}]$ and the covariance matrix $V[\hat{R}]$ of Eq. (7.6).
- Compare that covariance matrix $V[\hat{R}]$ with the KCR lower bound $\sigma^2\bar{\boldsymbol{H}}^{-1}$ of Eq. (7.45), where $\bar{\boldsymbol{H}}$ is defined by Eq. (7.17).
- Confirm that maximum likelihood estimation is very accurate and that its covariance matrix is close to the KCR lower bound.

8.5 LAND MOVEMENT COMPUTATION USING REAL GPS DATA

Geodetic scientists all over the world monitor the land movement using GPS data. For this purpose, a dense network of reference posts is built (Fig. 8.3). Each post receives GPS signals from multiple satellites over a long time, say, hours. By statistical procedures, its

FIGURE 8.3 GPS reference post (photographed by the author).

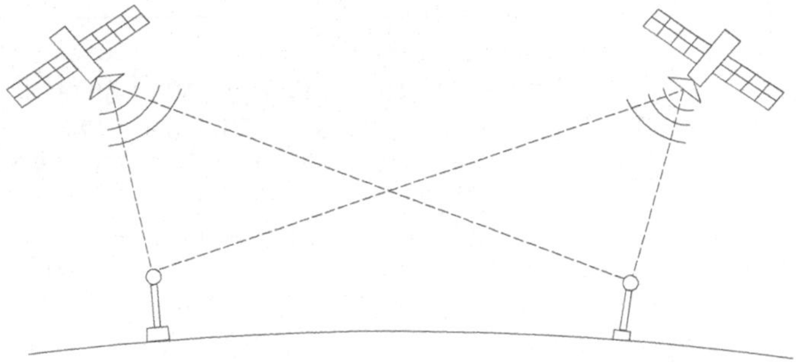

FIGURE 8.4 The landmark reference posts receive GPS signals from multiple satellites over a long time, and by statistical procedures, its position relative to the earth is computed very accurately. At the same time, the data covariance is also obtained.

position relative to the earth is computed very precisely up to millimeters (Fig. 8.4). At the same time, the data covariance is also obtained.

Table 8.1 shows the x, y, and z coordinates (in meters) with respect to the global earth coordinate system, called WGS84 (World Geodetic System 1984), of eight positions in northeast Japan (Fig. 8.5) in April 1, 2010, January 20, 2011, and January 20, 2012 provided by the Geospatial Information Authority of Japan[1]. The location IDs 0036, 0172, 0175, 0549, 0550, 0914, 0916, and 0918 in Table 8.1 correspond to Onagawa, Kesennuma, Shizugawa, Yamoto, Oshika, Towa, Minamikata, and Kahoku, respectively, as indicated in Fig. 8.5. The covariance matrices $\left(\sigma_{ij}\right)$ of each measurement are listed in Table 8.2. In this region, a massive earthquake of magnitude 9.0, the largest ever record in history, took place on March 11, 2011, causing more than 20,000 deaths and injuries.

From these data, readers can compute the land movement, using the methods described in this book. They can also evaluate the KCR lower bound of Eq. (7.45) by replacing the true values by their maximum likelihood estimates. Comparing the movement between April 1, 2010 and January 1, 2011 and the movement between January 1, 2011 and January 1, 2012, they can observe the effect of the earthquake in quantitative terms.

[11] http://www.gsi.go.jp/

TABLE 8.1 The 3D data (in meters) of eight locations in northeast Japan in April 1, 2010, January 20, 2011, and January 20, 2012 (from [23]).

ID	x	y	z
April 1, 2010			
0036	−3911124.6109	3117611.8596	3944663.0892
0172	−3893613.1472	3089073.9138	3983982.4425
0175	−3898936.7310	3106983.5744	3964933.7807
0549	−3899954.0638	3134197.0846	3942545.9721
0550	−3922366.9569	3119914.9630	3931806.3441
0914	−3888499.5166	3113285.6200	3970160.1127
0916	−3884406.9622	3127530.4255	3963000.4271
0918	−3900409.6500	3124326.0455	3949941.0937
January 20, 2011			
0036	−3911124.6161	3117611.8674	3944663.0891
0172	−3893613.1407	3089073.9247	3983982.4331
0175	−3898936.7224	3106983.5798	3964933.7745
0549	−3899954.0672	3134197.0985	3942545.9686
0550	−3922366.9488	3119914.9518	3931806.3269
0914	−3888499.5075	3113285.6240	3970160.1054
0916	−3884406.9628	3127530.4296	3963000.4215
0918	−3900409.6423	3124326.0532	3949941.0840
January 20, 2012			
0036	−3911128.3589	3117608.0272	3944661.2547
0172	−3893616.5621	3089070.9017	3983980.4920
0175	−3898940.3307	3106980.2371	3964931.9731
0549	−3899957.3856	3134193.9276	3942544.6596
0550	−3922370.7681	3119910.6783	3931804.3063
0914	−3888502.8233	3113282.7641	3970158.5816
0916	−3884410.1104	3127527.7274	3962999.1209
0918	−3900413.1310	3124322.7276	3949939.5679

TABLE 8.2 Covariance matrices ($\times 10^{-8}$) of the GPS measurements in Table 8.1 (from [23]).

ID	σ_{11}	σ_{22}	σ_{33}	σ_{23}	σ_{31}	σ_{12}
April 1, 2010						
0036	543.81468	425.88304	320.91074	204.01142	−262.01505	−143.09649
0172	2600.5301	2395.0165	1180.6302	655.80839	−765.87092	−145.37253
0175	588.95526	557.68621	306.88459	222.80817	−252.43021	−155.31865
0549	299.42994	206.77237	187.97368	129.75187	−173.89883	−117.32354
0550	2298.3728	2204.4857	970.31985	555.38549	−658.16237	−141.02400
0914	2580.3350	2378.9566	1113.2217	609.86213	−830.68293	−180.97003
0916	510.26601	473.90957	255.43911	181.32306	−225.06877	−143.14545
0918	2230.8269	2148.0015	958.60970	530.02453	−625.30146	−98.325922
January 20, 2011						
0036	287.87533	208.37832	186.80209	125.56468	−170.69383	−112.37926
0172	249.12117	192.85786	161.45344	110.72924	−143.73564	−93.520583
0175	452.82105	371.08918	230.58634	143.89346	−198.90161	−101.24319
0549	247.77608	189.61635	154.45629	106.81192	−139.79921	−90.106188
0550	2300.5173	1811.4054	869.80636	412.96236	−627.57330	−71.178480
0914	2509.0785	1958.3768	978.14059	417.99055	−766.42047	−71.479138
0916	1664.8206	1707.0988	822.11796	400.88891	−523.79020	−43.792427
0918	803.41570	592.74803	316.10716	182.73249	−261.03986	−84.101060
January 20, 2012						
0036	305.96250	215.96414	212.30943	135.52470	−190.15388	−122.02639
0172	250.29374	191.07272	161.34809	108.43137	−145.39350	−97.485117
0175	384.59613	222.83353	219.11424	141.58703	−211.37678	−130.11266
0549	250.86478	182.75383	157.11409	103.04156	−141.09274	−91.186199
0550	273.56924	195.10014	162.31885	111.27658	−154.20913	−103.82372
0914	2514.4584	1960.5877	1000.0640	42.292048	−771.60432	−58.595343
0916	586.20375	568.93574	300.81322	179.18146	−299.18962	−101.51431
0918	274.97742	178.45872	156.79702	101.31024	−140.78606	−89.699310

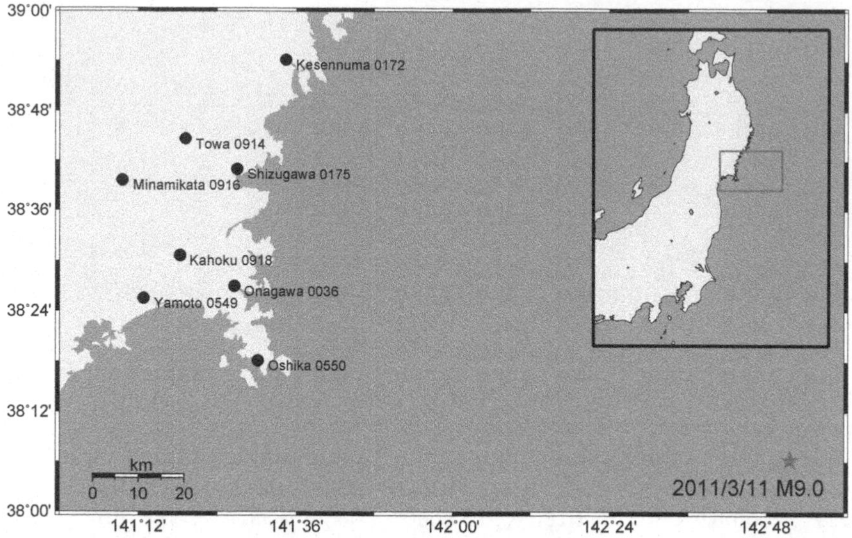

FIGURE 8.5 Eight locations (black circles) in northeast Japan and the epicenter (the star mark) of the earthquake on March 11, 2011 (from [23]).

8.6 SUPPLEMENTAL NOTES

Stereo vision is a method for reconstructing the 3D structure of a scene from corresponding points by triangulation; if the configuration of the cameras and their intrinsic parameters are known, one can compute the "ray" or the "line of sight" of each pixel, and the intersection of the corresponding rays gives their 3D position. In practice, however, correspondence detection entails uncertainty, so the corresponding rays may not meet in the scene. In the old days, this was handled by a practical compromise such as regarding the "midpoint" of the shortest line segment connecting the two rays as the intersection. Kanazawa and Kanatani [31] point out that an optimal method is to displace the corresponding pixels "minimally," i.e., the amount of displacement is minimum, so that their rays intersect. They not only optimally computed the 3D position but also evaluated the covariance matrix of thus reconstructed point. This is a typical instance of *optimal correction* of geometric estimation (see Kanatani [20] for general formulation).

The method of Kanazawa and Kanatani [31] is a first approximation to the true maximum likelihood estimate, although the difference is very small. Later, Kanatani et al. [30] modified it to obtain the true maximum likelihood solution using iterations as shown in Sec. 9.3 (↪ Exercise 8.1). Meanwhile, Hartley and Strum [14] presented a direct algebraic method, solving a 6th degree polynomial. The resulting solution is the same, but it has been pointed out that the optimal correction of Sec. 9.3 is much faster to compute [29, 30].

The mathematical principle of evaluating the covariance of stereo reconstruction was given by Kanazawa and Kanatani [31] and used by Ohta and Kanatani [35] for evaluating the accuracy and reliability of 3D rotation computation in their stereo simulation; they used a scheme called "renormalization" for their rotation computation, iterating eigenvalue computation (↪ Sec. 5.6). The covariance evaluation procedure of Sec. 8.4 is a reformulation of the method of Kanazawa and Kanatani [31] and was presented by Kanatani and Niitsuma [25].

The GPS data in Sec. 8.5 are from Kanatani and Matsunaga [23]. Using these data, they computed not only the rigid motion of the land but also considered various other motion modes, including similarity and affine transformation. To do that, they adopted the homogeneous constraint formulation of Sec. 5.5 and used the method called "EFNS " (↪ Sec. 5.5). Then, they compared different motion modes by "geometric model selection" (↪ Footnote 2 of Sec. 7.5), using the criteria called the "geometric AIC," the "geometric BIC," and the "geometric MDL," all of which balance the residual of the model fitting and the complexity of the model (the number of parameters involved). They concluded that between April 1, 2010 and January 20, 2011 the most reasonable interpretation was no motion, i.e., the land did not move at all, even though all motion modes have nonzero residuals. Between January 20, 2010 and January 20, 2012, however, they showed that all motion modes played nonnegligible roles.

8.7 EXERCISES

8.1. (1) If we represent points (x, y), (x', y'), $(\bar{x}, \bar{y})$ and $(\bar{x}', \bar{y}')$ by 3D vectors $\boldsymbol{x}$, $\boldsymbol{x}'$, $\bar{\boldsymbol{x}}$, and $\bar{\boldsymbol{x}}'$, respectively, as in Eq. (8.1) and write

$$\Delta\boldsymbol{x} = \boldsymbol{x} - \bar{\boldsymbol{x}}, \qquad \Delta\boldsymbol{x}' = \boldsymbol{x}' - \bar{\boldsymbol{x}}, \tag{8.23}$$

the reprojection error of Eq. (8.4) is written as

$$E = \frac{f_0^2}{2}\Big(\|\Delta\boldsymbol{x}\|^2 + \|\Delta\boldsymbol{x}'\|^2\Big). \tag{8.24}$$

Show that the $\Delta\boldsymbol{x}$ and $\Delta\boldsymbol{x}'$ that minimize Eq. (8.24) subject to the constraint that $\bar{\boldsymbol{x}}$ and $\bar{\boldsymbol{x}}'$ satisfy the epipolar equation of Eq. (6.49) are given by

$$\begin{aligned}\Delta\boldsymbol{x} &= \frac{\langle\boldsymbol{x}, \boldsymbol{F}\boldsymbol{x}'\rangle\boldsymbol{P}_{\boldsymbol{k}}\boldsymbol{F}\boldsymbol{x}'}{\|\boldsymbol{P}_{\boldsymbol{k}}\boldsymbol{F}\boldsymbol{x}'\|^2 + \|\boldsymbol{P}_{\boldsymbol{k}}\boldsymbol{F}^\top\boldsymbol{x}\|^2}, \\ \Delta\boldsymbol{x}' &= \frac{\langle\boldsymbol{x}, \boldsymbol{F}\boldsymbol{x}'\rangle\boldsymbol{P}_{\boldsymbol{k}}\boldsymbol{F}^\top\boldsymbol{x}}{\|\boldsymbol{P}_{\boldsymbol{k}}\boldsymbol{F}\boldsymbol{x}'\|^2 + \|\boldsymbol{P}_{\boldsymbol{k}}\boldsymbol{F}^\top\boldsymbol{x}\|^2},\end{aligned} \tag{8.25}$$

to a first approximation, i.e., by ignoring high order terms in $\Delta\boldsymbol{x}$ and $\Delta\boldsymbol{x}'$, where $\boldsymbol{P}_{\boldsymbol{k}} \equiv \mathrm{diag}(1, 1, 0)$.

(2) Using the $\Delta\boldsymbol{x}$ and $\Delta\boldsymbol{x}'$ obtained by Eq. (8.25), we define

$$\hat{\boldsymbol{x}} = \boldsymbol{x} - \Delta\boldsymbol{x}, \qquad \hat{\boldsymbol{x}}' = \boldsymbol{x}' - \Delta\boldsymbol{x}'. \tag{8.26}$$

Let $(\hat{x}, \hat{y})$ and $(\hat{x}', \hat{y}')$ be the points these vectors respectively represent. These are regarded as better approximations to $(\bar{x}, \bar{y})$ and $(\bar{x}', \bar{y}')$ than (x, y) and (x', y'). The reprojection error of Eq. (8.4) is now rewritten as

$$\begin{aligned}E &= \frac{1}{2}\Big((\hat{x} + (x - \hat{x}) - \bar{x})^2 + (\hat{y} + (y - \hat{y}) - \bar{y})^2 + (\hat{x}' + (x' - \hat{x}') - \bar{x}')^2 \\ &\quad + (\hat{y}' + (y' - \hat{y}') - \bar{y}')^2 \\ &= (\hat{x} + \tilde{x} - \bar{x})^2 + (\hat{y} + \tilde{y} - \bar{y})^2 + (\hat{x}' + \tilde{x}' - \bar{x}')^2 + (\hat{y}' + \tilde{y}' - \bar{y}')^2,\end{aligned} \tag{8.27}$$

where we define

$$\tilde{x} = x - \hat{x}, \qquad \tilde{y} = y - \hat{y}, \qquad \tilde{x}' = x' - \hat{x}', \qquad \tilde{y}' = y' - \hat{y}'. \tag{8.28}$$

If we represent points $(\tilde{x}, \tilde{y})$ and $(\tilde{x}', \tilde{y}')$ by 3D vectors $\tilde{\boldsymbol{x}}$ and $\tilde{\boldsymbol{x}}'$, respectively, as in Eq. (8.1) and write

$$\Delta\hat{\boldsymbol{x}} = \hat{\boldsymbol{x}} - \bar{\boldsymbol{x}}, \qquad \Delta\hat{\boldsymbol{x}}' = \hat{\boldsymbol{x}}' - \bar{\boldsymbol{x}}, \tag{8.29}$$

the reprojection error of Eq. (8.27) is written as

$$E = \frac{f_0^2}{2}\Big(\|\tilde{\boldsymbol{x}} + \Delta\hat{\boldsymbol{x}}\|^2 + \|\tilde{\boldsymbol{x}}' + \Delta\hat{\boldsymbol{x}}'\|^2\Big). \tag{8.30}$$

Show that the $\Delta\hat{\boldsymbol{x}}$ and $\Delta\hat{\boldsymbol{x}}'$ that minimize this subject to the constraint that $\bar{\boldsymbol{x}}$ and $\bar{\boldsymbol{x}}'$ satisfy the epipolar equation of Eq. (6.49) are given by

$$\Delta\hat{\boldsymbol{x}} = \frac{\Big(\langle\hat{\boldsymbol{x}}, \boldsymbol{F}\hat{\boldsymbol{x}}'\rangle + \langle\boldsymbol{F}\hat{\boldsymbol{x}}', \tilde{\boldsymbol{x}}\rangle + \langle\boldsymbol{F}^\top\hat{\boldsymbol{x}}, \tilde{\boldsymbol{x}}'\rangle\Big)\boldsymbol{P}_{\boldsymbol{k}}\boldsymbol{F}\hat{\boldsymbol{x}}'}{\langle\boldsymbol{F}\hat{\boldsymbol{x}}', \boldsymbol{P}_{\boldsymbol{k}}\boldsymbol{F}\hat{\boldsymbol{x}}'\rangle + \langle\boldsymbol{F}^\top\hat{\boldsymbol{x}}, \boldsymbol{P}_{\boldsymbol{k}}\boldsymbol{F}^\top\hat{\boldsymbol{x}}\rangle} - \tilde{\boldsymbol{x}},$$

$$\Delta\hat{\boldsymbol{x}}' = \frac{\Big(\langle\hat{\boldsymbol{x}}, \boldsymbol{F}\hat{\boldsymbol{x}}'\rangle + \langle\boldsymbol{F}\hat{\boldsymbol{x}}', \tilde{\boldsymbol{x}}\rangle + \langle\boldsymbol{F}^\top\hat{\boldsymbol{x}}, \tilde{\boldsymbol{x}}'\rangle\Big)\boldsymbol{P}_{\boldsymbol{k}}\boldsymbol{F}^\top\hat{\boldsymbol{x}}}{\langle\boldsymbol{F}\hat{\boldsymbol{x}}', \boldsymbol{P}_{\boldsymbol{k}}\boldsymbol{F}\hat{\boldsymbol{x}}'\rangle + \langle\boldsymbol{F}^\top\hat{\boldsymbol{x}}, \boldsymbol{P}_{\boldsymbol{k}}\boldsymbol{F}^\top\hat{\boldsymbol{x}}\rangle} - \tilde{\boldsymbol{x}}', \tag{8.31}$$

to a first approximation, i.e., by ignoring high order terms in $\Delta\hat{\boldsymbol{x}}$ and $\Delta\hat{\boldsymbol{x}}'$.

(3) Using the $\Delta\hat{\boldsymbol{x}}$ and $\Delta\hat{\boldsymbol{x}}'$ obtained by Eq. (8.31), we define

$$\hat{\hat{\boldsymbol{x}}} = \hat{\boldsymbol{x}} - \Delta\hat{\boldsymbol{x}}, \qquad \hat{\hat{\boldsymbol{x}}}' = \hat{\boldsymbol{x}}' - \Delta\hat{\boldsymbol{x}}'. \tag{8.32}$$

Let $(\hat{\hat{x}}, \hat{\hat{y}})$ and $(\hat{\hat{x}}', \hat{\hat{y}}')$ be the points these vectors respectively represent. These are regarded as better approximations to $(\bar{x}, \bar{y})$ and $(\bar{x}', \bar{y}')$ than $(\hat{x}, \hat{y})$ and $(\hat{x}'\hat{y}')$. Repeating this correction, we can improve the approximation to $(\bar{x}, \bar{y})$ and $(\bar{x}', \bar{y}')$ furthermore. Show that using the vectorized fundamental matrix $\boldsymbol{f}$ and the vector $\boldsymbol{\xi}^*$ defined by Eq. (8.6), we can rewrite Eq. (8.31) in the form

$$\begin{pmatrix}\hat{\hat{x}}\\ \hat{\hat{y}}\end{pmatrix} = \begin{pmatrix}x\\ y\end{pmatrix} - \frac{\langle\boldsymbol{f}, \boldsymbol{\xi}^*\rangle}{\langle\boldsymbol{f}, V_0[\hat{\boldsymbol{\xi}}]\boldsymbol{f}\rangle}\begin{pmatrix}F_{11} & F_{12} & F_{13}\\ F_{21} & F_{22} & F_{23}\end{pmatrix}\begin{pmatrix}\hat{x}'\\ \hat{y}'\\ f_0\end{pmatrix},$$

$$\begin{pmatrix}\hat{\hat{x}}'\\ \hat{\hat{y}}'\end{pmatrix} = \begin{pmatrix}x'\\ y'\end{pmatrix} - \frac{\langle\boldsymbol{f}, \boldsymbol{\xi}^*\rangle}{\langle\boldsymbol{f}, V_0[\hat{\boldsymbol{\xi}}]\boldsymbol{f}\rangle}\begin{pmatrix}F_{11} & F_{21} & F_{31}\\ F_{12} & F_{22} & F_{32}\end{pmatrix}\begin{pmatrix}\hat{x}\\ \hat{y}\\ f_0\end{pmatrix}, \tag{8.33}$$

where $V_0[\hat{\boldsymbol{\xi}}]$ is the matrix defined by Eq. (8.5).

8.2. (1) Show that the four equations of Eq. (8.11) are linearly dependent if and only if

$$\begin{vmatrix} P_{11} & P_{12} & P_{13} & P_{14} & x/f_0 & 0\\ P_{21} & P_{22} & P_{23} & P_{24} & y/f_0 & 0\\ P_{31} & P_{32} & P_{33} & P_{34} & 1 & 0\\ P'_{11} & P'_{12} & P'_{13} & P'_{14} & 0 & x'/f_0\\ P'_{21} & P'_{22} & P'_{23} & P'_{24} & 0 & y'/f_0\\ P'_{31} & P'_{32} & P'_{33} & P'_{34} & 0 & 1 \end{vmatrix} = 0. \tag{8.34}$$

(2) Show that Eq. (8.34) can be rewritten in the form of Eq. (6.49) for some matrix $\boldsymbol{F}$. Also, express each element of $\boldsymbol{F}$ in terms of P_{ij} and P'_{ij}, $i = 1, 2, 3$, $j = 1, 2, 3, 4$.

8.3. (1) Show that the nD vector $\boldsymbol{x}$ that minimizes $\|\boldsymbol{A}\boldsymbol{x} - \boldsymbol{b}\|^2$ for an $m \times n$ $(m > n)$ matrix $\boldsymbol{A}$ is obtained by solving the following *normal equation*:

$$\boldsymbol{A}^\top \boldsymbol{A}\boldsymbol{x} = \boldsymbol{A}^\top \boldsymbol{b}. \tag{8.35}$$

(2) If we define the *pseudoinverse* of an $n \times m$ $(m > n)$ $\boldsymbol{A}$ by $\boldsymbol{A}^- = (\boldsymbol{A}^\top \boldsymbol{A})^{-1}\boldsymbol{A}^\top$ when $\boldsymbol{A}^\top \boldsymbol{A}$ is nonsingular, show that the solution of the normal equation of Eq. (8.35) is written as

$$\boldsymbol{x} = \boldsymbol{A}^- \boldsymbol{b}. \tag{8.36}$$

8.4. (1) Let $\bar{\boldsymbol{x}}$ and $\bar{\boldsymbol{x}}'$ be the true values of the corresponding image points $\boldsymbol{x}$ and $\boldsymbol{x}'$, respectively (we use the 3D vector notation of eq. (8.1)), and let $\delta\boldsymbol{x}$ and $\delta\boldsymbol{x}'$ be their errors, i.e.,

$$\boldsymbol{x} = \bar{\boldsymbol{x}} + \delta\boldsymbol{x}, \qquad \boldsymbol{x}' = \bar{\boldsymbol{x}}' + \delta\boldsymbol{x}'. \tag{8.37}$$

Let $\Delta\hat{\boldsymbol{x}}$ and $\Delta\hat{\boldsymbol{x}}'$ be the errors of the optimally corrected points $\hat{\boldsymbol{x}}$ and $\hat{\boldsymbol{x}}'$, respectively, obtained by the procedure of Sec. 8.2, i.e.,

$$\hat{\boldsymbol{x}} = \bar{\boldsymbol{x}} + \Delta\hat{\boldsymbol{x}}, \qquad \hat{\boldsymbol{x}}' = \bar{\boldsymbol{x}}' + \Delta\hat{\boldsymbol{x}}'. \tag{8.38}$$

Show that $\Delta\hat{\boldsymbol{x}}$ and $\Delta\hat{\boldsymbol{x}}'$ are related to $\delta\boldsymbol{x}$ and $\delta\boldsymbol{x}'$ by

$$\begin{aligned}
\Delta\hat{\boldsymbol{x}} &= \delta\boldsymbol{x} - \frac{(\langle\delta\boldsymbol{x}, \boldsymbol{F}\boldsymbol{x}'\rangle + \langle\boldsymbol{x}, \boldsymbol{F}\delta\boldsymbol{x}'\rangle)\boldsymbol{P}_k\boldsymbol{F}\boldsymbol{x}'}{\|\boldsymbol{P}_k\boldsymbol{F}\boldsymbol{x}'\|^2 + \|\boldsymbol{P}_k\boldsymbol{F}^\top\boldsymbol{x}\|^2}, \\
\Delta\hat{\boldsymbol{x}}' &= \delta\boldsymbol{x}' - \frac{(\langle\delta\boldsymbol{x}, \boldsymbol{F}\boldsymbol{x}'\rangle + \langle\boldsymbol{x}, \boldsymbol{F}\delta\boldsymbol{x}'\rangle)\boldsymbol{P}_k\boldsymbol{F}\boldsymbol{x}'}{\|\boldsymbol{P}_k\boldsymbol{F}\boldsymbol{x}'\|^2 + \|\boldsymbol{P}_k\boldsymbol{F}^\top\boldsymbol{x}\|^2},
\end{aligned} \tag{8.39}$$

to a first approximation, i.e., up to higher order terms in $\delta\boldsymbol{x}$ and $\delta\boldsymbol{x}'$.

(2) Show that Eq. (8.13) holds.

8.5. For a 3D vector $\boldsymbol{a}$ and a 3×3 matrix $\boldsymbol{T}$, show that the following identity holds:

$$(\boldsymbol{a} \times \boldsymbol{T})^\top(\boldsymbol{a} \times \boldsymbol{T}) = \boldsymbol{T}^\top(\|\boldsymbol{a}\|^2\boldsymbol{I} - \boldsymbol{a}\boldsymbol{a}^\top)\boldsymbol{T}. \tag{8.40}$$

Hamilton's Quaternion Algebra

In Sec. 3.5, we showed that 3D rotations can be represented by quaternions first introduced by Hamilton as an extension of complex numbers for representing 2D rotations. We also showed that quaternions provide a convenient analytical tool for optimizing rotations as illustrated in Secs. 4.4 and 5.3. Beside being a useful analytical tool, quaternions have an important mathematical structure of its own. Here, we briefly summarize algebraic and geometric structures of the set of quaternions from a pure mathematical point of view. First of all, quaternions provide a typical algebraic approach of defining operations on symbols for describing geometry. A quaternion can be regarded as a combination of a scalar and a vector, and the quaternion product can be viewed as simultaneous computation of the inner product and the vector product. Also, division can be defined for quaternions. We introduce various mathematical facts about quaternions and their relationships to rotations. For more details, see [22].

A.1 QUATERNIONS

The expression

$$q = q_0 + q_1 i + q_2 j + q_3 k \tag{A.1}$$

for four real numbers q_0, q_1, q_2, and q_3 and the three "symbols" i, j, and k is called a *quaternion*. One may wonder how symbols can be multiplied by numbers or added to other symbols. However, additions and scalar multiplications are only formal without having particular meanings. For example, $2i$ only means that the symbol i is counted twice, and the addition "+" merely indicates the set of the summands. This is the same as defining complex numbers. For example, $2 + 3i$ is nothing but the "set" of a real number 2 and an imaginary number $3i$, i.e., the imaginary unit i counted three times; it is not that adding a real number and an imaginary number creates something new. Such a "set operation" is called a *formal sum*. However, a formal sum is not just a mere enumeration of elements. We require that the commutativity, the associativity, and the distributivity of real numbers also hold. In other words, we are allowed to change the order of additions and distribute a real coefficient to each term. Hence, if

$$q' = q'_0 + q'_1 i + q'_2 j + q'_3 k \tag{A.2}$$

is another quaternion, we can write

$$2q + 3q' = (2q_0 + 3q_0') + (2q_1 + 3q_1')i + (2q_2 + 3q_2')j + (2q_3 + 3q_3')k. \tag{A.3}$$

Mathematically, we say that the set of all quaternions constitutes a vector space *generated* by the basis $\{1, i, j, k\}$.

Thus, we are free to add quaternions and multiply them by scalars. Next, we define the product qq' of quaternions q and q'. After expansion using the commutativity, the associativity, and the distributivity of addition, the product reduces in the end to the sum of the pairwise products of the symbols i, j, and k. As in Eqs. (3.25) and (3.26), we define

$$i^2 = -1, \qquad j^2 = -1, \qquad k^2 = -1, \tag{A.4}$$

$$jk = i, \qquad ki = j, \qquad ij = k,$$

$$kj = -i, \qquad ik = -j, \qquad ji = -k. \tag{A.5}$$

Equation (A.4) implies that each of i, j, and k is an "imaginary unit." Equation (A.5) suggests that if i, j, and k are identified with the orthonormal coordinate basis vectors e_1, e_2, and e_3, respectively, then the rule of vector product $e_2 \times e_3 = e_1$, etc. applies. From Eqs. (A.4) and (A.5), the product of Eqs. (A.1) and (A.2) has the following expression:

$$\begin{aligned} qq' &= (q_0 + q_1 i + q_2 j + q_3 k)(q_0' + q_1' i + q_2' j + q_3' k) \\ &= q_0 q_0' + q_1 q_1' i^2 + q_2 q_2' j^2 + q_3 q_3' k^2 + (q_0 q_1' + q_1 q_0')i + (q_0 q_2' + q_2 q_0')j + (q_0 q_3' + q_3 q_0')k \\ &\quad + q_1 q_2' ij + q_1 q_3' ik + q_2 q_1' ji + q_2 q_3' jk + q_3 q_1' ki + q_3 q_2' kj \\ &= q_0 q_0' - q_1 q_1' - q_2 q_2' - q_3 q_3' + (q_0 q_1' + q_1 q_0')i + (q_0 q_2' + q_2 q_0')j + (q_0 q_3' + q_3 q_0')k \\ &\quad + q_1 q_2' k - q_1 q_3' j - q_2 q_1' k + q_2 q_3' i + q_3 q_1' j - q_3 q_2' i \\ &= (q_0 q_0' - q_1 q_1' - q_2 q_2' - q_3 q_3') + (q_0 q_1' + q_1 q_0' + q_2 q_3' - q_3 q_2')i \\ &\quad + (q_0 q_2' + q_2 q_0' + q_3 q_1' - q_1 q_3')j + (q_0 q_3' + q_3 q_0' + q_1 q_2' - q_2 q_1')k. \end{aligned} \tag{A.6}$$

A.2 QUATERNION ALGEBRA

Equation (A.6) states that the product of quaternions is again a quaternion. It can be confirmed from Eq. (A.6) that the associativity

$$(qq')q'' = q(q'q'') \tag{A.7}$$

holds. This can also be seen from Eqs (A.4) and (A.5), which imply that the multiplication rule of 1, i, j, and k is associative, i.e., $(ij)k = i(jk) = -1$, $(ij)i = i(ji) = j$, etc. However, the commutativity $qq' = q'q$ does not necessarily hold, as Eq. (A.5) shows. If associative multiplication is defined in a vector space, and if the space is closed under that multiplication, i.e., if the product of arbitrary elements also belongs to that space, the vector space is said to be an *algebra*. In this sense, the set of all quaternions is an algebra.

If we let $q_1 = q_2 = q_3 = 0$ in Eq. (A.1), then q $(= q_0)$ is a real number. Hence, the set of all real numbers is included in the set of quaternions, i.e., quaternions are an extension of real numbers. On the other hand, if we identify a quaternion $q = q_1 i + q_2 j + q_3 k$ for which $q_0 = 0$ with a vector $q_1 e_1 + q_2 e_2 + q_3 e_3$, the same rule applies for addition and scalar multiplication as in the case of vectors. In this sense, a quaternion is an extension of a 3D vector. In view of this, we call q_0 in Eq. (A.1) the *scalar part* of q and $q_1 i + q_2 j + q_3 k$ its *vector part*. We also say that a quaternion is a *scalar* if its vector part is 0 and a *vector* if its scalar part is 0.

If we put the scalar part q_0 of Eq. (A.1) to be $\alpha = q_0$ and its vector part to be $\boldsymbol{a} = q_1 i + q_2 j + q_3 k$, the quaternion q is expressed as a formal sum of the scalar α and the vector $\boldsymbol{a}$ in the form $q = \alpha + \boldsymbol{a}$. Then, as we showed in Sec. 3.5, the product of quaternions $q = \alpha + \boldsymbol{a}$ and $q' = \beta + \boldsymbol{b}$ is written, from Eq. (A.6), in the form

$$qq' = (\alpha\beta - \langle \boldsymbol{a}, \boldsymbol{b} \rangle) + \alpha\boldsymbol{b} + \beta\boldsymbol{a} + \boldsymbol{a} \times \boldsymbol{b}. \tag{A.8}$$

In particular, the product of their vector parts $\boldsymbol{a}$ and $\boldsymbol{b}$ is

$$\boldsymbol{a}\boldsymbol{b} = -\langle \boldsymbol{a}, \boldsymbol{b} \rangle + \boldsymbol{a} \times \boldsymbol{b}. \tag{A.9}$$

Here, $\langle \boldsymbol{a}, \boldsymbol{b} \rangle$ and $\boldsymbol{a} \times \boldsymbol{b}$ in Eqs. (A.8) and (A.9) are the inner and the vector products, respectively, computed by identifying $\{i, j, k\}$ with the orthonormal coordinate basis $\{e_1, e_2, e_3\}$ (see Eqs. (3.28) and (3.29) in Sec. 3.5). Equation (A.9) allows us to interpret the quaternion product $\boldsymbol{a}\boldsymbol{b}$ to be simultaneous computation of their inner product $\langle \boldsymbol{a}, \boldsymbol{b} \rangle$ and vector product $\boldsymbol{a} \times \boldsymbol{b}$.

A.3 CONJUGATE, NORM, AND INVERSE

From Eq. (A.4), we can interpret the quaternion q to be an extended complex number with three imaginary units i, j, and k. In view of this, we define the *conjugate* $q^\dagger$ of the quaternion q of Eq. (A.1) by

$$q^\dagger = q_0 - q_1 i - q_2 j - q_3 k. \tag{A.10}$$

Evidently, the conjugate of the conjugate is the original quaternion. For quaternions q and q', the following holds (↪ Problem 3.4):

$$q^{\dagger\dagger} = q, \qquad (qq')^\dagger = q'^\dagger q^\dagger. \tag{A.11}$$

From the definition of the conjugate of Eq. (A.10), we conclude that a quaternion q is a scalar or a vector if and only if

$$q^\dagger = q, \qquad q^\dagger = -q, \tag{A.12}$$

respectively (↪ Problem 3.5).

In view of the identity (↪ Problem 3.6)

$$qq^\dagger = q_0^2 + q_1^2 + q_2^2 + q_3^2 \ (= q^\dagger q), \tag{A.13}$$

we define the *norm* of quaternion q by

$$\|q\| = \sqrt{qq^\dagger} = \sqrt{q^\dagger q} = \sqrt{q_0^2 + q_1^2 + q_2^2 + q_3^2}. \tag{A.14}$$

For a vector $\boldsymbol{a}$ regarded as a quaternion, its quaternion norm $\|\boldsymbol{a}\|$ coincides with its vector norm $\|\boldsymbol{a}\|$.

We see that $q^\dagger/\|q\|^2$ is the *inverse* q^{-1} of q (↪ Problem 3.7):

$$q^{-1} = \frac{q^\dagger}{\|q\|^2}, \qquad qq^{-1} = q^{-1}q = 1. \tag{A.15}$$

In other words, every nonzero quaternion q has its inverse q^{-1}, which allows division by quaternions. An algebra is called a *field* if every nonzero element of it has its inverse and if it is closed under division by nonzero elements. The set of all real numbers is a field; so is the set of all quaternions.

The existence of an inverse that admits division means that $qq' = qq''$ for $q \neq 0$ implies $q' = q''$. This property, however, does not hold for the inner product and the vector product of vectors. In fact, $\langle \boldsymbol{a}, \boldsymbol{b} \rangle = \langle \boldsymbol{a}, \boldsymbol{c} \rangle$ for $\boldsymbol{a} \neq 0$ does not imply $\boldsymbol{b} = \boldsymbol{c}$, because we can add to $\boldsymbol{b}$ any vector that is orthogonal to $\boldsymbol{a}$. Similarly, $\boldsymbol{a} \times \boldsymbol{b} = \boldsymbol{a} \times \boldsymbol{c}$ for $\boldsymbol{a} \neq 0$ does not imply $\boldsymbol{b} = \boldsymbol{c}$, because we can add to $\boldsymbol{b}$ any vector that is parallel to $\boldsymbol{a}$. If we recall that the quaternion product of vectors can be regarded as simultaneous computation of the inner and the vector products, as shown in Eq. (A.9), the existence of an inverse is evident: if $\langle \boldsymbol{a}, \boldsymbol{b} \rangle = \langle \boldsymbol{a}, \boldsymbol{c} \rangle$ and $\boldsymbol{a} \times \boldsymbol{b} = \boldsymbol{a} \times \boldsymbol{c}$ at the same time for $\boldsymbol{a} \neq 0$, we must have $\boldsymbol{b} = \boldsymbol{c}$.

A.4 QUATERNION REPRESENTATION OF ROTATIONS

We call a quaternion q of unit norm a *unit quaternion*. Consider the product $q\boldsymbol{a}q^\dagger$ for a unit quaternion q and a vector $\boldsymbol{a}$ regarded as a quaternion. As shown in Problem 3.8, its conjugate is $(q\boldsymbol{a}q^\dagger)^\dagger = -q\boldsymbol{a}q^\dagger$, so $q\boldsymbol{a}q^\dagger$ is a vector as implied by Eq. (A.12). If we let this vector be

$$\boldsymbol{a}' = q\boldsymbol{a}q^\dagger, \tag{A.16}$$

its square norm is $\|\boldsymbol{a}'\|^2 = \|\boldsymbol{a}\|^2$, as shown in Problem 3.9. Thus, Eq. (A.16) defines a linear mapping of $\boldsymbol{a}$ that preserves the norm, and hence it is either a pure rotation or a composition of a rotation and a reflection. In Sec. 3.5, we showed that it is indeed a rotation by writing the unit quaternion q in the form of Eq. (3.33), i.e.,

$$q = \cos\frac{\Omega}{2} + \boldsymbol{l}\sin\frac{\Omega}{2}, \tag{A.17}$$

where q_0 and $\boldsymbol{l}$ (unit vector) are defined by Eq. (3.32); we showed that Eq. (A.16) reduces to the Rodrigues formula of Eq. (3.19) in Sec. 3.4 (see Eqs. (3.35)–(3.38)). Thus, Eq. (A.17) represents a rotation by angle Ω around axis $\boldsymbol{l}$.

The important thing is that a quaternion q acts on vector $\boldsymbol{a}$ by "sandwiching" $\boldsymbol{a}$ in the form of Eq. (A.16). To emphasize this face, we call Eq. (A.17) a *rotor* by angle Ω around axis $\boldsymbol{l}$. As we showed in Sec. 3.5, quaternions q and $-q$ define the same rotor; to be precise, $-q$ represents a rotation by angle $2\pi - \Omega$ around axis $-\boldsymbol{l}$ (see Eq. (3.45)), which is the same as the rotation around $\boldsymbol{l}$ by Ω.

A.5 COMPOSITION OF ROTATIONS

Let $\mathcal{R}$ symbolically denote the operation of rotating a vector by some angle around some axis. Suppose we perform a rotation $\mathcal{R}$ followed by another rotation $\mathcal{R}'$. We write the resulting rotation, i.e., the composition of the two rotations, as $\mathcal{R}' \circ \mathcal{R}$. If we apply a rotor q to vector $\boldsymbol{a}$ and then apply another rotor q', we obtain

$$\boldsymbol{a}' = q'(q\boldsymbol{a}q^\dagger)q'^\dagger = (q'q)\boldsymbol{a}(q'q)^\dagger. \tag{A.18}$$

Hence, if a rotor q defines rotation $\mathcal{R}$ and another rotor q' rotation $\mathcal{R}'$, their composition $\mathcal{R}' \circ \mathcal{R}$ is defined by the rotor $q'q$. We express this fact by saying that the product of rotors and the composition of rotations are *homomorphic* to each other, meaning that the rule of computation has the same form.

From Eq. (A.17), the composition of a rotation by angle Ω around axis $\boldsymbol{l}$ and a rotation by angle Ω' around axis $\boldsymbol{l}'$ is given by

$$
\begin{aligned}
&(\cos\frac{\Omega'}{2} + \boldsymbol{l}'\sin\frac{\Omega'}{2})(\cos\frac{\Omega}{2} + \boldsymbol{l}\sin\frac{\Omega}{2}) \\
&= \cos\frac{\Omega'}{2}\cos\frac{\Omega}{2} + \boldsymbol{l}\cos\frac{\Omega'}{2}\sin\frac{\Omega}{2} + \boldsymbol{l}'\sin\frac{\Omega'}{2}\cos\frac{\Omega}{2} + \boldsymbol{l}'\boldsymbol{l}\sin\frac{\Omega'}{2}\sin\frac{\Omega}{2} \\
&= \cos\frac{\Omega'}{2}\cos\frac{\Omega}{2} + \boldsymbol{l}\cos\frac{\Omega'}{2}\sin\frac{\Omega}{2} + \boldsymbol{l}'\sin\frac{\Omega'}{2}\cos\frac{\Omega}{2} + (-\langle\boldsymbol{l}',\boldsymbol{l}\rangle + \boldsymbol{l}'\times\boldsymbol{l})\sin\frac{\Omega'}{2}\sin\frac{\Omega}{2} \\
&= \Big(\cos\frac{\Omega'}{2}\cos\frac{\Omega}{2} - \langle\boldsymbol{l}',\boldsymbol{l}\rangle\sin\frac{\Omega'}{2}\sin\frac{\Omega}{2}\Big) + \boldsymbol{l}\cos\frac{\Omega'}{2}\sin\frac{\Omega}{2} + \boldsymbol{l}'\sin\frac{\Omega'}{2}\cos\frac{\Omega}{2} \\
&+\boldsymbol{l}'\times\boldsymbol{l}\sin\frac{\Omega'}{2}\sin\frac{\Omega}{2}. \qquad (A.19)
\end{aligned}
$$

From this, we see that the angle Ω'' and the axis $\boldsymbol{l}''$ of the composite rotation are given by

$$
\begin{aligned}
\cos\frac{\Omega''}{2} &= \cos\frac{\Omega'}{2}\cos\frac{\Omega}{2} - \langle\boldsymbol{l}',\boldsymbol{l}\rangle\sin\frac{\Omega'}{2}\sin\frac{\Omega}{2}, \\
\boldsymbol{l}''\cos\frac{\Omega''}{2} &= \boldsymbol{l}\sin\frac{\Omega'}{2}\sin\frac{\Omega}{2} + \boldsymbol{l}'\sin\frac{\Omega'}{2}\cos\frac{\Omega}{2} + \boldsymbol{l}'\times\boldsymbol{l}\sin\frac{\Omega'}{2}\sin\frac{\Omega}{2}. \qquad (A.20)
\end{aligned}
$$

A.6 TOPOLOGY OF ROTATIONS

Equation (A.16) defines a linear mapping such that $\|\boldsymbol{a}'\| = \|\boldsymbol{a}\|$. Hence, it is either a pure rotation or a composition of a rotation and a reflection, and we showed that it is a rotation by reducing Eq. (A.16) to the Rodrigues formula. However, it can be shown directly that Eq. (A.16) does not involve reflection by a simple consideration as follows. Evidently, $q = \pm 1$ acts as the identity, and an arbitrary unit quaternion $q = q_0 + q_1 i + q_2 j + q_3 k$ can be smoothly reduced to $q = \pm 1$ by varying $q_0 \to \pm 1$, $q_1 \to 0$, $q_2 \to 0$, and $q_3 \to 0$ without violating $q_0^2 + q_1^2 + q_2^2 + q_3^2 = 1$. If reflections are involved, q cannot be continuously reduced to the identity. The mathematical study of this type of reasoning based on "continuous variations" is called *topology*.

Since a set of four numbers q_0, q_1, q_2, q_3 such that $q_0^2 + q_1^2 + q_2^2 + q_3^2 = 1$ represents a rotation, the set of all rotations corresponds to the unit sphere S^3 around the origin in 4D. However, two quaternions q and $-q$ represent the same rotation, so the correspondence between S^3 and the set of rotations is two-to-one. This can be made one-to-one by considering a hemisphere, e.g., the part of S^3 for $q_0 \geq 0$. But then there arises a problem of continuity, because each point on the boundary and its antipode, i.e., the other end of the diametrical segment, represent the same rotation. Hence, if the trajectory of continuously varying rotations reaches the boundary, it then reappears from the antipode. In order to eliminate such a discontinuity, we need to paste each point on the boundary to its antipode (Fig. A.1). The resulting space is denoted by $\mathcal{P}^3$ and called, in topological terms, the 3D *projective space*. Thus, the set of all rotations continuously corresponds one-to-one to $\mathcal{P}^3$. We refer to this fact saying that the set of all rotations is *homeomorphic* to $\mathcal{P}^3$.

It is easy to see that a closed loop on this hemisphere that reaches the boundary and reappears from the antipode cannot be continuously shrunk to a point (Fig. A.1(a)). A space is said to be *connected* if any two points in it can be connected by a smooth path, and *simply connected* if any closed loop in it can be continuously shrunk to a point. Thus, $\mathcal{P}^3$ is connected but not simply connected. However, it is easy to mentally visualize that a closed loop that passes through the boundary twice (or an even number of times) can be continuously shrunk to a point (Fig. A.1(b)).

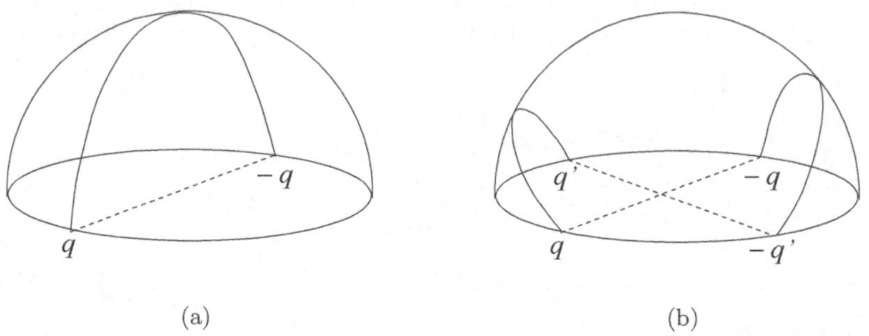

FIGURE A.1 The set of all quaternions that represents rotations corresponds to a hemisphere of radius 1 in 4D such that all antipodal points q and $-q$ on the boundary are pasted together. (a) If a closed path that represents continuous variations of rotation reaches the boundary, it reappears on the opposite side. This loop cannot be continuously shrunk to a point. (b) If a closed loop passes through the boundary twice, it can be continuously shrunk to a point: we first rotate the diametrical segment connecting q' and $-q'$ so that they coincide with q and $-q$ and then shrink the loop to q and $-q$, which represent the same point.

A.7 INFINITESIMAL ROTATIONS

We have seen that by expressing a unit quaternion q in the form of Eq. (A.17), we can derive the Rodrigues formula. Hence, Eq. (A.17) represents the rotation around axis $\boldsymbol{l}$ by angle Ω. However, we can directly show that a rotation around axis $\boldsymbol{l}$ by angle Ω must have the form of Eq. (A.17). To show this, let us consider infinitesimal rotations close to the identity. Since the identity corresponds to the rotor $q = 1$, the rotor for an infinitesimal rotation has the form

$$q = 1 + \delta q + O(\delta q^2), \qquad q^\dagger = 1 + \delta q^\dagger + O(\delta q^2). \tag{A.21}$$

Since q is a unit quaternion, its square norm

$$\|q\|^2 = qq^\dagger = (1 + \delta q + O(\delta q^2))(1 + \delta q^\dagger + O(\delta q^2)) = 1 + \delta q + \delta q^\dagger + O(\delta q^2) \tag{A.22}$$

must be identically 1. Hence, $\delta q^\dagger = -\delta q$, so δq is a vector from Eq. (A.12). From Eq. (A.9), an infinitesimal rotation of vector $\boldsymbol{a}$ is given by

$$\begin{aligned}\boldsymbol{a}' &= q\boldsymbol{a}q^\dagger = (1 + \delta q)\boldsymbol{a}(1 - \delta q) + O(\delta q^2) = \boldsymbol{a} + \delta q\boldsymbol{a} - \boldsymbol{a}\delta q + O(\delta q^2)\\ &= \boldsymbol{a} + 2\delta q \times \boldsymbol{a} + O(\delta q^2).\end{aligned} \tag{A.23}$$

Comparing this with Eq. (6.5) in Sec. 6.2, we can express δq in terms of an infinitesimal angle $\Delta\Omega$ and an axis $\boldsymbol{l}$ as $\Delta\Omega\boldsymbol{l}/2$. Hence, we can write

$$q = 1 + \frac{\Delta\Omega}{2}\boldsymbol{l} + O(\delta q^2). \tag{A.24}$$

Let $q_{\boldsymbol{l}}(\Omega)$ be the rotor by angle Ω around axis $\boldsymbol{l}$. Differentiating it with respect to Ω, we see that

$$\begin{aligned}\frac{dq_{\boldsymbol{l}}(\Omega)}{d\Omega} &= \lim_{\Delta\Omega\to 0}\frac{q_{\boldsymbol{l}}(\Omega + \Delta\Omega) - q_{\boldsymbol{l}}(\Omega)}{\Delta\Omega} = \lim_{\Delta\Omega\to 0}\frac{q_{\boldsymbol{l}}(\Delta\Omega)q_{\boldsymbol{l}}(\Omega) - q_{\boldsymbol{l}}(\Omega)}{\Delta\Omega}\\ &= \lim_{\Delta\Omega\to 0}\frac{q_{\boldsymbol{l}}(\Delta\Omega) - 1}{\Delta\Omega}q_{\boldsymbol{l}}(\Omega) = \frac{1}{2}\boldsymbol{l}q_{\boldsymbol{l}}(\Omega),\end{aligned} \tag{A.25}$$

where we have noted that $q_l(\Omega + \Delta\Omega) = q_l(\Delta\Omega)q_l(\Omega)$ and used Eq. (A.24) for $q_l(\Delta\Omega)$. Differentiating Eq. (A.25) many times, we obtain $d^2q_l(\Omega)/d\Omega^2 = (1/4)\boldsymbol{l}^2 q_l(\Omega)$, $d^3q_l(\Omega)/d\Omega^3 = (1/8)\boldsymbol{l}^3 q_l(\Omega)$, etc. Since $q_l(0) = 1$, we obtain the Taylor expression around $\Omega = 0$ (known to be absolutely convergent) in the following form:

$$q_l(\Omega) = 1 + \frac{\Omega}{2}\boldsymbol{l} + \frac{1}{2!}\frac{\Omega^2}{4}\boldsymbol{l}^2 + \frac{1}{3!}\frac{\Omega^3}{8}\boldsymbol{l}^3 + \cdots = \sum_{k=1}^{\infty}\frac{1}{k!}\Big(\frac{\Omega}{2}\boldsymbol{l}\Big)^k = \exp\frac{\Omega}{2}\boldsymbol{l}. \tag{A.26}$$

The last term is a symbolic expression of $\sum_{k=1}^{\infty}(\Omega\boldsymbol{l}/2)^k/k!$. Since $\boldsymbol{l}$ is a unit vector, we have $\boldsymbol{l}^2 = -1$ from Eq. (A.9). Hence Eq. (A.26) can be rewritten in the form of Eq. (A.17):

$$\begin{aligned} q_l(\Omega) &= \Big(1 - \frac{1}{2!}\Big(\frac{\Omega}{2}\Big)^2 + \frac{1}{4!}\Big(\frac{\Omega}{2}\Big)^4 + \cdots\Big) + \boldsymbol{l}\Big(\frac{\Omega}{2} - \frac{1}{3!}\Big(\frac{\Omega}{2}\Big)^3 + \frac{1}{5!}\Big(\frac{\Omega}{2}\Big)^5 - \cdots\Big) \\ &= \cos\frac{\Omega}{2} + \boldsymbol{l}\sin\frac{\Omega}{2}. \end{aligned} \tag{A.27}$$

A.8 REPRESENTATION OF GROUP OF ROTATIONS

A set of elements for which multiplication is defined is called a *group* if 1) the multiplication is associative, 2) there exists a unique *identity* whose multiplication does not change any element, and 3) each element has its *inverse* whose multiplication results in the identity (see Appendix C for more details). The set of all rotations is a group, called the *group of rotations* and denoted by $SO(3)$, where multiplication is defined by composition; the identity is the rotation by angle 0 and the inverse is the opposite rotation (sign reversal of the angle of rotation).

We have already seen that the action of rotors is homomorphic to the composition of rotations. In terms of rotation matrices, multiplication of rotation matrices is homomorphic to the composition of rotations. Namely, if matrices $\boldsymbol{R}$ and $\boldsymbol{R}'$ represent rotations $\mathcal{R}$ and $\mathcal{R}'$, respectively, the product $\boldsymbol{R}'\boldsymbol{R}$ represents their composition $\mathcal{R}' \circ \mathcal{R}$. In mathematical terms, if each element of a group corresponds to a matrix and if multiplication of group elements is homomorphic to multiplication of the corresponding matrices, we say that this correspondence is a *representation* of the group [22]. The matrix of Eq. (3.20) in Sec. 6.4 and the matrix of Eq. (3.40) in Sec. 3.5 are both representations of $SO(3)$, but there exist many other representations. Among them is the following expression of the quaternion $q = q_0 + q_1 i + q_2 j + q_3 k$ as a 2×2 matrix with complex components

$$\boldsymbol{U} = \begin{pmatrix} q_0 - iq_3 & -q_2 - iq_1 \\ q_2 - iq_1 & q_0 + iq_3 \end{pmatrix}. \tag{A.28}$$

To say that this is a representation is equivalent to saying

$$\begin{pmatrix} q_0'' - iq_3'' & -q_2'' - iq_1'' \\ q_2'' - iq_1'' & q_0'' + iq_3'' \end{pmatrix} = \begin{pmatrix} q_0' - iq_3' & -q_2' - iq_1' \\ q_2' - iq_1' & q_0' + iq_3' \end{pmatrix}\begin{pmatrix} q_0 - iq_3 & -q_2 - iq_1 \\ q_2 - iq_1 & q_0 + iq_3 \end{pmatrix}, \tag{A.29}$$

where the quaternion $q'' = q_0'' + q_1''i + q_2''j + q_3''k$ equals the product $q'q$ of the quaternions $q' = q_0' + q_1'i + q_2'j + q_3'k$ and $q = q_0 + q_1 i + q_2 j + q_3 k$. This can be easily confirmed by direct calculation, but the following argument is more informative. We can rewrite Eq. (A.28) in the form

$$\boldsymbol{U} = q_0\boldsymbol{I} + q_1\boldsymbol{S}_1 + q_2\boldsymbol{S}_2 + q_3\boldsymbol{S}_3, \tag{A.30}$$

where we define

$$\boldsymbol{I} = \begin{pmatrix} 1 & 0 \\ 0 & 1 \end{pmatrix}, \quad \boldsymbol{S}_1 = \begin{pmatrix} 0 & -i \\ -i & 0 \end{pmatrix}, \quad \boldsymbol{S}_2 = \begin{pmatrix} 0 & -1 \\ 1 & 0 \end{pmatrix}, \quad \boldsymbol{S}_3 = \begin{pmatrix} -i & 0 \\ 0 & i \end{pmatrix}. \tag{A.31}$$

Their pairwise products are

$$\begin{aligned} \boldsymbol{S}_1^2 &= -\boldsymbol{I}, & \boldsymbol{S}_2^2 &= -\boldsymbol{I}, & \boldsymbol{S}_3^2 &= -\boldsymbol{I}, \\ \boldsymbol{S}_2\boldsymbol{S}_3 &= \boldsymbol{S}_1, & \boldsymbol{S}_3\boldsymbol{S}_1 &= \boldsymbol{S}_2, & \boldsymbol{S}_1\boldsymbol{S}_2 &= \boldsymbol{S}_3, \end{aligned} \tag{A.32}$$

$$\boldsymbol{S}_3\boldsymbol{S}_2 = -\boldsymbol{S}_1, \qquad \boldsymbol{S}_1\boldsymbol{S}_3 = -\boldsymbol{S}_2, \qquad \boldsymbol{S}_2\boldsymbol{S}_1 = -\boldsymbol{S}_3. \tag{A.33}$$

In other words, pairwise multiplication of $\boldsymbol{I}$, $\boldsymbol{S}_1$, $\boldsymbol{S}_2$, and $\boldsymbol{S}_3$ has the same form as pairwise multiplication of 1, i, j, and k in Eqs. (A.4) and (A.5). Hence, we can identify the quaternion multiplication of 1, i, j, and k in Eqs. (A.4) and (A.5) with matrix multiplication of $\boldsymbol{I}$, $\boldsymbol{S}_1$, $\boldsymbol{S}_2$, and $\boldsymbol{S}_3$.

A.9 STEREOGRAPHIC PROJECTION

Let us write Eq. (A.28) as

$$\boldsymbol{U} = \begin{pmatrix} \alpha & \beta \\ \gamma & \delta \end{pmatrix}. \tag{A.34}$$

This matrix has the form of Eq. (A.28) with $q_0^2 + q_1^2 + q_2^2 + q_3^2 = 1$ if and only if

$$\gamma = -\beta^\dagger, \qquad \delta = -\alpha^\dagger, \qquad \alpha\delta - \beta\gamma = 1, \tag{A.35}$$

where † denotes the complex conjugate. Thus, a rotation can be specified by four complex numbers α, β, γ, and δ that satisfy Eq. (A.35). They are called the *Cayley–Klein parameters*. The group of matrices in the form of Eq. (A.34), for which Eq. (A.35) holds, is called the *special unitary group* of dimension 2 and denoted by $SU(2)$. The term "unitary" refers to the fact that $\boldsymbol{U}$ is a *unitary matrix*, i.e., $\boldsymbol{U}^\dagger\boldsymbol{U} = \boldsymbol{I}$, where † denotes the *Hermitian conjugate*, i.e., the transpose of the complex conjugate. The term "special" refers to the fact that the determinant is 1: $|\boldsymbol{U}| = \alpha\delta - \beta\gamma = 1$.

Equation (A.34) is not only a representation of the group of rotations but also a representation of the group of transformations of the complex plane in the form

$$z' = \frac{\gamma + \delta z}{\alpha + \beta z}. \tag{A.36}$$

A transformation of this form is called a *linear fractional transformation* or a *Möbius transformation*. If this transformation is followed by another transformation specified by α', β', γ', and δ', it is easy to show that the resulting transformation is a linear fractional transformation again. Namely, the set of linear fractional transformations forms a group with respect to composition. Let α'', β'', γ'', and δ'' be the parameters of that composite transformation, and let $\boldsymbol{U}''$ be the 2×2 matrix having them as its elements. Then, $\boldsymbol{U}'' = \boldsymbol{U}'\boldsymbol{U}$ holds, where $\boldsymbol{U}'$ is the 2×2 matrix consisting of α', β', γ', and δ', i.e.,

$$\begin{pmatrix} \alpha'' & \beta'' \\ \gamma'' & \delta'' \end{pmatrix} = \begin{pmatrix} \alpha' & \beta' \\ \gamma' & \delta' \end{pmatrix} \begin{pmatrix} \alpha & \beta \\ \gamma & \delta \end{pmatrix}. \tag{A.37}$$

This means that Eq. (A.34) is a representation of the group of linear fractional transformations. This suggests that Eq. (A.36) corresponds to a 3D rotation in some sense. In fact, this correspondence is given by the *stereographic projection* of a unit sphere at the origin: the point (x, y) obtained by projecting a point on the sphere from its "south pole" onto the xy plane is identified with the complex number $z = x + iy$ (Fig. A.2). It can be shown that if the sphere rotates by a rotation specified by the Cayley–Klein parameters α, β, γ, and δ, the corresponding transformation of the complex number z is given by the linear fractional transformation in the form of Eq. (A.36).

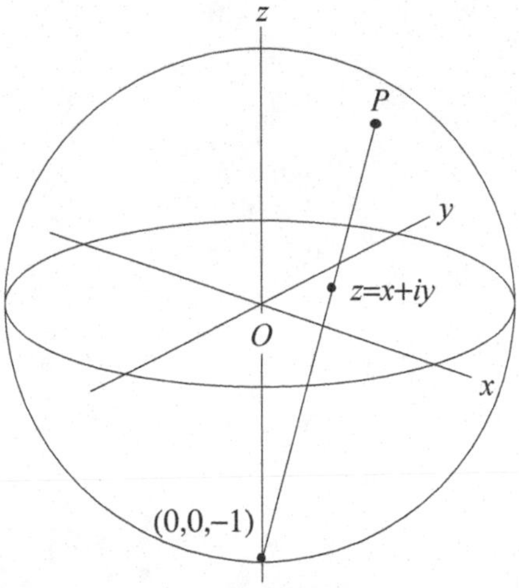

FIGURE A.2 Stereographic projection of a unit sphere onto a plane. The projection of a point P on the sphere from the "south pole" $(0, 0, -1)$ onto the xy plane can be regarded as a complex number $z = x + iy$. If the sphere rotates, the projected point on the xy plane undergoes a linear fractional transformation.

Topics of Linear Algebra

Here, we summarize topics of linear algebra related to analysis of 3D rotation. First, we review fundamentals of linear mapping and projection operation. Next, we describe basic facts about eigenvalues and spectral decomposition of symmetric matrices. We then show that these can be extended to general rectangular matrices in terms of singular values and singular value decomposition.

B.1 LINEAR MAPPING AND BASIS

A linear mapping from the nD space $\mathcal{R}^n$ to the mD space $\mathcal{R}^m$ is represented by an $m \times n$ matrix $\boldsymbol{A}$. One of the basic ways to specify it is to define an *orthonormal basis* $\{\boldsymbol{u}_1, ..., \boldsymbol{u}_n\}$, i.e., mutually orthogonal unit vectors, in $\mathcal{R}^n$, which is called the *domain*, and to specify the *image*, $\boldsymbol{a}_1$, ..., $\boldsymbol{a}_n$, i.e., the mD vectors to which the basis vectors are to be mapped (Fig. B.1). Then, we see that the matrix $\boldsymbol{A}$ is written in the form

$$\boldsymbol{A} = \boldsymbol{a}_1\boldsymbol{u}_1^\top + \cdots + \boldsymbol{a}_n\boldsymbol{u}_n^\top. \tag{B.1}$$

In fact, if we multiply Eq. (B.1) by $\boldsymbol{u}_i$ from right, we obtain $\boldsymbol{A}\boldsymbol{u}_i = \boldsymbol{a}_i$ due to the orthonormality

$$\boldsymbol{u}_i^\top\boldsymbol{u}_j = \delta_{ij}, \tag{B.2}$$

where δ_{ij} is the *Kronecker delta*, which takes the value 1 for $j = i$ and 0 otherwise.

If we use the *natural basis* (also called the *standard* or *canonical basis*) $\{\boldsymbol{e}_1, ... \boldsymbol{e}_n\}$ for $\{\boldsymbol{u}_1, ... \boldsymbol{u}_n\}$, where $\boldsymbol{e}_i$ is the nD vector whose ith component is 1 and whose other components are all 0, and if we write the vetor $\boldsymbol{a}_i$ as $\boldsymbol{a}_i = (a_{1i}, ..., a_{mi})^\top$, Eq. (B.1) is

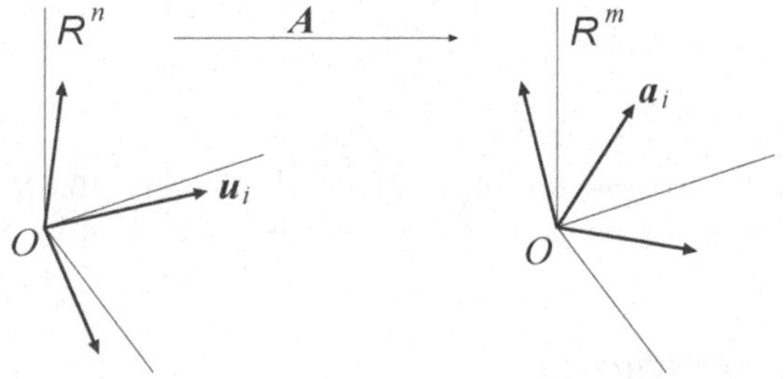

FIGURE B.1 The linear mapping that maps an orthonormal basis $\{\boldsymbol{u}_i\}$, $i = 1, ..., n$, of $\mathcal{R}^n$ to vectors $\boldsymbol{a}_i$, $i = 1, ..., n$, of $\mathcal{R}^m$ is given by the $m \times n$ matrix $\boldsymbol{A} = \sum_{i=1}^n \boldsymbol{a}_i\boldsymbol{u}_i^\top$.

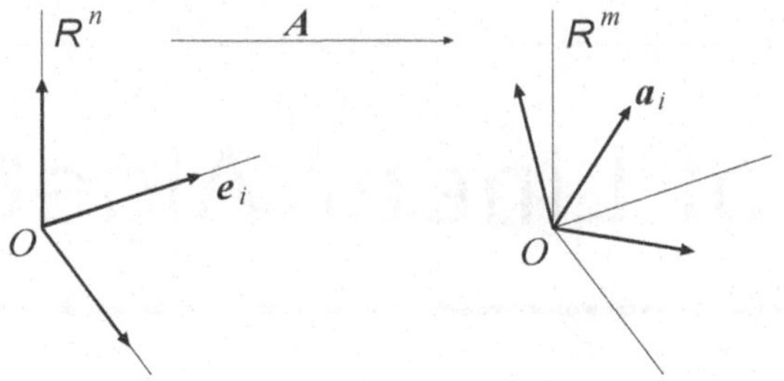

FIGURE B.2 The linear mapping that maps the natural basis $\{e_i\}$, $i = 1, ..., n$, of $\mathcal{R}^n$ to vectors $\boldsymbol{a}_i = (a_{1i}, ..., a_{mi})^\top$, $i = 1, ..., n$, of $\mathcal{R}^m$ is given by the $m \times n$ matrix $\boldsymbol{A} = \begin{pmatrix} a_{ij} \end{pmatrix}$.

expressed in the form

$$\boldsymbol{A} = \begin{pmatrix} a_{11} \\ \vdots \\ a_{m1} \end{pmatrix} \begin{pmatrix} 1 & 0 & \cdots & 0 \end{pmatrix} + \cdots + \begin{pmatrix} a_{1n} \\ \vdots \\ a_{mn} \end{pmatrix} \begin{pmatrix} 0 & \cdots & 0 & 1 \end{pmatrix}$$
$$= \begin{pmatrix} a_{11} & \cdots & a_{1n} \\ \vdots & \ddots & \vdots \\ a_{m1} & \cdots & a_{mn} \end{pmatrix}. \tag{B.3}$$

In other words, *the matrix* $\boldsymbol{A}$ *consists of the images* $\boldsymbol{a}_1, ..., \boldsymbol{a}_n$ *as its columns in that order* (Fig. B.2).

2D rotation

Rotation by angle θ (anti-clockwise) in two dimensions is a linear mapping. The natural basis vectors $\boldsymbol{e}_1 = (1, 0)^\top$ and $\boldsymbol{e}_2 = (0, 1)^\top$ are mapped to $\boldsymbol{a}_1 = (\cos\theta, \sin\theta)^\top$ and $\boldsymbol{a}_2 = (-\sin\theta, \cos\theta)^\top$, respectively (Fig. B.3). Hence, rotation by angle θ is represented by the matrix $\boldsymbol{R}(\theta) = \begin{pmatrix} \cos\theta & -\sin\theta \\ \sin\theta & \cos\theta \end{pmatrix}$.

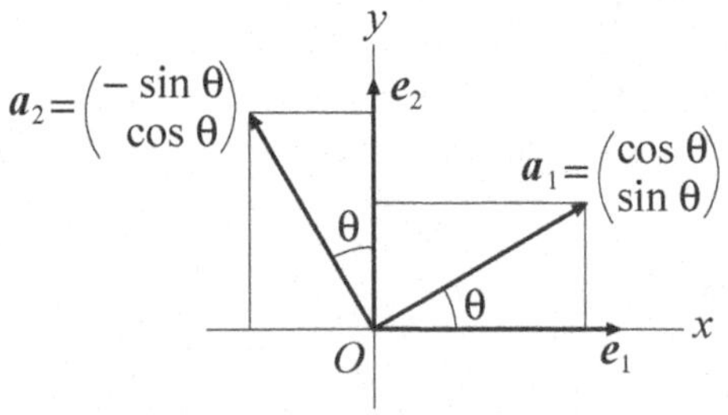

FIGURE B.3 The natural basis vectors $\boldsymbol{e}_1 = (1, 0)^\top$ and $\boldsymbol{e}_2 = (0, 1)^\top$ are mapped to $\boldsymbol{a}_1 = (\cos\theta, \sin\theta)^\top$ and $\boldsymbol{a}_2 = (-\sin\theta, \cos\theta)^\top$, respectively, after a rotation by angle θ.

B.2 PROJECTION MATRICES

Let $\boldsymbol{u}_1, ..., \boldsymbol{u}_r$ be a set of r linearly independent vectors in $\mathcal{R}^n$. The set $\mathcal{U} \subset \mathcal{R}^n$ of all linear combinations of these vectors is called the *subspace* of dimension r *spanned by* $\boldsymbol{u}_1, ..., \boldsymbol{u}_r$.

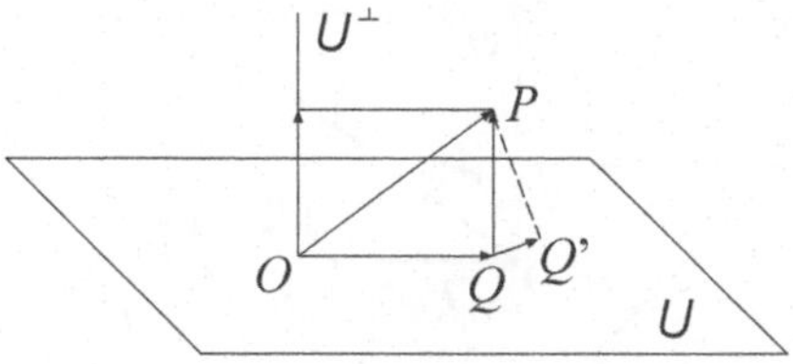

FIGURE B.4 The projection Q of point P onto the subspace $\mathcal{U}$ is the point of $\mathcal{U}$ closest to P. The vector $\overrightarrow{QP} \in \mathcal{U}^\perp$ is the rejection from $\mathcal{U}$.

For instance, the subspace spanned by one vector is a line that extends along it, and the subspace spanned by two vectors is the plane that passes through them.

Given a point P in $\mathcal{R}^n$ and a subpace $\mathcal{U} \subset \mathcal{R}^n$, the point $Q \in \mathcal{U}$ defined so that $\overrightarrow{PQ}$ is orthogonal to $\mathcal{U}$ is called the *projection*[1] of P onto $\mathcal{U}$, and $\overrightarrow{QP}$ is said to be the *rejection* of Q from $\mathcal{U}$ (Fig. B.4). If we move the point Q to another point Q' of $\mathcal{U}$, we see from the Pythagorean theorem that

$$\|PQ'\|^2 = \|PQ\|^2 + \|QQ'\|^2 > \|PQ\|^2. \tag{B.4}$$

In other words, *the projection Q is the closest point of $\mathcal{U}$ from point P.*

These facts are summarized as

$$\overrightarrow{OP} = \overrightarrow{OQ} + \overrightarrow{QP}, \qquad \overrightarrow{OQ} \in \mathcal{U}, \qquad \overrightarrow{QP} \in \mathcal{U}^\perp, \tag{B.5}$$

where $\mathcal{U}^\perp$ is the set of all vectors orthogonal to $\mathcal{U}$, called the *orthogonal complement* of $\mathcal{U}$, which is also a subspace of $\mathcal{R}^n$. Thus, any vector of $\mathcal{R}^n$ is expressed as the sum of its projection onto $\mathcal{U}$ and the rejection from it. Such an expression is unique and called the *direct sum decomposition* of $\overrightarrow{OP}$ to $\mathcal{U}$ and $\mathcal{U}^\perp$.

Let $\boldsymbol{P}_\mathcal{U}$ be the projection mapping onto subspace $\mathcal{U}$, and $\boldsymbol{P}_{\mathcal{U}^\perp}$ the projection mapping onto its orthogonal complement $\mathcal{U}^\perp$. By definition,

$$\boldsymbol{P}_\mathcal{U}\boldsymbol{x} = \begin{cases} \boldsymbol{x} & \boldsymbol{x} \in \mathcal{U} \\ \boldsymbol{0} & \boldsymbol{x} \in \mathcal{U}^\perp \end{cases}, \tag{B.6}$$

$$\boldsymbol{P}_{\mathcal{U}^\perp}\boldsymbol{x} = \begin{cases} \boldsymbol{0} & \boldsymbol{x} \in \mathcal{U} \\ \boldsymbol{x} & \boldsymbol{x} \in \mathcal{U}^\perp \end{cases}. \tag{B.7}$$

If we define an orthonormal basis $\{\boldsymbol{u}_1, ..., \boldsymbol{u}_r\}$ of the subspace $\mathcal{U}$, it can be extended to an orthonormal basis $\{\boldsymbol{u}_1, ..., \boldsymbol{u}_r, \boldsymbol{u}_{r+1}, ..., \boldsymbol{u}_n\}$ of $\mathcal{R}^n$. Equation (B.6) states that $\boldsymbol{P}_\mathcal{U}$ maps the orthonormal basis vectors $\{\boldsymbol{u}_1, ..., \boldsymbol{u}_n\}$ of $\mathcal{R}^n$ to $\boldsymbol{u}_1, ..., \boldsymbol{u}_r, \boldsymbol{0}, ..., \boldsymbol{0}$, respectively. Similarly, Eq. (B.7) states that $\boldsymbol{P}_{\mathcal{U}^\perp}$ maps $\{\boldsymbol{u}_1, ..., \boldsymbol{u}_n\}$ to $\boldsymbol{0}, ..., \boldsymbol{0}, \boldsymbol{u}_{r+1}, ..., \boldsymbol{u}_n$, respectively. Hence, from Eq. (B.1), the mappings $\boldsymbol{P}_\mathcal{U}$ and $\boldsymbol{P}_{\mathcal{U}^\perp}$ are expressed as matrices

$$\boldsymbol{P}_\mathcal{U} = \boldsymbol{u}_1\boldsymbol{u}_1^\top + \cdots + \boldsymbol{u}_r\boldsymbol{u}_r^\top, \tag{B.8}$$

$$\boldsymbol{P}_{\mathcal{U}^\perp} = \boldsymbol{u}_{r+1}\boldsymbol{u}_{r+1}^\top + \cdots + \boldsymbol{u}_n\boldsymbol{u}_n^\top, \tag{B.9}$$

respectively, where $\boldsymbol{P}_\mathcal{U}$ and $\boldsymbol{P}_{\mathcal{U}^\perp}$ are called the *projection matrices* onto subspaces $\mathcal{U}$ and $\mathcal{U}^\perp$, respectively.

[1]It is formally called "orthogonal projection," but we call it simply "projection," since we do not consider other types of projection in this book.

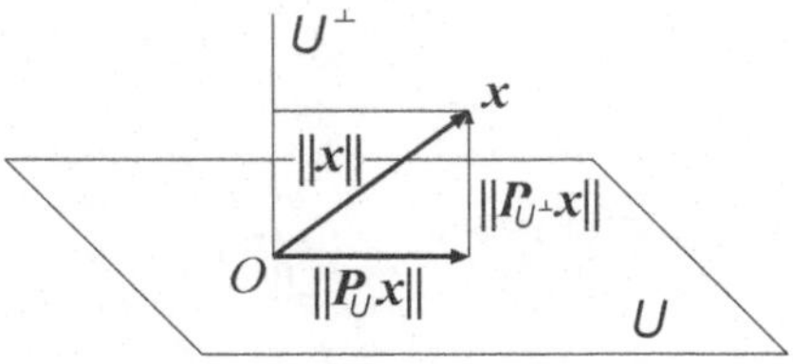

FIGURE B.5 The equality $\|\boldsymbol{x}\|^2 = \|\boldsymbol{P}_{\mathcal{U}}\boldsymbol{x}\|^2 + \|\boldsymbol{P}_{\mathcal{U}^{\perp}}\boldsymbol{x}\|^2$ holds for any vector $\boldsymbol{x}$.

Since $\overrightarrow{QP} = \boldsymbol{P}_{\mathcal{U}}\overrightarrow{QP} + \boldsymbol{P}_{\mathcal{U}^{\perp}}\overrightarrow{QP} = (\boldsymbol{P}_{\mathcal{U}} + \boldsymbol{P}_{\mathcal{U}^{\perp}})\overrightarrow{QP}$ for every point P, we see that

$$\boldsymbol{P}_{\mathcal{U}} + \boldsymbol{P}_{\mathcal{U}^{\perp}} = \boldsymbol{I}. \tag{B.10}$$

Hence, the identity matrix $\boldsymbol{I}$ is decomposed into the sum of the projection matrix onto the subspace $\mathcal{U}$ and the projection matrix onto its orthogonal complement $\mathcal{U}^{\perp}$ in the form

$$\boldsymbol{I} = \underbrace{\boldsymbol{u}_1\boldsymbol{u}_1^{\top} + \cdots + \boldsymbol{u}_r\boldsymbol{u}_r^{\top}}_{\boldsymbol{P}_{\mathcal{U}}} + \underbrace{\boldsymbol{u}_{r+1}\boldsymbol{u}_{r+1}^{\top} + \cdots + \boldsymbol{u}_n\boldsymbol{u}_n^{\top}}_{\boldsymbol{P}_{\mathcal{U}^{\perp}}}. \tag{B.11}$$

Note that the identity matrix itself is the projection matrix onto the entire space $\mathcal{R}^n$.

Since the vector $\overrightarrow{OQ} = \boldsymbol{P}_{\mathcal{U}}\overrightarrow{OP}$ on the right side of Eq. (B.5) and the vector $\overrightarrow{QP} = \boldsymbol{P}_{\mathcal{U}^{\perp}}\overrightarrow{OP}$ are orthogonal to each other, we have $\|\overrightarrow{OP}\|^2 = \|\overrightarrow{OQ}\|^2 + \|\overrightarrow{QP}\|^2$. Hence, we see that

$$\|\boldsymbol{x}\|^2 = \|\boldsymbol{P}_{\mathcal{U}}\boldsymbol{x}\|^2 + \|\boldsymbol{P}_{\mathcal{U}^{\perp}}\boldsymbol{x}\|^2 \tag{B.12}$$

for an arbitrary vector $\boldsymbol{x}$ (Fig. B.5).

For the projection matrix $\boldsymbol{P}_{\mathcal{U}}$, the following hold[2]:

$$\boldsymbol{P}_{\mathcal{U}}^{\top} = \boldsymbol{P}_{\mathcal{U}}, \tag{B.13}$$

$$\boldsymbol{P}_{\mathcal{U}}^2 = \boldsymbol{P}_{\mathcal{U}}. \tag{B.14}$$

Equation (B.13) states that $\boldsymbol{P}_{\mathcal{U}}$ is a symmetric matrix, as is evident from the definition of Eq. (B.8). Equation (B.14) states that the projected point is unchanged if it is projected again, which is evident from the meaning of projection. A matrix for which Eq. (B.14) holds is said to be *idempotent*. It can be easily shown that a matrix that is symmetric and idempotent represents the projection matrix onto some subspace.

B.3 PROJECTION ONTO A LINE AND A PLANE

A line l starting from the origin O and extending in the direction of unit vector $\boldsymbol{u}$ is a one-dimensional subspace.. The projection matrix $\boldsymbol{P}_l$ onto the line l is given by

$$\boldsymbol{P}_l = \boldsymbol{u}\boldsymbol{u}^{\top}. \tag{B.15}$$

Hence, the projection of $\overrightarrow{OP}$ onto l is given by

$$\boldsymbol{u}\boldsymbol{u}^{\top}\overrightarrow{OP} = \langle\overrightarrow{OP}, \boldsymbol{u}\rangle\boldsymbol{u}. \tag{B.16}$$

[2]Equation (B.14) is the defintion of the (not necessarily orthogonal) projection. The orthogonal projection is defined by adding Eq. (B.13).

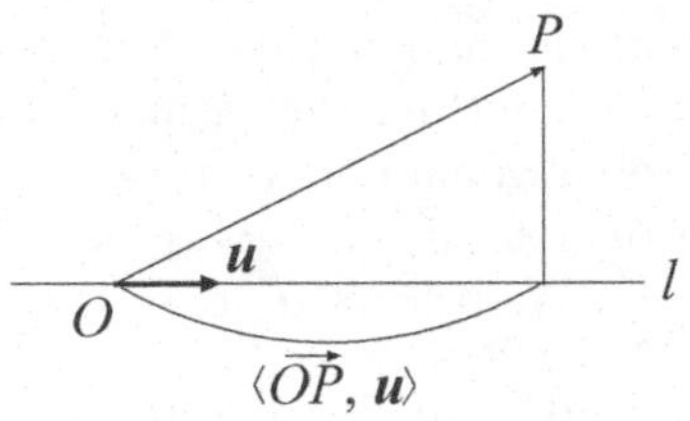

FIGURE B.6 The projected length of vector $\overrightarrow{OP}$ onto a line passing through the origin O and extending in the direction of the unit vector $\boldsymbol{u}$ is given by $\langle \overrightarrow{OP}, \boldsymbol{u} \rangle$.

The right side of Eq. (B.16) is the vector lying on the line l with length $\langle \overrightarrow{OP}, \boldsymbol{u} \rangle$ (Fig. B.6 ↪ Problem 2.3), signed so that it is positive in the direction of $\boldsymbol{u}$ and negative in the opposite direction. This signed length is called the *projected length*. Thus, we conclude that *the inner product with a unit vector is the projected length onto the line in that direction.*

A plane[3] Π passing through the origin O having a unit vector $\boldsymbol{n}$ as its surface normal is a subspace of dimension $n - 1$. The line along the surface normal $\boldsymbol{n}$ is the orthogonal complement to the plane Π. Hence, if $\boldsymbol{P_n}$ is the projection matrix onto Π, Eqs. (B.10) and (B.11) imply

$$\boldsymbol{P_n} = \boldsymbol{I} - \boldsymbol{n}\boldsymbol{n}^\top. \tag{B.17}$$

Thus, the projection of $\overrightarrow{OP}$ onto Π (Fig. B.7) is given by

$$\boldsymbol{P_n}\overrightarrow{OP} = \overrightarrow{OP} - \langle \overrightarrow{OP}, \boldsymbol{n} \rangle \boldsymbol{n}. \tag{B.18}$$

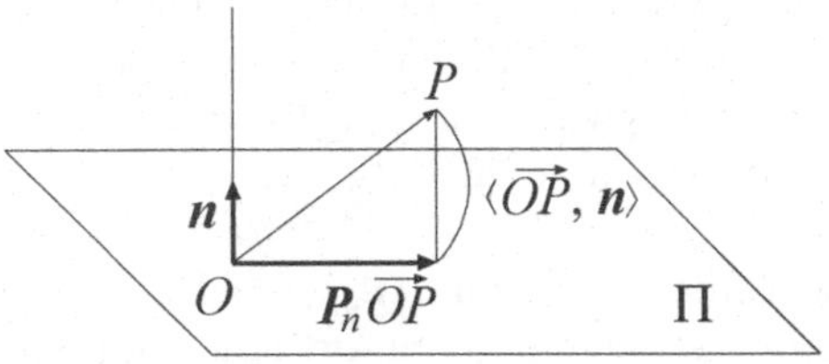

FIGURE B.7 Projection of vector $\overrightarrow{OP}$ onto plane Π passing through the origin O and having unit surface normal $\boldsymbol{n}$.

Schmidt Orthogonalization A set of mutually orthogonal unit vectors is said to be an *orthonormal system*. We can convert n given linearly independent vectors $\boldsymbol{a}_1$, ..., $\boldsymbol{a}_n$ to an orthonormal system $\boldsymbol{u}_1$, ..., $\boldsymbol{u}_n$ as follows. First, let $\boldsymbol{u}_1 = \boldsymbol{a}_1/\|\boldsymbol{a}_1\|$. From Eq. (B.17), the projection matrix onto the subspace orthogonal to $\boldsymbol{u}_1$, i.e., its orthogonal complement, is $\boldsymbol{I} - \boldsymbol{u}_1\boldsymbol{u}_1^\top$. We project $\boldsymbol{a}_2$ onto it to extract the component orthogonal to $\boldsymbol{u}_1$. We obtain

$$\boldsymbol{a}_2' = (\boldsymbol{I} - \boldsymbol{u}_1\boldsymbol{u}_1^\top)\boldsymbol{a}_2 = \boldsymbol{a}_2 - \langle \boldsymbol{u}_1, \boldsymbol{a}_2 \rangle \boldsymbol{u}_1. \tag{B.19}$$

Its normalization $\boldsymbol{u}_2 = \boldsymbol{a}_2'/\|\boldsymbol{a}_2'\|$ is a unit vector orthogonal to $\boldsymbol{u}_1$. By the same argument, the projection matrix onto the subspace orthogonal to $\boldsymbol{u}_1$ and $\boldsymbol{u}_2$, i.e., its orthogonal complement, is $\boldsymbol{I} - \boldsymbol{u}_1\boldsymbol{u}_1^\top - \boldsymbol{u}_2\boldsymbol{u}_2^\top$. We project $\boldsymbol{a}_3$ onto it to obtain

$$\boldsymbol{a}_3' = (\boldsymbol{I} - \boldsymbol{u}_1\boldsymbol{u}_1^\top - \boldsymbol{u}_2\boldsymbol{u}_2^\top)\boldsymbol{a}_3 = \boldsymbol{a}_3 - \langle \boldsymbol{u}_1, \boldsymbol{a}_3 \rangle \boldsymbol{u}_1 - \langle \boldsymbol{u}_2, \boldsymbol{a}_3 \rangle \boldsymbol{u}_2, \tag{B.20}$$

[3]Strictly speaking, a "hyperplane," but we call it simply a "plane" if confusion does not occur.

which is orthogonal to both $\boldsymbol{u}_1$ and $\boldsymbol{u}_2$; its normalization $\boldsymbol{u}_3 = \boldsymbol{a}'_3/\|\boldsymbol{a}'_3\|$ is a unit vector orthogonal to both $\boldsymbol{u}_1$ and $\boldsymbol{u}_2$. Repeating the same argument, we see that if we already have mutually orthogonal unit vectors $\boldsymbol{u}_1$, ..., $\boldsymbol{u}_{k-1}$, the projection matrix onto the subspace orthogonal to $\boldsymbol{u}_1$, ..., $\boldsymbol{u}_{k-1}$, i.e., its orthogonal complement, is $\boldsymbol{I} - \boldsymbol{u}_1\boldsymbol{u}_1^\top - \cdots - \boldsymbol{u}_{k-1}\boldsymbol{u}_{k-1}^\top$. We project $\boldsymbol{a}_k$ onto it to obtain

$$\boldsymbol{a}'_k = (\boldsymbol{I} - \boldsymbol{u}_1\boldsymbol{u}_1^\top - \cdots - \boldsymbol{u}_{k-1}\boldsymbol{u}_{k-1}^\top)\boldsymbol{a}_k = \boldsymbol{a}_k - \langle \boldsymbol{u}_1, \boldsymbol{a}_k\rangle\boldsymbol{u}_1 - \cdots - \langle \boldsymbol{u}_{k-1}, \boldsymbol{a}_k\rangle\boldsymbol{u}_k, \quad \text{(B.21)}$$

which is orthogonal to all of $\boldsymbol{u}_1$, ..., $\boldsymbol{u}_{k-1}$; its normalization $\boldsymbol{u}_k = \boldsymbol{a}'_k/\|\boldsymbol{a}'_k\|$ is a unit vector orthogonal to all of $\boldsymbol{u}_1$, ..., $\boldsymbol{u}_{k-1}$. Iterating this process for $k = 1$, ..., n, we end up with an orthonormal system $\boldsymbol{u}_1$, ..., $\boldsymbol{u}_n$. This procedure is called the *(Gram–)Schmidt orthogonalization*.

B.4 EIGENVALUES AND SINGULAR VALUE DECOMPOSITION

For an $n \times n$ symmetric matrix $\boldsymbol{A}$, there exist n real numbers λ, called the *eigenvalues*, and n nonzero vectors $\boldsymbol{u}$, called the *eigenvectors*, such that

$$\boldsymbol{A}\boldsymbol{u} = \lambda\boldsymbol{u}, \qquad \boldsymbol{u} \neq \boldsymbol{0}. \quad \text{(B.22)}$$

The n eigenvalues λ_1, ..., λ_n, which may have overlaps, are given as the solution of the nth degree equation

$$\phi(\lambda) \equiv |\lambda\boldsymbol{I} - \boldsymbol{A}| = 0, \quad \text{(B.23)}$$

called the *characteristic equation*, where $\boldsymbol{I}$ is the $n \times n$ identity matrix, and $|\cdots|$ denotes the determinant. The nth degree polynomial $\phi(\lambda)$ is called the *characteristic polynomial*. It is known that n eigenvectors $\{\boldsymbol{u}_i\}$, $i = 1$, ..., n, can be chosen as an orthonormal system.

However, we need not actually solve the characteristic equation to obtain eigenvalues and eigenvectors. Various software tools which allow us to compute them with high accuracy and high speed using iterations are available, including the *Jacobi method* and the *Householder method* [36].

Let λ_1, ..., λ_n be the eigenvalues of $\boldsymbol{A}$, and $\{\boldsymbol{u}_i\}$, $i = 1$, ..., n, the corresponding orthonormal system of its eigenvectors, which defines an orthonormal basis of $\mathcal{R}$. Eq. (B.22) implies that $\boldsymbol{A}$ maps the orthonormal basis vectors $\{\boldsymbol{u}_i\}$ of $\mathcal{R}^n$ to $\lambda_1\boldsymbol{u}_1$, ..., $\lambda_n\boldsymbol{u}_n$, respectively. Hence, From Eq. (B.1) the matrix $\boldsymbol{A}$ is written in the form

$$\boldsymbol{A} = \lambda_1\boldsymbol{u}_1\boldsymbol{u}_1^\top + \cdots + \lambda_n\boldsymbol{u}_n\boldsymbol{u}_n^\top. \quad \text{(B.24)}$$

In other words, *a symmetric matrix can be expressed in terms of its eigenvalues and eigenvectors*. This is called the *spectral decomposition*[4], or sometimes *eigenvalue decomposition*.

Since each term $\boldsymbol{u}_i\boldsymbol{u}_i^\top$ of Eq. (B.24) is the projection matrix onto the direction, called the *principal axis*, of each eigenvector $\boldsymbol{u}_i$, Eq. (B.24) expresses the matrix $\boldsymbol{A}$ as a linear combination of the projection matrices onto the principal axes. In other words, the transformation of the space by a symmetric matrix is interpreted to be *projections of each point onto the principal axis directions, followed by multiplication by the respective eigenvalues*, which are then summed over all the principal axes.

The identity matrix $\boldsymbol{I}$ maps any orthonormal basis $\{\boldsymbol{u}_i\}$, $i = 1$, ..., n, to itself, i.e., $\boldsymbol{I}\boldsymbol{u}_i = \boldsymbol{u}_i$. Hence, its eigenvalues are all 1, meaning that it has the spectral decomposition in the following form ($\hookrightarrow$ Eq. (B.11)):

$$\boldsymbol{I} = \boldsymbol{u}_1\boldsymbol{u}_1^\top + \cdots + \boldsymbol{u}_n\boldsymbol{u}_n^\top. \quad \text{(B.25)}$$

[4]This term is used because the "eigenvalue" λ is also called the "spectrum."

The number of linearly independent vectors among the n columns of matrix $\boldsymbol{A}$, or the number of linearly independent vectors among its n rows, is called the *rank* of that matrix. Consider an arbitrary linear combination of the columns $\boldsymbol{a}_1$, ..., $\boldsymbol{a}_n$ of $\boldsymbol{A}$, which has the form

$$c_1\boldsymbol{a}_1 + \cdots + c_n\boldsymbol{a}_n = \begin{pmatrix} \boldsymbol{a}_1 & \cdots & \boldsymbol{a}_n \end{pmatrix} \begin{pmatrix} c_1 \\ \vdots \\ c_n \end{pmatrix} = \boldsymbol{A}\boldsymbol{c}, \tag{B.26}$$

where we let $\boldsymbol{c} = \begin{pmatrix} c_i \end{pmatrix}$. If r of the n eigenvalues are nonzero, we can let $\lambda_{r+1} = \cdots = \lambda_n = 0$ in Eq. (B.24) and write $\boldsymbol{A}\boldsymbol{c}$ as

$$\boldsymbol{A}\boldsymbol{c} = \lambda_1\boldsymbol{u}_1\boldsymbol{u}_1^\top\boldsymbol{c} + \cdots + \lambda_r\boldsymbol{u}_r\boldsymbol{u}_r^\top\boldsymbol{c} = \lambda_1\langle\boldsymbol{u}_1, \boldsymbol{c}\rangle\boldsymbol{u}_1 + \cdots + \lambda_r\langle\boldsymbol{u}_r, \boldsymbol{c}\rangle\boldsymbol{u}_r. \tag{B.27}$$

This means that an arbitrary linear combination of the columns of $\boldsymbol{A}$ is written as a linear combination of mutually orthogonal, hence linearly independent, r vectors $\boldsymbol{u}_1$, ..., $\boldsymbol{u}_r$. Thus, the subspace spanned by $\boldsymbol{a}_1$, ..., $\boldsymbol{a}_n$ has dimension r, meaning that only r of the n columns are linearly independent. In other words, *the rank r of matrix $\boldsymbol{A}$ equals the number of its nonzero eigenvalues*. Since $\boldsymbol{A}$ is a symmetric matrix, this also holds for the rows, i.e., only r of the n rows are linearly independent.

B.5 MATRIX REPRESENTATION OF SPECTRAL DECOMPOSITION

Equation (B.24) is rewritten as

$$\begin{aligned} \boldsymbol{A} &= \begin{pmatrix} \lambda_1\boldsymbol{u}_1 & \cdots & \lambda_n\boldsymbol{u}_n \end{pmatrix} \begin{pmatrix} \boldsymbol{u}_1^\top \\ \vdots \\ \boldsymbol{u}_n^\top \end{pmatrix} = \begin{pmatrix} \boldsymbol{u}_1 & \cdots & \boldsymbol{u}_n \end{pmatrix} \begin{pmatrix} \lambda_1 & & \\ & \ddots & \\ & & \lambda_n \end{pmatrix} \begin{pmatrix} \boldsymbol{u}_1^\top \\ \vdots \\ \boldsymbol{u}_n^\top \end{pmatrix} \\ &= \boldsymbol{U} \begin{pmatrix} \lambda_1 & & \\ & \ddots & \\ & & \lambda_n \end{pmatrix} \boldsymbol{U}^\top, \end{aligned} \tag{B.28}$$

where

$$\boldsymbol{U} = \begin{pmatrix} \boldsymbol{u}_1 & \cdots & \boldsymbol{u}_n \end{pmatrix} \tag{B.29}$$

is the orthogonal matrix consisting of columns $\boldsymbol{u}_1$, ..., $\boldsymbol{u}_n$, for which

$$\boldsymbol{U}^\top\boldsymbol{U} = \boldsymbol{I} \tag{B.30}$$

holds. If $\boldsymbol{U}$ is an orthogonal matrix, so is its transpose. Hence, the rows of an orthogonal matrix are also an orthonormal system (see Eqs. (2.5) and (2.6) in the 3D case). Multiplying Eq. (B.28) by $\boldsymbol{U}^\top$ from left and $\boldsymbol{U}$ from right on both sides, we obtain, using Eq. (B.30), the equality

$$\boldsymbol{U}^\top\boldsymbol{A}\boldsymbol{U} = \begin{pmatrix} \lambda_1 & & \\ & \ddots & \\ & & \lambda_n \end{pmatrix}. \tag{B.31}$$

Namely, *a symmetric matrix is transformed by multiplying it by a matrix consisting of its eigenvectors as columns from right and its transpose from left into a diagonal matrix whose diagonal elements are the eigenvalues*. This process is called the *diagonalization* of a symmetric matrix.

If $\boldsymbol{A}$ is a nonsingular matrix, its eigenvalues are all nonzero[5]. Its rank is n, and it has its inverse $\boldsymbol{A}^{-1}$. Multiplying Eq. (B.22) by $\boldsymbol{A}^{-1}$ on both sides, we obtain $\boldsymbol{u} = \lambda\boldsymbol{A}^{-1}\boldsymbol{u}$, or $\boldsymbol{A}^{-1}\boldsymbol{u} = (1/\lambda)\boldsymbol{u}$. Hence, $\boldsymbol{A}^{-1}$ has the same eigenvectors as $\boldsymbol{A}$ with eigenvalues $1/\lambda$. It follows that $\boldsymbol{A}^{-1}$ has its spectral decomposition

$$\boldsymbol{A}^{-1} = \frac{1}{\lambda_1}\boldsymbol{u}_1\boldsymbol{u}_1^\top + \cdots + \frac{1}{\lambda_n}\boldsymbol{u}_n\boldsymbol{u}_n^\top. \tag{B.32}$$

In the same way as Eqs. (B.28) and (B.31), we obtain the relationships

$$\boldsymbol{A}^{-1} = \boldsymbol{U}\begin{pmatrix} 1/\lambda_1 & & \\ & \ddots & \\ & & 1/\lambda_n \end{pmatrix}\boldsymbol{U}^\top, \qquad \boldsymbol{U}^\top\boldsymbol{A}^{-1}\boldsymbol{U} = \begin{pmatrix} 1/\lambda_1 & & \\ & \ddots & \\ & & 1/\lambda_n \end{pmatrix}. \tag{B.33}$$

From Eq. (B.22), we see that $\boldsymbol{A}^2\boldsymbol{u} = \lambda\boldsymbol{A}\boldsymbol{u} = \lambda^2\boldsymbol{u}$, $\boldsymbol{A}^3\boldsymbol{u} = \lambda^2\boldsymbol{A}\boldsymbol{u} = \lambda^3\boldsymbol{u}$, ... , so that $\boldsymbol{A}^N\boldsymbol{u} = \lambda^N\boldsymbol{u}$. Hence, for an arbitrary natural number N, the matrix $\boldsymbol{A}^N$ has the same eigenvectors as $\boldsymbol{A}$ with eigenvalues λ^N. It follows that it has the spectral decomposition

$$\boldsymbol{A}^N = \lambda_1^N\boldsymbol{u}_1\boldsymbol{u}_1^\top + \cdots + \lambda_n^N\boldsymbol{u}_n\boldsymbol{u}_n^\top. \tag{B.34}$$

From this, we obtain, as in the case of Eq. (B.33), the expressions

$$\boldsymbol{A}^N = \boldsymbol{U}\begin{pmatrix} \lambda_1^N & & \\ & \ddots & \\ & & \lambda_n^N \end{pmatrix}\boldsymbol{U}^\top, \qquad \boldsymbol{U}^\top\boldsymbol{A}^N\boldsymbol{U} = \begin{pmatrix} \lambda_1^N & & \\ & \ddots & \\ & & \lambda_n^N \end{pmatrix}. \tag{B.35}$$

It is easy to see that this also applies to an arbitrary polynomial $f(x)$ so that we obtain

$$f(\boldsymbol{A}) = f(\lambda_1)\boldsymbol{u}_1\boldsymbol{u}_1^\top + \cdots + f(\lambda_n)\boldsymbol{u}_n\boldsymbol{u}_n^\top, \tag{B.36}$$

$$f(\boldsymbol{A}) = \boldsymbol{U}\begin{pmatrix} f(\lambda_1) & & \\ & \ddots & \\ & & f(\lambda_n) \end{pmatrix}\boldsymbol{U}^\top, \qquad \boldsymbol{U}^\top f(\boldsymbol{A})\boldsymbol{U} = \begin{pmatrix} f(\lambda_1) & & \\ & \ddots & \\ & & f(\lambda_n) \end{pmatrix}. \tag{B.37}$$

These equations can be extend to an arbitrary function $f(x)$ for which its power series expansion converges. Further more, for any function $f(x)$ for which $f(\lambda_i)$, $i = 1$, ..., n, are defined, we can "define" $f(\boldsymbol{A})$ via Eq. (B.36). For example, if all the eigenvalues of $\boldsymbol{A}$ is nonnegative[6], we can define its "square root" $\sqrt{\boldsymbol{A}}$ by

$$\sqrt{\boldsymbol{A}} = \sqrt{\lambda_1}\boldsymbol{u}_1\boldsymbol{u}_1^\top + \cdots + \sqrt{\lambda_n}\boldsymbol{u}_n\boldsymbol{u}_n^\top, \tag{B.38}$$

$$\sqrt{\boldsymbol{A}} = \boldsymbol{U}\begin{pmatrix} \sqrt{\lambda_1} & & \\ & \ddots & \\ & & \sqrt{\lambda_n} \end{pmatrix}\boldsymbol{U}^\top, \qquad \boldsymbol{U}^\top\sqrt{\boldsymbol{A}}\boldsymbol{U} = \begin{pmatrix} \sqrt{\lambda_1} & & \\ & \ddots & \\ & & \sqrt{\lambda_n} \end{pmatrix}. \tag{B.39}$$

We can view Eqs. (B.25) and (B.32) as special cases of Eq. (B.34) with $N = 0, -1$, where we define $\boldsymbol{A}^0 = \boldsymbol{I}$. For a nonsingular matrix $\boldsymbol{A}$, we can write $\boldsymbol{A}^{-N} = (\boldsymbol{A}^{-1})^N$ $(= (\boldsymbol{A}^N)^{-1})$ for a natural number N. Combining Eqs. (B.32) and (B.34), we see that Eq. (B.34) holds for an arbitrary integer N. If $\boldsymbol{A}$ is a positive definite symmetric matrix, N can be extended to an arbitrary real number.

---

[5]A matrix is nonsingular if its determinant is nonzero, and the determinant equals the product of all the eigenvalues.

[6]Such a matrix is said to be *positive semidefinite*; it is *positive definite* if all the eigenvalues are positive.

B.6 SINGULAR VALUES AND SINGULAR VALUE DECOMPOSITION

For an $m \times n$ matrix $\boldsymbol{A}$ which is not the zero matrix $\boldsymbol{O}$, there exist a positive number σ ($>$ 0), called the *singular value*, an mD vector $\boldsymbol{u}$ ($\neq \boldsymbol{0}$), called the *left singular vector*, and an nD vector $\boldsymbol{v}$ ($\neq \boldsymbol{0}$), called the *right singular vector*, such that

$$\boldsymbol{A}\boldsymbol{v} = \sigma\boldsymbol{u}, \qquad \boldsymbol{A}^\top\boldsymbol{u} = \sigma\boldsymbol{v}, \qquad \sigma > 0, \quad \boldsymbol{u} \neq \boldsymbol{0}, \quad \boldsymbol{v} \neq \boldsymbol{0}. \tag{B.40}$$

The left and right singular vectors are simply called the *singular vectors*. There exist r triplets $\{\sigma_i, \boldsymbol{u}_i, \boldsymbol{v}_i\}$, $i = 1, ..., r$, of such singular values and singular vectors, where r is the rank of the matrix $\boldsymbol{A}$, i.e. the number of linearly independent columns (= the number of linearly independent rows; we discuss this shortly).

Multiplying the second equation of Eq. (B.40) by $\boldsymbol{A}$ from left on both sides, and multiplying the first equation by $\boldsymbol{A}^\top$ from left on both sides, we see that

$$\boldsymbol{A}\boldsymbol{A}^\top\boldsymbol{u} = \sigma^2\boldsymbol{u}, \qquad \boldsymbol{A}^\top\boldsymbol{A}\boldsymbol{v} = \sigma^2\boldsymbol{v}. \tag{B.41}$$

Namely, the left singular vector $\boldsymbol{u}$ is the eigenvector of the $m \times m$ symmetric matrix $\boldsymbol{A}\boldsymbol{A}^\top$; the right singular vector $\boldsymbol{v}$ is the eigenvector of the $n \times n$ symmetric matrix $\boldsymbol{A}^\top\boldsymbol{A}$. The squared singular value σ^2 is the eigenvalue of both of them. It is easy to see that $\boldsymbol{A}\boldsymbol{A}^\top$ and $\boldsymbol{A}^\top\boldsymbol{A}$ have a common positive eigenvalue σ^2 and that their eigenvectors $\boldsymbol{u}$ and $\boldsymbol{v}$ are related by Eq. (B.40).

Let $\sigma_1 \geq \cdots \geq \sigma_r$ (> 0) be the singular values of $\boldsymbol{A}$, where some of them may overlap. Since corresponding r left singular vectors $\boldsymbol{u}_1, ..., \boldsymbol{u}_r$ and r right singular vectors $\boldsymbol{v}_1, ..., \boldsymbol{v}_r$ are both eigenvectors of symmetric matrices, they can be chosen to form orthonormal systems.

For actually computing the singular values and singular vectors, we need not compute the eigenvalues and eigenvectors of $\boldsymbol{A}\boldsymbol{A}^\top$ and $\boldsymbol{A}^\top\boldsymbol{A}$. Various software tools that can compute them with high speed and high accuracy are available. A typical one consists of transformation to a *bidiagonal matrix* by means of the Householder method and application of the *Golub–Reinsch method* [11, 36].

An $m \times n$ matrix $\boldsymbol{A}$ defines a linear mapping from the nD space $\mathcal{R}^n$ to the mD space $\mathcal{R}^m$. We can extend the orthonormal system $\boldsymbol{u}_1, ..., \boldsymbol{u}_r$ of the r left singular vectors to an orthonormal bais $\{\boldsymbol{u}_1, ..., \boldsymbol{u}_r, \boldsymbol{u}_{r+1}, ..., \boldsymbol{u}_m\}$ of $\mathcal{R}^m$. Similarly, we can extend the orthonormal system $\boldsymbol{v}_1, ..., \boldsymbol{v}_r$ of the r right singular vectors to an orthonormal basis $\{\boldsymbol{v}_1, ..., \boldsymbol{v}_r, \boldsymbol{v}_{r+1}, ..., \boldsymbol{v}_n\}$ of $\mathcal{R}^n$. As Eq. (B.41) implies, these are the eigenvectors of $\boldsymbol{A}\boldsymbol{A}^\top$ and $\boldsymbol{A}^\top\boldsymbol{A}$. Hence, $\boldsymbol{u}_{r+1}, ..., \boldsymbol{u}_m$ and $\boldsymbol{v}_{r+1}, ..., \boldsymbol{v}_n$ are identified with their eigenvectors with eigenvalue 0:

$$\begin{aligned} \boldsymbol{A}\boldsymbol{A}^\top\boldsymbol{u}_i &= \boldsymbol{0}, \qquad i = r+1, ..., m, \\ \boldsymbol{A}^\top\boldsymbol{A}\boldsymbol{v}_i &= \boldsymbol{0}, \qquad i = r+1, ..., n, \end{aligned} \tag{B.42}$$

The second equation implies[7] $\boldsymbol{A}\boldsymbol{v}_i = \boldsymbol{0}$, $i = r+1, ..., n$. This and the first equation of Eq. (B.40) state that $\boldsymbol{A}$ maps the orthonormal basis vectors $\{\boldsymbol{v}_1, ..., \boldsymbol{v}_n\}$ of $\mathcal{R}^n$ to $\sigma_1\boldsymbol{u}_1, ..., \sigma_r\boldsymbol{u}_r, \boldsymbol{0}, ..., \boldsymbol{0}$, respectively. Hence, from Eq. (B.1), we see that $\boldsymbol{A}$ is expressed as

$$\boldsymbol{A} = \sigma_1\boldsymbol{u}_1\boldsymbol{v}_1^\top + \cdots + \sigma_r\boldsymbol{u}_r\boldsymbol{v}_r^\top, \qquad \sigma_1 \geq \cdots \geq \sigma_r > 0. \tag{B.43}$$

Similarly, we see from the first equation of Eq. (B.42) that $\boldsymbol{A}^\top\boldsymbol{u}_i = \boldsymbol{0}$, $i = r+1, ..., m$. This and the second equation of Eq. (B.40) state that $\boldsymbol{A}^\top$ maps the orthonormal basis vectors $\{\boldsymbol{u}_1, ..., \boldsymbol{u}_n\}$ of $\mathcal{R}^m$ to $\sigma_1\boldsymbol{v}_1, ..., \sigma_r\boldsymbol{v}_r, \boldsymbol{0}, ..., \boldsymbol{0}$, respectively. So, from Eq. (B.1), $\boldsymbol{A}^\top$ is expressed in the form

$$\boldsymbol{A}^\top = \sigma_1\boldsymbol{v}_1\boldsymbol{u}_1^\top + \cdots + \sigma_r\boldsymbol{v}_r\boldsymbol{u}_r^\top, \qquad \sigma_1 \geq \cdots \geq \sigma_r > 0, \tag{B.44}$$

[7] In fact, $\|\boldsymbol{A}\boldsymbol{v}_i\|^2 = \langle \boldsymbol{A}\boldsymbol{v}_i, \boldsymbol{A}\boldsymbol{v}_i \rangle = \langle \boldsymbol{v}_i, \boldsymbol{A}^\top\boldsymbol{A}\boldsymbol{v}_i \rangle$ =0.

which is the transpose of Eq. (B.43) on both sides. Thus, *an arbitrary matrix is expressed in terms of its singular values and singular vectors*. The expression is called the *singular value decomposition*.

B.7 COLUMN AND ROW DOMAINS

Let $\mathcal{U}$ be the subspace spanned by the n columns of $\boldsymbol{A}$, and $\mathcal{V}$ the subspace spanned by its m rows. We call them *column domain* and the *row domain*, respectively.

Consider an arbitrary linear combination of the columns $\boldsymbol{a}_1$, ..., $\boldsymbol{a}_n$ of $\boldsymbol{A}$, which has the form of

$$c_1\boldsymbol{a}_1 + \cdots + c_n\boldsymbol{a}_n = \begin{pmatrix} \boldsymbol{a}_1 & \cdots & \boldsymbol{a}_n \end{pmatrix} \begin{pmatrix} c_1 \\ \vdots \\ c_n \end{pmatrix} = \boldsymbol{A}\boldsymbol{c}, \tag{B.45}$$

where we let $\boldsymbol{c} = \begin{pmatrix} c_i \end{pmatrix}$. From Eq. (B.43), $\boldsymbol{A}\boldsymbol{c}$ is rewritten as

$$\boldsymbol{A}\boldsymbol{c} = \sigma_1\boldsymbol{u}_1\boldsymbol{v}_1^\top\boldsymbol{c} + \cdots + \sigma_r\boldsymbol{u}_r\boldsymbol{v}_r^\top\boldsymbol{c} = \sigma_1\langle\boldsymbol{v}_1, \boldsymbol{c}\rangle\boldsymbol{u}_1 + \cdots + \sigma_r\langle\boldsymbol{v}_r, \boldsymbol{c}\rangle\boldsymbol{u}_r. \tag{B.46}$$

Namely, an arbitrary linear combination of the columns of $\boldsymbol{A}$ is a linear combination of mutually orthogonal, hence linearly independent, vectors $\boldsymbol{u}_1$, ..., $\boldsymbol{u}_r$. This means that the column domain $\mathcal{U}$ spanned by $\boldsymbol{a}_1$, ..., $\boldsymbol{a}_n$ is a subspace of dimension r, for which $\boldsymbol{u}_1$, ..., $\boldsymbol{u}_r$ are an orthonormal basis. It follows that *only r columns are linearly independent*.

The rows of $\boldsymbol{A}$ are the columns of $\boldsymbol{A}^\top$. Hence, from Eq. (B.44) an arbitrary linear combination of rows is expressed as a linear combination of $\boldsymbol{v}_1$, ..., $\boldsymbol{v}_r$. Thus, the row domain $\mathcal{V}$ spanned by rows of $\boldsymbol{A}$ is a subspace of dimension r, for which $\boldsymbol{v}_1$, ..., $\boldsymbol{v}_r$ are an orthonormal basis. It follows that *only r rows are linearly independent*.

From these considerations, we conclude that *the rank r of $\boldsymbol{A}$ equals the number of the singular values of $\boldsymbol{A}$* and that *the left singular vectors $\{\boldsymbol{u}_i\}$, i = 1, ..., r, and the right singular vectors $\{\boldsymbol{v}_i\}$, i = 1, ..., r, constitute the orthonormal bases of the column domain $\mathcal{U}$ and the row domain $\mathcal{V}$, respectively*.

From Eq. (B.8), the projection matrix of $\mathcal{R}^m$ onto the column domain $\mathcal{U}$ and the projection matrix of $\mathcal{R}^n$ onto the row domain $\mathcal{V}$ are respectively given by

$$\boldsymbol{P}_{\mathcal{U}} = \sum_{i=1}^{r} \boldsymbol{u}_i\boldsymbol{u}_i^\top, \qquad \boldsymbol{P}_{\mathcal{V}} = \sum_{i=1}^{r} \boldsymbol{v}_i\boldsymbol{v}_i^\top. \tag{B.47}$$

Since each $\boldsymbol{u}_i$, i = 1, ..., r, is $\boldsymbol{u}_i \in \mathcal{U}$, we have $\boldsymbol{P}_{\mathcal{U}}\boldsymbol{u}_i = \boldsymbol{u}_i$. Hence, operation of $\boldsymbol{P}_{\mathcal{U}}$ to Eq. (B.43) from left does not cause any change. Similarly, we have $\boldsymbol{P}_{\mathcal{V}}\boldsymbol{v}_i = \boldsymbol{v}_i$ for the rows. Hence, operation of $\boldsymbol{P}_{\mathcal{V}}$ to Eq. (B.43) from right does not cause any change. Thus,

$$\boldsymbol{P}_{\mathcal{U}}\boldsymbol{A} = \boldsymbol{A}, \qquad \boldsymbol{A}\boldsymbol{P}_{\mathcal{V}} = \boldsymbol{A}. \tag{B.48}$$

As in Eq. (B.28), Eq. (B.43) can be rewritten in the form

$$\begin{aligned} \boldsymbol{A} &= \begin{pmatrix} \sigma_1\boldsymbol{u}_1 & \cdots & \sigma_r\boldsymbol{u}_r \end{pmatrix} \begin{pmatrix} \boldsymbol{v}_1^\top \\ \vdots \\ \boldsymbol{v}_r^\top \end{pmatrix} = \begin{pmatrix} \boldsymbol{u}_1 & \cdots & \boldsymbol{u}_r \end{pmatrix} \begin{pmatrix} \sigma_1 & & \\ & \ddots & \\ & & \sigma_r \end{pmatrix} \begin{pmatrix} \boldsymbol{v}_1^\top \\ \vdots \\ \boldsymbol{v}_r^\top \end{pmatrix} \\ &= \boldsymbol{U} \begin{pmatrix} \sigma_1 & & \\ & \ddots & \\ & & \sigma_r \end{pmatrix} \boldsymbol{V}^\top, \qquad \sigma_1 \geq \cdots \geq \sigma_r > 0, \end{aligned} \tag{B.49}$$

where

$$U = \begin{pmatrix} u_1 & \cdots & u_r \end{pmatrix}, \qquad V = \begin{pmatrix} v_1 & \cdots & v_r \end{pmatrix}, \tag{B.50}$$

are $m \times r$ and $n \times r$ matrices consisting of singular vectors u_1, ..., u_r and v_1, ..., v_r as columns, respectively. Rewriting Eq. (B.44) in the same way results in the transpose of Eq. (B.49) on both sides.

Since the r columns of the matrices U and V are both orthonormal systems, we obtain

$$U^\top U = I, \qquad V^\top V = I, \tag{B.51}$$

where the right sides are the $r \times r$ identity matrix. We also obtain

$$UU^\top = P_{\mathcal{U}}, \qquad VV^\top = P_{\mathcal{V}}. \tag{B.52}$$

APPENDIX C

Lie Groups and Lie Algebras

As stated in Sec. 6.9, a "Lie group" is a "group" that has the structure of a continuous surface. By "continuous," we mean that a "topology" is defined. By "the structure of a surface," we mean a "topological space" for which a coordinate system, just as in the ordinary n-dimensional space $\mathcal{R}^n$, is defined in the "neighborhood," i.e., an "open set," around each point. Such a space is called a "manifold." A "Lie algebra" of a Lie group is a linear space defined in the "tangent space" of that Lie group viewed as a manifold and is invariant to the transformation of the Lie group viewed as a group. Such an intuitive description is sufficient to convey the meaning to those familiar with abstract mathematics. However, precise description of the exact meaning would require a large number of pages. Here, we briefly enumerate the definitions and terminologies of the underlying basic concepts.

C.1 GROUPS

A *group* is a set G in which *multiplication*, or *composition*, is defined. Namely, for elements a, $b \in G$, their *product* $ab \in G$ is defined and has the following properties.

(1) The product is *associative*:

$$a(bc) = (ab)c, \qquad a, b, c \in G. \tag{C.1}$$

(2) The set G has an *identity* e that satisfies[1]

$$ea = ae = a, \qquad a \in G. \tag{C.2}$$

(3) For each element $a \in G$, an element a^{-1} called its *inverse* exists and satisfies the following[2]:

$$a^{-1}a = aa^{-1} = e. \tag{C.3}$$

[1] Actually, either $ea = e$ or $ae = e$ is sufficient. If the former holds, e is called the *left identity*, while if the latter holds, e is called the *right identity*. For a group, it is easily shown that if one exists, the other also exists and that both coincide.

[2] Actually, either $a^{-1}a = e$ or $aa^{-1} = e$ is sufficient. If the former holds, a^{-1} is called the *left inverse* of a, while if the latter holds, it is called the *right inverse*. For a group, it is easily shown that if one exists, the other also exists and that both coincide.

Elements a and b are said to *commute*, or to be *commutative*, if $ab = ba$. By definition, any element a commutes with the identity e. If all elements are mutually commutative, the group G is said to be a *commutative group* or an *Abelian group*. For an commutative group, "multiplication" is called *addition*, and the "product" ab is written as $a + b$ and called the *sum*; the "identity" e is denoted by 0 and called the *zero*, and the "inverse" a^{-1} is denoted by $-a$ and called its *negative*.

For a specific element g_0 of group G, the set of the products of g_0 and all the elements $g \in G$ is written as $g_0G = \{g_0g|g \in G\}$. It is easy to see that $g_0G = G$, i.e., g_0G and G are the same set. In other words, $g_0 \in G$ acts on G as its *transformation*, i.e., a one-to-one and onto mapping. If G has a finite number of elements, G is said to be a *finite group*, and the number of its elements, written as $|G|$, is called its *order*. For a finite group G, its element $g_0 \in G$ acts on G as *permutation*.

A subset $H \subset G$ of a group G is said to be a *subgroup* if H is a group by itself. It is easy to see that $H \subset G$ is a subgroup of G if and only if $ab^{-1} \in H$ for any elements $a, b \in H$. Evidently, the set $\{e\}$ consisting of the identity e only and the group G itself are subgroups of G, called the *trivial subgroups*; other subgroups are called *proper subgroups*.

Let H_1, ..., H_r be subgroups of G. The group G is said to be the *direct product* of H_1, ..., H_r if the following condition holds.

(1) Distinct subgroups are mutually commutative:

$$h_ih_j = h_jh_i, \qquad h_i \in H_i, \qquad h_j \in H_j, \qquad i \neq j. \tag{C.4}$$

(2) Any element $g \in G$ can be uniquely written as the product of some elements of the subgroups:

$$g = h_1 \cdots h_r, \qquad h_i \in H_i, \qquad i = 1, ..., r. \tag{C.5}$$

In this case, we write[3]

$$G = H_1 \otimes \cdots \otimes H_r, \tag{C.6}$$

and each H_i is called the *direct factor*. By definition, the direct factors H_1, ..., H_r share the identity e alone.

Consider r groups H_1, ..., H_r, which may have overlapping. Consider the following set G consisting of r-tuples of their elements:

$$G = \{(h_1, ..., h_r)|h_i \in H_i, i = 1, ..., r\}. \tag{C.7}$$

If we define the product of two elements $(h_1, ..., h_r)$ and $(h'_1, ..., h'_r)$ by

$$(h_1, ..., h_r)(h'_1, ..., h'_r) = (h_1h'_1, ..., h_rh'_r), \tag{C.8}$$

then G is a group; its identity is $(e_1, ..., e_r)$, where e_i is the identity of the group H_i, and the inverse of $(h_1, ..., h_r)$ is $(h_1^{-1}, ..., h_r^{-1})$, where h_i^{-1} is the inverse of h_i in H_i.

For each H_i, consider the following group $\tilde{H}_i$:

$$\tilde{H}_i = \{(e_1, ..., e_{i-1}, h_i, e_{i+1}, ..., e_r)|h_i \in H_i\}. \tag{C.9}$$

The identity of $\tilde{H}_i$ is $(e_1, ..., e_r)$, and the multiplication is defined in the same way as in G. Evidently, $\tilde{H}_i$ is a subgroup of G, and the above statements (1) and (2) are satisfied. Hence, G is the direct product $\tilde{H}_1 \otimes \cdots \otimes \tilde{H}_r$ of $\tilde{H}_1$, ..., $\tilde{H}_r$. Usually, however, we identify $\tilde{H}_i$

[3]Some authors write this as $G = H_1 \times \cdots \times H_r$.

with H_i and write as Eq. (C.6). If H_1, ..., H_r are commutative groups, the direct product of Eq. (C.6) is also a commutative group. In this case, we call it the *direct sum* and write[4], instead of Eq. (C.6),

$$G = H_1 \oplus \cdots \oplus H_r. \tag{C.10}$$

C.2 MAPPINGS AND GROUPS OF TRANSFORMATION

For a mapping $T : S \to S'$ from set S to set S', the sets S and S' are called the *domain* and the *range* of T, respectively. If an element $x \in S$ is mapped by T to $y = T(x)$, the element y is called the *image* of x. For a subset $A \subset S$, the set $\{y|y = T(x), x \in A\}$ of all images $T(x)$ of elements $x \in A$ is called the *image* of the subset A and written as $T(A)$. For a subset $B \subset S'$, if there exists an element $x \in A$ such that $y = T(x)$ for all $y \in B$, the set of all such elements $\{x|y = T(x), y \in B\}$ is called the *inverse image*, or *preimage*, of the subset B and written as $T^{-1}(B)$.

A mapping $T : S \to S'$ from set S to set S' is said to be *one-to-one*, or an *injection*, if

$$T(x) \neq T(x') \tag{C.11}$$

for all x, $x' \in S$, $x \neq x'$. It is said to be *onto*, or a *surjection*, if there exists $x \in S$ such that $x' = Tx$ for all $x' \in S'$. A mapping that is both one-to-one and onto is said to be a *bijection*.

A mapping T from group G to group G' is a *homomorphism* if

$$T(ab) = T(a)T(b), \qquad a, b \in G. \tag{C.12}$$

Evidently, the identity e of G is mapped to the identity e' of G':

$$e' = T(e), \qquad T(a^{-1}) = (Ta)^{-1}. \tag{C.13}$$

If such a homomorphism exists, groups G and G' are said to be *homomorphic*. If T is, in addition, one-to-one and onto, it is an *isomorphism*. If T is an isomorphism from group G to group G', it is evident that T^{-1} is an isomorphism from group G' to group G, and we say that G and G' are *isomorphic* to each other. We write this as

$$G \cong G. \tag{C.14}$$

We can think of isomorphic groups as essentially identical. For example, Eq. (C.9) defines an isomorphism between group H_i and group $\tilde{H}_i$. A bijection T from a set S to itself is called a *transformation* of S. If the set G of transformations T form a group, i.e, if

(1) If T, $T \in G$, then $T \circ T' \in G$.

(2) The set G contains an identity transformation I.

(3) For any $T \in G$, its inverse T^{-1} is also contained in G.

we say that G is a *group of transformations* of the set S.

---

[4]Some authors write this as $G = H_1 + \cdots + H_r$ or $H_1 \dot{+} \cdots \dot{+} H_r$.

C.3 TOPOLOGY

A set X is a *topological space* if the following set $\mathcal{O}$ of its subsets is given.

(1) The set $\mathcal{O}$ contains the empty set $\emptyset$ and the set X itself: $\emptyset$, $X \in \mathcal{O}$.

(2) The set $\mathcal{O}$ contains an arbitrary union of its members: $U_i \in \mathcal{O}$, $i \in I$ (an arbitrary index set) $\to \cup_{i \in I} U_i \in \mathcal{O}$.

(3) The set $\mathcal{O}$ contains an arbitrary finite intersections of its members: $U_i \in \mathcal{O}$, $i \in J$ (an arbitrary finite index set) $\to \cap_{i \in J} U_i \in \mathcal{O}$.

This set $\mathcal{O}$ is called the *topology* of the set X, and its members are called *open sets*. The complement $X - U$ of an open set U is said to be a *closed set*. A subset $X' \subset X$ of the set X with topology $\mathcal{O}$ is also a topological space with the topology $\mathcal{O}' = \{X' \cap U \mid U \in \mathcal{O}\}$, which is called the *relative topology*.

For a given set X, we can define many different topologies. The topology consisting only of the empty set $\emptyset$ and the set X itself is the *trivial topology*. The topology consisting of all subsets of X is called the *discrete topology*. We say that a topology that contains more subsets (with respect to inclusion) is *stronger*; a topology is *weaker* if it contains less subsets. The discrete topology is the strongest topology, and the trivial topology is the weakest topology.

For the n-dimensional space $\mathcal{R}^n$, we can define a topology generated by *open balls* $\{(x_1, ..., x_n) \mid \sqrt{\sum_{i=1}^{n} (x_i - c_i)^2} | < r\}$ for all c_i, $r \in \mathcal{R}$, $r > 0$. This is called the *Euclidean topology*. By "generate," we mean that we are considering an arbitrary number of unions and an arbitrary finite number of intersections. Instead of open balls, we may use all *open boxes* $\{(x_1, ..., x_n) \mid a_i < x_i < b_i, i = 1, ..., n\}$ for all a_i, $b_i \in \mathcal{R}$. These two are *equivalent* in the sense that both generate the same topology. In the following, we assume this topology for $\mathcal{R}^n$ unless otherwise stated, and the relative topology for all its subsets. A subset A of $\mathcal{R}^n$ is said to be *bounded* if it is included in some open ball, or equivalently in some open box.

A member of a topological space is usually referred to as a *point*. An open set that contains a point x of a topological space X is called a *neighborhood* of x. For a subset $A \subset X$, a point $x \in A$ is said to be an *interior* (or *inner*) *point* of A if x has a neighborhood included in A. The set A° of all interior points of A is called the *interior* of A. If any neighborhoods of a point $x \in X$ have an intersection with $A \subset X$, x is called a *limit* (or *accumulation*) *point*. The set $\bar{A}$ of all limit points of $A \subset X$ is called the *closure* of A, and $\bar{A} - A^\circ$ is called the *boundary* of A. When we say that a point sequence $\{x_i\}$, $i = 1, 2, ...$ *converges* to a *limit point* $x \in X$, we mean that any neighborhood U of x contains a subsequence $\{x_k\}$, $k = N, N+1, ...$ for some integer N.

C.4 MAPPINGS OF TOPOLOGICAL SPACES

A topological space X is said to be *Hausdorff*, or *separable*, if any distinct points x_1, $x_2 \in X$ have disjoint neighborhoods U_1, U_2, $U_1 \cap U_2 = \emptyset$. Any point x of a Hausdorff space is itself a closed set. The n-dimensional space $\mathcal{R}^n$ with Euclidean topology is Hausdorff.

A set $\{U_i\}$, $i \in I$, of open sets of a Hausdorff space X is a *covering* of X if any point $x \in X$ is contained in at least one U_i, i.e., if $\cup_{i \in I} U_i = X$. A Hausdorff space is *compact* if for any covering $\{U_i\}$, $i \in I$, we can choose finite members that cover X, i.e., a finite index set $J \subset I$ exists such that $\cup_{j \in J} U_j = X$. Any sequence $\{x_i\}$, $i = 1, 2, ...$, of a compact space X has a convergent subsequence. Its limit point is called an *accumulation point* of the sequence $\{x_i\}$, $i = 1, 2, ...$. A bounded closed set of $\mathcal{R}^n$ is compact (the *Heine–Borel theorem*).

Hence, any infinitely many points of a bounded closed set of $\mathcal{R}^n$ has an accumulation point (the *Bolzano–Weierstrass theorem*).

A topological space X is *disconnected* if it consists of two disjoint nonempty open sets X_1 and X_2, and *connected* otherwise. For a disconnected topological space $X = X_1 \cup X_2$, $X_1 \cap X_2 = \emptyset$, the open sets X_1 and X_2 are complements of each other, so they are also closed sets by definition. If each of them is connected, they are called the *connected components*. Otherwise, they are decomposed into smaller connected components. A topological space X is *locally connected* if any neighborhood of each point $x \in X$ includes a connected neighborhood.

Consider a mapping $f : X \to Y$ from a topological space X to a topological space Y. Suppose it maps a point $x \in X$ to a point $y \in Y$. If for any neighborhood V_y of y, there exists a neighborhood U_x of x such that $f(U_x) \subset V_y$, then the mapping f is said to be *continuous* at x. If it is continuous at all points $x \in X$, it is said to be a continuous mapping from X to Y. This is equivalent to saying that for any open set V of Y, its inverse image $f^{-1}(V)$ is an open set of X. An image of a compact set by a continuous mapping is also compact.

A mapping $f : X \to Y$ from a topological space X to a topological space Y is a *homeomorphism* if it is one-to-one and onto, i.e., a bijection, and if both f and f^{-1} are continuous. If such a mapping exists, X and Y are said to be *homeomorphic*. Since the image and inverse image of any open set of one is an open set of the other, we say that X and Y *have the same topology* in the sense that their open sets correspond one-to-one. A quantity that characterizes a topological space X is a *topological invariant* if it does not change by a homeomorphism. For example, the number of connected components is a topological invariant. Other well known topological invariants include the *Euler–Poincaré characteristic*, or simply the *Euler number*, and the *Betti number*.

C.5 MANIFOLDS

A Hausdorff space M is a *manifold* if the following are satisfied.

(1) Any point $x \in M$ has a neighborhood U such that there exists a homeomorphism ϕ, called the *coordinate map*, from U to an open set of $\mathcal{R}^n$.

(2) If point $x \in M$ belongs to two neighborhood U_1 and U_2 equipped with respective coordinate maps ϕ_1 and ϕ_2, the mapping $\phi_2\phi_1^{-1}$ is a homeomorphism from $\phi_1(U_1 \cap U_2) \subset \mathcal{R}^n$ to $\phi_2(U_1 \cap U_2) \subset \mathcal{R}^n$.

Here, n is a fixed integer, called the *dimension* of the manifold M. The coordinate map ϕ given in (1) defines the *coordinates* $\phi(x) = (x_1, ..., x_n) \in \mathcal{R}^n$ of point x. The pair (U, ϕ)

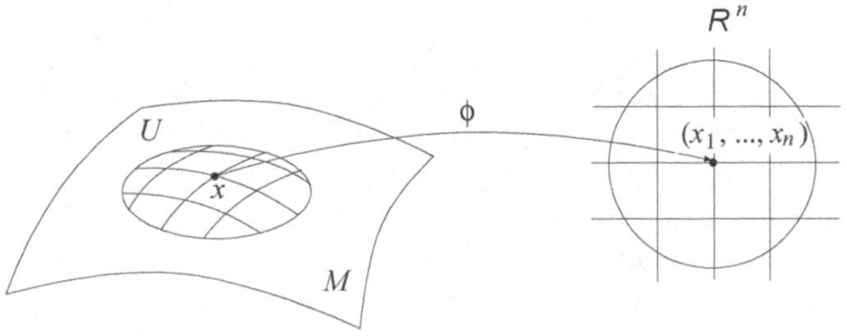

FIGURE C.1 Each point $x \in M$ of manifold M is given coordinates $(x_1, ..., x_n)$, specified by an homeomorphism (coordinate map) from a neighborhood U of x to $\mathcal{R}^n$.

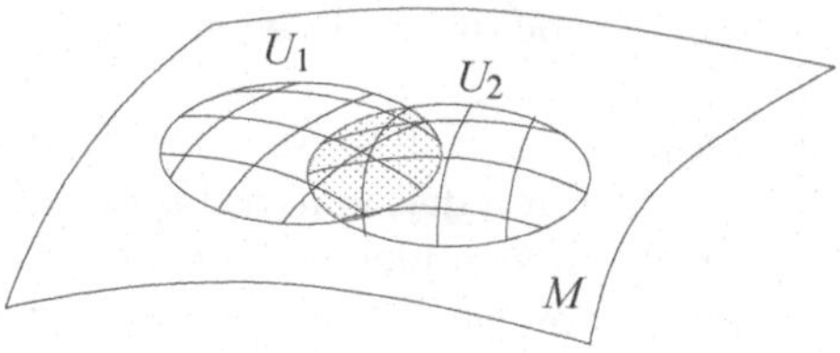

FIGURE C.2 Different local coordinate systems are continuously mapped to each other.

is called the *local coordinate system*, or the *chart*, of point x. If a point x is described by two local coordinate systems, the homeomorphism $\phi_2\phi_1^{-1}$ given in (2) defines a *coordinate change* from the local coordinate system (U_1, ϕ_1) to the local coordinate system (U_2, ϕ_2). In short, a manifold is a space in which *a local coordinate system is defined around each point* (Fig. C.1) such that *different coordinate systems are linked by a continuous mapping* (Fig. C.2). For $n = 2$, we can imagine pasting planar patches by continuously deforming them.

If at every point $x \in M$ the coordinate change $\phi_2\phi_1^{-1}$ is k-differentiable, i.e., has continuous derivatives up to order k, for some integer k, M is said to be a *differentiable manifold* and is *C^k-differentiable* for that k. If M is C^∞-differentiable, it is said to be *smooth*.

A continuous mapping f from a smooth manifold M to a smooth manifold N is said to be C^k-differentiable if it is a C^k-differentiable function of chosen coordinates. This property does not depend on the choice of the local coordinate systems of M and N. If a mapping $f : M \to N$ is C^∞-differentiable and has a C^∞-differentiable inverse f^{-1}, it is said to be a *diffeomorphism*, and we say M and N are *diffeomorphic* to each other.

C.6 LIE GROUPS

A group G is called a *Lie group* if it is also a differential manifold. This means, to be precise, that the multiplication $(a, b) \in G \times G \to ab \in G$ and the inverse $a \in G \to a^{-1} \in G$ are both differentiable mappings[5]. To be specific, the mapping $f : \phi_a(U_a) \times \phi_b(U_b) \to \phi_{ab}(U_{ab})$ defined by $f(\boldsymbol{x}, \boldsymbol{y}) = \phi_{ab}(\phi_a^{-1}(\boldsymbol{x})\phi_b^{-1}(\boldsymbol{y}))$, $\boldsymbol{x}, \boldsymbol{y} \in \mathcal{R}^n$ and the mapping $g : \phi_a(U_a) \to \phi_{a^{-1}}(U_{a^{-1}})$ defined by $g(\boldsymbol{x}) = \phi_{a^{-1}}(\phi_a(\boldsymbol{x})^{-1})$, $\boldsymbol{x} \in \mathcal{R}^n$ are both differentiable functions with respect to the coordinates of $\mathcal{R}^n$, where (ϕ_a, U_a), (ϕ_b, U_b), (ϕ_{ab}, U_{ab}), and $(\phi_{a^{-1}}, U_{a^{-1}})$ are the local coordinate systems around points a, b, ab, $a^{-1} \in G$, respectively.

The set $GL(n, \mathcal{R})$ of all $n \times n$ nonsingular matrices is a group of transformations of $\mathcal{R}^n$, called the n-dimensional *general linear group*. This is a subset of the n^2-dimensional space $\mathcal{R}^{n^2}$, where n^2 elements of each matrix are regarded as its coordinates, consisting of points of $\mathcal{R}^{n^2}$ at which the determinant is not 0. The set of points of $\mathcal{R}^{n^2}$ at which the determinant is 0 is a hypersurface of $\mathcal{R}^{n^2}$, which is a closed set with respect to the Euclidean topology. Since $GL(n, \mathcal{R})$ is its complement, it is an open set.

The general linear group $GL(n, \mathcal{R}) \subset \mathcal{R}^{n^2}$ is a topological space with respect to the relative topology. Defining the coordinate map ϕ by the *inclusion mapping* from $GL(n, \mathcal{R})$ to $\mathcal{R}^{n^2}$, i.e., the identity mapping, we can regard $GL(n, \mathcal{R})$ as a manifold. Since the identity mapping can be differentiable to any degree, it is a C^∞-differentiable. The elements of matrix products are polynomials in the elements of the matrices, so it is a differentiable mapping from $\mathcal{R}^{n^2} \times \mathcal{R}^{n^2}$ to $\mathcal{R}^{n^2}$. The elements of inverse matrices are rational functions

[5]Actually, this is a redundant expression; it is sufficient to say the mapping $(a, b) \to ab^{-1}$ is differentiable.

of the elements of the original matrices, so they define a differentiable mapping from $\mathcal{R}^{n^2}$ to itself. Thus, $GL(n, \mathcal{R})$ is a Lie group.

The set $O(n)$ of all $n \times n$ orthogonal matrices and its subset $SO(n)$ consisting matrices of determinant 1 are both groups of transformations of $\mathcal{R}^n$ and called the n-dimensional *orthogonal group* and the n-dimensional *special orthogonal group*, respectively. They are both subgroups of $GL(n, \mathcal{R})$, topological spaces with respect to the relative topology, and C^∞ manifolds. Since matrix multiplication and matrix inverse are differentiable mapping, they are also Lie groups.

From the definition of an orthogonal matrix, each of its elements is within the range of ± 1, so $O(n)$ is included in a bounded subset of $\mathcal{R}^{n^2}$ and hence a compact Lie group. Since the determinant of each element is either 1 or -1, $O(n)$ consists of two connected components, one with determinant 1 and the other -1, and $SO(n)$ is a connected Lie group consisting of the connected component of $O(n)$ with determinant 1. Lie groups that are subgroups of $GL(n, \mathcal{R})$, such as $O(n)$ and $SO(n)$, and their extensions to complex numbers are called *classical groups* or *linear Lie groups*. Besides $O(n)$ and $SO(n)$, they include among others the *special linear group*[6] $SL(n)$, the *unitary group*[7] $U(n)$, *special unitary group*[8] $SU(n)$, the *Lorenz group*[9], and the *symplectic group*[10] $Sp(2n)$.

C.7 LIE ALGEBRAS

An operation $[\cdot, \cdot] : V \times V \to V$ between two elements of a linear space, or a vector space, V is called a *Lie bracket* if the following rules[11] hold for any $\boldsymbol{x}$, $\boldsymbol{y}$, $\boldsymbol{z} \in V$ and any real number $c \in \mathcal{R}$:

$$[\boldsymbol{x}, \boldsymbol{y}] = -[\boldsymbol{y}, \boldsymbol{x}], \tag{C.15}$$

$$[c\boldsymbol{x}, \boldsymbol{y}] = c[\boldsymbol{x}, \boldsymbol{y}], \qquad [\boldsymbol{x}, c\boldsymbol{y}] = c[\boldsymbol{x}, \boldsymbol{y}], \tag{C.16}$$

$$[\boldsymbol{x} + \boldsymbol{y}, \boldsymbol{z}] = [\boldsymbol{x}, \boldsymbol{z}] + [\boldsymbol{y}, \boldsymbol{z}], \qquad [\boldsymbol{x}, \boldsymbol{y} + \boldsymbol{z}] = [\boldsymbol{x}, \boldsymbol{y}] + [\boldsymbol{x}, \boldsymbol{z}], \tag{C.17}$$

$$[\boldsymbol{x}, [\boldsymbol{y}, \boldsymbol{z}]] + [\boldsymbol{y}, [\boldsymbol{z}, \boldsymbol{x}]] + [\boldsymbol{z}, [\boldsymbol{x}, \boldsymbol{y}]] = \boldsymbol{0}. \tag{C.18}$$

Equation (C.15) states that the Lie bracket is *anticommutative*, and Eqs. (C.16) and (C.17) state that it is *bilinear*. Eqution (C.18) is called the *Jacobi identity*.

A linear space is called an *algebra* if multiplication (subject to standard rules) is defined between its elements. In particular, a linear space whose multiplication is defined by a Lie bracket is called a *Lie algebra*. The vector product $\boldsymbol{a} \times \boldsymbol{b}$ of $\mathcal{R}^3$ satisfies the rules of Eqs. (C.15)–(C.18). Hence, $\mathcal{R}^3$ is a Lie algebra with the Lie bracket $[\boldsymbol{a}, \boldsymbol{b}] = \boldsymbol{a} \times \boldsymbol{b}$.

The group G of transformations of a liner space V is itself a linear space with the following operations:

$$(cT)(\boldsymbol{x}) = T(c\boldsymbol{x}), \qquad (T_1 + T_2)(\boldsymbol{x}) = T_1(\boldsymbol{x}) + T_2(\boldsymbol{x}),$$

---

[6] The set of all matrices of determinant 1.

[7] The set of $n \times n$ complex matrices that satisfy $\boldsymbol{U}\boldsymbol{U}^\dagger = \boldsymbol{I}$, called *unitary matrices*, that appear in quantum mechanics, where $\boldsymbol{U}^\dagger$ denotes *Hermitian conjugate* (transpose of complex conjugate) of $\boldsymbol{U}$.

[8] The set of all unitary matrices of determinant 1.

[9] The set of 4×4 matrices that preserve a quadratic form, called the *Lorenz metric*, of 4-dimensional space-time that appear in the special theory of relativity.

[10] The set of $2n \times 2n$ matrices equipped with a special type of symmetry and antisymmetry between two types of coordinate components, one corresponding to positions and the other momentums. They appear in the analysis of generalized mechanics.

[11] Actually, this is a redundant description. The second equation of Eq. (C.16) and the second equation of Eq. (C.17) are obtained from Eq. (C.15), the first equation of Eq. (C.16), and the first equation of Eq. (C.17).

$$T, T_1, T_2 \in G, \qquad \boldsymbol{x} \in V, \qquad c \in \mathcal{R}. \tag{C.19}$$

The *commutator* defined by

$$[T_1, T_2] \equiv T_1 T_2 - T_2 T_1 \tag{C.20}$$

satisfies Eqs. (C.15)–(C.18). Hence, the group G of transformations is a Lie algebra with the Lie bracket defined by the commutator.

Let $\{\boldsymbol{e}_i\}$, $i = 1, ..., n$, be the basis of Lie algebra V viewed as a linear space. Since the Lie bracket is an element of V, it is specified by the Lie brackets of the basis elements. So, we put

$$[\boldsymbol{e}_i, \boldsymbol{e}_j] = \sum_{k=1}^{n} c_{ij}^k \boldsymbol{e}_k, \qquad i, j = 1, ..., n. \tag{C.21}$$

The n^3 constants c_{ij}^k, $i, j, k = 1, ...\ n$, are called the *structure constants*. In terms of them the Lie bracket $[\boldsymbol{x}, \boldsymbol{y}]$ of elements $\boldsymbol{x} = \sum_{i=1}^n x_i \boldsymbol{e}_i \in V$ and $\boldsymbol{y} = \sum_{i=1}^n y_i \boldsymbol{e}_i \in V$ is given as follows:

$$[\sum_{i=1}^{n} x_i \boldsymbol{e}_i, \sum_{j=1}^{n} y_j \boldsymbol{e}_j] = \sum_{k=1}^{n} \Big(\sum_{i,j=1}^{n} c_{ij}^k x_i y_j \Big) \boldsymbol{e}_k. \tag{C.22}$$

Equations (C.16) and (C.17) automatically hold for by any constants c_{ij}^k, but for Eqs. (C.15) and (C.18) to be satisfied the structural constants c_{ij}^k must satisfy

$$c_{ij}^k = -c_{jk}^k, \qquad i, j, k = 1, ..., n, \tag{C.23}$$

$$\sum_{l=1}^{n} c_{ij}^l c_{lk}^m + \sum_{l=1}^{n} c_{jk}^l c_{li}^m + \sum_{l=1}^{n} c_{ki}^k c_{lj}^m = 0, \qquad i, j, k.m = 1, ..., n. \tag{C.24}$$

A linear mapping $f : V \to V'$ between Lie algebras V and V' is called a *homomorphism* if

$$f([\boldsymbol{x}, \boldsymbol{y}]) = [f(\boldsymbol{x}), f(\boldsymbol{y})], \qquad \boldsymbol{x}, \boldsymbol{y} \in V. \tag{C.25}$$

If it is in addition one-to-one and onto, it is called an *isomorphism*. If an isomorphism exists, we say Lie algebras V and V' are *isomorphic* and write $V \cong V'$. Evidently, V and V' are isomorphic if and only if we can define their bases for which the structural constants coincide.

C.8 LIE ALGEBRAS OF LIE GROUPS

For a given Lie group, we can define an associated Lie algebra. In Sec. C.6, we defined a Lie group to be a differentiable manifold on which its group action is a differentiable mapping. Its Lie algebra is defined in terms of its differentiability. To be specific, we first define *tangent vectors* of a Lie group, viewed as a manifold, as differentiation operators on it and then *tangent spaces* at all points, or more generally a *fiber bundle*, in such a way that they are continuously and differentiably mapped to each other by the group action; we can imagine this by defining a tangent space around the identity e and copying it to all other points via the group action. Its Lie algebra is defined as the set of *invariant vector fields* in the sense that they are mapped to themselves by the group action. We define their Lie bracket by the commutator of differentiation operators. As a result, the relationships between the Lie group and its Lie algebra are described in terms *differential forms*, or *Pfaffians*, and their *integrability conditions* (*Frobenius theorem*).

However, such mathematical descriptions of general Lie groups and their Lie algebras are rather complicated. Here, we simplify the discussion by restricting the Lie group G to subgroups of $GL(n, \mathcal{R})$ (and of $GL(n, \mathcal{C})$) and defining their Lie algebras L in terms of their matrix representations.

For a Lie group G described by matrices, we consider the set L of all $n \times n$ matrices $\boldsymbol{X}$ such that

$$\exp(t\boldsymbol{X}) \quad (\equiv \sum_{k=0}^{\infty} \frac{t^k}{k!}\boldsymbol{X}^k) \in G \tag{C.26}$$

for an arbitrary real number t. Note that the exponential function of a matrix is always (absolutely) convergent. We can easily see that the set L is a (real) linear space, satisfying

$$\boldsymbol{X} \in L \;\rightarrow\; c\boldsymbol{X} \in L, \qquad c \in \mathcal{R}, \tag{C.27}$$

$$\boldsymbol{X}, \boldsymbol{Y} \in L \;\rightarrow\; \boldsymbol{X} + \boldsymbol{Y} \in L. \tag{C.28}$$

We can also see that L is a Lie algebra with the commutator $[\boldsymbol{X}, \boldsymbol{Y}] \equiv \boldsymbol{XY} - \boldsymbol{YX}$:

$$\boldsymbol{X}, \boldsymbol{Y} \in L \;\rightarrow\; [\boldsymbol{X}, \boldsymbol{Y}] \in L. \tag{C.29}$$

To show this, we use the identities (we omit the derivation)

$$\exp(t\boldsymbol{X})\exp(t\boldsymbol{Y}) = \exp(t(\boldsymbol{X} + \boldsymbol{Y}) + \frac{t^2}{2}[\boldsymbol{X}, \boldsymbol{Y}] + O(t^3)), \qquad t \in \mathcal{R}, \tag{C.30}$$

$$\{\exp(t\boldsymbol{X}), \exp(t\boldsymbol{Y})\} = \exp(t^2[\boldsymbol{X}, \boldsymbol{Y}] + O(t^3)), \qquad t \in \mathcal{R}, \tag{C.31}$$

where we define $\{\boldsymbol{A}, \boldsymbol{B}\} \equiv \boldsymbol{ABA}^{-1}\boldsymbol{B}^{-1}$, which is also called the *commutator*. The resulting algebra L is called the *Lie algebra of the Lie group G*. Its elements $\boldsymbol{X}$ are called, mainly by physicists, *infinitesimal generators*.

From the argument of Secs. 6.2 and 6.3, we can easily understand why the matrix $\boldsymbol{X}$ of Eq. (C.26) represents an infinitesimal transformation. In fact, if we write an element g of G close to the identity as $g = \boldsymbol{I} + t\boldsymbol{X} + O(t^2)$ for some small number t (≈ 0), we can see, by the reasoning of Eq. (6.1) and Eqs. (6.9)–(6.11), that g is written in the form of Eq. (C.26). Unlike in Chapter 6, however, $\boldsymbol{X}$ is no longer necessarily an antisymmetric matrix. As we will discuss below, it has some specific form that characterizes the Lie group G.

Here, the important thing to note is that Eq. (C.26) can express only elements in the connected component of G that contains the identity e. Hence, if two Lie groups have the same connected component that includes the identity e, their Lie algebras are identical.

The Lie algebra of the general linear group $GL(n, \mathcal{R})$ (or $GL(n, \mathcal{R})$) is the set of all $n \times n$ (real or complex) matrices and denoted by $gl(n, \mathcal{R})$ (or $gl(n, \mathcal{R})$). The Lie algebra of the special linear group $SL(n)$ is the set of all $n \times n$ (real) matrices $\boldsymbol{X}$ of trace 0 ($\mathrm{tr}(\boldsymbol{X}) = 0$) and denoted by $sl(n)$. The Lie algebra of the orthogonal group $O(n)$ is the set of all $n \times n$ (real) antisymmetric matices $\boldsymbol{X}$ ($\boldsymbol{X}^\top = -\boldsymbol{X}$) and denoted by $o(n)$. The special orthogonal group $SO(n)$ is the connected component of $O(n)$ that contains the identity e, so its Lie algebra $so(n)$ is the same as $o(n)$. The Lie algebra of the unitary group $U(n)$ is the set of all $n \times n$ (complex) *anti-Hermitian matrices*, $\boldsymbol{X}$ ($\boldsymbol{X}^\dagger = -\boldsymbol{X}$), and denoted by $u(n)$. The Lie algebra of the special unitary group $SU(n)$ is the set of the matrices $\boldsymbol{X}$ of $u(n)$ that have trace 0 ($\mathrm{tr}(\boldsymbol{X}) = 0$). All these are found, just as deriving Eq. (6.3) from Eqs. (6.1) and (6.2), by substituting $g = \boldsymbol{I} + t\boldsymbol{X} + O(t^2)$ into the relationship that defines the respective Lie group G, expanding it, and taking up terms that are linear in t.

The importance of Lie algebras L is that the Lie groups G are uniquely (though locally) determined by their Lie algebras L. What we mean by this is that we can find a neighborhood U_e of the identity e of G such that any of its element $g \in U_e$ is uniquely expressed in term of some fixed elements $\boldsymbol{A}_1, ..., \boldsymbol{A}_n \in L$ of the Lie algebra L in the form $g = \exp(\sum_{i=1}^{n} t_i \boldsymbol{A}_i)$, $|t_i| < 1$, $i = 1, ..., n$.

If the Lie group G is connected, the neighborhood U_e of the identity e generates all the elements g of G, i.e., any $g \in G$ is written as $g = u_1 \cdots u_N$ in terms of a finite number of elements $u_i \in U_e$, $i = 1, ..., N$. Hence, any $g \in G$ is written as $g = \exp(\boldsymbol{X}_1) \cdots \exp(\boldsymbol{X}_N)$ in terms of a finite number of elements $X_i \in L$, $i = 1, ..., N$, of the Lie algebra L, although the expression is not necessarily unique. In particular, the Lie group G is commutative if and only if its Lie algebra is commutative.

Suppose there is a neighborhood $U_e \subset G$ of the identity e of Lie group G that contains elements g, g', $gg' \in U_e$. Then, a mapping $f : G \to G'$ from Lie group G to Lie group G' is a *local homomorphism* from G to G' if

$$f(g)f(g') = f(gg'). \tag{C.32}$$

If in addition this is one-to-one and $f^{-1} : G' \to G$ is also a local homomorphism, f is a *local isomorphism*, and we say that G and G' are *locally isomorphic*. Lie groups G and G' are locally isomorphic if and only if they have the same, i.e., isomorphic, Lie algebras[12].

If two connected Lie groups G and G' have the same Lie algebra (hence locally isomorphic) and if G is *simply connected*[13], G is called the *universal covering group*[14] of G'. For example, $SO(3)$ and $SU(2)$ share the same Lie algebra, so they are locally isomorphic, and $SU(2)$ is known to be simply connected. Hence, it is a universal covering group of $SO(3)$.

[12]To be specifc, for a local isomorphism $f : G \to G'$ between Lie groups G and G', the isomorphism $df : L \to L'$ beteween their Lie algebras L and L' is given by the *derivation* $(df)(\boldsymbol{X}) = df(\exp(t\boldsymbol{X}))/dt|_{t=0}$.

[13]This means that an arbitrary loop in G can be continuously shrunk to a point.

[14]This means that there exists a many-to-one continuous mapping such that the mapping is locally isomorphic in the neighborhood of corresponding points, i.e., a *projection*. One can imagine that G is winding around G' many times.

Answers

Chapter 2

2.1. Let a_{ij} be the (i, j) element of matrix $\boldsymbol{A}$, and x_i and y_i the ith components of vectors $\boldsymbol{x}$ and $\boldsymbol{y}$, respectively. The definition of the product of a matrix and a vector implies that $\langle \boldsymbol{x}, \boldsymbol{A}\boldsymbol{y} \rangle$ and $\langle \boldsymbol{A}^\top \boldsymbol{x}, \boldsymbol{y} \rangle$ are both equal to $\sum_{i,j=1}^{3} a_{ij} x_i y_j$.

2.2. (1) Let λ be an eigenvalue of $\boldsymbol{A}$, and $\boldsymbol{u}$ $(\neq \boldsymbol{0})$ the corresponding eigenvector. Rewriting the definition $\boldsymbol{A}\boldsymbol{u} = \lambda \boldsymbol{u}$ of eigenvalues and eigenvectors, we obtain $(\lambda \boldsymbol{I} - \boldsymbol{A})\boldsymbol{u} = \boldsymbol{0}$. This is a linear equation in $\boldsymbol{u}$, which has a nontrivial solution if and only if the coefficient matrix has determinant 0, i.e., $|\lambda \boldsymbol{I} - \boldsymbol{A}| = 0$.

(2) If we let a_{ij} be the (i, j) element of $\boldsymbol{A}$, the characteristic polynomial $\phi(\lambda)$ has the form

$$\phi(\lambda) = \left| \lambda \begin{pmatrix} 1 & & \\ & 1 & \\ & & 1 \end{pmatrix} - \begin{pmatrix} a_{11} & a_{12} & a_{13} \\ a_{21} & a_{22} & a_{23} \\ a_{31} & a_{32} & a_{33} \end{pmatrix} \right| = \begin{vmatrix} \lambda - a_{11} & -a_{12} & -a_{13} \\ -a_{21} & \lambda - a_{22} & -a_{23} \\ -a_{31} & -a_{32} & \lambda - a_{33} \end{vmatrix}$$
$$= \lambda^3 - a\lambda^2 + b\lambda - c.$$

Expanding the determinant, we see that $a = a_{11} + a_{22} + a_{33}$ $(= \mathrm{tr}\boldsymbol{A})$. Letting $\lambda = 0$ in $\phi(\lambda) = |\lambda \boldsymbol{I} - \boldsymbol{A}|$, we obtain $\phi(0) = |-\boldsymbol{A}| = -|\boldsymbol{A}|$ and hence $c = |\boldsymbol{A}|$. Let λ_1, λ_2, and λ_3 be the three roots of $\phi(\lambda)$. We can write $\phi(\lambda)$ as

$$\begin{aligned}\phi(\lambda) &= (\lambda - \lambda_1)(\lambda - \lambda_2)(\lambda - \lambda_3) \\ &= \lambda^3 - (\lambda_1 + \lambda_2 + \lambda_3)\lambda^2 + (\lambda_2\lambda_3 + \lambda_3\lambda_1 + \lambda_1\lambda_2)\lambda - \lambda_1\lambda_2\lambda_3.\end{aligned}$$

Comparing the above two expressions, we obtain Eq. (2.20).

2.3. (1) Let θ be the angle made by the vector $\boldsymbol{a}$ and the line l. Since $\boldsymbol{u}$ is a unit vector, we see that $\langle \boldsymbol{u}, \boldsymbol{a} \rangle = \|\boldsymbol{u}\| \cdot \|\boldsymbol{a}\| \cos\theta = \|\boldsymbol{a}\| \cos\theta$. Hence, from Fig. 2.6, the projected length of $\boldsymbol{a}$ onto the line l is $\|\boldsymbol{a}\| \cos\theta = \langle \boldsymbol{u}, \boldsymbol{a} \rangle$, where the length is regarded as positive in the direction of $\boldsymbol{u}$ and negative in the opposite direction.

(2) From Fig. 2.6, we see that the projection $\overrightarrow{OH}$ of the vector $\boldsymbol{a} = \overrightarrow{OA}$ onto the line l is in the direction of the unit vector $\boldsymbol{u}$ and has length $\langle \boldsymbol{u}, \boldsymbol{a} \rangle$. So, $\overrightarrow{OH} = \langle \boldsymbol{u}, \boldsymbol{a} \rangle \boldsymbol{u}$, and hence $|AH| = \|\boldsymbol{a} - \langle \boldsymbol{u}, \boldsymbol{a} \rangle \boldsymbol{u}\|$.

Chapter 3

3.1. (1) From Eq. (2.19), we obtain

$$\langle \boldsymbol{x}, (\boldsymbol{A}_1\boldsymbol{A}_2 \cdots \boldsymbol{A}_N)\boldsymbol{y} \rangle = \langle (\boldsymbol{A}_1\boldsymbol{A}_2 \cdots \boldsymbol{A}_N)^\top \boldsymbol{x}, \boldsymbol{y} \rangle.$$

On the other hand, applying Eq. (2.19) successively, we obtain

$$\langle \boldsymbol{x}, \boldsymbol{A}_1\boldsymbol{A}_2\cdots\boldsymbol{A}_N\boldsymbol{y}\rangle = \langle \boldsymbol{A}_1^\top\boldsymbol{x}, \boldsymbol{A}_2\cdots\boldsymbol{A}_N\boldsymbol{y}\rangle = \cdots = \langle \boldsymbol{A}_N\cdots\boldsymbol{A}_2^\top\boldsymbol{A}_1^\top\boldsymbol{x}, \boldsymbol{y}\rangle.$$

These equalities are identities in $\boldsymbol{x}$ and $\boldsymbol{y}$, holding for any $\boldsymbol{x}$ and $\boldsymbol{y}$. Hence, Eq. (3.46) follows.

(2) To prove Eq. (3.47), it suffices to show that the product of $\boldsymbol{A}_1\boldsymbol{A}_2\cdots\boldsymbol{A}_N$ and $\boldsymbol{A}_N^{-1}\cdots\boldsymbol{A}_2^{-1}\boldsymbol{A}_1^{-1}$ is the identity $\boldsymbol{I}$. This is confirmed as follows:

$$\begin{aligned}\boldsymbol{A}_1\boldsymbol{A}_2\cdots\underbrace{\boldsymbol{A}_N\boldsymbol{A}_N^{-1}}_{\boldsymbol{I}}\cdots\boldsymbol{A}_2^{-1}\boldsymbol{A}_1^{-1} &= \boldsymbol{A}_1\boldsymbol{A}_2\cdots\underbrace{\boldsymbol{A}_{N-1}\boldsymbol{A}_{N-1}^{-1}}_{\boldsymbol{I}}\cdots\boldsymbol{A}_2^{-1}\boldsymbol{A}_1^{-1}\\ &= \cdots = \underbrace{\boldsymbol{A}_1\boldsymbol{A}_1^{-1}}_{\boldsymbol{I}} = \boldsymbol{I}.\end{aligned}$$

Hence, $\boldsymbol{A}_1\boldsymbol{A}_2\cdots\boldsymbol{A}_N$ and $\boldsymbol{A}_N^{-1}\cdots\boldsymbol{A}_2^{-1}\boldsymbol{A}_1^{-1}$ are the inverse of each other.

3.2. In terms of the components of the vectors $\boldsymbol{a}$ and $\boldsymbol{l}$, the components of Eq. (3.19) have the following expressions:

$$\begin{aligned}a_1' &= a_1\cos\Omega + (l_2a_3 - l_3a_2)\sin\Omega + (a_1l_1 + a_2l_2 + a_3l_3)l_1(1-\cos\Omega),\\ a_2' &= a_2\cos\Omega + (l_3a_1 - l_1a_3)\sin\Omega + (a_1l_1 + a_2l_2 + a_3l_3)l_2(1-\cos\Omega),\\ a_3' &= a_3\cos\Omega + (l_1a_2 - l_2a_1)\sin\Omega + (a_1l_1 + a_2l_2 + a_3l_3)l_3(1-\cos\Omega).\end{aligned}$$

These are written as $\boldsymbol{a}' = \boldsymbol{R}\boldsymbol{a}$ if the matrix $\boldsymbol{R}$ is defined by Eq. (3.20).

3.3. Using the rule of Eqs. (3.25) and (3.26), we can write the product of $q = \alpha + a_1i + a_2j + a_3k$ and $q' = \beta + a_1'i + b_2j + b_3k$ as follows:

$$\begin{aligned}qq' &= (\alpha + a_1i + a_2j + a_3k)(\beta + b_1i + b_2j + b_3k)\\ &= \alpha\beta + a_1b_1i^2 + a_2b_2j^2 + a_3b_3k^2 + (\alpha b_1 + a_1\beta)i + (\alpha b_2 + a_2\beta)j + (\alpha b_3 + a_3\beta)k\\ &\quad + a_1b_2ij + a_1b_3ik + a_2b_1ji + a_2b_3jk + a_3b_1ki + a_3b_2kj\\ &= \alpha\beta - a_1b_1 - a_2b_2 - a_3b_3 + (\alpha b_1 + a_1\beta)i + (\alpha b_2 + a_2\beta)j + (\alpha b_3 + a_3\beta)k\\ &\quad + a_1b_2k - a_1b_3j - a_2b_1k + a_2b_3i + a_3b_1j - a_3b_2i\\ &= \alpha\beta - (a_1b_1 + a_2b_2 + a_3b_3) + \alpha(b_1i + b_2j + b_3k) + \beta(a_1i + a_2j + a_3k)\\ &\quad + (a_2b_3 - a_3b_2)i + (a_3b_1 - a_1b_3)j + (a_1b_2 - a_2b_1)k\\ &= \alpha\beta - \langle\boldsymbol{a}, \boldsymbol{b}\rangle + \alpha\boldsymbol{b} + \beta\boldsymbol{a} + \boldsymbol{a}\times\boldsymbol{b}.\end{aligned}$$

3.4. The first condition is evident from the definition of the conjugate quternion $q^\dagger$. If we let $q = \alpha + \boldsymbol{a}$ and $q' = \beta + \boldsymbol{b}$, we obtain from Eq. (3.28)

$$(qq')^\dagger = \alpha\beta - \langle\boldsymbol{a}, \boldsymbol{b}\rangle - \alpha\boldsymbol{b} - \beta\boldsymbol{a} - \boldsymbol{a}\times\boldsymbol{b}.$$

Since $q^\dagger = \alpha - \boldsymbol{a}$ and $q'^\dagger = \beta - \boldsymbol{b}$, on the other hand, we obtain from Eq. (3.28)

$$q'^\dagger q^\dagger = \beta\alpha - \langle\boldsymbol{b}, \boldsymbol{a}\rangle - \beta\boldsymbol{a} - \alpha\boldsymbol{b} + \boldsymbol{b}\times\boldsymbol{a}.$$

Hence, $(qq')^\dagger = q'^\dagger q^\dagger$ follows.

3.5. This is an immediate consequence of the definition of the conjugate quternion $q^\dagger$.

3.6. If we let $q = \alpha + \boldsymbol{a}$, then $q^\dagger = \alpha - \boldsymbol{a}$. Hence, we see from Eq. (3.28) that

$$qq^\dagger = \alpha^2 + \|\boldsymbol{a}\|^2 - \alpha\boldsymbol{a} + \alpha\boldsymbol{a} - \boldsymbol{a}\times\boldsymbol{a} = \alpha^2 + \|\boldsymbol{a}\|^2.$$

Similarly,

$$q^\dagger q = \alpha^2 + \|\boldsymbol{a}\|^2 + \alpha\boldsymbol{a} - \alpha\boldsymbol{a} - \boldsymbol{a}\times\boldsymbol{a} = \alpha^2 + \|\boldsymbol{a}\|^2.$$

Thus, Eq. (3.50) holds.

3.7. If $q \neq 0$, then $\|q\| > 0$. Hence, Eq. (3.50) implies

$$q\Big(\frac{q^\dagger}{\|q\|^2}\Big) = \Big(\frac{q^\dagger}{\|q\|^2}\Big)q = 1.$$

This means that if we let $q^{-1} = q^\dagger/\|q\|^2$, Eq. (3.51) holds.

3.8. From Eq. (3.48), we see that

$$(q\boldsymbol{a}q^\dagger)^\dagger = q^{\dagger\dagger}\boldsymbol{a}^\dagger q^\dagger = -q\boldsymbol{a}q^\dagger.$$

Since the second equation of Eq. (3.49) holds, the scalar part of $\boldsymbol{a}'$ is 0.

3.9. The square norm of Eq. (3.34) is written as follows:

$$\|\boldsymbol{a}'\|^2 = \boldsymbol{a}'\boldsymbol{a}'^\dagger = q\boldsymbol{a}q^\dagger q\boldsymbol{a}^\dagger q^\dagger = q\boldsymbol{a}\|q\|^2\boldsymbol{a}^\dagger q^\dagger = q\boldsymbol{a}\boldsymbol{a}^\dagger q^\dagger = q\|\boldsymbol{a}\|^2 q^\dagger = \|\boldsymbol{a}\|^2 qq^\dagger = \|\boldsymbol{a}\|^2.$$

3.10. The first component of the left side of Eq. (3.37) is

$$\begin{aligned} & a_2(b_1c_2 - b_2c_1) - a_3(b_3c_1 - b_1c_3) = (a_2c_2 + a_3c_3)b_1 - (a_2b_2 + a_3b_3c_1) \\ &= (a_1c_1 + a_2c_2 + a_3c_3)b_1 - (a_1b_1 + a_2b_2 + a_3b_3c_1) \\ &= \langle\boldsymbol{a},\boldsymbol{c}\rangle b_1 - \langle\boldsymbol{a},\boldsymbol{b}\rangle c_1. \end{aligned}$$

Similarly, the second and third components are $\langle\boldsymbol{a},\boldsymbol{c}\rangle b_2 - \langle\boldsymbol{a},\boldsymbol{b}\rangle c_2$ and $\langle\boldsymbol{a},\boldsymbol{c}\rangle b_3 - \langle\boldsymbol{a},\boldsymbol{b}\rangle c_3$, respectively. Hence, Eq. (3.37) is obtained.

3.11. If we let $\boldsymbol{q} = q_1 i + q_2 j + q_3 k$, Eq. (3.34) is written as

$$\boldsymbol{a}' = (q_0 + \boldsymbol{q})\boldsymbol{a}(q_0 - \boldsymbol{q}) = q_0^2\boldsymbol{a} + q_0(\boldsymbol{q}\boldsymbol{a} - \boldsymbol{a}\boldsymbol{q}) - \boldsymbol{q}\boldsymbol{a}\boldsymbol{q}.$$

From Eq. (3.29), we can write $\boldsymbol{q}\boldsymbol{a} - \boldsymbol{a}\boldsymbol{q}$ as

$$\begin{aligned} \boldsymbol{q}\boldsymbol{a} - \boldsymbol{a}\boldsymbol{q} &= \boldsymbol{q}\times\boldsymbol{a} - \boldsymbol{a}\times\boldsymbol{q} = 2\boldsymbol{q}\times\boldsymbol{a} \\ &= 2(q_2a_3 - q_3a_2)i + 2(q_3a_1 - q_1a_3)j + 2(q_1a_2 - q_2a_1)k. \end{aligned}$$

For $\boldsymbol{q}\boldsymbol{a}\boldsymbol{q}$, we can rewrite it, using the same procedure as in Eq. (3.36), in the form

$$\boldsymbol{q}\boldsymbol{a}\boldsymbol{q} = \|\boldsymbol{q}\|^2\boldsymbol{a} - 2\langle\boldsymbol{q},\boldsymbol{a}\rangle\boldsymbol{q}.$$

Hence, letting $\boldsymbol{a}' = a_1' i + a_2' j + a_3' k$, we see that a_1' has the form

$$\begin{aligned} a_1' &= q_0^2 a_1 + 2q_0(q_2a_3 - q_3a_2) - \|\boldsymbol{q}\|^2 a_1 + 2\langle\boldsymbol{q},\boldsymbol{a}\rangle q_1 \\ &= q_0^2 a_1 + 2q_0q_2a_3 - 2q_0q_3a_2 - \|\boldsymbol{q}\|^2 a_1 + 2(q_1a_1 + q_2a_2 + q_3a_3)q_1 \\ &= (q_0^2 - \|\boldsymbol{q}\|^2 + 2q_1^2)a_1 + (-2q_0q_3 + 2q_2q_1)a_2 + (2q_0q_2 + 2q_3q_1)a_3 \\ &= (q_0^2 + q_1^2 - q_2^2 - q_3^2)a_1 + 2(q_1q_2 - q_0q_3)a_2 + 2(q_1q_3 + q_0q_2)a_3. \end{aligned}$$

Similarly, a_2' and a_3' have the form

$$a_2' = 2(q_2q_1 + q_0q_3)a_1 + (q_0^2 - q_1^2 + q_2^2 - q_3^2)a_2 + 2(q_2q_3 - q_0q_1)a_3,$$
$$a_3' = 2(q_3q_1 - q_0q_2)a_1 + 2(q_3q_2 + q_0q_1)a_2 + (q_0^2 - q_1^2 - q_2^2 + q_3^2)a_3.$$

In terms of the matrix $\boldsymbol{R}$ of Eq. (3.40), these are written as $\boldsymbol{a}' = \boldsymbol{R}\boldsymbol{a}$.

Chapter 4

4.1. Let $\boldsymbol{\lambda}_\alpha$ be the Lagrange multiplier vector for the constraint $\bar{\boldsymbol{a}}_\alpha' = \boldsymbol{R}\bar{\boldsymbol{a}}_\alpha$, and consider

$$\frac{1}{2}\sum_{\alpha=1}^{N}(\|\boldsymbol{a}_\alpha - \bar{\boldsymbol{a}}_\alpha\|^2 + \|\boldsymbol{a}_\alpha' - \bar{\boldsymbol{a}}_\alpha'\|^2) - \sum_{\alpha=1}^{N}\langle\boldsymbol{\lambda}_\alpha, \bar{\boldsymbol{a}}_\alpha' - \boldsymbol{R}\bar{\boldsymbol{a}}_\alpha\rangle.$$

Differentiating this with respect to $\bar{\boldsymbol{a}}_\alpha$ and $\bar{\boldsymbol{a}}_\alpha'$ and letting the results be $\boldsymbol{0}$, we obtain

$$\boldsymbol{a}_\alpha - \bar{\boldsymbol{a}}_\alpha - \boldsymbol{R}^\top\boldsymbol{\lambda}_\alpha = \boldsymbol{0}, \qquad \boldsymbol{a}_\alpha' - \bar{\boldsymbol{a}}_\alpha' + \boldsymbol{\lambda}_\alpha = \boldsymbol{0}.$$

Hence, $\bar{\boldsymbol{a}}_\alpha$ are $\bar{\boldsymbol{a}}_\alpha'$ written, respectively, as

$$\bar{\boldsymbol{a}}_\alpha = \boldsymbol{a}_\alpha - \boldsymbol{R}^\top\boldsymbol{\lambda}_\alpha, \qquad \bar{\boldsymbol{a}}_\alpha' = \boldsymbol{a}_\alpha' + \boldsymbol{\lambda}_\alpha.$$

From $\bar{\boldsymbol{a}}_\alpha' = \boldsymbol{R}\bar{\boldsymbol{a}}_\alpha$, we obtain

$$\boldsymbol{a}_\alpha' + \boldsymbol{\lambda}_\alpha = \boldsymbol{R}\boldsymbol{a}_\alpha - \boldsymbol{\lambda}_\alpha,$$

and hence

$$\boldsymbol{\lambda}_\alpha = -\frac{1}{2}(\boldsymbol{a}_\alpha' - \boldsymbol{R}\boldsymbol{a}_\alpha).$$

Thus, we can write the Mahalanobis distance J of Eq. (4.11) as

$$J = \frac{1}{2}\sum_{\alpha=1}^{N}(\|\boldsymbol{R}^\top\boldsymbol{\lambda}_\alpha\|^2 + \|\boldsymbol{\lambda}_\alpha\|^2) = \sum_{\alpha=1}^{N}\|\boldsymbol{\lambda}_\alpha\|^2 = \frac{1}{4}\sum_{\alpha=1}^{N}\|\boldsymbol{a}_\alpha' - \boldsymbol{R}\boldsymbol{a}_\alpha\|^2.$$

Note that since $\boldsymbol{R}^\top$ is a rotation matrix, the norm of a vector is unchanged by its multiplication.

4.2. (1) The statement that $\boldsymbol{z}$ has probability density $p_z(\boldsymbol{z})$ means that the probability of the value of $\boldsymbol{z}$ being in the interval $[\boldsymbol{z}, \boldsymbol{z}+d\boldsymbol{z}]$ (abbreviation of the direct sum for their components) is $p_z(\boldsymbol{z})d\boldsymbol{z}$. This is equal to the probability of the event that $\boldsymbol{y}$ is in the interval $[\boldsymbol{z}-\boldsymbol{x}, \boldsymbol{z}-\boldsymbol{x}+d\boldsymbol{z}]$ (whose probability is $p_y(\boldsymbol{z}-\boldsymbol{x})d\boldsymbol{z}$), where $\boldsymbol{x}$ assumes an arbitrary value. Since $\boldsymbol{x}$ and $\boldsymbol{y}$ are mutually independent, that probability equals $\left(\int_{-\infty}^{\infty} p_x(\boldsymbol{x})p_z(\boldsymbol{z}-\boldsymbol{x})d\boldsymbol{x}\right)d\boldsymbol{z}$. Hence, the probability density of $\boldsymbol{z}$ is given by Eq. (4.44).

(2) The probability densities of $\boldsymbol{x}$ and $\boldsymbol{y}$ are both given in the form

$$p(\boldsymbol{x}) = \frac{1}{\sqrt{(2\pi)^n}\sigma^n}e^{-\|\boldsymbol{x}\|^2/2\sigma^2},$$

which is an extension of Eq. (4.8) to n dimensions. Hence, the probability density $p_z(\boldsymbol{z})$ of $\boldsymbol{z}$ is given by

$$\begin{aligned}
p_z(\boldsymbol{z}) &= \int_{-\infty}^{\infty} p(\boldsymbol{x})p(\boldsymbol{z}-\boldsymbol{x})d\boldsymbol{x} = \frac{1}{(2\pi)^n\sigma^{2n}}\int_{-\infty}^{\infty} e^{-(\|\boldsymbol{x}\|^2+\|\boldsymbol{z}-\boldsymbol{x}\|^2)/2\sigma^2}d\boldsymbol{x} \\
&= \frac{1}{(2\pi)^n\sigma^{2n}}\int_{-\infty}^{\infty} e^{-(\|\boldsymbol{x}\|^2+\|\boldsymbol{z}\|^2-2\langle\boldsymbol{z},\boldsymbol{x}\rangle+\|\boldsymbol{x}\|^2)/2\sigma^2}d\boldsymbol{x} \\
&= \frac{1}{(2\pi)^n\sigma^{2n}}\int_{-\infty}^{\infty} e^{-(2\|\boldsymbol{x}\|^2-2\langle\boldsymbol{z},\boldsymbol{x}\rangle+\|\boldsymbol{z}\|^2/2+\|\boldsymbol{z}\|^2/2)/2\sigma^2}d\boldsymbol{x} \\
&= \frac{1}{(2\pi)^n\sigma^{2n}}\int_{-\infty}^{\infty} e^{-(2\|\boldsymbol{x}-\boldsymbol{z}/2\|^2+\|\boldsymbol{z}\|^2/2)/2\sigma^2}d\boldsymbol{x} \\
&= \frac{1}{\sqrt{(2\pi)^n(\sigma/\sqrt{2})^n}}\int_{-\infty}^{\infty} e^{-\|\boldsymbol{x}-\boldsymbol{z}/2\|^2/\sigma^2}d\boldsymbol{x}\frac{1}{\sqrt{(2\pi)^n(\sqrt{2}\sigma)^n}}e^{-\|\boldsymbol{z}\|^2/4\sigma^2} \\
&= \frac{1}{\sqrt{(2\pi)^n(\sigma/\sqrt{2})^n}}\int_{-\infty}^{\infty} e^{-\|\boldsymbol{w}\|^2/2(\sigma^2/2)}d\boldsymbol{w}\frac{1}{\sqrt{(2\pi)^n(\sqrt{2}\sigma)^n}}e^{-\|\boldsymbol{z}\|^2/2(2\sigma^2)},
\end{aligned}$$

where we have put $\boldsymbol{w} = \boldsymbol{x} - \boldsymbol{z}/2$ and changed the integration variable from $\boldsymbol{x}$ to $\boldsymbol{w}$. The first part equals the integration of the Gaussian random variable $\boldsymbol{w}$ of expectation $\boldsymbol{0}$ and variance $\sigma^2/2$ over the entire space and hence equals 1. Thus,

$$p_z(\boldsymbol{z}) = \frac{1}{\sqrt{(2\pi)^n(\sqrt{2}\sigma)^n}}e^{-\|\boldsymbol{z}\|^2/2(2\sigma^2)},$$

which is equal to the probability density of a Gaussian random variable of expectation $\boldsymbol{0}$ and variance $2\sigma^2$.

4.3. Evidently, the (i,j) element of the product $\boldsymbol{a}\boldsymbol{b}^\top$ is a_ib_j by the definition of matrix multiplication operation. Hence, $\mathrm{tr}(\boldsymbol{a}\boldsymbol{b}^\top) = \sum_{i=1}^n a_ib_i = \langle\boldsymbol{a},\boldsymbol{b}\rangle$.

4.4. From the definition of matrix multiplication operation, both $\mathrm{tr}(\boldsymbol{A}\boldsymbol{B})$ and $\mathrm{tr}(\boldsymbol{B}\boldsymbol{A})$ are evidently equal to $\sum_{i,j=1}^n A_{ij}B_{ij}$.

4.5. Let $\boldsymbol{A} = \begin{pmatrix}\boldsymbol{a}_1 & \cdots & \boldsymbol{a}_N\end{pmatrix}$ be the $3\times N$ matrix consisting of columns $\boldsymbol{a}_1$, ..., $\boldsymbol{a}_N$. From the definition of the matrix norm of Eq. (4.33), $\|\boldsymbol{A}\|^2$ equals the sum of squares of all the elements of $\boldsymbol{A}$. Hence, $\|\boldsymbol{A}\|^2 = \sum_{\alpha=1}^N \|\boldsymbol{a}_\alpha\|^2$. Therefore, if $\boldsymbol{A}'$ is the $3\times N$ matrix consisting of columns $\boldsymbol{a}'_1$, ..., $\boldsymbol{a}'_N$, we can write $\|\boldsymbol{A}'-\boldsymbol{R}\boldsymbol{A}\|^2$ as

$$\begin{aligned}
\|\boldsymbol{A}'-\boldsymbol{R}\boldsymbol{A}\|^2 &= \|\begin{pmatrix}\boldsymbol{a}'_1 & \cdots & \boldsymbol{a}'_N\end{pmatrix} - \boldsymbol{R}\begin{pmatrix}\boldsymbol{a}_1 & \cdots & \boldsymbol{a}_N\end{pmatrix}\|^2 \\
&= \|\begin{pmatrix}\boldsymbol{a}'_1 & \cdots & \boldsymbol{a}'_N\end{pmatrix} - \begin{pmatrix}\boldsymbol{R}\boldsymbol{a}_1 & \cdots & \boldsymbol{R}\boldsymbol{a}_N\end{pmatrix}\|^2 \\
&= \|\begin{pmatrix}\boldsymbol{a}'_1-\boldsymbol{R}\boldsymbol{a}_1 & \cdots & \boldsymbol{a}'_N-\boldsymbol{R}\boldsymbol{a}_N\end{pmatrix}\|^2 \\
&= \sum_{\alpha=1}^N \|\boldsymbol{a}'_\alpha-\boldsymbol{R}\boldsymbol{a}_\alpha\|^2.
\end{aligned}$$

4.6. For a matrix $\boldsymbol{A} = \begin{pmatrix}A_{ij}\end{pmatrix}$, we can easily confirm from the definition of matrix multiplication operation that $\mathrm{tr}(\boldsymbol{A}\boldsymbol{A}^\top)$ and $\mathrm{tr}(\boldsymbol{A}^\top\boldsymbol{A})$ are both equal to $\sum_{i=1}^m\sum_{j=1}^n A_{ij}^2$.

4.7. (1) If we let

$$\boldsymbol{T}^{(s)} = \frac{1}{2}(\boldsymbol{T}+\boldsymbol{T}^\top), \qquad \boldsymbol{T}^{(a)} = \frac{1}{2}(\boldsymbol{T}-\boldsymbol{T}^\top),$$

$\boldsymbol{T}^{(s)}$ is a symmetric matrix and $\boldsymbol{T}^{(a)}$ is an antisymmetric matrix. Evidently, $\boldsymbol{T}^{(s)} + \boldsymbol{T}^{(a)} = \boldsymbol{T}$, so we obtain the decomposition of Eq. (4.49). Conversely, if $\boldsymbol{T}$ is decomposed to the sum of a symmetric matrix $\boldsymbol{T}^{(s)}$ and an antisymmetric matrix $\boldsymbol{T}^{(a)}$, it is evident that $(\boldsymbol{T}+\boldsymbol{T}^\top)/2 = \boldsymbol{T}^{(s)}$ and $(\boldsymbol{T}-\boldsymbol{T}^\top)/2 = \boldsymbol{T}^{(a)}$.

(2) If $\boldsymbol{S}$ is a symmetric matrix and $\boldsymbol{A}$ an antisymmetric matrix, then

$$(\boldsymbol{SA})^\top = \boldsymbol{A}^\top\boldsymbol{S}^\top = -\boldsymbol{AS}.$$

Since the trace of a square matrix is unchanged by transpose, we see from from Eq. (4.47) that

$$\mathrm{tr}(\boldsymbol{SA}) = \mathrm{tr}(-\boldsymbol{AS}) = -\mathrm{tr}(\boldsymbol{SA}).$$

Hence, $\mathrm{tr}(\boldsymbol{SA}) = 0$.

(3) If we decompose $\boldsymbol{T}$ into the sum of a symmetric matrix $\boldsymbol{T}^{(s)}$ and an antisymmetric matrix $\boldsymbol{T}^{(a)}$ as in Eq. (4.49), we see from the above (2) that

$$\mathrm{tr}(\boldsymbol{ST}) = \mathrm{tr}(\boldsymbol{ST}^{(s)} + \boldsymbol{ST}^{(a)}) = \mathrm{tr}(\boldsymbol{ST}^{(s)}) = 0.$$

Since $\boldsymbol{S}$ is an arbitrary symmetric matrix, this also holds for $\boldsymbol{S} = \boldsymbol{T}^{(s)}$. Hence, from Eq. (4.34), we see that

$$\mathrm{tr}(\boldsymbol{T}^{(s)}\boldsymbol{T}^{(s)}) = \mathrm{tr}(\boldsymbol{T}^{(s)}\boldsymbol{T}^{(s)\top}) = \|\boldsymbol{T}^{(s)}\|^2 = 0,$$

which implies $\boldsymbol{T}^{(s)} = \boldsymbol{O}$, i.e., $\boldsymbol{T} = \boldsymbol{T}^{(a)}$. Hence, $\boldsymbol{T}$ is an antisymmetric matrix.

(4) If we decompose $\boldsymbol{T}$ into he sum of a symmetric matrix $\boldsymbol{T}^{(s)}$ and an antisymmetric matrix $\boldsymbol{T}^{(a)}$ as in Eq. (4.49), we see from the above (2) that

$$\mathrm{tr}(\boldsymbol{AT}) = \mathrm{tr}(\boldsymbol{AT}^{(s)} + \boldsymbol{AT}^{(a)}) = \mathrm{tr}(\boldsymbol{AT}^{(a)}) = 0.$$

Since $\boldsymbol{A}$ is an arbitrary symmetric matrix, this also holds for $\boldsymbol{A} = \boldsymbol{T}^{(a)}$. Hence, from Eq. (4.34), we see that

$$\mathrm{tr}(\boldsymbol{T}^{(a)}\boldsymbol{T}^{(a)}) = -\mathrm{tr}(\boldsymbol{T}^{(a)}\boldsymbol{T}^{(a)\top}) = -\|\boldsymbol{T}^{(a)}\|^2 = 0,$$

which implies $\boldsymbol{T}^{(a)} = \boldsymbol{O}$, i.e., $\boldsymbol{T} = \boldsymbol{T}^{(s)}$. Hence, $\boldsymbol{T}$ is a symmetric matrix.

4.8. Let $\boldsymbol{Au} = \lambda\boldsymbol{u}$. If all the eigenvalues are distinct, all the eigenvectors for eigenvalue λ are nonzero scalar multiples of $\boldsymbol{u}$. Since $\boldsymbol{A}$ and $\boldsymbol{B}$ commute, we have

$$\boldsymbol{ABu} = \boldsymbol{BAu} = \lambda\boldsymbol{Bu}.$$

This implies that $\boldsymbol{Bu}$ is an eigenvector of $\boldsymbol{A}$ for eigenvalue λ. Hence, $\boldsymbol{Bu} = \mu\boldsymbol{u}$ holds for some nonzero constant μ.

Chapter 5

5.1. Introduce Lagrange multiplier vector $\boldsymbol{\lambda}$ for the constraint of Eq. (5.7) and consider

$$J - \sum_{\alpha=1}^{N}\langle\boldsymbol{\lambda}, \bar{\boldsymbol{a}}'_\alpha - \boldsymbol{R}\bar{\boldsymbol{a}}_\alpha\rangle = J - \sum_{\alpha=1}^{N}\langle\boldsymbol{\lambda}, \bar{\boldsymbol{a}}'_\alpha\rangle + \sum_{\alpha=1}^{N}\langle\boldsymbol{R}^\top\boldsymbol{\lambda}, \bar{\boldsymbol{a}}_\alpha\rangle.$$

Differentiating this with respect to $\bar{\boldsymbol{a}}_\alpha$ and $\bar{\boldsymbol{a}}'_\alpha$ and letting the result be $\boldsymbol{0}$, we obtain

$$-V_0[\boldsymbol{a}_\alpha]^{-1}(\boldsymbol{a}_\alpha - \bar{\boldsymbol{a}}_\alpha) + \boldsymbol{R}^\top \boldsymbol{\lambda} = \boldsymbol{0}, \qquad -V_0[\boldsymbol{a}'_\alpha]^{-1}(\boldsymbol{a}'_\alpha - \bar{\boldsymbol{a}}'_\alpha) - \boldsymbol{\lambda} = \boldsymbol{0},$$

from which $\bar{\boldsymbol{a}}$ and $\bar{\boldsymbol{a}}'$ are determined in the form

$$\bar{\boldsymbol{a}}_\alpha = \boldsymbol{a}_\alpha - V_0[\boldsymbol{a}_\alpha]\boldsymbol{R}^\top \boldsymbol{\lambda}, \qquad \bar{\boldsymbol{a}}'_\alpha = \boldsymbol{a}'_\alpha + V_0[\boldsymbol{a}'_\alpha]\boldsymbol{\lambda}.$$

Substituting these into Eq. (5.7), we obtain

$$\boldsymbol{a}'_\alpha + V_0[\boldsymbol{a}'_\alpha]\boldsymbol{\lambda} = \boldsymbol{R}(\boldsymbol{a}_\alpha - V_0[\boldsymbol{a}_\alpha]\boldsymbol{R}^\top \boldsymbol{\lambda}).$$

Using the matrix $\boldsymbol{V}_\alpha$ of Eq. (5.12), we can write this as

$$-\boldsymbol{V}_\alpha \boldsymbol{\lambda} = \boldsymbol{a}'_\alpha - \boldsymbol{R}\boldsymbol{a}_\alpha.$$

Using the matrix $\boldsymbol{W}_\alpha$ of Eq. (5.34), we can express $\boldsymbol{\lambda}$ in the form

$$\boldsymbol{\lambda} = -\boldsymbol{W}_\alpha(\boldsymbol{a}'_\alpha - \boldsymbol{R}\boldsymbol{a}_\alpha).$$

Substituting this into the expressions of $\bar{\boldsymbol{a}}$ and $\bar{\boldsymbol{a}}'$, we obtain

$$\begin{aligned} \bar{\boldsymbol{a}}_\alpha &= \boldsymbol{a}_\alpha - V_0[\boldsymbol{a}_\alpha]\boldsymbol{R}^\top \boldsymbol{W}_\alpha(\boldsymbol{a}'_\alpha - \boldsymbol{R}\boldsymbol{a}_\alpha), \\ \bar{\boldsymbol{a}}'_\alpha &= \boldsymbol{a}'_\alpha + V_0[\boldsymbol{a}'_\alpha]\boldsymbol{W}_\alpha(\boldsymbol{a}'_\alpha - \boldsymbol{R}\boldsymbol{a}_\alpha). \end{aligned}$$

Substituting these into Eq. (5.10), we can express J in the form

$$\begin{aligned} J &= \frac{1}{2}\sum_{\alpha=1}^{N}\langle V_0[\boldsymbol{a}_\alpha]\boldsymbol{R}^\top \boldsymbol{W}_\alpha(\boldsymbol{a}'_\alpha - \boldsymbol{R}\boldsymbol{a}_\alpha), V_0[\boldsymbol{a}_\alpha]^{-1}V_0[\boldsymbol{a}_\alpha]\boldsymbol{R}^\top \boldsymbol{W}_\alpha(\boldsymbol{a}'_\alpha - \boldsymbol{R}\boldsymbol{a}_\alpha)\rangle \\ &\quad + \frac{1}{2}\sum_{\alpha=1}^{N}\langle V_0[\boldsymbol{a}'_\alpha]\boldsymbol{W}_\alpha(\boldsymbol{a}'_\alpha - \boldsymbol{R}\boldsymbol{a}_\alpha), V_0[\boldsymbol{a}'_\alpha]^{-1}V_0[\boldsymbol{a}'_\alpha]\boldsymbol{W}_\alpha(\boldsymbol{a}'_\alpha - \boldsymbol{R}\boldsymbol{a}_\alpha) \\ &= \frac{1}{2}\sum_{\alpha=1}^{N}\langle \boldsymbol{a}'_\alpha - \boldsymbol{R}\boldsymbol{a}_\alpha, \boldsymbol{W}_\alpha \boldsymbol{R}V_0[\boldsymbol{a}_\alpha]\boldsymbol{R}^\top \boldsymbol{W}_\alpha(\boldsymbol{a}'_\alpha - \boldsymbol{R}\boldsymbol{a}_\alpha)\rangle \\ &\quad + \frac{1}{2}\sum_{\alpha=1}^{N}\langle \boldsymbol{a}'_\alpha - \boldsymbol{R}\boldsymbol{a}_\alpha, \boldsymbol{W}_\alpha V_0[\boldsymbol{a}'_\alpha]\boldsymbol{W}_\alpha(\boldsymbol{a}'_\alpha - \boldsymbol{R}\boldsymbol{a}_\alpha)\rangle \\ &= \frac{1}{2}\sum_{\alpha=1}^{N}\langle \boldsymbol{a}'_\alpha - \boldsymbol{R}\boldsymbol{a}_\alpha, \boldsymbol{W}_\alpha(\boldsymbol{R}V_0[\boldsymbol{a}_\alpha]\boldsymbol{R}^\top + V_0[\boldsymbol{a}'_\alpha])\boldsymbol{W}_\alpha(\boldsymbol{a}'_\alpha - \boldsymbol{R}\boldsymbol{a}_\alpha)\rangle \\ &= \frac{1}{2}\sum_{\alpha=1}^{N}\langle \boldsymbol{a}'_\alpha - \boldsymbol{R}\boldsymbol{a}_\alpha, \boldsymbol{W}_\alpha \boldsymbol{V}_\alpha \boldsymbol{W}_\alpha(\boldsymbol{a}'_\alpha - \boldsymbol{R}\boldsymbol{a}_\alpha)\rangle \\ &= \frac{1}{2}\sum_{\alpha=1}^{N}\langle \boldsymbol{a}'_\alpha - \boldsymbol{R}\boldsymbol{a}_\alpha, \boldsymbol{W}_\alpha(\boldsymbol{a}'_\alpha - \boldsymbol{R}\boldsymbol{a}_\alpha)\rangle, \end{aligned}$$

where we have noted that $V_0[\boldsymbol{a}_\alpha]$, $V_0[\boldsymbol{a}'_\alpha]$, and $\boldsymbol{W}$ are symmetric matrices and applied Eq. (2.19).

5.2. (1) Let $\boldsymbol{a} = \overrightarrow{OP}$ and $\boldsymbol{a}' = \overrightarrow{OP'}$, and let M be the midpoint of P and P'. Let H be the foot of the perpendicular from M to the axis of rotation, and θ the angle made by vectors $\boldsymbol{l}$ and $\overrightarrow{OM}$. Since $HM = OM\sin\theta$, we see that

$$MP' = HM\tan\frac{\Omega}{2} = OM\sin\theta\tan\frac{\Omega}{2}.$$

Let $\boldsymbol{m}$ be the unit vector in the direction of $\overrightarrow{PP'}$. Since vector $\boldsymbol{l}\times\overrightarrow{OM}$ is orthogonal to vectors $\boldsymbol{l}$ and $\overrightarrow{OM}$, it is in the direction of $\boldsymbol{m}$. Since l is a unit vector, we have $\|\boldsymbol{l}\times\overrightarrow{OM}\| = OM\sin\theta$ and hence

$$\boldsymbol{m} = \frac{\boldsymbol{l}\times\overrightarrow{OM}}{OM\sin\theta}.$$

It follows that

$$\overrightarrow{PP'} = 2MP'\boldsymbol{m} = 2OM\sin\theta\tan\frac{\Omega}{2}\frac{\boldsymbol{l}\times\overrightarrow{OM}}{OM\sin\theta} = 2\tan\frac{\Omega}{2}\boldsymbol{l}\times\overrightarrow{OM}.$$

Since $\overrightarrow{PP'} = \boldsymbol{a}' - \boldsymbol{a}$ and $\overrightarrow{OM} = (\boldsymbol{a}+\boldsymbol{a}')/2$, we obtain Eq. (5.67).

(2) From Eqs. (3.32) and (3.33), we see that $q_0 = \cos\Omega/2$ and $\boldsymbol{q}_l = \boldsymbol{l}\sin(\Omega/2)$. Hence, Eq. (5.67) is rewritten as

$$\boldsymbol{a}' - \boldsymbol{a} = 2\frac{\sin\Omega/2}{\cos\Omega/2}\boldsymbol{l}\times\frac{\boldsymbol{a}'+\boldsymbol{a}}{2}.$$

Multiplying both sides by $q_0 = \cos\Omega/2$, we obtain

$$q_0(\boldsymbol{a}'-\boldsymbol{a}) = \boldsymbol{q}_l\times(\boldsymbol{a}'+\boldsymbol{a}),$$

and hence Eq. (5.20).

5.3. Differentiating $\boldsymbol{V}_\alpha\boldsymbol{W}_\alpha = \boldsymbol{I}$ with respect to q_i, $i = 0, 1, 2, 3$, we obtain

$$\frac{\partial\boldsymbol{V}_\alpha}{\partial q_i}\boldsymbol{W}_\alpha + \boldsymbol{V}_\alpha\frac{\partial\boldsymbol{W}_\alpha}{\partial q_i} = \boldsymbol{O}.$$

Multiplying both sides by $\boldsymbol{W}_\alpha$ from left and noting that $\boldsymbol{W}_\alpha\boldsymbol{V}_\alpha = \boldsymbol{I}$, we obtain

$$\frac{\partial\boldsymbol{W}_\alpha}{\partial q_i} = -\boldsymbol{W}_\alpha\frac{\partial\boldsymbol{V}_\alpha}{\partial q_i}\boldsymbol{W}_\alpha.$$

In elements,

$$\frac{\partial W_\alpha^{(kl)}}{\partial q_i} = -\sum_{m,n=1}^{3} W_\alpha^{(km)}\frac{\partial V_\alpha^{(mn)}}{\partial q_i}W_\alpha^{(nl)},$$

or

$$\nabla_{\boldsymbol{q}}W_\alpha^{(kl)} = -\sum_{m,n=1}^{3} W_\alpha^{(km)}\nabla_{\boldsymbol{q}}V_\alpha^{(mn)}W_\alpha^{(nl)}.$$

Differentiating the expression $V_\alpha^{(mn)} = \langle\boldsymbol{q}, V_0^{(mn)}[\boldsymbol{\xi}_\alpha]\boldsymbol{q}\rangle$, which is obtained from Eq. (5.32), with respect to $\boldsymbol{q}$, we obtain $\nabla_{\boldsymbol{q}}V_\alpha^{(mn)} = 2V_0^{(mn)}[\boldsymbol{\xi}_\alpha]\boldsymbol{q}$. Substituting this into the above expression, we obtain Eq. (5.36).

5.4. Computing the inner product of Eq. (5.42) with $\boldsymbol{q}$ on both sides, we obtain $\langle \boldsymbol{q}, \boldsymbol{X}\boldsymbol{q}\rangle = \lambda\|\boldsymbol{q}\|^2 = \lambda$. On the other hand, we see from Eq. (5.43) that $W_\alpha^{(kl)} = \Big(\langle \boldsymbol{q}, V_0^{(kl)}[\boldsymbol{\xi}_\alpha]\boldsymbol{q}\rangle\Big)^{-1}$ holds when the iterations have converged. From Eqs. (5.39) and (5.41), we see that

$$\langle \boldsymbol{q}, \boldsymbol{X}\boldsymbol{q}\rangle = \sum_{\alpha=1}^{N}\sum_{k,l=1}^{3} W_\alpha^{(kl)}\langle \boldsymbol{\xi}_\alpha^{(k)}, \boldsymbol{q}\rangle\langle \boldsymbol{\xi}_\alpha^{(l)}, \boldsymbol{q}\rangle - \sum_{\alpha=1}^{N}\sum_{k,l=1}^{3} v_\alpha^{(k)} v_\alpha^{(l)}\langle \boldsymbol{q}, V_0^{(kl)}[\boldsymbol{\xi}_\alpha]\boldsymbol{q}\rangle.$$

If we let $V_\alpha^{(kl)} = \langle \boldsymbol{q}, V_0^{(kl)}[\boldsymbol{\xi}_\alpha]\boldsymbol{q}\rangle$ (= the (k,l) element of the matrix $\boldsymbol{V}_\alpha$ of Eq. (5.32)), we obtain from Eq. (5.38)

$$\begin{aligned}\sum_{k,l=1}^{3} v_\alpha^{(k)} v_\alpha^{(l)} V_\alpha^{(kl)} &= \sum_{k,l=1}^{3}\Big(\sum_{m=1}^{3} W_\alpha^{(km)}\langle \boldsymbol{\xi}_\alpha^{(m)}, \boldsymbol{q}\rangle\Big)\Big(\sum_{n=1}^{3} W_\alpha^{(kn)}\langle \boldsymbol{\xi}_\alpha^{(n)}, \boldsymbol{q}\rangle\Big)V_\alpha^{(kl)}\\ &= \sum_{m,n=1}^{3}\Big(\sum_{k,l=1}^{3} W_\alpha^{(km)} V_\alpha^{(kl)} W_\alpha^{(ln)}\Big)\langle \boldsymbol{\xi}_\alpha^{(m)}, \boldsymbol{q}\rangle\langle \boldsymbol{\xi}_\alpha^{(n)}, \boldsymbol{q}\rangle\\ &= \sum_{m,n=1}^{3} W_\alpha^{(mn)}\langle \boldsymbol{\xi}_\alpha^{(m)}, \boldsymbol{q}\rangle\langle \boldsymbol{\xi}_\alpha^{(n)}, \boldsymbol{q}\rangle,\end{aligned}$$

where we have noted that $\boldsymbol{V}_\alpha = \Big(V_\alpha^{(kl)}\Big)$ and $\boldsymbol{W}_\alpha = \Big(W_\alpha^{(kl)}\Big)$ are the inverse of each other (see Eq. (5.34)). Thus, $\langle \boldsymbol{q}, \boldsymbol{X}\boldsymbol{q}\rangle = 0$, and hence $\lambda = 0$.

Chapter 6

6.1. If we let $\Omega = \omega t$ in Eq. (3.20) and regard $\boldsymbol{R}$ as a function of t, we obtain

$$\boldsymbol{R}(t) = \begin{pmatrix} \cos\omega t + l_1^2(1-\cos\omega t) & l_1 l_2(1-\cos\omega t) - l_3\sin\omega t & l_1 l_3(1-\cos\omega t) + l_2\sin\omega t \\ l_2 l_1(1-\cos\omega t) + l_3\sin\omega t & \cos\omega t + l_2^2(1-\cos\omega t) & l_2 l_3(1-\cos\omega t) - l_1\sin\omega t \\ l_3 l_1(1-\cos\omega t) - l_2\sin\omega t & l_3 l_2(1-\cos\omega t) + l_1\sin\omega t & \cos\omega t + l_3^2(1-\cos\omega t) \end{pmatrix}.$$

Differentiation with respect to t yields

$$\dot{\boldsymbol{R}}(t) = \begin{pmatrix} -\omega\sin\omega t + l_1^2\omega\sin\omega t & l_1 l_2\omega\sin\omega t - l_3\omega\cos\omega t & l_1 l_3\omega\sin\omega t + l_2\omega\cos\omega t \\ l_2 l_1\omega\sin\omega t + l_3\omega\cos\omega t & -\omega\sin\omega t + l_2^2\omega\sin\omega t & l_2 l_3\omega\sin\omega t - l_1\omega\cos\omega t \\ l_3 l_1\omega\sin\omega t - l_2\omega\cos\omega t & l_3 l_2\omega\sin\omega t + l_1\omega\cos\omega t & -\omega\sin\omega t + l_3^2\omega\sin\omega t \end{pmatrix}.$$

Letting $t = 0$, obtain

$$\dot{\boldsymbol{R}}(0) = \begin{pmatrix} 0 & -\omega l_3 & \omega l_2 \\ \omega l_3 & 0 & -\omega l_1 \\ -\omega l_2 & \omega l_1 & 0 \end{pmatrix}.$$

Hence, the time differentiation of $\boldsymbol{a}(t) = \boldsymbol{R}(t)\boldsymbol{a}$ has the following form at $t = 0$:

$$\dot{\boldsymbol{a}}|_{t=0} = \frac{d\boldsymbol{R}\boldsymbol{a}}{dt}\bigg|_{t=0} = \dot{\boldsymbol{R}}(0)\boldsymbol{a} = \omega\boldsymbol{l}\times\boldsymbol{a}.$$

6.2. From the definition of the commutator, we obtain

$$\begin{aligned}[\boldsymbol{A},[\boldsymbol{B},\boldsymbol{C}]] &= \boldsymbol{A}(\boldsymbol{BC}-\boldsymbol{CB})-(\boldsymbol{BC}-\boldsymbol{CB})\boldsymbol{A}\\ &= \boldsymbol{ABC}-\boldsymbol{ACB}-\boldsymbol{BCA}+\boldsymbol{CBA}.\end{aligned}$$

Similarly, we obtain

$$\begin{aligned}[\boldsymbol{B},[\boldsymbol{C},\boldsymbol{A}]] &= \boldsymbol{BCA}-\boldsymbol{BAC}-\boldsymbol{CAB}+\boldsymbol{ACB},\\ [\boldsymbol{C},[\boldsymbol{A},\boldsymbol{B}]] &= \boldsymbol{CAB}-\boldsymbol{CBA}-\boldsymbol{ABC}+\boldsymbol{BAC}.\end{aligned}$$

The sum of these vanishes.

6.3. The first equation is obtained as follows:

$$\begin{aligned}[\boldsymbol{A}_2,\boldsymbol{A}_3] &= \begin{pmatrix}0&0&1\\0&0&0\\-1&0&0\end{pmatrix}\begin{pmatrix}0&-1&0\\1&0&0\\0&0&0\end{pmatrix}-\begin{pmatrix}0&-1&0\\1&0&0\\0&0&0\end{pmatrix}\begin{pmatrix}0&0&1\\0&0&0\\-1&0&0\end{pmatrix}\\ &= \begin{pmatrix}0&0&0\\0&0&0\\0&1&0\end{pmatrix}-\begin{pmatrix}0&0&0\\0&0&1\\0&0&0\end{pmatrix}=\begin{pmatrix}0&0&0\\0&0&-1\\0&1&0\end{pmatrix}=\boldsymbol{A}_1.\end{aligned}$$

The second and third equations are similarly obtained.

6.4. The first equation is obtained as follows:

$$\begin{aligned}\boldsymbol{a}\times(\boldsymbol{b}\times\boldsymbol{c}) &= \begin{pmatrix}a_1\\a_2\\a_3\end{pmatrix}\times\begin{pmatrix}b_2c_3-b_3c_2\\b_3c_1-b_1c_3\\b_1c_2-b_2c_1\end{pmatrix}\\ &= \begin{pmatrix}a_2(b_1c_2-b_2c_1)-a_3(b_3c_1-b_1c_3)\\a_3(b_2c_3-b_3c_2)-a_1(b_1c_2-b_2c_1)\\a_1(b_3c_1-b_1c_3)-a_2(b_2c_3-b_3c_2)\end{pmatrix}\\ &= \begin{pmatrix}(a_2c_2+a_3c_3)b_1-(a_2b_2+a_3b_3)c_1\\(a_3c_3+a_1c_1)b_2-(a_3b_3+a_1b_1)c_2\\(a_1c_1+a_2c_2)b_3-(a_1b_1+a_2b_2)c_3\end{pmatrix}\\ &= \begin{pmatrix}(a_1c_1+a_2c_2+a_3c_3)b_1-(a_1b_1+a_2b_2+a_3b_3)c_1\\(a_1c_1+a_2c_2+a_3c_3)b_2-(a_1b_1+a_2b_2+a_3b_3)c_2\\(a_1c_1+a_2c_2+a_3b_3)b_3-(a_1b_1+a_2b_2+c_1c_2)c_3\end{pmatrix}\\ &= (a_1c_1+a_2c_2+a_3c_3)\begin{pmatrix}b_1\\b_2\\b_3\end{pmatrix}-(a_1b_1+a_2b_2+a_3b_3)\begin{pmatrix}c_1\\c_2\\c_3\end{pmatrix}\\ &= \langle\boldsymbol{a},\boldsymbol{c}\rangle\boldsymbol{b}-\langle\boldsymbol{a},\boldsymbol{b}\rangle\boldsymbol{c}.\end{aligned}$$

Using this, we obtain the second equation as follows:

$$(\boldsymbol{a}\times\boldsymbol{b})\times\boldsymbol{c}=-\boldsymbol{c}\times(\boldsymbol{a}\times\boldsymbol{b})=-\langle\boldsymbol{c},\boldsymbol{b}\rangle\boldsymbol{a}+\langle\boldsymbol{c},\boldsymbol{a}\rangle\boldsymbol{b}=\langle\boldsymbol{a},\boldsymbol{c}\rangle\boldsymbol{b}-\langle\boldsymbol{b},\boldsymbol{c}\rangle\boldsymbol{a}.$$

6.5. The definition of the vector product implies that it is antisymmetric so that $\boldsymbol{a}\times\boldsymbol{b}=-\boldsymbol{b}\times\boldsymbol{a}$ holds. Also, $(\boldsymbol{a}+\boldsymbol{b})\times\boldsymbol{c}=\boldsymbol{a}\times\boldsymbol{c}+\boldsymbol{b}\times\boldsymbol{c}$ and $(c\boldsymbol{a})\times\boldsymbol{b}=c(\boldsymbol{a}\times\boldsymbol{b})$ are evident from the definition of the vector product. Meanwhile, Eq. (6.80) for the vector triple product implies

$$\begin{aligned}\boldsymbol{a} \times (\boldsymbol{b} \times \boldsymbol{c}) &= \langle \boldsymbol{a}, \boldsymbol{c} \rangle \boldsymbol{b} - \langle \boldsymbol{a}, \boldsymbol{b} \rangle \boldsymbol{c}, \\ \boldsymbol{b} \times (\boldsymbol{c} \times \boldsymbol{a}) &= \langle \boldsymbol{b}, \boldsymbol{a} \rangle \boldsymbol{c} - \langle \boldsymbol{b}, \boldsymbol{c} \rangle \boldsymbol{a}, \\ \boldsymbol{c} \times (\boldsymbol{b} \times \boldsymbol{b}) &= \langle \boldsymbol{c}, \boldsymbol{b} \rangle \boldsymbol{a} - \langle \boldsymbol{c}, \boldsymbol{a} \rangle \boldsymbol{b}.\end{aligned}$$

The sum of these is $\mathbf{0}$. Hence, the following identity holds:

$$\boldsymbol{a} \times (\boldsymbol{b} \times \boldsymbol{c}) + \boldsymbol{b} \times (\boldsymbol{c} \times \boldsymbol{a}) + \boldsymbol{c} \times (\boldsymbol{b} \times \boldsymbol{b}) = \mathbf{0}.$$

6.6. Expanding Eq. (6.80) using the definition of the vector product and the inner product, we see that all terms are equal to

$$a_1 b_2 c_3 + b_1 c_2 a_3 + c_1 a_2 b_3 - c_1 b_2 a_3 - b_1 a_2 c_3 - a_1 c_2 b_3 = |\boldsymbol{a}, \boldsymbol{b}, \boldsymbol{c}|,$$

i.e., the determinant of the matrix with columns $\boldsymbol{a}$, $\boldsymbol{b}$, and $\boldsymbol{c}$.

6.7. From Eq. (2.19), $\langle \boldsymbol{x}, \boldsymbol{A}^\top \boldsymbol{x} \rangle = \langle \boldsymbol{A}\boldsymbol{x}, \boldsymbol{x} \rangle = \langle \boldsymbol{x}, \boldsymbol{A}\boldsymbol{x} \rangle$ holds. If $\boldsymbol{A} = \boldsymbol{A}^{(s)} + \boldsymbol{A}^{(a)}$, we see that $\langle \boldsymbol{x}, \boldsymbol{A}\boldsymbol{x} \rangle = \langle \boldsymbol{x}, (\boldsymbol{A}^{(s)} + \boldsymbol{A}^{(a)})\boldsymbol{x} \rangle = \langle \boldsymbol{x}, \boldsymbol{A}^{(s)}\boldsymbol{x} \rangle + \langle \boldsymbol{x}, \boldsymbol{A}^{(a)}\boldsymbol{x} \rangle$. If we write $\boldsymbol{A}^{(a)} = \left(A_{ij}^{(a)}\right)$, then $A_{ii}^{(a)} = 0$ and $A_{ji}^{(a)} = -A_{ij}^{(a)}$, $i, j = 1, \ldots, n$. Hence, if we write $\boldsymbol{x} = \left(x_i\right)$, terms $A_{ij}^{(a)} x_i x_j$ and terms $A_{ji}^{(a)} x_j x_i$ in $\langle \boldsymbol{x}, \boldsymbol{A}^{(a)}\boldsymbol{x} \rangle = \sum_{i,j=1}^n A_{ij}^{(a)} x_i x_j$ cancel each other, so that $\langle \boldsymbol{x}, \boldsymbol{A}^{(a)}\boldsymbol{x} \rangle = 0$. Thus, $\langle \boldsymbol{x}, \boldsymbol{A}\boldsymbol{x} \rangle = \langle \boldsymbol{x}, \boldsymbol{A}^{(s)}\boldsymbol{x} \rangle$.

6.8. (1) The following holds:

$$\begin{aligned}\boldsymbol{\omega} \times \boldsymbol{T} &= \boldsymbol{A}(\boldsymbol{\omega}) \begin{pmatrix} \boldsymbol{t}_1 & \boldsymbol{t}_2 & \boldsymbol{t}_3 \end{pmatrix} = \begin{pmatrix} \boldsymbol{A}(\boldsymbol{\omega})\boldsymbol{t}_1 & \boldsymbol{A}(\boldsymbol{\omega})\boldsymbol{t}_2 & \boldsymbol{A}(\boldsymbol{\omega})\boldsymbol{t}_3 \end{pmatrix} \\ &= \begin{pmatrix} \boldsymbol{\omega} \times \boldsymbol{t}_1 & \boldsymbol{\omega} \times \boldsymbol{t}_2 & \boldsymbol{\omega} \times \boldsymbol{t}_3 \end{pmatrix}.\end{aligned}$$

(2) The following holds:

$$\begin{aligned}\boldsymbol{T} \times \boldsymbol{\omega} &= \begin{pmatrix} \boldsymbol{t}_1 & \boldsymbol{t}_2 & \boldsymbol{t}_3 \end{pmatrix}^\top \boldsymbol{A}(\boldsymbol{\omega})^\top = \Big(\boldsymbol{A}(\boldsymbol{\omega}) \begin{pmatrix} \boldsymbol{t}_1 & \boldsymbol{t}_2 & \boldsymbol{t}_3 \end{pmatrix}\Big)^\top \\ &= \begin{pmatrix} \boldsymbol{A}(\boldsymbol{\omega})\boldsymbol{t}_1 & \boldsymbol{A}(\boldsymbol{\omega})\boldsymbol{t}_2 & \boldsymbol{A}(\boldsymbol{\omega})\boldsymbol{t}_3 \end{pmatrix}^\top \\ &= \begin{pmatrix} \boldsymbol{\omega} \times \boldsymbol{t}_1 & \boldsymbol{\omega} \times \boldsymbol{t}_2 & \boldsymbol{\omega} \times \boldsymbol{t}_3 \end{pmatrix}^\top = \begin{pmatrix} (\boldsymbol{\omega} \times \boldsymbol{t}_1)^\top \\ (\boldsymbol{\omega} \times \boldsymbol{t}_2)^\top \\ (\boldsymbol{\omega} \times \boldsymbol{t}_3)^\top \end{pmatrix}.\end{aligned}$$

6.9. Let $\boldsymbol{x}_\alpha$ and $\boldsymbol{x}'_\alpha$ be the vectors defined in Eq. (6.51), and let $\bar{\boldsymbol{x}}_\alpha$ and $\bar{\boldsymbol{x}}'_\alpha$ be the vectors similarly defined for their true values $(\bar{x}_\alpha, \bar{y}_\alpha)$ and $(\bar{x}'_\alpha, \bar{y}'_\alpha)$. If we let $\Delta\boldsymbol{x}_\alpha = \boldsymbol{x}_\alpha - \bar{\boldsymbol{x}}_\alpha$ and $\Delta\boldsymbol{x}' = \boldsymbol{x}'_\alpha - \bar{\boldsymbol{x}}'_\alpha$, Eq. (6.85) is written as

$$J = \frac{f_0^2}{2} \sum_{\alpha=1}^N \Big(\|\Delta\boldsymbol{x}_\alpha\|^2 + \|\Delta\boldsymbol{x}'_\alpha\|^2 \Big).$$

The epipolar equation of Eq. (6.49) now has the form

$$\langle \boldsymbol{x}_\alpha - \Delta\boldsymbol{x}_\alpha, \boldsymbol{F}(\boldsymbol{x}'_\alpha - \Delta\boldsymbol{x}'_\alpha) \rangle = 0.$$

Expanding this and ignoring second order terms in $\Delta\boldsymbol{x}_\alpha$ and $\Delta\boldsymbol{x}'_\alpha$, we obtain

$$\langle \boldsymbol{F}\boldsymbol{x}'_\alpha, \Delta\boldsymbol{x}_\alpha\rangle + \langle \boldsymbol{F}^\top\boldsymbol{x}_\alpha, \Delta\boldsymbol{x}'_\alpha\rangle = \langle \boldsymbol{x}_\alpha, \boldsymbol{F}\boldsymbol{x}'_\alpha\rangle. \qquad (*)$$

Since the third components of $\boldsymbol{x}_\alpha$, $\bar{\boldsymbol{x}}_\alpha$, $\boldsymbol{y}'_\alpha$, and $\bar{\boldsymbol{y}}'_\alpha$ are all 1, the third components of $\Delta\boldsymbol{x}_\alpha$, and $\Delta\boldsymbol{x}'_\alpha$ are 0. This fact is written as $\langle \boldsymbol{k}, \Delta\boldsymbol{x}_\alpha\rangle = 0$ and $\langle \boldsymbol{k}, \Delta\boldsymbol{x}'_\alpha\rangle = 0$, using $\boldsymbol{k} = (0,0,1)^\top$. Introducing Lagrange multipliers for minimizing J, consider

$$\frac{f_0^2}{2}\sum_{\alpha=1}^{N}(\|\Delta\boldsymbol{x}_\alpha\|^2 + \|\Delta\boldsymbol{x}'_\alpha\|^2) - \sum_{\alpha=1}^{N}\lambda_\alpha\Big(\langle \boldsymbol{F}\boldsymbol{x}'_\alpha, \Delta\boldsymbol{x}_\alpha\rangle + \langle \boldsymbol{F}^\top\boldsymbol{x}_\alpha, \Delta\boldsymbol{x}'_\alpha\rangle$$
$$-\langle \boldsymbol{x}_\alpha, \boldsymbol{F}\boldsymbol{x}'_\alpha\rangle\Big) - \sum_{\alpha=1}^{N}\mu_\alpha\langle \boldsymbol{k}, \Delta\boldsymbol{x}_\alpha\rangle - \sum_{\alpha=1}^{N}\mu'_\alpha\langle \boldsymbol{k}, \Delta\boldsymbol{x}'_\alpha\rangle.$$

Differentiating this with respect to $\Delta\boldsymbol{x}_\alpha$ and $\Delta\boldsymbol{x}'_\alpha$ and letting the result be 0, we obtain

$$f_0^2\Delta\boldsymbol{x}_\alpha - \lambda_\alpha\boldsymbol{F}\boldsymbol{x}'_\alpha - \mu_\alpha\boldsymbol{k} = \boldsymbol{0}, \qquad f_0^2\Delta\boldsymbol{x}'_\alpha - \lambda_\alpha\boldsymbol{F}^\top\boldsymbol{x}_\alpha - \mu'_\alpha\boldsymbol{k} = \boldsymbol{0}.$$

Multiplying this by $\boldsymbol{P}_{\boldsymbol{k}}$ from left on both sides and noting that $\boldsymbol{P}_{\boldsymbol{k}}\Delta\boldsymbol{x}_\alpha = \Delta\boldsymbol{x}_\alpha$, $\boldsymbol{P}_{\boldsymbol{k}}\Delta\boldsymbol{x}'_\alpha = \Delta\boldsymbol{x}'_\alpha$, and $\boldsymbol{P}_{\boldsymbol{k}}\boldsymbol{k} = \boldsymbol{0}$, we obtain

$$f_0^2\Delta\boldsymbol{x}_\alpha - \lambda_\alpha\boldsymbol{P}_{\boldsymbol{k}}\boldsymbol{F}\boldsymbol{x}'_\alpha = \boldsymbol{0}, \qquad f_0^2\Delta\boldsymbol{x}'_\alpha - \lambda_\alpha\boldsymbol{P}_{\boldsymbol{k}}\boldsymbol{F}^\top\boldsymbol{x}_\alpha = \boldsymbol{0}.$$

Hence,

$$\Delta\boldsymbol{x}_\alpha = \frac{\lambda_\alpha}{f_0^2}\boldsymbol{P}_{\boldsymbol{k}}\boldsymbol{F}\boldsymbol{x}'_\alpha, \qquad \Delta\boldsymbol{x}'_\alpha = \frac{\lambda_\alpha}{f_0^2}\boldsymbol{P}_{\boldsymbol{k}}\boldsymbol{F}^\top\boldsymbol{x}_\alpha.$$

Substituting these into Eq. $(*)$, we obtain

$$\langle \boldsymbol{F}\boldsymbol{x}'_\alpha, \frac{\lambda_\alpha}{f_0^2}\boldsymbol{P}_{\boldsymbol{k}}\boldsymbol{F}\boldsymbol{x}'_\alpha\rangle + \langle \boldsymbol{F}^\top\boldsymbol{x}_\alpha, \frac{\lambda_\alpha}{f_0^2}\boldsymbol{P}_{\boldsymbol{k}}\boldsymbol{F}^\top\boldsymbol{x}_\alpha\rangle = \langle \boldsymbol{x}_\alpha, \boldsymbol{F}\boldsymbol{x}'_\alpha\rangle,$$

from which λ_α is given by

$$\frac{\lambda_\alpha}{f_0^2} = \frac{\langle \boldsymbol{x}_\alpha, \boldsymbol{F}\boldsymbol{x}'_\alpha\rangle}{\langle \boldsymbol{F}\boldsymbol{x}'_\alpha, \boldsymbol{P}_{\boldsymbol{k}}\boldsymbol{F}\boldsymbol{x}'_\alpha\rangle + \langle \boldsymbol{F}^\top\boldsymbol{x}_\alpha, \boldsymbol{P}_{\boldsymbol{k}}\boldsymbol{F}^\top\boldsymbol{x}_\alpha\rangle} = \frac{\langle \boldsymbol{x}_\alpha, \boldsymbol{F}\boldsymbol{x}'_\alpha\rangle}{\|\boldsymbol{P}_{\boldsymbol{k}}\boldsymbol{F}\boldsymbol{x}'_\alpha\|^2 + \|\boldsymbol{P}_{\boldsymbol{k}}\boldsymbol{F}^\top\boldsymbol{x}_\alpha\|^2},$$

where we have noted that the matrix $\boldsymbol{P}_{\boldsymbol{k}}^2$ is symmetric and satisfies $\boldsymbol{P}_{\boldsymbol{k}}^2 = \boldsymbol{P}_{\boldsymbol{k}}$ and that $\langle \boldsymbol{a}, \boldsymbol{P}_{\boldsymbol{k}}\boldsymbol{a}\rangle = \langle \boldsymbol{a}, \boldsymbol{P}_{\boldsymbol{k}}^2\boldsymbol{a}\rangle = \langle \boldsymbol{P}_{\boldsymbol{k}}\boldsymbol{a}, \boldsymbol{P}_{\boldsymbol{k}}\boldsymbol{a}\rangle = \|\boldsymbol{P}_{\boldsymbol{k}}\boldsymbol{a}\|^2$ for an arbitrary vector $\boldsymbol{a}$. Hence, we can write $\Delta\boldsymbol{x}_\alpha$ and $\Delta\boldsymbol{x}'_\alpha$ as

$$\Delta\boldsymbol{x}_\alpha = \frac{\langle \boldsymbol{x}_\alpha, \boldsymbol{F}\boldsymbol{x}'_\alpha\rangle\boldsymbol{P}_{\boldsymbol{k}}\boldsymbol{F}\boldsymbol{x}'_\alpha}{\|\boldsymbol{P}_{\boldsymbol{k}}\boldsymbol{F}\boldsymbol{x}'_\alpha\|^2 + \|\boldsymbol{P}_{\boldsymbol{k}}\boldsymbol{F}^\top\boldsymbol{x}_\alpha\|^2}, \qquad \Delta\boldsymbol{x}'_\alpha = \frac{\langle \boldsymbol{x}_\alpha, \boldsymbol{F}\boldsymbol{x}'_\alpha\rangle\boldsymbol{P}_{\boldsymbol{k}}\boldsymbol{F}^\top\boldsymbol{x}_\alpha}{\|\boldsymbol{P}_{\boldsymbol{k}}\boldsymbol{F}\boldsymbol{x}'_\alpha\|^2 + \|\boldsymbol{P}_{\boldsymbol{k}}\boldsymbol{F}^\top\boldsymbol{x}_\alpha\|^2}.$$

Thus, J has the form

$$J = \frac{f_0^2}{2}\sum_{\alpha=1}^{N}\frac{\langle \boldsymbol{x}_\alpha, \boldsymbol{F}\boldsymbol{x}'_\alpha\rangle^2(\|\boldsymbol{P}_{\boldsymbol{k}}\boldsymbol{F}\boldsymbol{x}'_\alpha\|^2 + \|\boldsymbol{P}_{\boldsymbol{k}}\boldsymbol{F}^\top\boldsymbol{x}_\alpha\|^2)}{(\|\boldsymbol{P}_{\boldsymbol{k}}\boldsymbol{F}\boldsymbol{x}'_\alpha\|^2 + \|\boldsymbol{P}_{\boldsymbol{k}}\boldsymbol{F}^\top\boldsymbol{x}_\alpha\|^2)^2}$$
$$= \frac{f_0^2}{2}\sum_{\alpha=1}^{N}\frac{\langle \boldsymbol{x}_\alpha, \boldsymbol{F}\boldsymbol{x}'_\alpha\rangle^2}{\|\boldsymbol{P}_{\boldsymbol{k}}\boldsymbol{F}\boldsymbol{x}'_\alpha\|^2 + \|\boldsymbol{P}_{\boldsymbol{k}}\boldsymbol{F}^\top\boldsymbol{x}_\alpha\|^2}.$$

6.10. As in the above exercise, we write $\boldsymbol{x}_\alpha$ and $\boldsymbol{x}'_\alpha$ as in Eq. (6.51) and let $\bar{\boldsymbol{x}}_\alpha$ and $\bar{\boldsymbol{x}}'_\alpha$ be the corresponding vectors for their true values $(\bar{x}_\alpha, \bar{y}_\alpha)$ and $(\bar{x}'_\alpha, \bar{y}'_\alpha)$. Also, let $\Delta\boldsymbol{x}_\alpha = \boldsymbol{x}_\alpha - \bar{\boldsymbol{x}}_\alpha$ and $\Delta\boldsymbol{x}' = \boldsymbol{x}'_\alpha - \bar{\boldsymbol{x}}'_\alpha$. Let ε_α be the left side $\langle \boldsymbol{x}_\alpha, \boldsymbol{F}\boldsymbol{x}'_\alpha \rangle$ of the epipolar equation of Eq. (6.49) for the αth data. Since this is 0 for the true data values, we can write

$$\begin{aligned}\varepsilon_\alpha &= \langle \boldsymbol{x}_\alpha, \boldsymbol{F}\boldsymbol{x}'_\alpha \rangle = \langle \bar{\boldsymbol{x}}_\alpha + \Delta\boldsymbol{x}_\alpha, \boldsymbol{F}(\bar{\boldsymbol{x}}'_\alpha + \Delta\boldsymbol{x}'_\alpha) \rangle \\ &= \langle \bar{\boldsymbol{x}}_\alpha, \boldsymbol{F}\Delta\boldsymbol{x}'_\alpha \rangle + \langle \Delta\boldsymbol{x}_\alpha, \boldsymbol{F}\bar{\boldsymbol{x}}'_\alpha \rangle + \langle \Delta\boldsymbol{x}_\alpha, \boldsymbol{F}\Delta\boldsymbol{x}'_\alpha \rangle.\end{aligned}$$

Ignoring the last term, which is quadratic in the noise terms, we can evaluate the variance of ε_α in the form

$$\begin{aligned}V[\varepsilon_\alpha] &= E[\varepsilon_\alpha^2] = E[\langle \bar{\boldsymbol{x}}_\alpha, \boldsymbol{F}\Delta\boldsymbol{x}'_\alpha \rangle^2] + 2E[\langle \bar{\boldsymbol{x}}_\alpha, \boldsymbol{F}\Delta\boldsymbol{x}'_\alpha \rangle \langle \Delta\boldsymbol{x}_\alpha, \boldsymbol{F}\bar{\boldsymbol{x}}'_\alpha \rangle] + E[\langle \Delta\boldsymbol{x}_\alpha, \boldsymbol{F}\bar{\boldsymbol{x}}'_\alpha \rangle^2] \\ &= E[(\bar{\boldsymbol{x}}_\alpha^\top \boldsymbol{F}\Delta\boldsymbol{x}'_\alpha)(\boldsymbol{F}\Delta\boldsymbol{x}'_\alpha)^\top \bar{\boldsymbol{x}}_\alpha] + E[(\boldsymbol{F}\bar{\boldsymbol{x}}'_\alpha)^\top \Delta\boldsymbol{x}_\alpha \Delta\boldsymbol{x}_\alpha^\top \boldsymbol{F}\bar{\boldsymbol{x}}'_\alpha] \\ &= \bar{\boldsymbol{x}}_\alpha^\top \boldsymbol{F} E[\Delta\boldsymbol{x}'_\alpha \Delta\boldsymbol{x}'^\top_\alpha] \boldsymbol{F}^\top \bar{\boldsymbol{x}}_\alpha + \bar{\boldsymbol{x}}'^\top_\alpha \boldsymbol{F}^\top E[\Delta\boldsymbol{x}_\alpha \Delta\boldsymbol{x}_\alpha^\top] \boldsymbol{F}\bar{\boldsymbol{x}}'_\alpha,\end{aligned}$$

where we have noted that $\Delta\boldsymbol{x}_\alpha$ and $\Delta\boldsymbol{x}'_\alpha$ are assumed to be mutually independent. Using the matrix $\boldsymbol{P_k}$ defined in Eq. (6.51) and recalling our assumptions about noise, we can write $E[\Delta\boldsymbol{x}_\alpha \Delta\boldsymbol{x}_\alpha^\top]$ in the form

$$\begin{aligned}E[\Delta\boldsymbol{x}_\alpha \Delta\boldsymbol{x}_\alpha^\top] &= E[\begin{pmatrix} \Delta x_\alpha/f_0 \\ \Delta y_\alpha/f_0 \\ 0 \end{pmatrix} \begin{pmatrix} \Delta x_\alpha/f_0 \\ \Delta y_\alpha/f_0 \\ 0 \end{pmatrix}^\top] \\ &= \frac{1}{f_0^2} \begin{pmatrix} E[\Delta x_\alpha^2] & E[\Delta x_\alpha \Delta y_\alpha] & 0 \\ E[\Delta y_\alpha \Delta x_\alpha] & E[\Delta y_\alpha^2] & 0 \\ 0 & 0 & 0 \end{pmatrix} = \frac{\sigma^2}{f_0^2} \boldsymbol{P_k}.\end{aligned}$$

Similarly,

$$E[\Delta\boldsymbol{x}'_\alpha \Delta\boldsymbol{x}'^\top_\alpha] = \frac{\sigma^2}{f_0^2} \boldsymbol{P_k}.$$

Hence, the covariance matrix $V[\varepsilon_\alpha]$ has the form

$$\begin{aligned}V[\varepsilon_\alpha] &= \frac{\sigma^2}{f_0^2} (\bar{\boldsymbol{x}}_\alpha^\top \boldsymbol{F}\boldsymbol{P_k}\boldsymbol{F}^\top \bar{\boldsymbol{x}}_\alpha + \bar{\boldsymbol{x}}'^\top_\alpha \boldsymbol{F}^\top \boldsymbol{P_k}\boldsymbol{F}\bar{\boldsymbol{x}}'_\alpha) \\ &= \frac{\sigma^2}{f_0^2} (\|\boldsymbol{P_k}\boldsymbol{F}^\top \bar{\boldsymbol{x}}_\alpha\|^2 + \|\boldsymbol{P_k}\boldsymbol{F}\bar{\boldsymbol{x}}'_\alpha\|^2),\end{aligned}$$

where we have used the identity $\langle \boldsymbol{a}, \boldsymbol{P_k}\boldsymbol{a} \rangle = \|\boldsymbol{P_k}\boldsymbol{a}\|^2$ shown in the previous exercise. Replacing the true values $\bar{\boldsymbol{x}}_\alpha$ and $\bar{\boldsymbol{x}}'_\alpha$ in the above expression by their observations $\boldsymbol{x}_\alpha$ and $\boldsymbol{x}'_\alpha$, we can approximate the probability density of ε_α, $\alpha = 1, ..., N$, in the form

$$\prod_{\alpha=1}^N \frac{e^{-\varepsilon_\alpha^2/2V[\varepsilon_\alpha]}}{\sqrt{2\pi}\sigma} = \frac{e^{-\sum_{\alpha=1}^N \varepsilon_\alpha^2/2V[\varepsilon_\alpha]}}{(\sqrt{2\pi}\sigma)^N}.$$

Maximizing this is equivalent to minimizing the following J:

$$J = \sigma^2 \sum_{\alpha=1}^N \frac{\varepsilon_\alpha^2}{2V[\varepsilon_\alpha]} = \frac{f_0^2}{2} \sum_{\alpha=1}^N \frac{\langle \boldsymbol{x}_\alpha, \boldsymbol{F}\boldsymbol{x}'_\alpha \rangle^2}{\|\boldsymbol{P_k}\boldsymbol{F}\boldsymbol{x}'_\alpha\|^2 + \|\boldsymbol{P_k}\boldsymbol{F}^\top \boldsymbol{x}_\alpha\|^2}.$$

6.11. Let $\boldsymbol{A} = \boldsymbol{U}\boldsymbol{\Sigma}\boldsymbol{V}^\top$ be the singular value decomposition of matrix $\boldsymbol{A}$, where $\boldsymbol{U}$ and $\boldsymbol{V}$ are, respectively, $n \times r$ and $m \times r$ matrices, having left and right singular vectors (r is the rank of $\boldsymbol{A}$), and $\boldsymbol{\Sigma}$ is an $r \times r$ diagonal matrix having the r singular values as its diagonal elements. Using Eq. (4.34) for the matrix norm, we can write $\|\boldsymbol{A}\|^2$ in the form

$$\begin{aligned}\|\boldsymbol{A}\|^2 &= \mathrm{tr}((\boldsymbol{U}\boldsymbol{\Sigma}\boldsymbol{V}^\top)(\boldsymbol{U}\boldsymbol{\Sigma}\boldsymbol{V}^\top)^\top) = \mathrm{tr}(\boldsymbol{U}\boldsymbol{\Sigma}\boldsymbol{V}^\top\boldsymbol{V}\boldsymbol{\Sigma}\boldsymbol{U}^\top)\\ &= \mathrm{tr}(\boldsymbol{U}^\top\boldsymbol{U}\boldsymbol{\Sigma}\boldsymbol{V}^\top\boldsymbol{V}\boldsymbol{\Sigma}) = \mathrm{tr}(\boldsymbol{\Sigma}^2),\end{aligned}$$

where we have used the identity $\mathrm{tr}(\boldsymbol{AB}) = \mathrm{tr}(\boldsymbol{BA})$ for the matrix trace and noted that left and right singular vectors define orthonormal systems so that $\boldsymbol{U}^\top\boldsymbol{U}$ and $\boldsymbol{V}^\top\boldsymbol{V}$ are both the $r \times r$ identity matrix. The above expression means that $\|\boldsymbol{A}\|^2$ is the sum of square singular values.

Chapter 7

7.1. Equation (7.25) is written as $\delta\bar{\boldsymbol{a}}'_\alpha - \bar{\boldsymbol{R}}\delta\bar{\boldsymbol{a}}_\alpha = \delta\boldsymbol{\omega} \times \bar{\boldsymbol{R}}\bar{\boldsymbol{a}}_\alpha$. Substituting Eq. (7.33) into the left side, we obtain

$$\begin{aligned}\delta\bar{\boldsymbol{a}}'_\alpha - \bar{\boldsymbol{R}}\delta\bar{\boldsymbol{a}}_\alpha &= V_0[\boldsymbol{a}'_\alpha]\bar{\boldsymbol{W}}_\alpha(\delta\boldsymbol{\omega} \times \bar{\boldsymbol{R}}\bar{\boldsymbol{a}}_\alpha) + \bar{\boldsymbol{R}}V_0[\boldsymbol{a}_\alpha]\bar{\boldsymbol{R}}^\top\bar{\boldsymbol{W}}_\alpha(\delta\boldsymbol{\omega} \times \bar{\boldsymbol{R}}\bar{\boldsymbol{a}}_\alpha)\\ &= (V_0[\boldsymbol{a}'_\alpha] + \bar{\boldsymbol{R}}V_0[\boldsymbol{a}_\alpha]\bar{\boldsymbol{R}}^\top)\bar{\boldsymbol{W}}_\alpha(\delta\boldsymbol{\omega} \times \bar{\boldsymbol{R}}\bar{\boldsymbol{a}}_\alpha) = \bar{\boldsymbol{V}}_\alpha\bar{\boldsymbol{W}}_\alpha(\delta\boldsymbol{\omega} \times \bar{\boldsymbol{R}}\bar{\boldsymbol{a}}_\alpha)\\ &= \delta\boldsymbol{\omega} \times \bar{\boldsymbol{R}}\bar{\boldsymbol{a}}_\alpha,\end{aligned}$$

where we have used the definitions $\bar{\boldsymbol{V}}_\alpha \equiv (V_0[\boldsymbol{a}'_\alpha] + \bar{\boldsymbol{R}}V_0[\boldsymbol{a}_\alpha]\bar{\boldsymbol{R}}^\top)$ and $\bar{\boldsymbol{W}}_\alpha \equiv \bar{\boldsymbol{V}}_\alpha^{-1}$.

7.2. Evidently, $\boldsymbol{A}$ is a symmetric matrix. For an arbitrary vector $\boldsymbol{x}$, we have $\langle \boldsymbol{x}, \boldsymbol{A}\boldsymbol{x}\rangle = \boldsymbol{x}^\top\boldsymbol{a}\boldsymbol{a}^\top\boldsymbol{x} = \langle \boldsymbol{a}, \boldsymbol{x}\rangle \geq 0$. Hence, the matrix $\boldsymbol{A}$ is positive semidefinite.

7.3. (1) The positive semidefiniteness of $\boldsymbol{A}$ is defined by $\langle \boldsymbol{x}, \boldsymbol{A}\boldsymbol{x}\rangle \geq 0$ for an arbitrary vector $\boldsymbol{x}$. For the matrix $\boldsymbol{B} = \boldsymbol{U}^\top\boldsymbol{A}\boldsymbol{U}$, which is evidently symmetric, Eq. (2.19) implies that

$$\langle \boldsymbol{x}, \boldsymbol{B}\boldsymbol{x}\rangle = \langle \boldsymbol{x}, \boldsymbol{U}^\top\boldsymbol{A}\boldsymbol{U}\boldsymbol{x}\rangle = \langle \boldsymbol{U}\boldsymbol{x}, \boldsymbol{A}\boldsymbol{U}\boldsymbol{x}\rangle = \langle \boldsymbol{y}, \boldsymbol{A}\boldsymbol{y}\rangle \geq 0,$$

where we let $\boldsymbol{y} = \boldsymbol{U}\boldsymbol{x}$. Hence, $\boldsymbol{B}$ is also positive semidefinite.

(2) We are assuming that $\boldsymbol{M}$ is nonsingular, so the matrix $\begin{pmatrix} \boldsymbol{I} & \boldsymbol{O} \\ \boldsymbol{M}^{-1} & \boldsymbol{M}^{-1}\end{pmatrix}$ has determinant $|\boldsymbol{I}||\boldsymbol{M}^{-1}| = 1/|\boldsymbol{M}| \neq 0$ and hence it is nonsingular. Since Eq. (7.37) is a positive semidefinite matrix, the matrix

$$\begin{pmatrix} \boldsymbol{I} & \boldsymbol{M}^{-1} \\ \boldsymbol{O} & \boldsymbol{M}^{-1}\end{pmatrix}\begin{pmatrix} V[\tilde{\boldsymbol{R}}] & -\boldsymbol{I} \\ -\boldsymbol{I} & \boldsymbol{M}\end{pmatrix}\begin{pmatrix} \boldsymbol{I} & \boldsymbol{O} \\ \boldsymbol{M}^{-1} & \boldsymbol{M}^{-1}\end{pmatrix} = \begin{pmatrix} V[\tilde{\boldsymbol{R}}] - \boldsymbol{M}^{-1} & \boldsymbol{O} \\ \boldsymbol{O} & \boldsymbol{M}^{-1}\end{pmatrix}$$

is also positive semidefinite. Hence, the upper left block is also a positive semidefinite matrix, from which Eq. (7.39) follows.

7.4. Since the covariance matrix $\boldsymbol{\Sigma}$ is positive definite, it is diagonalized in the form

$$\boldsymbol{U}^\top\boldsymbol{\Sigma}\boldsymbol{U} = \begin{pmatrix} \sigma_1^2 & & \\ & \ddots & \\ & & \sigma_n^2\end{pmatrix},$$

where $\boldsymbol{U}$ is the orthogonal matrix consisting of the unit eigenvectors of $\boldsymbol{\Sigma}$ as columns. If we let $\boldsymbol{y} = \boldsymbol{U}^\top \boldsymbol{x}$, each component y_i of $\boldsymbol{y}$ is a linear combination of $\boldsymbol{x}$. Hence, $\boldsymbol{y}$ is also a Gaussian variable. Evidently, $\boldsymbol{y}$ has expectation $\boldsymbol{0}$. Its covariance matrix $V[\boldsymbol{y}]$ is given by

$$V[\boldsymbol{y}] = E[\boldsymbol{y}\boldsymbol{y}^\top] = E[\boldsymbol{U}^\top \boldsymbol{x}\boldsymbol{x}^\top \boldsymbol{U}] = \boldsymbol{U}^\top E[\boldsymbol{x}\boldsymbol{x}^\top]\boldsymbol{U} = \boldsymbol{U}^\top \boldsymbol{\Sigma} \boldsymbol{U} = \mathrm{diag}(\sigma_1^2, ..., \sigma_n^2).$$

Hence, each component y_i of $\boldsymbol{y}$ is an independent Gaussian variable of mean 0 and variance σ_i^2. We see that

$$\langle \boldsymbol{x}, \boldsymbol{\Sigma}^{-1}\boldsymbol{x}\rangle = \langle \boldsymbol{U}\boldsymbol{y}, \boldsymbol{\Sigma}^{-1}\boldsymbol{U}\boldsymbol{y}\rangle = \langle \boldsymbol{y}, \boldsymbol{U}^\top \boldsymbol{\Sigma}^{-1}\boldsymbol{U}\boldsymbol{y}\rangle = \langle \boldsymbol{y}, V[\boldsymbol{y}]^{-1}\boldsymbol{y}\rangle = \frac{y_1^2}{\sigma_1^2} + \cdots + \frac{y_n^2}{\sigma_n^2},$$

where we have noted that the inverse of $\boldsymbol{U}^\top \boldsymbol{\Sigma} \boldsymbol{U}$ is $\boldsymbol{U}^\top \boldsymbol{\Sigma}^{-1} \boldsymbol{U}$ (their product is $\boldsymbol{I}$ due to $\boldsymbol{U}\boldsymbol{U}^\top = \boldsymbol{I}$). Each y_i/σ_i is an independent Gaussian variable of mean 0 and variance 1. Since the above expression is their sum, it is, from the definition of the χ^2 distribution, a χ^2 variable with n degrees of freedom. Evidently, its expectation is $E[y_1^2]/\sigma_1^2 + \cdots + E[y_n^2]/\sigma_n^2 = \sigma_1^2/\sigma_1^2 + \cdots + \sigma_n^2/\sigma_n^2 = n$.

Chapter 8

8.1. (1) In terms of the $\Delta\boldsymbol{x}$ and $\Delta\boldsymbol{x}'$ of Eq. (8.23), the epipolar equation of Eq. (6.49) is written as

$$\langle \boldsymbol{x} - \Delta\boldsymbol{x}, \boldsymbol{F}(\boldsymbol{x}' - \Delta\boldsymbol{x}')\rangle = 0.$$

As shown in the answer to Exercise 6.9, the $\Delta\boldsymbol{x}$ and $\Delta\boldsymbol{x}'$ that minimize Eq. (8.24) subject to the constraint that $\bar{\boldsymbol{x}}$ and $\bar{\boldsymbol{x}}'$ satisfy the epipolar equation of Eq. (6.49) are given by Eq. (8.25) by ignoring high order terms in $\Delta\boldsymbol{x}$ and $\Delta\boldsymbol{x}'$.

(2) In terms of the $\Delta\boldsymbol{x}$ and $\Delta\boldsymbol{x}'$ of Eq. (8.26), the epipolar equation of Eq. (6.49) is written as

$$\langle \hat{\boldsymbol{x}} - \Delta\hat{\boldsymbol{x}}, \boldsymbol{F}(\hat{\boldsymbol{x}}' - \Delta\hat{\boldsymbol{x}}')\rangle = 0.$$

Expanding this and ignoring second order terms in $\Delta\hat{\boldsymbol{x}}$ and $\Delta\hat{\boldsymbol{x}}'$, we obtain

$$\langle \boldsymbol{F}\hat{\boldsymbol{x}}', \Delta\hat{\boldsymbol{x}}\rangle + \langle \boldsymbol{F}^\top\hat{\boldsymbol{x}}, \Delta\hat{\boldsymbol{x}}'\rangle = \langle \hat{\boldsymbol{x}}, \boldsymbol{F}\hat{\boldsymbol{x}}'\rangle. \qquad (**)$$

Since the third components of $\Delta\hat{\boldsymbol{x}}$ and $\Delta\hat{\boldsymbol{x}}'$ are 0, we obtain the constraints $\langle \boldsymbol{k}, \Delta\boldsymbol{x}\rangle = 0$ and $\langle \boldsymbol{k}, \Delta\boldsymbol{x}'\rangle = 0$, where $\boldsymbol{k} = (0,0,1)^\top$. Introduce Lagrange multipliers and consider

$$\frac{f_0^2}{2}\Big(\|\tilde{\boldsymbol{x}} + \Delta\hat{\boldsymbol{x}}\|^2 + \|\tilde{\boldsymbol{x}}' + \Delta\hat{\boldsymbol{x}}'\|^2\Big) - \lambda\Big(\langle \boldsymbol{F}\hat{\boldsymbol{x}}', \Delta\hat{\boldsymbol{x}}\rangle + \langle \boldsymbol{F}^\top\hat{\boldsymbol{x}}, \Delta\hat{\boldsymbol{x}}'\rangle\Big)$$
$$-\mu\langle \boldsymbol{k}, \Delta\hat{\boldsymbol{x}}\rangle - \mu'\langle \boldsymbol{k}, \Delta\hat{\boldsymbol{x}}'\rangle.$$

Differentiating this with respect to $\Delta\hat{\boldsymbol{x}}$ and $\Delta\hat{\boldsymbol{x}}'$ and letting the result be 0, we obtain

$$f_0^2(\tilde{\boldsymbol{x}} + \Delta\hat{\boldsymbol{x}}) - \lambda\boldsymbol{F}\hat{\boldsymbol{x}}' - \mu\boldsymbol{k} = \boldsymbol{0}, \qquad f_0^2(\tilde{\boldsymbol{x}}' + \Delta\hat{\boldsymbol{x}}' - \lambda\boldsymbol{F}^\top\hat{\boldsymbol{x}} - \mu'\hat{\boldsymbol{k}} = \boldsymbol{0}.$$

Multiplying this by $\boldsymbol{P}_{\boldsymbol{k}} \equiv \mathrm{diag}(1,1,0)$ from left on both sides and noting that $\boldsymbol{P}_{\boldsymbol{k}}\Delta\hat{\boldsymbol{x}} = \Delta\hat{\boldsymbol{x}}$, $\boldsymbol{P}_{\boldsymbol{k}}\Delta\hat{\boldsymbol{x}}' = \Delta\hat{\boldsymbol{x}}'$, and $\boldsymbol{P}_{\boldsymbol{k}}\boldsymbol{k} = \boldsymbol{0}$, we obtain

$$f_0^2(\tilde{\boldsymbol{x}} + \Delta\hat{\boldsymbol{x}}) - \lambda\boldsymbol{P}_{\boldsymbol{k}}\boldsymbol{F}\hat{\boldsymbol{x}}' = \boldsymbol{0}, \qquad f_0^2(\tilde{\boldsymbol{x}} + \Delta\hat{\boldsymbol{x}}) - \lambda\boldsymbol{P}_{\boldsymbol{k}}\boldsymbol{F}^\top\boldsymbol{x} = \boldsymbol{0}.$$

Hence,

$$\Delta\hat{\boldsymbol{x}} = \frac{\lambda}{f_0^2}\boldsymbol{P}_k\boldsymbol{F}\hat{\boldsymbol{x}}' - \tilde{\boldsymbol{x}}, \qquad \Delta\hat{\boldsymbol{x}}' = \frac{\lambda}{f_0^2}\boldsymbol{P}_k\boldsymbol{F}^\top\hat{\boldsymbol{x}} - \tilde{\boldsymbol{x}}'.$$

Substituting these into Eq. (∗∗), we obtain

$$\langle \boldsymbol{F}\hat{\boldsymbol{x}}', \frac{\lambda}{f_0^2}\boldsymbol{P}_k\boldsymbol{F}\hat{\boldsymbol{x}}' - \tilde{\boldsymbol{x}}\rangle + \langle \boldsymbol{F}^\top\hat{\boldsymbol{x}}, \frac{\lambda}{f_0^2}\boldsymbol{P}_k\boldsymbol{F}^\top\hat{\boldsymbol{x}} - \tilde{\boldsymbol{x}}'\rangle = \langle \hat{\boldsymbol{x}}, \boldsymbol{F}\hat{\boldsymbol{x}}'\rangle,$$

from which λ is given by

$$\frac{\lambda}{f_0^2} = \frac{\langle \hat{\boldsymbol{x}}, \boldsymbol{F}\hat{\boldsymbol{x}}'\rangle + \langle \boldsymbol{F}\hat{\boldsymbol{x}}', \tilde{\boldsymbol{x}}\rangle + \langle \boldsymbol{F}^\top\hat{\boldsymbol{x}}, \tilde{\boldsymbol{x}}'\rangle}{\langle \boldsymbol{F}\hat{\boldsymbol{x}}', \boldsymbol{P}_k\hat{\boldsymbol{F}}\hat{\boldsymbol{x}}'\rangle + \langle \boldsymbol{F}^\top\hat{\boldsymbol{x}}, \boldsymbol{P}_k\hat{\boldsymbol{F}}^\top\hat{\boldsymbol{x}}\rangle}.$$

Hence, we can write $\Delta\hat{\boldsymbol{x}}$ and $\Delta\hat{\boldsymbol{x}}'$ in the form of Eq. (8.31).

(3) We can confirm that the identities

$$\langle \hat{\boldsymbol{x}}, \boldsymbol{F}\hat{\boldsymbol{x}}'\rangle + \langle \boldsymbol{F}\hat{\boldsymbol{x}}', \tilde{\boldsymbol{x}}\rangle + \langle \boldsymbol{F}^\top\hat{\boldsymbol{x}}, \tilde{\boldsymbol{x}}'\rangle = \frac{\langle \boldsymbol{\xi}^*, \boldsymbol{f}\rangle}{f_0^2},$$

$$\langle \boldsymbol{F}\hat{\boldsymbol{x}}', \boldsymbol{P}_k\boldsymbol{F}\hat{\boldsymbol{x}}'\rangle + \langle \boldsymbol{F}^\top\hat{\boldsymbol{x}}, \boldsymbol{P}_k\boldsymbol{F}^\top\hat{\boldsymbol{x}}\rangle = \frac{\langle \boldsymbol{f}, V_0[\hat{\boldsymbol{\xi}}]\boldsymbol{f}\rangle}{f_0^2}$$

by substituting the definitions of the vectors $\boldsymbol{f}$ and $\boldsymbol{\xi}^*$ and the matrix $V_0[\hat{\boldsymbol{\xi}}]$ on the right sides. Substituting these into Eq. (8.31), we can easily see that it is rewritten in the form of Eq. (8.33).

8.2. (1) The four equations of Eq. (8.11) are linearly dependent if and only if the determinant of the 4×4 coefficient matrix vanishes, i.e.,

$$\begin{vmatrix} f_0P_{11} - xP_{31} & f_0P_{12} - xP_{32} & f_0P_{13} - xP_{33} & f_0P_{14} - xP_{34} \\ f_0P_{21} - yP_{31} & f_0P_{22} - yP_{32} & f_0P_{23} - yP_{33} & f_0P_{24} - yP_{34} \\ f_0P'_{11} - x'P'_{31} & f_0P'_{12} - x'P'_{32} & f_0P'_{13} - x'P'_{33} & f_0P'_{14} - x'P'_{34} \\ f_0P'_{21} - y'P'_{31} & f_0P'_{22} - y'P'_{32} & f_0P'_{23} - y'P'_{33} & f_0P'_{24} - y'P'_{34} \end{vmatrix} = 0.$$

We add to this a diagonal block consisting of the identity matrix, which does not the determinant. The determinant is also unchanged by adding a non-diagonal block consisting of 0. Hence, the left side of the above equation is rewritten as

$$\begin{vmatrix} P_{11} - xP_{31}/f_0 & P_{12} - xP_{32}/f_0 & P_{13} - xP_{33}/f_0 & P_{14} - xP_{34}/f_0 & 0 & 0 \\ P_{21} - yP_{31}/f_0 & P_{22} - yP_{32}/f_0 & P_{23} - yP_{31}/f_0 & P_{24} - yP_{33}/f_0 & 0 & 0 \\ P'_{11} - x'P'_{31}/f_0 & P'_{12} - x'P'_{32}/f_0 & P'_{13} - x'P'_{33}/f_0 & P'_{14} - x'P'_{34}/f_0 & 0 & 0 \\ P'_{21} - y'P'_{31}/f_0 & P'_{22} - y'P'_{32}/f_0 & P'_{23} - y'P'_{33}/f_0 & P'_{24} - y'P'_{34}/f_0 & 0 & 0 \\ P_{31} & P_{32} & P_{33} & P_{34} & 1 & 0 \\ P'_{31} & P'_{32} & P'_{33} & P'_{34} & 0 & 1 \end{vmatrix}$$
$$= \begin{vmatrix} P_{11} & P_{12} & P_{13} & P_{14} & x/f_0 & 0 \\ P_{21} & P_{22} & P_{23} & P_{24} & y/f_0 & 0 \\ P_{31} & P_{32} & P_{33} & P_{34} & 1 & 0 \\ P'_{11} & P'_{12} & P'_{13} & P'_{14} & 0 & x'/f_0 \\ P'_{21} & P'_{22} & P'_{23} & P'_{24} & 0 & y'/f_0 \\ P'_{31} & P'_{32} & P'_{33} & P'_{34} & 0 & 1 \end{vmatrix},$$

where we have multiplied the fifth row by x/f_0 and y/f_0 and added the resulting rows to the first and the second rows, respectively. Also, we have multiplied the sixth row by x'/f_0 and y'/f_0 and added the resulting rows to the third and the fourth rows, respectively. These operations do not change the determinant. We have finally interchanged rows; the sign alters each time two rows are interchanged.

(2) Doing cofactor expansion on the left side of Eq. (8.34) with respect to the fifth column and then doing cofactor expansion of the result with respect to the sixth column, we obtain

$$
\begin{aligned}
&\begin{vmatrix} P_{21} & P_{22} & P_{23} & P_{24} & 0 \\ P_{31} & P_{32} & P_{33} & P_{34} & 0 \\ P'_{11} & P'_{12} & P'_{13} & P'_{14} & x'/f_0 \\ P'_{21} & P'_{22} & P'_{23} & P'_{24} & y'/f_0 \\ P'_{31} & P'_{32} & P'_{33} & P'_{34} & 1 \end{vmatrix} \frac{x}{f_0} - \begin{vmatrix} P_{11} & P_{12} & P_{13} & P_{14} & 0 \\ P_{31} & P_{32} & P_{33} & P_{34} & 0 \\ P'_{11} & P'_{12} & P'_{13} & P'_{14} & x'/f_0 \\ P'_{21} & P'_{22} & P'_{23} & P'_{24} & y'/f_0 \\ P'_{31} & P'_{32} & P'_{33} & P'_{34} & 1 \end{vmatrix} \frac{y}{f_0} \\
&+ \begin{vmatrix} P_{11} & P_{12} & P_{13} & P_{14} & 0 \\ P_{21} & P_{22} & P_{23} & P_{24} & 0 \\ P'_{11} & P'_{12} & P'_{13} & P'_{14} & x'/f_0 \\ P'_{21} & P'_{22} & P'_{23} & P'_{24} & y'/f_0 \\ P'_{31} & P'_{32} & P'_{33} & P'_{34} & 1 \end{vmatrix} \\
&= \left(\begin{vmatrix} P_{21} & P_{22} & P_{23} & P_{24} \\ P_{31} & P_{32} & P_{33} & P_{34} \\ P'_{21} & P'_{22} & P'_{23} & P'_{24} \\ P'_{31} & P'_{32} & P'_{33} & P'_{34} \end{vmatrix} \frac{x'}{f_0} - \begin{vmatrix} P_{21} & P_{22} & P_{23} & P_{24} \\ P_{31} & P_{32} & P_{33} & P_{34} \\ P'_{11} & P'_{12} & P'_{13} & P'_{14} \\ P'_{31} & P'_{32} & P'_{33} & P'_{34} \end{vmatrix} \frac{y'}{f_0} \right. \\
&\left. + \begin{vmatrix} P_{21} & P_{22} & P_{23} & P_{24} \\ P_{31} & P_{32} & P_{33} & P_{34} \\ P'_{11} & P'_{12} & P'_{13} & P'_{14} \\ P'_{21} & P'_{22} & P'_{23} & P'_{24} \end{vmatrix} \right) \frac{x}{f_0} - \left(\begin{vmatrix} P_{11} & P_{12} & P_{13} & P_{14} \\ P_{31} & P_{32} & P_{33} & P_{34} \\ P'_{21} & P'_{22} & P'_{23} & P'_{24} \\ P'_{31} & P'_{32} & P'_{33} & P'_{34} \end{vmatrix} \frac{x'}{f_0} \right. \\
&\left. - \begin{vmatrix} P_{11} & P_{12} & P_{13} & P_{14} \\ P_{31} & P_{32} & P_{33} & P_{34} \\ P'_{11} & P'_{12} & P'_{13} & P'_{14} \\ P'_{31} & P'_{32} & P'_{33} & P'_{34} \end{vmatrix} \frac{y'}{f_0} + \begin{vmatrix} P_{11} & P_{12} & P_{13} & P_{14} \\ P_{31} & P_{32} & P_{33} & P_{34} \\ P'_{11} & P'_{12} & P'_{13} & P'_{14} \\ P'_{21} & P'_{22} & P'_{23} & P'_{24} \end{vmatrix} \right) \frac{y}{f_0} \\
&+ \left(\begin{vmatrix} P_{11} & P_{12} & P_{13} & P_{14} \\ P_{21} & P_{22} & P_{23} & P_{24} \\ P'_{21} & P'_{22} & P'_{23} & P'_{24} \\ P'_{31} & P'_{32} & P'_{33} & P'_{34} \end{vmatrix} \frac{x'}{f_0} - \begin{vmatrix} P_{11} & P_{12} & P_{13} & P_{14} \\ P_{21} & P_{22} & P_{23} & P_{24} \\ P'_{11} & P'_{12} & P'_{13} & P'_{14} \\ P'_{31} & P'_{32} & P'_{33} & P'_{34} \end{vmatrix} \frac{y'}{f_0} \right. \\
&\left. + \begin{vmatrix} P_{11} & P_{12} & P_{13} & P_{14} \\ P_{21} & P_{22} & P_{23} & P_{24} \\ P'_{11} & P'_{12} & P'_{13} & P'_{14} \\ P'_{21} & P'_{22} & P'_{23} & P'_{24} \end{vmatrix} \right) \\
&= F_{11}\left(\frac{x}{f_0}\right)\left(\frac{x'}{f_0}\right) + F_{12}\left(\frac{x}{f_0}\right)\left(\frac{y'}{f_0}\right) + F_{13}\left(\frac{x}{f_0}\right) + F_{21}\left(\frac{y}{f_0}\right)\left(\frac{x'}{f_0}\right) + F_{22}\left(\frac{y}{f_0}\right)\left(\frac{y'}{f_0}\right) \\
&\quad + F_{23}\left(\frac{y}{f_0}\right) + F_{31}\left(\frac{x}{f_0}\right) + F_{32}\left(\frac{x}{f_0}\right) + F_{33},
\end{aligned}
$$

where we define (with appropriate interchanges of rows)

$$F_{11} = \begin{vmatrix} P_{21} & P_{22} & P_{23} & P_{24} \\ P_{31} & P_{32} & P_{33} & P_{34} \\ P'_{21} & P'_{22} & P'_{23} & P'_{24} \\ P'_{31} & P'_{32} & P'_{33} & P'_{34} \end{vmatrix}, \qquad F_{12} = \begin{vmatrix} P_{21} & P_{22} & P_{23} & P_{24} \\ P_{31} & P_{32} & P_{33} & P_{34} \\ P'_{31} & P'_{32} & P'_{33} & P'_{34} \\ P'_{11} & P'_{12} & P'_{13} & P'_{14} \end{vmatrix},$$

$$F_{33} = \begin{vmatrix} P_{21} & P_{22} & P_{23} & P_{24} \\ P_{31} & P_{32} & P_{33} & P_{34} \\ P'_{11} & P'_{12} & P'_{13} & P'_{14} \\ P'_{21} & P'_{22} & P'_{23} & P'_{24} \end{vmatrix}, \qquad F_{21} = \begin{vmatrix} P_{31} & P_{32} & P_{33} & P_{34} \\ P_{11} & P_{12} & P_{13} & P_{14} \\ P'_{21} & P'_{22} & P'_{23} & P'_{24} \\ P'_{31} & P'_{32} & P'_{33} & P'_{34} \end{vmatrix},$$

$$F_{22} = \begin{vmatrix} P_{11} & P_{12} & P_{13} & P_{14} \\ P_{31} & P_{32} & P_{33} & P_{34} \\ P'_{11} & P'_{12} & P'_{13} & P'_{14} \\ P'_{31} & P'_{32} & P'_{33} & P'_{34} \end{vmatrix}, \qquad F_{23} = \begin{vmatrix} P_{31} & P_{32} & P_{33} & P_{34} \\ P_{11} & P_{12} & P_{13} & P_{14} \\ P'_{11} & P'_{12} & P'_{13} & P'_{14} \\ P'_{21} & P'_{22} & P'_{23} & P'_{24} \end{vmatrix},$$

$$F_{31} = \begin{vmatrix} P_{11} & P_{12} & P_{13} & P_{14} \\ P_{21} & P_{22} & P_{23} & P_{24} \\ P'_{21} & P'_{22} & P'_{23} & P'_{24} \\ P'_{31} & P'_{32} & P'_{33} & P'_{34} \end{vmatrix}, \qquad F_{32} = \begin{vmatrix} P_{11} & P_{12} & P_{13} & P_{14} \\ P_{21} & P_{22} & P_{23} & P_{24} \\ P'_{31} & P'_{32} & P'_{33} & P'_{34} \\ P'_{11} & P'_{12} & P'_{13} & P'_{14} \end{vmatrix},$$

$$F_{33} = \begin{vmatrix} P_{11} & P_{12} & P_{13} & P_{14} \\ P_{21} & P_{22} & P_{23} & P_{24} \\ P'_{11} & P'_{12} & P'_{13} & P'_{14} \\ P'_{21} & P'_{22} & P'_{23} & P'_{24} \end{vmatrix}.$$

Using the thus defined matrix $\boldsymbol{F} = (F_{ij})$, we can write Eq. (8.34) in the form of Eq. (6.49).

8.3. (1) The square norm $\|\boldsymbol{A}\boldsymbol{x} - \boldsymbol{b}\|^2$ is expanded into

$$\begin{aligned} \|\boldsymbol{A}\boldsymbol{x} - \boldsymbol{b}\|^2 &= \langle \boldsymbol{A}\boldsymbol{x} - \boldsymbol{b}, \boldsymbol{A}\boldsymbol{x} - \boldsymbol{b}\rangle = \langle \boldsymbol{A}\boldsymbol{x}, \boldsymbol{A}\boldsymbol{x}\rangle - 2\langle \boldsymbol{A}\boldsymbol{x}, \boldsymbol{b}\rangle + \langle \boldsymbol{b}, \boldsymbol{b}\rangle \\ &= \langle \boldsymbol{x}, \boldsymbol{A}^\top \boldsymbol{A}\boldsymbol{x}\rangle - 2\langle \boldsymbol{x}, \boldsymbol{A}^\top \boldsymbol{b}\rangle + \|\boldsymbol{b}\|^2. \end{aligned}$$

Differentiating this with respect to each component of $\boldsymbol{x}$, and letting the result be $\boldsymbol{0}$, we obtain Eq. (8.35).

(2) If the left side matrix of Eq. (8.35) is nonsingular, we multiply the right side by its inverse from left to obtain

$$\boldsymbol{x} = (\boldsymbol{A}^\top \boldsymbol{A})^{-1}\boldsymbol{A}^\top \boldsymbol{b} = \boldsymbol{A}^- \boldsymbol{b}.$$

8.4. (1) From Eqs. (8.23) and (8.25), we can write $\hat{\boldsymbol{x}}$ as

$$\begin{aligned} \hat{\boldsymbol{x}} &= \bar{\boldsymbol{x}} + \delta\boldsymbol{x} - \frac{\langle \bar{\boldsymbol{x}} + \delta\boldsymbol{x}, \boldsymbol{F}(\bar{\boldsymbol{x}}' + \delta\boldsymbol{x})\rangle \boldsymbol{P}_{\boldsymbol{k}}\boldsymbol{F}\boldsymbol{x}'}{\|\boldsymbol{P}_{\boldsymbol{k}}\boldsymbol{F}\boldsymbol{x}'\|^2 + \|\boldsymbol{P}_{\boldsymbol{k}}\boldsymbol{F}^\top \boldsymbol{x}\|^2} \\ &= \bar{\boldsymbol{x}} + \delta\boldsymbol{x} - \frac{(\langle \bar{\boldsymbol{x}}, \boldsymbol{F}\bar{\boldsymbol{x}}'\rangle + \langle \delta\boldsymbol{x}, \boldsymbol{F}\bar{\boldsymbol{x}}'\rangle + \langle \bar{\boldsymbol{x}}, \boldsymbol{F}\delta\boldsymbol{x}'\rangle + \langle \delta\boldsymbol{x}, \boldsymbol{F}\delta\boldsymbol{x}'\rangle)\boldsymbol{P}_{\boldsymbol{k}}\boldsymbol{F}\boldsymbol{x}'}{\|\boldsymbol{P}_{\boldsymbol{k}}\boldsymbol{F}\boldsymbol{x}'\|^2 + \|\boldsymbol{P}_{\boldsymbol{k}}\boldsymbol{F}^\top \boldsymbol{x}\|^2} \\ &= \bar{\boldsymbol{x}} + \delta\boldsymbol{x} - \frac{(\langle \delta\boldsymbol{x}, \boldsymbol{F}\bar{\boldsymbol{x}}'\rangle + \langle \bar{\boldsymbol{x}}, \boldsymbol{F}\delta\boldsymbol{x}'\rangle)\boldsymbol{P}_{\boldsymbol{k}}\boldsymbol{F}\boldsymbol{x}'}{\|\boldsymbol{P}_{\boldsymbol{k}}\boldsymbol{F}\boldsymbol{x}'\|^2 + \|\boldsymbol{P}_{\boldsymbol{k}}\boldsymbol{F}^\top \boldsymbol{x}\|^2} + \cdots, \end{aligned}$$

where $\cdots$ denotes terms of errors of second and higher orders. Note that $\langle \bar{\boldsymbol{x}}, \boldsymbol{F}\bar{\boldsymbol{x}}'\rangle = 0$ and that since $\langle \bar{\boldsymbol{x}}, \boldsymbol{F}\bar{\boldsymbol{x}}'\rangle$ is a small quantity, the errors $\delta\boldsymbol{x}$ and $\delta\boldsymbol{x}'$ in the terms

$\boldsymbol{P_k F x'}$ and $\boldsymbol{P_k F^\top x}$ in the denominator need not be considered; the discrepancies are all subsumed in the final terms of $\cdots$. Similarly, we obtain

$$\hat{\boldsymbol{x}}' = \bar{\boldsymbol{x}} + \delta\boldsymbol{x} - \frac{(\langle\delta\boldsymbol{x}, \boldsymbol{F}\bar{\boldsymbol{x}}'\rangle + \langle\bar{\boldsymbol{x}}, \boldsymbol{F}\delta\boldsymbol{x}'\rangle)\boldsymbol{P}_k\boldsymbol{F}^\top\boldsymbol{x}}{\|\boldsymbol{P}_k\boldsymbol{F}\boldsymbol{x}'\|^2 + \|\boldsymbol{P}_k\boldsymbol{F}^\top\boldsymbol{x}\|^2} + \cdots.$$

Hence, we obtain Eq. (8.39) to a first approximatio, where we replace $\bar{\boldsymbol{x}}$ and $\bar{\boldsymbol{x}}'$ by $\hat{\boldsymbol{x}}$ and $\hat{\boldsymbol{x}}'$, respectively; the discrepancies are subsumed in the omitted higher order terms. Note that the above analysis starts with Eq. (8.25). Strictly speaking, we should start with Eq. (8.31) for the optimally corrected solution, since we iteratively improve the solution using Eq. (8.31). However, the effect of subsequent iterations is of higher order in $\delta\boldsymbol{x}$ and $\delta\boldsymbol{x}'$ so that it can be omitted.

(2) Consider $V[\hat{\boldsymbol{x}}]$. We see that

$$\begin{aligned}
V[\hat{\boldsymbol{x}}] &= E[\Delta\hat{\boldsymbol{x}}\Delta\hat{\boldsymbol{x}}^\top] \\
&= E\Big[\Big(\delta\boldsymbol{x} - \frac{(\langle\delta\boldsymbol{x}, \boldsymbol{F}\hat{\boldsymbol{x}}'\rangle + \langle\hat{\boldsymbol{x}}, \boldsymbol{F}\delta\boldsymbol{x}'\rangle)\boldsymbol{P}_k\boldsymbol{F}\hat{\boldsymbol{x}}'}{\|\boldsymbol{P}_k\boldsymbol{F}\hat{\boldsymbol{x}}'\|^2 + \|\boldsymbol{P}_k\boldsymbol{F}^\top\hat{\boldsymbol{x}}\|^2}\Big) \\
&\quad \Big(\delta\boldsymbol{x} - \frac{(\langle\delta\boldsymbol{x}, \boldsymbol{F}\hat{\boldsymbol{x}}'\rangle + \langle\hat{\boldsymbol{x}}, \boldsymbol{F}\delta\boldsymbol{x}'\rangle)\boldsymbol{P}_k\boldsymbol{F}\hat{\boldsymbol{x}}'}{\|\boldsymbol{P}_k\boldsymbol{F}\hat{\boldsymbol{x}}'\|^2 + \|\boldsymbol{P}_k\boldsymbol{F}^\top\hat{\boldsymbol{x}}\|^2}\Big)^\top\Big] \\
&= E[\delta\boldsymbol{x}\delta\boldsymbol{x}^\top] - \frac{E[\langle\delta\boldsymbol{x}, \boldsymbol{F}\hat{\boldsymbol{x}}'\rangle\delta\boldsymbol{x}(\boldsymbol{P}_k\boldsymbol{F}\hat{\boldsymbol{x}}')^\top]}{\|\boldsymbol{P}_k\boldsymbol{F}\hat{\boldsymbol{x}}'\|^2 + \|\boldsymbol{P}_k\boldsymbol{F}^\top\hat{\boldsymbol{x}}\|^2} - \frac{E[\langle\delta\boldsymbol{x}, \boldsymbol{F}\hat{\boldsymbol{x}}'\rangle\boldsymbol{P}_k\boldsymbol{F}\hat{\boldsymbol{x}}'\delta\boldsymbol{x}^\top]}{\|\boldsymbol{P}_k\boldsymbol{F}\hat{\boldsymbol{x}}'\|^2 + \|\boldsymbol{P}_k\boldsymbol{F}^\top\hat{\boldsymbol{x}}\|^2} \\
&\quad + \frac{E\Big[\Big(\langle\delta\boldsymbol{x}, \boldsymbol{F}\hat{\boldsymbol{x}}\rangle^2 + \langle\hat{\boldsymbol{x}}, \boldsymbol{F}\delta\boldsymbol{x}'\rangle^2\Big)(\boldsymbol{P}_k\boldsymbol{F}\hat{\boldsymbol{x}})(\boldsymbol{P}_k\boldsymbol{F}\hat{\boldsymbol{x}})^\top\Big]}{\Big(\|\boldsymbol{P}_k\boldsymbol{F}\hat{\boldsymbol{x}}'\|^2 + \|\boldsymbol{P}_k\boldsymbol{F}^\top\hat{\boldsymbol{x}}\|^2\Big)^2}.
\end{aligned}$$

The reason that the right side does not include linear terms in $\delta\boldsymbol{x}$ and $\delta\boldsymbol{x}'$ is that $\delta\boldsymbol{x}$ and $\delta\boldsymbol{x}'$ are assumed to be independent and both have expectation 0 so that the expectation of their product vanishes. Note that we can write $\delta\boldsymbol{x} = (\delta x/f_0, \delta y/f_0, 0)^\top$. From our assumption that δx and δy are independent, both having expectation 0 and variance σ^2, we see that

$$E[\delta\boldsymbol{x}\delta\boldsymbol{x}^\top] = \frac{\sigma^2}{f_0^2}\boldsymbol{P}_k.$$

Thus,

$$\begin{aligned}
V[\hat{\boldsymbol{x}}] &= E[\delta\boldsymbol{x}\delta\boldsymbol{x}^\top] - \frac{E[\delta\boldsymbol{x}\delta\boldsymbol{x}^\top\boldsymbol{F}\hat{\boldsymbol{x}}'(\boldsymbol{P}_k\boldsymbol{F}\hat{\boldsymbol{x}}')^\top]}{\|\boldsymbol{P}_k\boldsymbol{F}\hat{\boldsymbol{x}}'\|^2 + \|\boldsymbol{P}_k\boldsymbol{F}^\top\hat{\boldsymbol{x}}\|^2} - \frac{E[\boldsymbol{P}_k\boldsymbol{F}\hat{\boldsymbol{x}}'(\boldsymbol{F}\hat{\boldsymbol{x}}')^\top\delta\boldsymbol{x}\delta\boldsymbol{x}^\top]}{\|\boldsymbol{P}_k\boldsymbol{F}\hat{\boldsymbol{x}}'\|^2 + \|\boldsymbol{P}_k\boldsymbol{F}^\top\hat{\boldsymbol{x}}\|^2} \\
&\quad + \frac{E\Big[\Big((\boldsymbol{F}\hat{\boldsymbol{x}}')^\top\delta\boldsymbol{x}\delta\boldsymbol{x}^\top\boldsymbol{F}\hat{\boldsymbol{x}} + \hat{\boldsymbol{x}}^\top\boldsymbol{F}\delta\boldsymbol{x}\delta\boldsymbol{x}^\top\boldsymbol{F}^\top\hat{\boldsymbol{x}}\Big)(\boldsymbol{P}_k\boldsymbol{F}\hat{\boldsymbol{x}}')(\boldsymbol{P}_k\boldsymbol{F}\hat{\boldsymbol{x}}')^\top\Big]}{\Big(\|\boldsymbol{P}_k\boldsymbol{F}\hat{\boldsymbol{x}}'\|^2 + \|\boldsymbol{P}_k\boldsymbol{F}^\top\hat{\boldsymbol{x}}\|^2\Big)^2} \\
&= E[\delta\boldsymbol{x}\delta\boldsymbol{x}^\top] - \frac{E[\delta\boldsymbol{x}\delta\boldsymbol{x}^\top]\boldsymbol{F}\hat{\boldsymbol{x}}'(\boldsymbol{P}_k\boldsymbol{F}\hat{\boldsymbol{x}}')^\top}{\|\boldsymbol{P}_k\boldsymbol{F}\hat{\boldsymbol{x}}'\|^2 + \|\boldsymbol{P}_k\boldsymbol{F}^\top\hat{\boldsymbol{x}}\|^2} - \frac{\boldsymbol{P}_k\boldsymbol{F}\hat{\boldsymbol{x}}'(\boldsymbol{F}\hat{\boldsymbol{x}}')^\top E[\delta\boldsymbol{x}\delta\boldsymbol{x}^\top]}{\|\boldsymbol{P}_k\boldsymbol{F}\hat{\boldsymbol{x}}'\|^2 + \|\boldsymbol{P}_k\boldsymbol{F}^\top\hat{\boldsymbol{x}}\|^2} \\
&\quad + \frac{\Big((\boldsymbol{F}\hat{\boldsymbol{x}}')^\top E[\delta\boldsymbol{x}\delta\boldsymbol{x}^\top]\boldsymbol{F}\hat{\boldsymbol{x}} + \hat{\boldsymbol{x}}^\top\boldsymbol{F}E[\delta\boldsymbol{x}\delta\boldsymbol{x}^\top]\boldsymbol{F}^\top\hat{\boldsymbol{x}}\Big)(\boldsymbol{P}_k\boldsymbol{F}\hat{\boldsymbol{x}}')(\boldsymbol{P}_k\boldsymbol{F}\hat{\boldsymbol{x}}')^\top}{\Big(\|\boldsymbol{P}_k\boldsymbol{F}\hat{\boldsymbol{x}}'\|^2 + \|\boldsymbol{P}_k\boldsymbol{F}^\top\hat{\boldsymbol{x}}\|^2\Big)^2} \\
&= \frac{\sigma^2}{f_0^2}\boldsymbol{P}_k - \frac{\sigma^2}{f_0^2}\frac{\boldsymbol{P}_k\boldsymbol{F}\hat{\boldsymbol{x}}'(\boldsymbol{P}_k\boldsymbol{F}\hat{\boldsymbol{x}}')^\top}{\|\boldsymbol{P}_k\boldsymbol{F}\hat{\boldsymbol{x}}'\|^2 + \|\boldsymbol{P}_k\boldsymbol{F}^\top\hat{\boldsymbol{x}}\|^2} - \frac{\sigma^2}{f_0^2}\frac{\boldsymbol{P}_k\boldsymbol{F}\hat{\boldsymbol{x}}'(\boldsymbol{F}\hat{\boldsymbol{x}}')^\top\boldsymbol{P}_k}{\|\boldsymbol{P}_k\boldsymbol{F}\hat{\boldsymbol{x}}'\|^2 + \|\boldsymbol{P}_k\boldsymbol{F}^\top\hat{\boldsymbol{x}}\|^2}
\end{aligned}$$

$$+\frac{\sigma^2}{f_0^2}\frac{\left((\boldsymbol{F}\hat{\boldsymbol{x}}')^\top \boldsymbol{P}_k\boldsymbol{F}\hat{\boldsymbol{x}} + \hat{\boldsymbol{x}}^\top \boldsymbol{F}\boldsymbol{P}_k\boldsymbol{F}^\top \hat{\boldsymbol{x}}\right)(\boldsymbol{P}_k\boldsymbol{F}\hat{\boldsymbol{x}}')(\boldsymbol{P}_k\boldsymbol{F}\hat{\boldsymbol{x}}')^\top}{\left(\|\boldsymbol{P}_k\boldsymbol{F}\hat{\boldsymbol{x}}'\|^2 + \|\boldsymbol{P}_k\boldsymbol{F}^\top \hat{\boldsymbol{x}}\|^2\right)^2}$$

$$= \frac{\sigma^2}{f_0^2}\boldsymbol{P}_k - \frac{\sigma^2}{f_0^2}\frac{(\boldsymbol{P}_k\boldsymbol{F}\hat{\boldsymbol{x}}')(\boldsymbol{P}_k\boldsymbol{F}\hat{\boldsymbol{x}}')^\top}{\|\boldsymbol{P}_k\boldsymbol{F}\hat{\boldsymbol{x}}'\|^2 + \|\boldsymbol{P}_k\boldsymbol{F}^\top \hat{\boldsymbol{x}}\|^2} - \frac{\sigma^2}{f_0^2}\frac{(\boldsymbol{P}_k\boldsymbol{F}\hat{\boldsymbol{x}}')(\boldsymbol{P}_k\boldsymbol{F}\hat{\boldsymbol{x}}')^\top}{\|\boldsymbol{P}_k\boldsymbol{F}\hat{\boldsymbol{x}}'\|^2 + \|\boldsymbol{P}_k\boldsymbol{F}^\top \hat{\boldsymbol{x}}\|^2}$$

$$+\frac{\sigma^2}{f_0^2}\frac{(\|\boldsymbol{P}_k\boldsymbol{F}\hat{\boldsymbol{x}}'\|^2 + \|\boldsymbol{P}_k^F U\hat{\boldsymbol{x}}\|^2)(\boldsymbol{P}_k\boldsymbol{F}\hat{\boldsymbol{x}}')(\boldsymbol{P}_k\boldsymbol{F}\hat{\boldsymbol{x}}')^\top}{\left(\|\boldsymbol{P}_k\boldsymbol{F}\hat{\boldsymbol{x}}'\|^2 + \|\boldsymbol{P}_k\boldsymbol{F}^\top \hat{\boldsymbol{x}}\|^2\right)^2}$$

$$= \frac{\sigma^2}{f_0^2}\left(\boldsymbol{P}_k - \frac{(\boldsymbol{P}_k\boldsymbol{F}\hat{\boldsymbol{x}}')(\boldsymbol{P}_k\boldsymbol{F}\hat{\boldsymbol{x}}')^\top}{\|\boldsymbol{P}_k\boldsymbol{F}\hat{\boldsymbol{x}}'\|^2 + \|\boldsymbol{P}_k\boldsymbol{F}^\top \hat{\boldsymbol{x}}\|^2}\right).$$

Removing σ^2, we obtain the normalized covariance matrix $V_0[\hat{\boldsymbol{x}}]$. The normalized covariance matrix $V_0[\hat{\boldsymbol{x}}']$ and the normalized correlation matrices $V_0[\hat{\boldsymbol{x}}, \hat{\boldsymbol{x}}']$ and $V_0[\hat{\boldsymbol{x}}', \hat{\boldsymbol{x}}]$ are similarly obtained.

8.5. We see that

$$(\boldsymbol{a}\times\boldsymbol{T})^\top(\boldsymbol{a}\times\boldsymbol{T}) = ((\boldsymbol{a}\times\boldsymbol{I})\boldsymbol{T})^\top(\boldsymbol{a}\times\boldsymbol{I}\boldsymbol{T}) = \boldsymbol{T}^\top(\boldsymbol{a}\times\boldsymbol{I})^\top(\boldsymbol{a}\times\boldsymbol{I})\boldsymbol{T}$$
$$= \boldsymbol{T}^\top(\|\boldsymbol{a}\|^2\boldsymbol{I} - \boldsymbol{a}\boldsymbol{a}^\top)\boldsymbol{T},$$

where we have noted that the definition of Eq. (6.44) implies $\boldsymbol{a}\times\boldsymbol{I} = \boldsymbol{A}(\boldsymbol{a})$ in the form of Eq. (6.25), i.e., for $\boldsymbol{a} = (a_i)$

$$\boldsymbol{a}\times\boldsymbol{I} = \begin{pmatrix} 0 & -a_3 & a_2 \\ a_3 & 0 & -a_1 \\ -a_2 & a_1 & 0 \end{pmatrix},$$

from which we can easily confirm that

$$(\boldsymbol{a}\times\boldsymbol{I})^\top(\boldsymbol{a}\times\boldsymbol{I}) = \|\boldsymbol{a}\|^2\boldsymbol{I} - \boldsymbol{a}\boldsymbol{a}^\top.$$

Bibliography

[1] K. S. Arun, T. S. Huang, and S. D. Blostein, Least-squares fitting of two 3-D point sets, *IEEE Transactions on Pattern Analysis and Machine Intelligence*, **9**-5 (1987), 698–700.

[2] A. Bartoli and P. Sturm, Nonlinear estimation of fundamental matrix with minimual parameters, *IEEE Transactions on Pattern Analysis and Machine Intelligence*, **26**-3 (2004), 426–432.

[3] S. Benhimane and E. Malis, Homography-based 2D Visual Tracking and Servoing *International Journal of Robotics Research*, **26**-7 (2007), 661–676.

[4] A. Chatterjee and V. M. Govindu, Robust relative rotation averaging, *IEEE Transactions on Pattern Analysis and Machine Intelligence*, **40**-4 (2018), 958–972.

[5] N. Chernov and C. Lesort, Statistical efficiency of curve fitting algorithms, *Computational Statistics and Data Analysis*, **47**-4 (2004), 713–728.

[6] W. Chojnacki, M. J. Brooks, A. van den Hengel, and D. Gawley, On the fitting of surfaces to data with covariance, *IEEE Transactions on Pattern Analysis and Machine Intelligence*, **22**-11 (2000), 1294–1302.

[7] W. Chojnacki, M. J. Brooks, A. van den Hengel, and D. Gawley, A new constrained parameter estimator for computer vision applications, *Image and Vision Computing/*, **22**-2 (2004), 85–91.

[8] H. C. Corben and P. Stehle, *Classical Mechanics*, 2nd ed. Dover, New York, NY, U.S. (2013).

[9] T. Drummond and R. Cipolla, Application of Lie algebra to visual servoing, *International Journal of Computer Vision*, **37**-1 (2000), 65–78.

[10] H. Goldstein, C. P. Poole, and J. L. Safko, *Classical Mechanics*, 3rd ed. Addison–Wesley, Reading, MA, U.S. (2001).

[11] G. H. Golub, C. F. Van Loan, *Matrix Computations*, The Johns Hopkins University Press, Baltimore, MD, U.S., 3rd ed. (1996), 4th ed., (2012).

[12] V. M. Govindu, Motion averaging in 3D reconstruction problems, in P. K. Turaga and A. Srivastava (eds.), *Riemannian Computing in Computer Vision*, Springer, Cham, Switzerland (2018), pp. 145–186.

[13] R. Hartley, In defense of the eight-point algorithm, *IEEE Transactions on Pattern Analysis and Machine Intelligence*, **19**-6 (1997), 580–593.

[14] R. Hartley and P. Sturm, Triangulation, *Computer Vision and Image Understanding*, **68**-2 (1997), 146–167.

[15] R. Hartley and A. Zisserman, *Multiple View Geometry in Computer Vision*, 2nd Ed., Cambridge University Press, Cambridge, UK (2003).

[16] B. K. P. Horn, Closed-form solution of absolute orientation using unit quaternions, *Journal of the Optical Society of America*, **A4**-4 (1987), 629–642.

[17] K. Kanatani, *Group-Theoretical Methods in Image Understanding*. Springer, Berlin, Germany (1990).

[18] K. Kanatani, *Geometric Computation for Machine Vision*, Oxford University Press, Oxford, U.K. (1993).

[19] K. Kanatani, Analysis of 3-D rotation fitting, *IEEE Transactions on Pattern Analysis and Machine Intelligence*, **16**-5 (1994), 543–549.

[20] K. Kanatani, *Statistical Optimization for Geometric Computation: Theory and Practice*, Elsevier, Amsterdam, The Netherlands (1996). Reprinted by Dover, New York, U.S. (2005).

[21] K. Kanatani, Statistical optimization for geometric fitting: Theoretical accuracy bound and high order error analysis, *International Journal of Computer Vision*, **80**-2 (2008), 167–188.

[22] K. Kanatani, *Understanding Geometric Algebra: Hamilton, Grassmann, and Clifford for Vision and Graphics*, CRC Press, Boca Raton, FL., U.S. (2015).

[23] K. Kanatani and C. Matsunaga, Computing internally constrained motion of 3-D sensor data for motion interpretation, *Pattern Recognition*, **46**-6 (2013), 1700–1709.

[24] K. Kanatani and H. Niitsuma, Optimal two-view planar triangulation, *JPSJ Transactions on Computer Vision and Applications*, **3**, (2011), 67–79.

[25] K. Kanatani and H. Niitsuma, Optimal computation of 3-D similarity: Gauss-Newton vs. Gauss-Helmert, *Computational Statistics and Data Analysis*, **56**-12, (2012), 4470–4483.

[26] K. Kanatani and Y. Sugaya, Compact fundamental matrix computation, *IPSJ Transactions on Computer Vision and Applications*, **2** (2010), 59–70.

[27] K. Kanatani and Y. Sugaya, Unified computation of strict maximum likelihood for geometric fitting, *Journal of Mathematical Imaging and Vision*, **38**-1 (2010), 1–13.

[28] K. Kanatani, Y. Sugaya, and Y. Kanazawa, *Ellipse Fitting for Computer Vision: Implementation and Applications*, Morgan-Claypool, San Rafael, CA, U.S. (2016).

[29] K. Kanatani, Y. Sugaya, and Y. Kanazawa, *Guide to 3D Vision Computation: Geometric Analysis and Implementation*, Springer, Cham, Switzerland (2016).

[30] K. Kanatani, Y. Sugaya, and N. Niitsuma, Triangulation from two views revisited: Hartley-Sturm vs. optimal correction, *Proc. 19th British Machine Vision Conference*, Leeds, U.K. (2008), pp. 173–182.

[31] Y. Kanazawa and K. Kanatani, Reliability of 3-D reconstruction by stereo vision, *IEICE Transactions on Information and Systems*, **E780-D**-19 (1995), 1301–1306.

[32] L. D. Laundau and E. M. Lifshitz, *Mechanics*, 3rd ed. Butterworth–Heinemann, Oxford, U.K. (1976).

[33] M. I. A. Lourakis and A. A. Argyros, SBA: A software package for generic sparse bundle adjustment, *ACM Transactions on Mathematical Software*, **36**-1 (2009), 2:1–30.

[34] S. J. Maybank, Detection of image structures using Fisher information and the Rao metric, *IEEE Transactions on Pattern Analysis and Machine Intelligence*, **26**-12 (2004), 49–62.

[35] N. Ohta and K. Kanatani, Optimal estimation of three-dimensional rotation and reliability evaluation, *IEICE Transactions of Information and Systems*, **E81-D**-11 (1998), 1243–1252.

[36] W. H. Press, S. A. Teukolsky, W. T. Vetterling, and B. P. Flannery, *Numerical Recipes: The Art of Scientific Computing*, Cambridge University Press, Cambridge, U.K., 3rd ed. (2007);

[37] M. Sakamoto, Y. Sugaya, and K. Kanatani, Homography optimization for consistent circular panorama generation, *Proc. 2006 IEEE Pacific-Rim Symposium on Image and Video Technology* Hsinchu, Taiwan (2006), 1195-1205.

[38] O. Sergiyenko, W. Flores-Fuentes and P. Mercorelli (eds.), *Machine Vision and Navigation*, Springer, Cham, Switzerland (2020).

[39] N. Snavely, S. Seitz and R. Szeliski, Photo tourism: Exploring photo collections in 3d, *ACM Transactions on Graphics*, **25**-8 (1995), 835–846.

[40] N. Snavely, S. Seitz and R. Szeliski, Modeling the world from internet photo collections, *International Journal of Computer Vision*, **80**-22 (2008), 189–210.

[41] Y. Sugaya and K. Kanatani, High accuracy fcomputation of rank-constrained fundamental matrix, *Proc. 18th British Machine Vision Conference*, Vol. 1, Coventry, U.K. (2007), 282–291.

[42] B. Triggs, P. F. McLauchlan, R. I. Hartley, A. Fitzgibbon, Bundle adjustment—A modern synthesis, in: B. Triggs, A. Zisserman, R. Szeliski (eds.), *Vision Algorithms: Theory and Practice*, Springer, Berlin (2000), 298–375.

[43] R. Tron and K. Daniilidis, The space of essential matrices as a Riemannian quotient manifold, *Siam Journal of Imaging Sciences*, **10**-3 (2017), 1416–1445.

Index